Fodor's

BAHAMAS

Welcome to The Bahamas

Made up of 700 islands—some busy and bustling, some isolated and inhabited by no one but hermit crabs and seagulls—The Bahamas offers an alluring mix of land and sea activities. From Nassau to Eleuthera, you can play golf on a seaside fairway, dive dramatic wrecks and reefs, and sail in crystal clear water. Accommodations run the gamut from simple inns to sophisticated retreats, from practical fishing lodges to romantic honeymoon hideaways. And for those who look a little closer, there's a fascinating and diverse culture to be explored. As you plan your upcoming travels, please confirm that places are still open and let us know when we need to make updates at editors@fodors.com.

TOP REASONS TO GO

★ **Beaches.** The powdery, soft sand creates some of the world's best strands.

★ **Boating.** Ideal conditions draw small dinghies, serious sailboats, and luxury yachts.

★ **Family fun.** From sprawling water parks to horseback rides along the beach.

★ **The Family (Out) Islands.** Quiet and uncrowded, these islands are hard to reach but worth the trip.

★ **Fishing.** From fly-casting for tarpon and bonefish to fighting with a giant marlin.

Contents

MAPS

Fodor's Features

Chapter 1

EXPERIENCE THE BAHAMAS

19 ULTIMATE EXPERIENCES

The Bahamas offers terrific experiences that should be on every traveler's list. Here are Fodor's top picks for a memorable trip.

1 Scuba diving

Discover aquatic wonders when you explore the region's ultra-clear waters, from the shallows of the world's third-largest barrier reef to the ocean depths. Coral, blue holes, drop-offs, and sea gardens abound here. *(Ch. 4)*

2 Lucayan National Park

Kayak through wild tamarind and gumbo-limbo trees, a mangrove swamp, and one of the world's largest underwater cave systems on Grand Bahama Island. *(Ch. 4)*

3 The Family Islands

Seek refuge at these sparsely populated islands, where you can ascend the cut-stone staircase to Mt. Alvernia, the country's highest natural point. *(Ch. 9)*

4 Rum drinks

Revisit the bootlegging days of the Prohibition Era, and treat yourself to a Goombay Smash. *(Ch. 1)*

5 Horseback riding

Even without prior experience, visitors can take guided tours of several of the islands on horseback; gallop across the sand and even into the sea. *(Ch. 7)*

6 Sailing

In July, Grand Bahama hosts a Regatta and Heritage Festival with sailing races and more. *(Ch. 4)*

7 Nurse sharks

Interact with harmless nurse sharks in their natural habitat at Compass Cay in The Exumas, where a handful of them swim and sunbathe at the private island marina. *(Ch. 8)*

8 Swimming with pigs

World-famous pigs live on Big Major Cay in The Exumas. The animals swim out to greet tourists, but be respectful on their home turf, and don't pick any up for selfies. *(Ch. 8)*

9 Aquaventure at the Atlantis Resort

This 141-acre aquatic wonderland on Paradise Island has river rides, a 200-foot body slide, and pools, the ultimate playground for kids and adventurous adults. *(Ch. 3)*

10 Bonefishing

Shallow waters and mangroves filled with "gray ghosts," silvery white fish, make bonefishing the fly-fishing sport of choice in the Bahamas. *(Ch. 6, 9)*

11 Private resorts

Complete your island getaway with a stay at a secluded, all-inclusive luxury resort like Fowl Cay, just a 7-minute boat transfer from Staniel Cay Airport. *(Ch. 8)*

12 Dolphin spotting

Take a boat into Freeport, and a pod of dolphins may splash and dive along beside you; jump into the water to swim with them in their natural environment. *(Ch. 4)*

13 Fish fry

At Arawak Cay, brightly colored restaurants serve local fish specialties like fried fish and cracked conch. Wash it down with "sky juice" (gin, coconut water, and milk). *(Ch. 3)*

14 Junkanoo Festival

This celebration with dancing, brass bands, and vibrant costumes is The Bahamas' most anticipated event of the year, held on Boxing Day and New Year's Day mornings. *(Ch. 3)*

15 Snorkeling

Explore Thunderball Grotto and its limestone cave in The Exumas or Paradise Point in Bimini, where dolphins and black coral await you just offshore. *(Ch. 6, 8)*

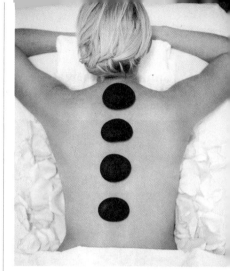

16 Spas

Retreat to top-rated spas in idyllic settings throughout the region, where you can indulge in massages, body treatments, aromatherapy, and much more. *(Ch. 3)*

17 The Exumas

Across the Tropic of Cancer lies this chain of hundreds of islands with white sand and calm blue water, home to exquisite wildlife: giant starfish, iguanas, and pigs. *(Ch. 8)*

18 Beaches

With powdery white and pink sand and blue water, beaches extend for a total of 800 miles in The Bahamas and offer parties on the sand or complete solitude. *(Ch. 1)*

19 Harbour Island

Modern but with an old-world feel, Harbour Island is home to pastel-colored clapboard houses, a 3½-mile pink sand beach, and the mysterious Lone Tree. *(Ch. 7)*

WHAT'S WHERE

1 New Providence and Paradise Island. New Providence—commonly referred to by the name of its capital, Nassau—is the busiest and most densely populated island, and it is conveniently connected to Paradise Island by two bridges. From flashy megaresorts like Atlantis and Baha Mar to fine dining and high-end shopping, these islands are fast-paced and have highly active tourist areas.

2 Grand Bahama. Urban and deserted vibes mix to create a quieter alternative to fast-paced Nassau. Shopping, golfing, scuba diving, and the vast expanses of untouched nature appeal to adventurous travelers.

3 The Abacos. Shallow, translucent waters, exotic marine animals, top-notch marinas, and idyllic, historic settlements spread over 120 miles of cays (some uninhabited) give the Abacos the apt title of "Sailing Capital of The Bahamas."

0 ——————— 50 miles

0 ——————— 75 km

ATLANTIC OCEAN

Cat
Island
▲ Mt. Alvernia
Port Howe ○ San
Salvador
Sound
Rum Cay
SOUTHERN
FAMILY ISLANDS
Long
Island [7] Samana Cay
Clarence ○
Town Crooked Mayaguana
Crooked Island Passage Island Island
Acklins
Islands Mayaguana Passage
Caicos Passage
Providenciales

Little Inagua Island

Great Inagua
Island

Lake
Rose

4 **Andros, Bimini, and the Berry Islands.** In the northwestern corner of The Bahamas, these islands share many characteristics, most notably excellent fishing and diving. Each exudes a casual, old-island atmosphere and abundant natural beauty.

5 **Eleuthera and Harbour Island.** Harbour Island—home of the legendary pink-sand beach—is a chic, must-visit Family Island. Eleuthera has historic churches; small, comfort-able inns; and upscale, intimate beach resorts.

6 **The Exumas.** Hundreds of islands are scattered across the Tropic of Cancer, all with gorgeous white beaches and the most beautiful water in The Bahamas. Great Exuma has friendly locals, great beach parties, and popular Pig Beach, where you can go swimming with the friendly pigs.

7 **The Southern Family Islands.** The Bahamas' southernmost islands have fewer visitors and many natural wonders. Cat Island boasts the highest natural point in the country, Mt. Alvernia, and Inagua is home to one of the largest flamingo colonies in the world.

What to Eat and Drink in The Bahamas

Rum Cake

CRACKED CONCH

Cracked conch is made from the meat of the shelled marine mollusk found in Bahamian waters, and it is guaranteed to be on every Bahamian restaurant's menu.

CONCH SALAD

You haven't had a taste of authentic Bahamian cuisine until you've had a conch salad. Onions, green pepper, tomato, and conch meat are diced to create a colorful bowl, then kicked up a notch with goat pepper. Salt and pepper are added, along with freshly squeezed lime and sour-orange juice. Conch salad is often prepared right in front of customers.

GUAVA DUFF

Guava duff is one of the most popular desserts in The Bahamas. The soft, cake-like treat is made with guava, a tropical fruit that is grown on trees in many Caribbean islands. The guava is peeled, cooked, and seasoned, then mixed into dough or spread on it before it is rolled. The dough is then placed in cheesecloth and boiled. It's sliced, and then crowned with a delicious

Conch Fritters

guava butter sauce (which usually has rum in it).

JOHNNY CAKE
The Bahamian johnny cake falls somewhere between a dense bread and a slightly sweet cake. It's made with flour, milk, butter, sugar, and baking powder, and baked in a round baking tin.

PEAS AND RICE
This dish is the country's most popular staple, traditionally served with heavy lunches or dinners alongside fish, meat, or chicken with two or three side dishes. The ingredients of the dish are in its name: white rice and pigeon peas. Bahamians will typically add thyme, diced vegetables, tomato paste, and salt pork or pieces of bacon.

MACARONI
Bahamian macaroni is a flavorful baked version of mac-and-cheese that includes diced onions, bell peppers, spices, and goat pepper. It's cut into squares for serving as a side dish in restaurants and homes for lunch and dinner.

RUM PUNCH
Rum punch in The Bahamas is made with orange juice, pineapple juice, grenadine, Angostura bitters, and gold rum. You can order one at most bars and restaurants.

CONCH FRITTERS
These small, round bites are a favorite appetizer, perfect for sharing, and a great introduction to conch for the hesitant. Flour batter is mixed with chopped vegetables, seasoning, and conch meat, then fried. Calypso sauce for dipping is a must!

GOOMBAY SMASH
The Goombay Smash is the unofficial cocktail of The Bahamas and was created in the 1960s by Emily Cooper, aka "Miss Emily," the owner of Miss Emily's Blue Bee Bar in Green Turtle Cay, Abaco. The official recipe of the drink contains pineapple juice, coconut rum, and gold rum, but you can expect your bartender to put their own twist on it with ingredients like coconut cream, orange juice, or other dark rums.

RUM CAKE
Bahamian rum cake is moist and buttery, like a sponge cake. The popular dessert is made with dark or light rum and is baked in a Bundt baking pan. The coating is made using white rum, sugar, butter, and sometimes pineapple juice. Nuts are also sometimes added. Bahamian rum cakes are produced at Purity Bakery in Nassau.

10 Animals to Meet in The Bahamas

SEA STARS
One of the most recognizable underwater creatures is the large, spiny, orange Bahama sea star. Tour guides are often outfitted with at least one sea star to show to visitors. Snorkeling is the best way to view the sea star in its natural habitat, thriving among the coral reefs and in seagrasses.

SPIDER CRABS
Crabs roam all over The Bahamas, especially on Andros Island, known as "The Land of the Crabs." This island hosts The Bahamas' largest population of land crabs, many of which are threatened due to overdevelopment. All crabs are influenced by the ocean's cycles.

IGUANAS
On the small shore of Allan's Cay, the familiar rumble of approaching boats summons a reptilian army of rock iguanas to the water where the tourists wait, armed with bananas and grapes. Rock iguanas are indigenous to only three islands in the world, all in The Bahamas.

DOLPHINS
Bimini is where the wild dolphins are. When sailing around these islands, a pod of wild Atlantic spotted dolphins might decide to swim alongside the boat and play in the wake, making the trip a memorable one.

SHARKS
At the marina in Compass Cay, nurse sharks congregate in the shallow waters where free meals are sprinkled from above, their only inconvenience being the tourists who stand among them while they feed.

FLAMINGOS
Preferring an isolated existence, the West Indian flamingo can be found balancing in the salt flats of Lake Rosa on the Inagua Islands. Roughly 70,000 flamingos flock to these marshes to feast on the fly larvae and brine shrimp that are packed to the gills with beta carotene, imparting their deep pink hue into the flamingos' plumage.

PIGS
Visitors to the beach at Big Major Cay in Exuma witness a sight that is highly unusual in any part of the world. A litter of pigs in varying colors and sizes splashes and waddles along an idyllic white sand beach on their own island, surrounded by the electric blue waters of the Caribbean. The pigs look very out of place against this backdrop, and most visitors become downright gleeful at the strange existence and enviable lifestyle of these tropical pigs.

The famous swimming pigs of The Bahamas

FISH

Strap on a snorkel for an immersive experience in the caves and coral reefs of Thunderball Grotto. What appears to be a not very interesting rock is actually a system of small caves that is home to lively, colorful coral reefs and many brightly colored tropical fish.

Made famous by a cameo in two James Bond films, Thunderball Grotto is a popular stop for many visitors to Exuma. Visitors arrive at the Grotto via boat and then snorkel or dive their way inside the cavernous rock. Low tide is easier to navigate, as there are five entrances that can only be accessed by diving underwater and two entrances that are accessible above water. Streams of light find their way into the cave, illuminating the calm blue water and the array of wildlife that darts in and out of reefs on the shallow sea floor. Spot some of The Bahamas's finest, such as triggerfish, rock beauty, angelfish, yellowtail snappers, and sergeant majors.

CONCH

The most celebrated ocean floor resident and a staple of Bahamian cuisine, the Queen Conch (pronounced "konk") is a sea snail that thrives in these warm blue waters. Conch shells are distinct in appearance and can be found strewn about many Bahamian beaches. A large, spiny outside is turned over to reveal a smooth, bright pink opening.

TURTLES

The sea turtles in The Bahamas can be found in their largest concentration on Eleuthera Island. Four of the world's seven turtle species live here, and each species has its own preferred habitat—mangrove forests, shallow coastal areas, coral reefs, and the open ocean.

Ways to Explore the Myths and Mysticism of The Bahamas

PRETTY MOLLY BAY

Pretty Molly Bay is a tiny, unoccupied beach located on Little Exuma, whose namesake was allegedly an enslaved woman who drowned here in the 1800s. Locals say that she still visits the beach at night, haunting the island. Some say she was a young woman who was turned into a mermaid.

MYSTERIOUS BLUE HOLES

Created over thousands of years, the limestone bedrock of the island eroded to form intricate cave systems, and Andros is known to have the largest collection in the world. Thus far, 178 blue holes on land and at least 50 in the sea have been discovered, and they provide habitat for unusual cave fish and invertebrates found nowhere else on earth. Fossils, shipwrecks, and the remains of a crocodile not native to The Bahamas have also been found. Noted oceanographer and conservationist Jacques Cousteau visited the island in 1970 to film these wonders, and divers from around the world continue to be drawn to them. When in South Andros, be sure to book a tour with Barbara Moore (☎ 242/475–0354).

LOST ISLAND OF ATLANTIS

For centuries, the fictional city of Atlantis has been the subject of focus by marine researchers. Many have speculated that the legendary underwater city would be located somewhere in Europe, while others have found evidence that suggests Atlantis could have been in North Bimini.

BUSH MEDICINE AND USE OF LOVE POTIONS

The use of plants for medicinal purposes is a tradition brought by enslaved Africans to The Bahamas in the 18th and 19th centuries and passed on to younger generations by parents and grandparents. Cures for ailments can be found all over The Bahamas.

LUSCA: MYTHICAL UNDERWATER CREATURE

Androsians believe that a gigantic half-octopus, half-shark dwells in the depths of the blue holes. They have named it Lusca, and folklore suggests it's 75 feet long and uses its strong tentacles to drag humans and boats into its underwater lair.

Pirates of Nassau Museum

THE CHICKCHARNIE

Sightings of the mysterious Chickcharnie, a feathered three-foot-tall creature with one red eye, three-toed claws, a prehensile tail, and a 360-degree rotating head are still being reported. This flightless bird may have a basis in the large, 3.3-foot-tall barn owl, *Tyto pollens*, whose remains were found on Andros. That species, however, disappeared in the 16th century due to hunting and habitat destruction.

PIRATES OF NASSAU

During the Golden Age of Piracy (1650–1730), Nassau was notorious for being a pirate haven. The city once served as the capital of the "Pirate Republic," a pirate-run colony that existed in The Bahamas between 1706 and 1718. Edward Teach, better known as Blackbeard, was the leader of the pirates that lived and "worked" in New Providence. They ran the colony until the British invaded the island in 1718. Blackbeard was killed in battle.

HAUNTED HOUSE ON HARBOUR ISLAND

In 1945, a young newlywed couple moved into this mansion. According to locals, they had a terrible argument shortly after and left everything just as it was and never returned. Children playing on the grounds talked of seeing two figures in white floating about the house. The table was set for dinner; the food on the stove and all their clothing and wedding gifts were left behind.

Kids and Families

It might not be an exaggeration to say that The Bahamas is a playground for children—or anyone else who likes building castles in the sand, searching for the perfect seashell, and playing tag with ocean waves.

Although water-related activities are the most obvious enticements, these relaxed and friendly islands also offer a variety of land-based options, particularly in Nassau and on adjacent Paradise Island. For tales of the high seas, **Pirates of Nassau** has artifacts and interactive exhibits of the original pirates of the Caribbean.

The **Ardastra Gardens & Wildlife Conservation Centre** is home to a variety of animals, like pink flamingos, a pair of guenons, and Madagascar lemurs.

Let the kids pick out their favorite horse at the **Surrey Horse Pavilion** on Prince George Wharf and take a leisurely clip-clopping ride through the old city of Nassau. For a few extra dollars, most guides will extend your tour beyond the typical route to include other sites.

Megaresort **Atlantis** has lots of appeal, with everything from pottery painting to making and racing remote-control cars, to an 8,000-square-foot, state-of-the-art kids' camp, plus The Bahamas' and Caribbean's largest casino and water park.

In Freeport, older children and adults can spend a day learning how dolphins are trained from **UNEXSO** (one of whose founders was Jacques Cousteau) at Sanctuary Bay, a refuge for dolphins.

For water-sports enthusiasts, snorkeling, parasailing, and boating opportunities abound. In The Exumas, rent a power-boat and take the kids to Big Major Cay to see the famous **swimming pigs**. If you are staying in Nassau, book a day trip to see the pigs with **Harbour Safaris**. Don't forget some scraps! Kids will also get a kick out of the hundreds of **iguanas** on nearby Allan's Cay and the **giant starfish** near mainland Great Exuma.

Much of The Bahamas' most incredible scenery is underwater, but kids of all ages can enjoy the scenes beneath the sea without even getting wet. At **Stuart Cove's Dive Bahamas** in Nassau, kids 12 and up can go 15 feet under with a SUB (Scenic Underwater Bubble) and zoom around the reefs. **Seaworld Explorer**'s semi-submarine explores Nassau Harbour and Paradise Island for 1½ hours with sightseeing above and below water.

Those with a sweet tooth should stop by **Mortimer's Candy Kitchen** on Nassau's East Street. In business since 1928, it delights customers with popcorn, snow cones, roasted peanuts, and handmade Bahamian treats like coconut cakes and giant lollipops.

GREAT WATER ADVENTURES

In an archipelago nation named for shallow seas that amaze even astronauts in space, don't miss having a close marine encounter. Water adventures range from a splash at the beach to shark diving. Or, stay between the extremes with fishing and snorkeling.

by Justin Higgs

WHERE TO DIVE AND SNORKEL IN THE BAHAMAS

Although most water in The Bahamas is clear enough to see to the bottom from your boat, snorkeling or diving gets you that much closer to the country's true natives. Coral reefs, blue holes, drop-offs, and sea gardens abound.

KEY

🤿 Best dive sites
🤿 Best snorkel sites

BEST DIVE SITES

Andros Barrier Reef/Tongue of the Ocean. Go from the shallows of the world's third-largest barrier reef to the depths of the ocean.

Shark Wall, New Providence. Off southwest New Providence, this drop is a must for experienced divers. James Bond movies *Thunderball* and *Never Say Never Again* were filmed here.

The Wall, Crooked Island. The famed dive site about 50 yards off Crooked Island's coast drops from 45 feet to thousands.

Diving near New Providence Island

BEST SNORKEL SITES

The Current Cut, Eleuthera. Near the Current settlement in North Eleuthera there is great drift snorkel with the right tide.

Exuma Cays Land and Sea Park. This 176-square-mile park was the first of its kind. Since the park is protected and its waters have essentially never been fished, you can see what the ocean looked like before humanity.

Paradise Point, Bimini. Off northern Bimini, this area is rich in sea life and is famous for the underwater stone path some believe marks the road to the lost city of Atlantis. Dolphins and black coral gardens are just offshore.

Thunderball Grotto, the Exumas. This three-story limestone-ceiling cave at the northern end of the Exumas chain was featured in the James Bond movie of the same name.

Diving near Bimini

EXTREME DIVING ADVENTURES

Various outfitters on Grand Bahama and New Providence offer shark dives. With **Caribbean Divers** (☎ 242/373–9111 ⊕ www.bellchannelinn.com) and **UNEXSO** in Grand Bahama and **Stuart Cove's** in New Providence, you'll watch dive masters feed reef sharks which brush by you—no cage included. Dive masters control the ferocity and location of the frenzy, so the sharks' attention is on the food.

Incredible Adventures (☎ 800/644–7382 ⊕ www.incredible-adventures.com) in Grand Bahama offers cage diving with tiger sharks. You'll sit in the water as giant sharks come breathtakingly close, the only thing between you a few strips of metal.

Feeding sharks when humans are present make these dives controversial, especially when multiple sharks are involved and there's the possibility of a frenzy. Dive operators doing these extreme adventures are experienced and knowledgeable about shark-feeding patterns and signs of aggression, but partake in these dives at your own risk.

San Salvador

Rum Cay

Long I.

Crooked Island Passage

Samana Cay

The Wall

Crooked Island

Acklins Island

Mayaguana Passage

Mayaguana Island

0   50 mi
0   50 km

Little Inagua Island

Great Inagua Island

French Angelfish | Four-eyed Butterflyfish | Grunt

Nassau Grouper | Parrotfish | Queen Triggerfish

Sergeant Major | Snapper | Tang

Barracuda* | Lionfish* | Shark*

* dangerous fish

WHAT YOU'LL SEE UNDER THE SEA

Reefs in The Bahamas are alive with colorful life. Vibrant hard corals—such as star, brain, staghorn, and elk—and waving purple sea fans are home to schools of myriad fish, some pictured above. Be on the lookout for lionfish; a prick from the fins of this poisonous fish is painful and could send you to the hospital. The most common sharks in The Bahamas are nurse sharks (typically non-threatening to humans) and Caribbean reef sharks. The deeper you dive, the bigger and more varied shark species get.

Generally, the further the reef is from a developed area the more abundant the marine life, but even sites around developed islands might surprise you.

TOUR THE EXUMA CAYS BY BOAT

The Bahamas is a boater's paradise, with shallow protected waters and secluded, safe harbors. In small island groups, travel takes just a few hours, even minutes.

THE EXUMA CAYS

To really get off the beaten path, the Exuma Cays are where it's at. This 120-mile archipelago is made up of small cays, many of which are still uninhabited or privately owned, and inter-spersed with sand banks and spits. Throughout is excellent diving and snorkel-ing. Boaters usually stock up and clear customs in Nassau, cross the yellow banks to the north of the chain, and slowly make their way south.

BOAT TOURS

If you don't have your own boat, these outfitters will take you on island-hopping adventures.

Exuma Water Sports
Come here for guided Jet Ski tours through the Exuma Cays, as well as a scenic boat cruise that includes snorkeling at Thunderball Grotto.
☎ 242/357-0770
⊕ www.exumawatertours. com.

Highbourne Cay at the chain's northern end has a marina and food store. You can explore many of the surrounding cays by tender if you prefer to dock here. Nearby, **Allan's Cay** is home to hundreds of iguanas that readily accept food.

Norman's Cay has an airstrip and Norman's Cay Beach Club has a fantastic restaurant and bar. Just south is the 176-sq-mile **Exuma Cays Land and Sea Park**. It has some of the country's best snorkel-ing and diving. Warderick Wells Cay houses the park headquarters, which has nature trail maps and a gift shop. Just below, **Compass Cay** has a marina known for its friendly nurse sharks and a small convenience store. **Pipe Creek**, which winds between Compass and Staniel Cays, has great shelling, snorkeling, diving, and bonefishing. **Staniel Cay** is the hub of activity in these parts and a favorite destination of yachters. That's thanks to the Staniel Cay Yacht Club, the only full-service marina in the cays. It makes a good base for visiting **Big Major Cay**,

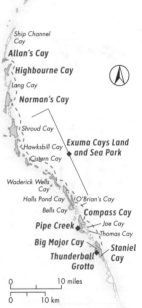

where wild pigs swim out to meet you, and **Thunderball Grotto,** a beautiful marine cave that snorkelers (at low tide) and experienced scuba divers can explore.

SAILING

Sailing is popular in The Bahamas, and there are many regattas held here throughout the year. Various outfitters in New Providence and Paradise Island offer relaxing sailing cruises.

BONEFISHING

WHAT IS BONEFISHING?

Bonefishing is the fly-fishing sport of choice in The Bahamas. The country is full of pristine shallow flats and mangroves where stealthy "gray ghosts"—silvery white, sleek fish—school in large groups. Hooking one is a challenge, as the fish are fast, strong, and perfectly camouflaged to the sand and water.

To catch bonefish you need the right mix of knowledge, instinct, and patience. Guides are the best way to go, as their knowledge of the area and schooling patterns gives them an uncanny ability to find bonefish quickly.

EQUIPMENT

Basics include a fly-fishing rod and reel and the right lure. Experienced anglers, guides, and fishing-supply dealers can help you gear up with the best and latest technology. Bonefishing is catch and release, so always use barbless hooks and work quickly when removing them to avoid stressing the fish. Wear comfortable, light clothing that protects much of your body from the sun, as you'll be out for hours without shade.

In many places you can just walk offshore onto the flats. Some anglers use shallow draft boats with a raised platform in the back, where they pole into extremely shallow areas.

BEST PLACES TO BONEFISH

Bonefish hang out in shallow flats and mangrove areas. Andros, Bimini, and the Exumas have the best bonefishing; Abaco, Eleuthera, and Long Island also provide excellent adventures. If you have the time, visit the southernmost islands, like Crooked, Acklins, or Inagua, where these gray ghosts are "uneducated" to anglers.

WHERE TO STAY

Bonefishing lodges are common in the Bahamas and often include top-notch guides. Accommodations are usually basic. Here are our top bonefishing lodges:

- **Andros Island Bonefish Club, Cargill Creek, Central Andros**
- **Crooked Island Lodge**
- **Peace and Plenty Bonefish Lodge, Georgetown, Exuma**
- **Small Hope Bay Lodge, Fresh Creek, Andros**

OTHER TYPES OF FISHING

Make sure you are familiar with fishing regulations before you begin your adventure. Visit ⊕ www.bahamas.com/things-do/fishing.

DEEP-SEA FISHING

Deep water is just a few miles off most islands, where anglers try for large ocean fish—tuna, wahoo, mahi mahi, shark, and marlin. Like bonefishing, the fight is what most anglers are after; however, a day on the ocean can provide a great meal. The Abacos has great deep-sea fishing, and many tournaments are held there each year.

REEF/SHOAL FISHING

Fishing with a rod, or Bahamian "hand-lining" can be a great family fishing adventure. Anchoring near a shoal or reef, or even trolling with a lure, can be relaxing. The Out Islands are home to shoals, reefs, and wrecks that are less visited by fishing enthusiasts.

SPEARFISHING

Most reefs are okay for free-dive spear fishing, but spear guns (guns that fire spears) are illegal in The Bahamas. Spear is the traditional Bahamian fishing method, so reefs close to more developed islands tend to have fewer fish. The Out Islands still have lesser-known spots good for spearfishing.

(opposite page) Bonefishing in Andros.
(right) A prize catch.

What to Watch and Read

ISLANDS IN THE STREAM
BY ERNEST HEMINGWAY

First published in 1970, nine years after Ernest Hemingway's death, *Islands in the Stream* follows the adventures of Thomas Hudson, a wandering artist, from his experiences as a painter on the Gulf Stream island of Bimini, where he is paid a visit by his three young sons, to the coast of Cuba during World War II. This book is the first of the posthumously published works of Ernest Hemingway. It has his sparse, to-the-point writing style, so it is easy to relax into the writing and wait for the big moments to come, with plenty of drinking, camaraderie, fishing, dialogue, and extensive time at sea in between.

THUNDERBALL BY IAN FLEMING

Published in 1961, *Thunderball* is the ninth book in Ian Fleming's James Bond series and the eighth full-length Bond novel. The book is where we first meet Bond's number one enemy, SPECTRE (Special Executive for Counterintelligence, Terrorism, Revenge, and Extortion) leader Ernst Stavro Blofeld, who steals two atomic bombs and attempts to blackmail Western powers for their return. James Bond, Secret Service operative 007, travels to The Bahamas to work with his friend Felix Leiter, for the CIA's investigation.

THE NOBEL PIRATES
BY RIMA JEAN

Rima Jean's time-travel romance novel *The Nobel Pirates* (2014) tells the story of a workaholic attorney named Sabrina who, on vacation in The Bahamas in 2009, gets transported back in time to 1718 amidst the pirates of Nassau. Surrounded by the notorious bad boys of the Golden Age of Piracy, Edward England,

Howell Davis, and "Black Bart" Roberts, Sabrina has to learn how to survive in the present-past and figure out how to get back to her own time.

CASINO ROYALE

In *Casino Royale* (2006), Daniel Craig suited up as secret agent James Bond for the first time. His first mission as 007 is to defeat a private banker to terrorists in a high stakes game of poker at Casino Royale, Montenegro, but he quickly finds out that things are not what they seem. The 21st-century film was the third screen adaption of Ian Fleming's 1953 *Casino Royale* novel. It was filmed at The Ocean Club, A Four Seasons Resort in The Bahamas.

SPLASH

In the 1984 fantasy/romance movie *Splash*, Daryl Hannah plays a mermaid who saves a young boy from drowning. Twenty years later, the same young man (Tom Hanks) is reunited with the mermaid, not knowing who or what she is, and falls in love with her. The movie was filmed on the former Gorda Cay in The Bahamas, which now is known as Castaway Cay, the private island of Disney Cruise Line.

COCOON

Cocoon, a science-fiction/comedy and drama, is one of the most popular movies filmed in The Bahamas. The 1985 film follows senior citizens living in a Florida rest home when they stumble across an alien "fountain of youth" at the swimming pool of the home next door. Unbeknownst to them, aliens have been using the swimming pool in the house to store their cocooned brethren, giving the waters a powerful, rejuvenating quality. Parts of the film were shot in Nassau.

AFTER THE SUNSET

Having already stolen two from the set of three priceless Napoléon diamonds, expert jewel thief Max Burdett (Pierce Brosnan) decides to retire on a tropical island with his girlfriend Lola (Salma Hayek). When Max discovers the third and final diamond is sitting on a docked cruise ship on his very island, an FBI agent shows up to investigate him, which spells trouble for Max and his girlfriend. *After the Sunset* (2004) was shot in Paradise Island and Nassau.

CARNIVAL OF LOVE—A TALE OF A BAHAMIAN FAMILY BY ERNESTIA FRASIER

Ernestia Fraser's literary memoir *Carnival of Love: A Tale of a Bahamian Family* is set in The Bahamas and told through the perspective of Maria, one of 10 siblings. When Maria's parents divorce, she must contend with a new reality. The story takes a deep look at various aspects of the Bahamian landscape and Bahamian culture. *Carnival of Love* is also a prescribed text for The Bahamas General Certificate for Secondary Schools literature syllabus, so it is certainly a great book for teens.

BOUGAINVILLEA RINGPLAY BY MARION BETHEL

Bougainvillea Ringplay by Bahamian lawyer, poet, and activist Marion Bethel is a collection of finely crafted poems that are sensual, bringing to mind the sounds of the sea, the aroma of delicious meals, and the carnival of color that is The Bahamas. Bethel, through her poetry, presents The Bahamas as more than a tourist destination, solidifying it as a place in its own right. She explores history, relationships, and scenery while eschewing all clichés. Full in its scope and light in weight, this is the perfect book to order for in-flight reading or poolside indulgence.

WHO KILLED SIR HARRY OAKES? BY JAMES LEASOR

Who Killed Sir Harry Oakes? by James Leasor is for the real mystery fans; it pieces together events around the brutal 1934 murder of a multimillionaire in The Bahamas. There are many theories about what happened to Sir Harry Oakes, and there was even a television miniseries in 1989. Pick up a copy, and if it's your cup of tea, take notes, connect the dots, and come up with your own theory. When you get to The Bahamas, you just may find a few Bahamians to spin a yarn with you.

CHILDREN OF GOD

Children of God, written and directed by Bahamian Kareem Mortimor, is a 2010 romantic drama set on the island of Eleuthera. The awkward Johnny, a white artist who has been bullied, meets Romeo, a Black musician, on a boat from Nassau to Eleuthera. The film has received rave reviews for its portrayal and direct challenge of homophobia and religious fundamentalism. It has received numerous awards from film festivals, including the Aruba International Film Festival and Festival del Mar in Mallorca, Spain.

The Bahamas Today

Despite the economic shock of COVID-19 and a few rough hurricane seasons, development continues in The Bahamas. One of the island's five-star resorts, Baha Mar, took more than 10 years to open, but once it officially opened its doors in 2017, the resort started attracting visitors from around the world, which led to a boost in the country's tourism industry. Many other new hotels, restaurants, and other tourist attractions are underway across all the islands, and Bahamians are using the increase in tourism as an opportunity to spruce up existing properties and improve infrastructure.

THE BRITISH FEEL REMAINS

From driving on the left side of the road, to tea parties, to the wig-wearing lawyers who stroll into court, British influence is still apparent in The Bahamas. Though the country gained independence from the UK in 1973, Bahamians learn British spelling in school, and the country still uses the Westminster style of government. At the same time, a constant diet of American media has had an impact on the country. Bahamians measure temperature in Fahrenheit instead of Celsius, and although the English gentleman's cricket is the national sport, you'll be hard-pressed to find a local who plays the game.

A PLAYGROUND FOR THE RICH AND FAMOUS

With its year-round near-perfect weather, modern infrastructure and amenities, and proximity to the United States, it's no wonder that The Bahamas is a home away from Hollywood for many celebrities. Tim McGraw and Faith Hill, David Copperfield, and Nicolas Cage own private islands in The Exumas. Mariah Carey once owned a private Eleuthera estate, and the island is also home to Lenny Kravitz.

MANY DIFFERENT DESTINATIONS

The majority of the 6 million tourists who visit The Bahamas each year experience only Nassau, Paradise Island, or perhaps Grand Bahama. But with more than 700 islands, there's so much more to see and do. Each island has a different way of life; none of them have the liveliness of big-city life experienced in the capital. The farther south you venture, the slower the pace.

STILL DEVELOPING

Bay Street, once Nassau's Madison Avenue, is on the road to recovery after years of neglect. The esplanade just west of downtown has seen the addition of new hotels and restaurants, the renovation of existing establishments, and new shopping areas, with other major additions currently underway. Lynden Pindling International Airport is now a modern gateway that truly welcomes visitors. The multibillion-dollar Baha Mar transformed the Cable Beach strip when it opened in 2017. As Nassau continues to develop, many parts of the Family Islands remain untouched, preserving the quaint nature that attracts adventure travelers each year.

SUSTAINABLE DEVELOPMENT

The government works closely with the Bahamas National Trust to identify and develop protected green spaces, adding more and more land each year to the National Park System, and any developer interested in putting up a sizable or potentially environmentally sensitive project anywhere in the country is required to pay for and submit an Environmental Impact Assessment before consideration is granted.

Chapter 2

TRAVEL SMART

Updated by
Alicia Wallace

★ **CAPITAL:**
Nassau

POPULATION:
389,482

$ **CURRENCY:**
Bahamian dollar; pegged to
U.S. dollar

LANGUAGE:
English

COUNTRY CODE:
1 242

⚠ **EMERGENCIES:**
919 or 911

🚗 **DRIVING:**
On the left

⚡ **ELECTRICITY:**
120v/60 cycles; plugs U.S.
2- and 3-prong

🕐 **TIME:**
EST

🌐 **WEBSITES:**
www.bahamas.com,
www.myoutislands.com,
www.bahamasvisitorsguide.
com

FLORIDA

ATLANTIC
OCEAN

Straits of
Florida

★ Nassau

BAHAMAS

CUBA

CARIBBEAN
SEA

JAMAICA

HAITI

DOMINICAN
REPUBLIC

Know Before You Go

Before you head to The Bahamas for a vacation, there are a few things you should know that will make your visit even better. Here are the answers to the questions you're afraid to ask, plus all the essentials.

DRIVE ON THE LEFT
One of many practices remaining from The Bahamas' days under British colonization is driving on the left. This has its roots in medieval times when it was important to keep your right hand free to draw your sword if necessary. Today, The Bahamas is one of the few countries that still keeps left. The majority of the cars on the road used to be imported from the United States, but there are now many cars from Japan, so the driver could be on the left or the right.

There aren't always marked pedestrian crossings, so it's important to be extra cautious of cars when you are a pedestrian.

BAHAMIANS ARE FRIENDLY AND POLITE
Bahamians are polite, so it's not unusual for locals to greet you in passing along the street or when you walk into a room. You'll make more friends if you return the courtesy with a "good morning," "good afternoon," or "good evening." You'll win extra points if you are the first to greet a local.

If you need assistance, Bahamians are generally happy to lend a hand, but it's always best to offer a courteous greeting before presenting your question or concern. To enjoy the real hospitality of Bahamians and get a true understanding of how they live, consider signing up with the Ministry of Tourism's People-to-People program, which matches visitors with local families, couples, or individuals for some unique and authentic experiences.

THERE ARE MORE THAN 700 ISLANDS
Although many of the country's 6 million annual visitors only get to New Providence, there are hundreds of other islands and cays that make up The Bahamas. Sixteen of them are considered major islands, with populations running from a few hundred to a few hundred thousand. The different islands and settlements have very different natural features: thick, towering pine forests and bonefish flats in the north and low-lying scrubland in

the south. There are also unique traits in the population from island to island. Accents, physical features, and last names often give clues as to which island or settlement a Bahamian or their parents or grandparents come from. The islands and cays range from sizable land masses to rocks that jut out of the ocean at low tide.

THE BAHAMAS IS A CARIBBEAN COUNTRY
The Bahamas is considered part of the Caribbean, but geographically speaking, the islands are surrounded by the Atlantic Ocean and situated hundreds of miles away from the Caribbean Sea. Politically, the country aligns with the other small countries in the English-speaking Caribbean and is a member of CARICOM (the Caribbean Community). The Bahamas is an independent country and remains a part of the British Commonwealth.

THE U.S. DOLLAR IS ACCEPTED EVERYWHERE
If you are visiting from the United States, great news— there's no need to exchange your currency. The Bahamian dollar is pegged to the U.S. dollar, so both currencies are accepted everywhere. If you are nearing the end of your trip, you can ask for change in USD and most cashiers will assist. In highly frequented tourist areas, such as Bay Street in New Providence, you will also find ATMs that dispense U.S. dollars.

It's important to note that smaller shops and vendors are not set up to accept credit cards. Some stores and restaurants roll the 10% value-added tax into the price of goods, while others add it at the cash register. Be sure to ask if there's no sign making it clear.

CULTURE
While the majority of the country's residents are of African descent, this little island nation is, as Bahamians like to say, mixed up like conch salad! You'll find Bahamians of English, Greek, Chinese, Filipino, Haitian, and Jamaican descent as well as many other corners of the earth. Bahamians share their islands with thousands of expatriate residents who also call The Bahamas home. Each October, there is an incredible display to showcase the best food, culture, and entertainment from different countries at the International Culture, Wine, and Food Festival.

PRE-CLEARANCE AND CUSTOMS
When you arrive in The Bahamas, you will have to clear Bahamian Immigration regardless of where you enter. You'll also go through Customs. If you arrive at Nassau's Lynden Pindling International Airport, tourists are usually waved through without having to produce forms or open luggage for inspection.

When flying out of the country's main airport, be sure to arrive at least two hours ahead of your scheduled flight. Depending on the time of day and the number of flights departing, security lines can be long. You will also need to allow extra time to go through the U.S. Customs and Immigration pre-clearance facility. The good news is that this process generally takes a lot less time than it would in major U.S. airports when you land.

LANGUAGE
Conch, that delicious sea snail you'll see on just about every menu, is pronounced "konk" or "kunk." The popular locally brewed beer is Kah- *lik*, not *Kay*-lick. Bahamians speak English and Bahamian Creole, retaining some features of the language of the Africans who were enslaved in The Bahamas. When speaking to you, most Bahamians will use "standard English."

HURRICANE SEASON
Hurricane season runs from June 1 through November 30, but there's no reason to avoid traveling there during this time. It is rare for storms to impact any part of The Bahamas in the initial summer months of the season, and the most likely time that a storm will make its way to or through the Bahama island chain is in September and October. Even then, it is important

to understand the country's unique archipelagic geography before changing or cancelling travel plans. Even with category 5 hurricanes, much of the island chain will not be directly impacted, so pay attention to the path of the storm. Most hotels have hurricane policies that will allow you to cancel without penalty if your trip and a storm coincide. Track storms at ⊕ *www.nhc.noaa.gov* and always heed warnings and evacuation orders.

ENVIRONMENTAL PROGRESS
In January 2020, The Bahamas banned the consumption and sale of single-use plastic items, including straws, cutlery, grocery bags, and styrofoam containers. It's also illegal to deliberately release balloons into the air. The Bahamas National Trust is the steward of more than a million acres of protected land and sea in a series of national parks that span the entire country. To further protect marine resources, The Bahamas has made it illegal to catch turtles and sharks and has closed seasons to give the popular Nassau grouper and crawfish time to procreate.

Getting Here and Around

Air

Most international flights to The Bahamas connect through airports in Florida, New York, North Carolina (Charlotte), and Georgia (Atlanta). The busiest airport in The Bahamas is in Nassau, which has the most connections to the more remote Family Islands. If you're traveling to the Family Islands, you might have to make a connection in both Florida and Nassau. In some cases, a short ferry or a water taxi to your final destination may be involved.

A direct flight from New York City to Nassau takes approximately three hours. The flight from Charlotte to Nassau is two hours, and the flight from Miami to Nassau takes less than an hour. Flights between the islands of The Bahamas can take from 20 minutes to 2½ hours.

⬤ Boat

If you're adventurous and have time to spare, take a ferry or one of the tradition-al mail boats that regularly leave Nassau from Potter's Cay, under the Paradise Island Bridge. Although faster air-con-ditioned boats now make some of the trips, certain remote destinations are still served by slower vessels. Especially if you choose the mail-boat route, you may find yourself sharing company with goats or chickens, or piles of lumber and crates of cargo; on these lumbering mail boats, expect to spend 5 or more hours making your way between islands. These boats operate on a schedule, but they can be affected by bad weather. Mail boats can-not generally be booked in advance, and services are limited. In Nassau, check details with the Dockmaster's Office at Potter's Cay. One-way trips can cost from $35 to $100.

Within The Bahamas, Bahamas Ferries has a few options for island-hopping on air-conditioned boats that have food and beverages available for purchase. Sched-ules can change, so if you're planning to ferry back to an island to catch a flight, double-check the departure times and planned routes. Ferries serve most of the major tourist destinations from Nassau, including Spanish Wells, Governor's Harbour, Harbour Island, and Exuma. The high-speed ferry that runs between Nassau and Spanish Wells, Governor's Harbour, and Harbour Island costs less than $100 and takes about two hours each way.

Local ferries in the Family Islands trans-port islanders and visitors from the main island to smaller cays. Usually, these ferries make several round-trips daily and keep a more punctual schedule than the longer-haul ferries.

It's possible to get to Grand Bahama and Bimini by ferry from Florida. Balearia Bahamas Express sails from Fort Laud-erdale's Port Everglades (Terminal 1) and provides fast ferry service for less than $100 one-way, while Bahamas Paradise Cruise Line sails from the Port of Palm Beach in Riviera Beach and offers a two-night getaway.

If you're setting sail yourself, note that cruising boats must clear customs at the nearest port of entry before beginning any diving or fishing. The fee depends on vessel size and number of occupants. Stays of longer than 12 months must be arranged with Bahamas customs and immigration officials.

Car

International rental agencies are generally in Nassau, and you will rent from privately owned companies on the small islands. Thoroughly check the vehicle before you leave as many are not in great condition. Bring your own car seats as companies do not often provide these.

To rent a car, you must be 21 years of age or older.

It's common to hire a driver with a van, and prices are negotiable. Most drivers charge by the half day or full day. Prices depend on the stops and distance, but the cost for a half-day tour is generally $50 to $100 for one to four people, and $100 to $200 for a full-day tour. It's customary to pay for the driver's lunch. All tour guides in The Bahamas are required to take a tourism course and pass an exam; they must also get a special license to operate a taxi.

GASOLINE

The cost of fuel in The Bahamas is usually about twice that in the United States; be prepared to pay in cash before the attendant pumps your gas. It's good practice to tip the pump attendant at least $1, and tip more if they clean the windshield. You can ask for a handwritten receipt if printed ones are not available. You may also go inside to pay using a credit or debit card. Stations are few and far between on the Family Islands, so keep the tank full. Gas stations may be closed on Sunday.

PARKING

Parking spaces are hard to find in Nassau, so be prepared to pay for parking or park on a side street and walk. Most hotels offer off-street parking for guests. There are few parking lots not associated with hotels.

ROADSIDE EMERGENCIES

In case of a road emergency, stay in your vehicle with your emergency flashers engaged and wait for help, especially after dark. If someone stops to help, relay information through a small opening in the window. If it's daylight and help does not arrive, walk to the nearest phone and call for help. In The Bahamas, motorists readily stop to help drivers in distress.

Ask for emergency numbers at the rental office when you pick up your car. These numbers vary from island to island. On smaller islands, the owner of the company may want you to call them at their home.

RULES OF THE ROAD

You must drive on the left side of the road. Be attentive to signs and other drivers as many streets in downtown Nassau are one-way. At roundabouts, keep left and yield to oncoming traffic as you enter the roundabout and at "Give Way" signs.

Taxi

There are taxis waiting at every airport and outside all the main hotels and cruise-ship docks. Sometimes you can negotiate a fare, but you must do so before you enter the taxi. Beware of drivers who don't display their license (and may not have one).

You'll find that Bahamian taxi drivers are more talkative than their U.S. counterparts. When you take a taxi to dinner or to town, you can ask the driver to return for you at a particular time. A 15% tip is suggested.

Essentials

🍴 Dining

The restaurants we list are the top-rated in each price category. You'll find all types, from cosmopolitan to the most casual, serving all types of cuisine. Unless otherwise noted, the restaurants listed in this guide are open daily for lunch and dinner.

PAYING

The U.S. dollar is on par with the Bahamian dollar and both currencies are accepted in restaurants. Most credit cards are also accepted in most restaurants, although more and more frequently local businesses are shunning American Express. Typically, you will have to ask for your check when you are finished.

What It Costs in U.S. Dollars			
$	$$	$$$	$$$$
RESTAURANTS			
under $20	$20–$30	$31–$40	over $40

RESERVATIONS AND DRESS

Reservations are recommended in Nassau and on the more remote islands, where restaurants may close early if no one shows up or has a table reserved. We mention dress only when men are required to wear a jacket or a jacket and tie. Otherwise, you can assume that dining out is a casual affair.

TIPPING

In The Bahamas, service staff and hotel workers expect to be tipped. The usual tip for service from a taxi driver or waiter is 15%, and $2 per bag is standard for porters. Most travelers leave $3–$5 per day for housekeeping, usually every morning since the staff may rotate. Many hotels and restaurants automatically add a 15% gratuity to your bill; if not, a 15% to 20% tip at a restaurant is appropriate (more for a high-end establishment). A reasonable tip for bartenders is $1–$2 per drink. It's also customary to tip the gas station attendant who fills your rental car $1–$2, especially if they clean the windshield. Grocery store packers are also usually given a few dollars—more if you have lots of bags for them to pack and carry to the car.

WINES, BEER, AND SPIRITS

Kalik and Sands beers are brewed in The Bahamas and are available at most restaurants for lunch and dinner.

📍 Hours

Banks are generally open Monday–Thursday 9 or 9:30 to 3, and Friday 9 to 5. However, on the Family Islands, banks may keep shorter hours—on the less populated islands, they may be open only a day or two each week. Some small islands and settlements no longer have a local bank, so it's always a good idea to take enough cash with you.

Hours for attractions vary. Most open between 9 and 10 am and close around 5 pm.

Pharmacies typically abide by normal store hours, some staying open until 8 or 9 pm.

Most stores, with the exception of straw markets and malls, close on Sunday, although a number of Bay Street stores will open if cruise ships are in port.

Generally, prices in The Bahamas are higher than in the United States. Businesses accept U.S. and Bahamian dollars as they are the same value, but they may not be able to give you change in U.S. currency. On the Family Islands, meals and simple goods can be expensive; prices are high due to the remoteness of the islands and the costs of importing.

🛏 Lodging

The lodgings we list are the top-rated in each price category. Depending on the island, top-rated could be a glitzy resort with a spa and casino or a two-cottage secluded getaway with lots of charm but little in the way of amenities. We always list the facilities that are available—but we don't specify whether they cost extra: when pricing accommodations, always ask what's included.

What It Costs in U.S. Dollars			
$	$$	$$$	$$$$
HOTELS			
under $200	$200–$300	$301–$400	over $400

💲 Money

CREDIT CARDS

Some smaller hotels in the islands do not take plastic.

It's a good idea to inform your credit-card company before you travel, especially if you don't travel internationally very often. Otherwise, the credit-card company might put a hold on your card owing to unusual activity.

Although it's usually cheaper (and safer) to use a credit card abroad for large purchases (so you can cancel payments or be reimbursed if there's a problem), note that some credit-card companies, and the banks that issue them, add substantial percentages to all foreign transactions, whether they're in a foreign currency or not. Check on these fees before leaving home.

CURRENCY AND EXCHANGE

The U.S. dollar is on par with the Bahamian dollar and is accepted all over The Bahamas. Bahamian money runs in bills of $1, $5, $10, $20, $50, and $100. Because U.S. currency is accepted everywhere, there really is no need to change to Bahamian. You won't incur any transaction fees for currency exchange. Carry small bills when bargaining at straw markets.

TAXES

There's no sales tax in The Bahamas, but a 10% VAT (down from 12%, effective January 2022) is added to most goods and services; the departure tax is included in the price of commercial airline tickets.

Tax on your hotel room is 6% to 12% in addition to VAT, depending on the island visited; at some resorts, a small service charge of up to 5% may be added to cover housekeeping and bellman service.

Comprehensive policies typically cover trip cancellation and interruption, letting you cancel or cut your trip short because of illness. Such policies might also cover evacuation and medical care. (For trips abroad you should have at least medical-only coverage.⇨ *See Medical Insurance and Assistance under Health.*) Some also cover you for trip delays because of bad weather or mechanical problems, as well as for lost or delayed luggage.

Another type of coverage to consider is financial default—that is, when your trip is disrupted because a tour operator, airline, or cruise line goes out of business. Generally you must buy this insurance when you book your trip or shortly thereafter, and it's available to you only if your operator isn't on a list of excluded companies.

Essentials

➕ Health and Safety

COVID-19

COVID-19 brought travel to a virtual standstill for most of 2020 and into 2021, but vaccinations have made travel possible and safe again. However, each destination (and each business within that destination) may have its own requirements and regulations. Travelers may expect to continue to wear a mask in some places and obey any other rules (and non-vaccinated travelers may face certain restrictions). Given how abruptly travel was curtailed at the onset of the pandemic, it is wise to consider protecting yourself by purchasing a travel insurance policy that will reimburse you for cancellation costs related to COVID-19. Not all travel insurance policies protect against pandemic-related cancellations, so always read the fine print.

FOOD AND WATER

The major health risk in The Bahamas is traveler's diarrhea. This is most often caused by ingesting fruit, shellfish, and drinks to which your body is unaccustomed. Go easy at first on new foods such as mangoes, conch, and rum punch.

If you're susceptible to digestive problems, avoid uncooked food and unpasteurized milk and milk products, and stick to bottled water, or water that has been boiled for several minutes, even when brushing your teeth.

Drink plenty of purified water or tea; chamomile is a good remedy. In severe cases, rehydrate yourself with a salt-sugar solution (½ teaspoon salt and 4 tablespoons sugar per quart of water).

DIVING

Do not fly within 24 hours of scuba diving. Always know where your nearest decompression chamber is before you embark on a dive expedition, and know how you would get there in an emergency. The only chambers in The Bahamas are in Nassau and San Salvador, and emergency cases are often sent to Miami.

INSECTS

No-see-ums (sand fleas) and mosquitoes can be bothersome. Some travelers have allergies to sand-flea bites. To prevent the bites, use a recommended bug repellent. To ease the itching, rub alcohol on the bites. Some Family Island hotels provide sprays or repellents, but it's a good idea to bring your own.

MEDICAL INSURANCE AND ASSISTANCE

The most serious accidents and illnesses may require an airlift to the United States—most likely to a hospital in Florida. The costs of a medical evacuation can quickly run into the thousands of dollars, and your personal health insurance may not cover such costs or require you to pay upfront and file for reimbursement later. If you plan to pursue inherently risky activities, such as scuba diving, or if you have an existing medical condition, check your policy to see what's covered.

Consider buying trip insurance with medical-only coverage. Neither Medicare nor some private insurers cover medical expenses anywhere outside the United States. Medical-only policies typically reimburse you for medical care (excluding that related to preexisting conditions) and hospitalization abroad, and provide for evacuation. Note that you still have to pay the bills and await reimbursement from the insurer.

Another option is to sign up with a medical-evacuation assistance company. A membership in one of these companies gets you doctor referrals, emergency evacuation or repatriation, 24-hour hotlines for medical consultation, and other assistance. International SOS and AirMed International provide evacuation services and medical referrals. MedjetAssist offers medical evacuation.

SUNBURN
Basking in the sun is one of the great pleasures of a Bahamian vacation, but take precautions against sunburn and sunstroke.

On a sunny day, even people who are not normally bothered by strong sun should cover up with a long-sleeve shirt, hat, and pants or a beach wrap while on a boat or at the beach. Carry UVA/UVB sunblock (with an SPF of at least 15) for your face and other sensitive areas. If you're engaging in water sports, be sure the sunscreen is waterproof.

Wear sunglasses because eyes are particularly vulnerable to direct sun and reflected rays. Drink enough liquids—water or fruit juice—and avoid coffee, tea, and alcohol. Above all, limit your sun time for the first few days until you become accustomed to the rays. Do not be fooled by an overcast day. The safest hours for sunbathing are 4–6 pm, but even then it's wise to limit initial exposure.

SAFETY
As in all destinations, exercise caution at night and in secluded areas. Be aware of your wallet or handbag at all times, and keep your valuables in the hotel safe. Always lock your rental vehicle.

Great Itineraries

Grand Bahama

IF YOU HAVE 3 DAYS

Rent a car for easy island touring at your own pace and schedule. Have breakfast and head out on your diving excursion at **UNEXSO.** Once back above water, head to Banana Bay on **Fortune Beach** to have lunch and unwind. For your evening's entertainment, stroll through the **Port Lucaya Marketplace,** have drinks at Pelican Bay's Bones Bar, then dine on the dock at Flying Fish GastroBar. On Day 3, drive to **West End** for the day, stopping at Lover's Beach for sea glass and **Paradise Cove** for a good snorkel around Deadman's Reef, and continuing on to West End's northeastern water's edge to sample a variety of fresh, made-in-front-of-you conch salads and fritters. End the night with dinner at East Sushi at Pier One to watch the sunset and feed the sharks.

IF YOU HAVE 5 DAYS

Book ecotours on Days 4 and 5 to kayak through the mangroves, snorkel around Peterson Cay, or go birding or feed stingrays with Keith Cooper's West End Ecology Tours. Reserve one night's romantic dinner at the elegant Dolphin Cove Clubhouse and wind down with a gourmet pizza or spicy curry at Pisces in the Port Lucaya Marketplace the next.

IF YOU HAVE 7 DAYS

Save your last two days for more private, quiet relaxation away from the tourist crowds at Old Bahama Bay, West End. If several days on a beach lounger or hammock is too slow for you, this spot has access to some of the best fishing on the island, plus the best fishing guides.

Eleuthera

IF YOU HAVE 3 DAYS

Fly into North Eleuthera and take the ferry to **Harbour Island.** Base yourself at a hotel near the famous 3-mile pink-sand beach or in historic Dunmore Town. Relax on the beach and have lunch at an oceanside restaurant. Stroll through **Dunmore Town** in the afternoon, stopping at craft stands and fashionable shops, admiring colonial houses along Bay Street, and visiting historic churches. At night, dine at one of the island's fine restaurants, such as Sip Sip, Rock House, Pink Sands, or Acquapazza. On Day 2, go scuba diving or snorkeling, or hire a guide and try to snag a canny bonefish. Visit the conch shacks on Bay Street for a low-key beachside dinner. On Day 3 get some last-minute color on the beach or some in-room spa pampering; stop by Gusty's for late-night music.

IF YOU HAVE 5 DAYS

Head back to **Eleuthera** for the next two days. Rent a car at the North Eleuthera Airport (reserve in advance) and drive south past the **Glass Window Bridge,** where you can stand in one spot and see the brilliantly blue and often fierce Atlantic Ocean to the east and the placid Bight of Eleuthera to the west. Continue to **Governor's Harbour,** the island's largest town, and grab lunch at Tippy's. Stay at one of the beach resorts and enjoy the water views. Head into town for nightlife or dining options.

IF YOU HAVE 7 DAYS

On your last two days, drive back to **North Eleuthera,** base yourself at The Cove, and relax on the resort's two beaches. On your final day take the ferry to **Spanish Wells,** where you can rent a golf cart and spend a half day exploring the tiny town and relaxing on a white-sand beach with no tourists. If you'd rather stay put, exploring Surfer's Beach is a great option.

Exuma

IF YOU HAVE 3 DAYS

Fly into **George Town**, relax on the beach or at the pool and, if it's a Friday night, drive to The Fish Fry, a collection of fish shacks and bars just north of George Town; eat at a picnic table next to the beach. Finish the night at Peace & Plenty, the heart of George Town for more than 50 years. On Day 2, pick an activity: golfing at Sandals Emerald Bay; diving, snorkeling, or kayaking (make arrangements the night before at your resort); bonefishing; or driving to a beautiful secluded beach. Get gussied up (sundresses and linen shirts) for a nice dinner in town. On Day 3, head out to **Stocking Island** for some beach volleyball and that it's-five-o'clock-somewhere cocktail. Stay for dinner and sunset. If it's Sunday, a pig roast at noon brings all the islanders over.

IF YOU HAVE 5 DAYS

On Day 4, head to the **Exuma Cays** for some island-hopping: snorkel in Thunderball Grotto, feed swimming pigs and the rare Bahamian iguanas, or find your own secluded sandbar. Spend the night at Staniel Cay Yacht Club and enjoy a festive dinner at the bar. On Day 5, head to the Exuma Cays Land and Sea Park, and spend the day snorkeling, hiking, and relaxing on the beach.

New Providence and Paradise Islands

IF YOU HAVE 3 DAYS

We're guessing you came to The Bahamas to get some sun, so don't waste any time. Decide whether you'd prefer a secluded stretch of sand or a beach right in the middle of the action, such as **Goodman's Bay** or **Junkanoo Beach**—New Providence has both. In the evening, check out the downtown bar and club scene. Spend Day 2 taking in the markets, gardens, and historic sites of **Nassau**. A good starting point is **Rawson Square**, in the heart of the commercial area. Do your shopping in the morning, hitting **Bay Street**, the capital's main street, and Festival Place at **Prince George Wharf.** To avoid the afternoon heat, visit the **National Art Gallery of The Bahamas,** checking out the colonial architecture along the way. When it's time to eat, head to Arawak Cay (the Fish Fry to locals) for an authentic Bahamian meal of fried snapper (served whole) washed down with a cold Kalik or Sands or sky juice. On your third day, tour Paradise Island. Try your luck at the **Atlantis** casino or explore the giant aquariums (non-resort guests will have to purchase day passes). For your final night, book a table at one of Atlantis's fancier restaurants; Nobu or Café Martinique will serve a last supper to remember. Alternately, head west and spend that final day exploring **Baha Mar.** You can play a round of golf, snorkel in the Sanctuary marine park, or book a massage at the impressive spa. With 40 restaurants and bars on-site, the hardest part of your day will be choosing one for that final meal.

IF YOU HAVE 5 DAYS

On Day 4, consider a day trip to one of the Family Islands. Harbour Island is two hours away on the fast ferry (☎ 242/323–2166), or book seats on one of the large speedboats that will take you to a private island in The Exumas. For your final day, rent a car or scooters and head to **Western New Providence,** stopping for fresh conch salad at **Dino's Gourmet Conch Salad** stall on your way to **Clifton Heritage National Park.**

Great Itineraries

Island-Hopping for One Week

The Bahamas is comprised of more than 700 islands, yet many visitors experience just one in a single visit. With limited scheduled transportation between the islands, it's difficult to island-hop without going back to Nassau for each leg, but this itinerary shows how you can use mail boats, speedboats, and scheduled flights to experience Nassau, Paradise Island, Rose Island, Sandals Island, mainland Exuma, and a handful of the Exuma Cays in just a week, provided you arrive in Nassau on a Monday since the mail boat to George Town leaves on Tuesday.

DAY 1: NASSAU
Explore the sprawling marine habitat, face your fears on the exhilarating waterslides (including a clear acrylic slide that plunges through a shark tank), and get up close with sea lions and dolphins at the iconic Atlantis Resort. Aquaventure passes can be limited if occupancy is high, so guarantee access by booking a night at the sprawling resort or the Comfort Suites next door. Dine at one of the 21 restaurants on-property, and then dance the night away at Aura nightclub.

DAY 2: MAIL-BOAT PASSAGE
On Day 2, head downtown and take in the history, architecture, culture, and (most importantly) the food of historic Nassau on the Bites of Nassau Food Tour or with Tru Bahamian Food Tours. With your belly full, head to the eastern side of Potter's Cay Dock to the *Grand Master* mail boat (☎ *242/393–1041*). Once you get your tickets (no need to book in

advance), head over to the colorful stalls to enjoy a game of dominoes and an ice-cold Sands or Kalik beer. The mail boat, which leaves port at 3 pm every Tuesday, will be your transportation, overnight accommodations, and dinner restaurant on your way to George Town, Exuma, all for $50 per person one-way. Don't expect anything fancy; you'll get only a basic bunk in one of two small and stark (yet air-conditioned) cabins. For dinner, it's a plate full of the same hearty meal enjoyed by the crew.

DAY 3: GEORGE TOWN, EXUMA
Following your 14-hour overnight passage—complete with unbelievable sunsets, a strong possibility of dolphin spotting, and space shared with everything from cars to mail to sheep and goats—you'll arrive in George Town bright and early. Make Peace & Plenty your first stop for a Bahamian breakfast staple: boiled fish and johnny cakes. Drop your bags at the hotel, and take the water taxi

from the Government Dock for a day of sun and fun at Chat 'N' Chill on Stocking Island, just a mile offshore. Swim with some wild stingrays that pop in daily for lunch, and treat yourself to tropical libations and conch salad prepared right before your eyes. After, head back over to the mainland for a restful night; evening activities are more or less limited to Fish Fry Friday or the annual Regatta.

DAY 4: EXUMA CAYS

The next day, island-hop the stunning Exuma Cays on a half-day excursion with Exuma Water Sports (☎ 242/357–0770 ⊕ exumawatersports.com ⇨ See Activities in The Exumas).

Skim through the azure, crystal-clear waters from island to island, feeding iguanas on Allan's Cay, petting the swimming pigs on Big Major Cay, taking the perfect selfie at one of the beautiful beaches, and snorkeling in ocean blue holes. Catch the last scheduled flight back to Nassau, where you'll spend another night.

DAY 5: ROSE ISLAND

Just 8 miles off the eastern coast of New Providence lies Rose Island. A popular weekend boating drop for locals, the long island is uninhabited. Book a night at the Sandy Toes Retreat (☎ 242/363–8637 ⊕ www.sandytoesroseisland.com ✉ From $795 a night), a beautifully appointed two-bedroom cottage with unbelievable ocean views. Your boat transportation is included, and once the excursion day-trippers leave at 3:45, you'll have the island to yourself.

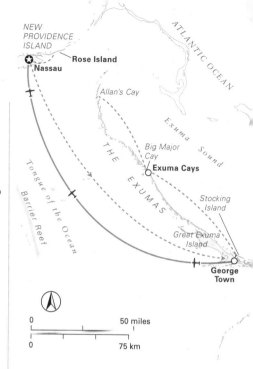

DAY 6: NASSAU

Catch the 20-minute boat ride back to Nassau, and head west to end your island-hopping week with a luxurious massage on the Sandals resort's private island. A day pass gives you access to an array of restaurants, unlimited beverages, and all the amenities, including a private offshore island where you can be pampered in a tiki hut as the waves break on the northern shore. Explore the three beaches or lounge in the pool. Then either head home late in the afternoon or in the early evening or spend one final night on New Providence.

On the Calendar

⇨ *See an expanded list of events in each chapter.*

Winter

Festival Noel. Since 1993, Festival Noel has marked the official start to the Christmas season. Traditionally held the first Friday evening in December at the Rand Nature Centre, this wine- and food-tasting event and art show displays local talent. Proceeds aid the Bahamas National Trust for the development and restoration of national parks on Grand Bahama Island. ⊠ *Rand Nature Centre, East Settler's Way, Freeport* ✛ *Across street from Sir Jack Hayward Junior High School* ☎ *242/352–5438* ⊕ *bnt.bs* ✉ *$55.*

Junkanoo. Once Christmas dinner is over, the focus shifts to Junkanoo. The first major parade of the season starts just after midnight in downtown Nassau. There's a second parade on New Year's Day that starts just after 1 am. ⊠ *Bay St.*

North Eleuthera/Harbour Island Sailing Regatta. The North Eleuthera/Harbour Island Sailing Regatta in October provides five days of exciting competition of Bahamian Class A, B, and C boats. Onshore activities based on Harbour Island include live bands, Bahamian music, cultural shows, food, and drink.

Spring

Bahamian Music and Heritage Festival. March's Bahamian Music and Heritage Festival brings local and nationally known musicians to George Town, along with arts and crafts, Bahamas sloop exhibitions, storytelling, singing, poetry reading, and gospel music. ⊠ *George Town.*

Bahamas International Film Festival. In early May, the Bahamas International Film Festival in Nassau celebrates cinema in paradise, with screenings, receptions, and movie-industry panels. ⊕ *www.bintlfilmfest.com.*

Summer

Conch Fest. Deep Creek's annual, six-day Conch Fest in June means talent shows, Rake 'n' Scrape music, arts and crafts, and, of course, lots of conch. The event was designed to promote the Deep Creek settlement and to share its cultural heritage with the younger members of the community, descendants, and visitors. ⊠ *Rock Sound.*

Cat Island Rake 'n' Scrape Festival. The annual Cat Island Rake 'n' Scrape Festival celebrating indigenous music is held in early June on Bahamian Labour Day weekend. Each day the festivities begin with breakfast and lunch in the park, with games of dominoes and checkers. At 7 pm, the site is cleared for the Battle of the Rake 'n' Scrape Bands. You can also enjoy a gospel concert, cultural dance troupes, a children's corner with games, arts and crafts, and a fishers' and farmers' market. Nearby restaurants expand their menus for the after-parties. Between 1,000 and 2,000 people attend and fill local hotels, inns, and guesthouses, so book early. Two mail boats, Bahamasair, and private charters serve the festival, which takes place in the town square near Arthur's Town Airport. ⊠ *Arthur's Town Square, North Cat Island, Arthur's Town* ✉ *$20.*

Tours

⇨ *See specific chapters for an expanded list of outfitters in each region.*

Bahamas Out-Island Adventures. This tour operator offers full-day, half-day, and over-night kayaking, snorkeling, and surfing trips, and offers accommodations at its headquarters at Surfer's Beach. ⊠ *Gregory Town* ☎ *242/551–9635, 242/335–0349* ⊕ *www.bahamasadventures.com.*

Blue Lagoon Island. Learn about dolphins, sea lions, stingrays, and sharks in their all-natural habitat at this American Humane Certified private-island attraction. Three of their dolphins starred in the movie *Flipper*, and their sea lions played the lead in a number of Hollywood films. Ferry transportation is included with departure from the Paradise Island Ferry Terminal. All programs include beach access, loungers, and a grilled lunch. They also boast the largest inflatable aqua park in Nassau. Beach Day and adults-only VIP Beach Day packages are also available, as is a fun Segway Safari tour and a historic cultural excursion that combines a tour of downtown Nassau with a delicious curated and narrated local lunch accompanied by rum drinks and a bush-tea bar. ⊠ *Paradise Island* ☎ *242/363–1003, 866/448–9535 toll-free from the US* ⊕ *www.dolphinencounters. com* ⊠ *Dolphin Swim $220; Dolphin Encounter $150; Sea Lion Encounter $144; Beach Day $70; Segway Safari $115.*

Island Boy Adventures. Island Boy Adventures offers fishing charters, beach tours, snorkeling, and other ocean adventures in Exuma. ☎ *242/357–0459* ⊕ *www. islandboyadventures.com.*

Powerboat Adventures. The company offers speed-filled day trips to the Exuma Cays on two custom-made powerboats. You can feed wild iguanas and stingrays, go on a snorkeling safari where you are pushed along by the ocean currents, and watch the daily shark-feeding. They even have some swimming pigs. Enjoy an open bar, a filling Bahamian lunch, and conch salad made fresh on the beach. For a true adventure, book an overnight stay on the company's private island, Ship Channel Cay. ⊠ *Paradise Island* ☎ *242/363–2265* ⊕ *www.powerboatadventures.com* ⊠ *$260.*

Seafari Dive Center at Club Med Columbus Isle. The diving operation at Club Med is now run separately by Seafari International, and all dive trips and certifications (PADI and CMAS) are open to Club Med guests and other visitors to the island. This professional dive center consistently offers three dives a day except Thursday, in addition to a weekly night dive, to more than 35 dive sites with permanent moorings. Divers go out on one of two catamarans, 54 and 52 feet. A hyperbaric chamber is on-site, and the staff consists of 11 dive instructors and 4 dive masters. All necessary equipment is available for rent, including Udive computers and Nitrox. ⊠ *Club Med, Cockburn Town* ☎ *242/331–2000, 242/331–2195* ⊕ *www. clubmed.us.*

Tours

Tru Bahamian Food Tours. If you have three hours in Nassau, this is a great way to spend it. These ecofriendly walking tours combine the food, history, and culture of The Bahamas in a way that's sure to leave you satisfied. The five-tasting-stop Bites of Nassau tour includes some popular hot spots as well as some off-the-beaten-path gems. Adults may opt for the two- to three-hour-long Savor Old Nassau food and cocktail tour offered on Sunday. ⊠ *George St. and King St., Nassau* ✛ *Meet outside Christ Church Cathedral* ☎ *242/825–2759* ⊕ *www. trubahamianfoodtours.com* ⊠ *Food tour $75; Food and Cocktail tour $100* ☞ *Not suitable for visitors in wheelchairs; must be at least 18 to join cocktail tour.*

UNEXSO (Underwater Explorers Society). This world-renowned scuba-diving facility provides rental equipment, guides, and boats. Facilities include a 17-foot-deep training pool with windows that look out on the harbor, changing rooms and showers, docks, an outdoor bar and grill, and an air-tank filling station. Daily dive offerings range from one-day discovery courses and dives to specialty shark, dolphin, and cave-diving excursions. Both the facility and its dive masters have been featured in international and U.S. magazines for their work with sharks and cave exploration. UNEXSO and its sister company, The Dolphin Experience, are known for their work with Atlantic bottlenose dolphins. ⊠ *Port Lucaya, Lucaya* ✛ *Next to Pelican Bay Hotel* ☎ *242/373–1244, 800/992–3483* ⊕ *unexso.com* ⊠ *One-tank reef dives $59, Discover Scuba course $129, night dives $79, dolphin dives $219, shark dives $109.*

Contacts

Air

AIRLINE SECURITY
Transportation Security Administration. ⊕ www.tsa.gov.

MAJOR AIRLINES
American Airlines. ☎ 800/433–7300 ⊕ www.aa.com. **Delta Airlines.** ☎ 800/221–1212 ⊕ www.delta.com. **JetBlue.** ☎ 800/538–2583 ⊕ www.jetblue.com. **Southwest.** ☎ 800/435–9792 ⊕ www.southwest.com. **United.** ☎ 800/864–8331 ⊕ www.united.com.

SMALLER AIRLINES
Apollo Jets. ☎ 954/239–7204 ⊕ www.apollojets.com. **Bahamasair.** ☎ 242/702–4140, 800/222–4262 ⊕ www.bahamasair.com. **Cherokee Air.** ☎ 242/367–1920 ⊕ www.cherokeeair.com. **Eastern Air Express.** ☎ 954/772–3363 ⊕ www.easternairexpress.com. **Flamingo Air.** ☎ 242/351–4963, 954/839-8688 ⊕ www.flamingoairbah.com. **Glen Air.** ⊠ Andros Town ☎ 242/368–2116. **Golden Wings Charter.** ☎ 242/377–0039 ⊕ www.goldenwingscharter.com. **Island Air.** ☎ 954/359–9942 ⊕ www.islandaircharters.com. **LeAir.** ☎ 242/377–2356 ⊕ www.flyleair.com. **Miami Seaplane.** ⊠ 3401 Rickenbacker Causeway, Miami ☎ 305/361–3909 ⊕ www.miamiseaplane.com. **Monarch Air Group.** ☎ 954/359–0059, 877/281–3051 ⊕ monarchairgroup.com. **Pineapple Air.** ☎ 242/328–1329 ⊕ www.pineappleair.com. **Silver Airlines.** ☎ 801/401–9100 in U.S. and Canada, 844/674–5837 toll-free from The Bahamas ⊕ www.silverairways.com. **Southern Air.** ☎ 242/323–7217 ⊕ www.southernaircharter.com. **Stella Maris Air Service.** ⊠ Stella Maris Airport ☎ 242/338–2050 reservations, 242/357–1182 pilot's cell phone ⊕ www.stellamarisresort.com/air-service. **Trans Island Airways.** ⊠ Odyssey Aviation, Lynden Pindling International Airport, Nassau ☎ 242/362–4006 in Nassau, 954/727–3377 in Fort Lauderdale ⊕ www.tia.aero. **Triton Airways.** ☎ 844/359–8748 ⊕ www.tritonairways.com. **Tropic Ocean Airways.** ⊠ Sheltair Aviation, 1100 Lee Wagener Blvd., Fort Lauderdale ☎ 954/210–5569, 800/767–0897 ⊕ flytropic.com. **Watermakers Air.** ⊠ 2331 N.W. 55th Court, Hangar 19, Fort Lauderdale ☎ 954/771–0330 ⊕ www.watermakersair.com.

Western Air. ☎ 242/377–2222 ⊕ www.westernair-bahamas.com.

AIRPORT INFORMATION
Grand Bahama International Airport. ⊠ Freeport ☎ 242/352–6020. **Lynden Pindling International Airport.** ☎ 242/702–1010 ⊕ www.nassaulpia.com.

Ferry

Bahamas Ferries. ☎ 242/323–2166 ⊕ www.bahamasferries.com. **Bahamas Paradise Cruise Line.** ⊠ 1 E. 11th St., Riviera Beach ☎ 800/995–3201 reservations, 800/374–4363 customer service ⊕ www.bahamasparadisecruise.com. **Balearia Bahamas Express.** ⊠ Port Everglades, Terminal 1, Fort Lauderdale ☎ 866/699–6988 ⊕ www.baleariacaribbean.com. **Potter's Cay Dockmaster.** ☎ 242/393–1064.

Emergency

Bahamas Air Sea Rescue Association. ☎ 242/325–8864, 242/322–7412.

Contacts

Health

DECOMPRESSION CHAMBER Bahamas Hyperbaric Centre. ☎ *242/362–5765.* **Bahamas Medical Center.** ✉ *Gambier Village* ☎ *242/302–4610* ⊕ *www.doctorshosp.com.*

🛏 Lodging

CONTACTS Bahamas Vacation Homes. ☎ *242/333–4080* ⊕ *www.bahamasvacationhomes.com.*

VISITOR INFORMATION Ministry of Agriculture and Marine Resources. ☎ *242/397–7400.*

🛂 Passport

U.S. Customs and Border Protection. ⊕ *www.cbp.gov.* **U.S. Department of State.** ☎ *202/501–4444* ⊕ *travel.state.gov/content/travel/en/contact-us/Emergencies-Abroad.html.* **U.S. Embassy.** ☎ *242/322–1181* ⊕ *bs.usembassy.gov.*

📍 Visitor Information

Bahamas Ministry of Tourism. ☎ *800/224–2627* ⊕ *www.bahamas.com.* **Bahama Out Islands Promotion Board.** ☎ *954/475–8315* ⊕ *www.myoutislands.com.* **Caribbean Tourism Organization.** ✉ *New York* ☎ *212/635–9530* ⊕ *www.onecaribbean.org.* **Grand Bahama Island Tourist Board.** ☎ *242/352–8356* ⊕ *www.grandbahamavacations.com.* **Harbour Island Tourism.** ⊕ *www.harbourislandguide.com.* **Nassau/Paradise Island Promotion Board.** ✉ *Nassau* ⊕ *www.nassauparadiseisland.com.*

GENERAL INFORMATION AND WARNINGS U.S. Department of State. ⊕ *www.travel.state.gov/travel.*

Chapter 3

NEW PROVIDENCE AND PARADISE ISLANDS

3

Updated by
Jessica Robertson

⊙ Sights	⊕ Restaurants	🛏 Hotels	🛍 Shopping	🍸 Nightlife
★★★★★	★★★★★	★★★★★	★★★★☆	★★★☆☆

WELCOME TO NEW PROVIDENCE AND PARADISE ISLANDS

TOP REASONS TO GO

★ **Beach-hop:** New Providence beaches, though less secluded than those on The Family Islands, still tempt travelers with their balmy breezes and aquamarine water. Choose between the more remote beaches on the island's western end, the action-packed strips of Cable Beach, or the public beaches in downtown Nassau.

★ **Dine with the best of 'em:** New Providence is the country's culinary capital. Eat at a grungy local dive for one meal, then feast at a celebrity-chef restaurant for the next.

★ **Experience Atlantis:** Explore the world's largest outdoor aquarium, splash around in the something-for-everyone water park, or dine at one of the 40-plus restaurants, all while never leaving the resort property.

★ **Celebrate Junkanoo:** This Bahamian carnival takes place the day after Christmas and again on New Year's Day. If you miss the main event in Nassau, there are often smaller parades in Marina Village on Paradise Island.

New Providence Island is often referred to by the name of its historic capital city, Nassau. More than two dozen hotels and at least twice as many restaurants lure nearly 8 million tourists annually to the city and nearby Paradise Island and Cable Beach. The heart of commerce and government and the bulk of the country's 400,000 people are crammed onto the 21-mile by 7-mile island, less than 200 miles from Miami. Venturing outside the three main tourist areas will give you a better idea of true Bahamian life and a glimpse at some under-visited attractions that are worth the trek.

1 Nassau. Pink buildings dating back to the colonial era are interspersed with modern-day office complexes; horses pull their wooden carriages alongside stretch limousines; and tourists browse the local craft-centric straw market or shop for luxurious designer handbags, all in this historic capital city.

2 Paradise Island. P. I. (as locals call the island) is connected to downtown Nassau's east end by a pair of bridges. Atlantis is a beachfront resort complete with a gamut of dining options, a huge casino, and some of the region's fanciest shops. Most memorable, however, are the resort's water-based activities, slides,

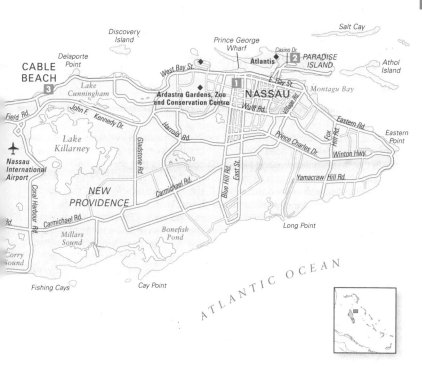

and aquariums, which make it a perfect family destination. Love it or hate it, it's today's face of paradise.

3 Cable Beach. The crescent-shape stretch of sand west of Nassau has been transformed into Baha Mar, a 1,000-acre destination to rival Paradise Island. Three luxurious resorts, a top-class golf course, the largest casino in the Caribbean, a sprawling upscale spa, a new beachfront water park, and a vast array of restaurants, bars, and nightlife guarantee there is something to suit everyone. A short walk west of the resort complex is a smattering of restaurants and cafés.

4 Western New Providence. West of Cable Beach's high-rise hotels, New Providence becomes primarily residential, with small restaurants and bars along the way. West Bay Street hugs the coastline, providing spectacular ocean views. This part of the island is the least developed, so it's the perfect spot to find a secluded beach or go bird-watching.

An incongruous mix of glitzy casinos and quiet shady lanes, splashy megaresorts and tiny settlements that recall a distant simpler age, and land development unrivaled elsewhere in The Bahamas and vast stretches of untrammeled territory. This is New Providence Island, a grab-bag destination.

The island, home to two-thirds of all Bahamians, provides fast-paced living, nightlife that lasts until dawn, and high-end shopping strips. And when all the hustle and bustle becomes too much, it's easy to find quiet stretches of sandy white beach where the only noise is the waves rolling in. In the course of its history, the island has weathered the comings and goings of lawless pirates, Spanish invaders, slave-holding British Loyalists who fled the United States after the Revolutionary War, Civil War–era Confederate blockade runners, and Pro-hibition rumrunners. Nevertheless, New Providence remains most influenced by England, which sent its first royal governor to the island in 1718. Although Bahamians won government control in 1964 and independence six years later, British influence is felt to this day.

Nassau is the nation's capital and transportation hub, as well as its banking and commercial center. The fortuitous combination of tourist-friendly enter-prise, tropical weather, and island flavor with a European overlay has not gone unnoticed: each year more than 4 million cruise-ship passengers arrive at Nassau Cruise Port, which recently underwent a $300 million transformation into a desti-nation in and of itself.

There's a definite liveliness in this capital city that's not found elsewhere in the country, but that doesn't mean you have to follow suit. From shark diving and snorkeling to bicycle tours, horseback riding, tennis, and golf, active pursuits abound in New Providence. Avid water-sports fans will find a range of possibil-ities, including paddleboarding, sailing, kayaking, and deep-sea fishing. Or, simply cruise the clear Bahamian waters on a day trip or an evening excursion.

Planning

When to Go

With the warm Gulf Stream currents swirling and balmy trade winds blowing, New Providence is an appealing year-round destination. Temperatures usually hover in the 70s and 80s and rarely get above 90°F on a midsummer's day or below 60°F on a winter's night. June to October tend to be the hottest and wettest months, although rain is often limited to periodic afternoon showers.

The best time to visit the island is December to May, especially if you're escaping the cold. Don't mind the locals, who'll likely tell you it's too chilly to hit the beach in winter, but you may want to pack a light sweater if you plan on dining outdoors. Visitors from colder climates may find the humid summer days and nights a bit stifling. Be aware that tropical depressions, tropical storms, and hurricanes are a possibility in New Providence during the Atlantic hurricane season from early June to late November, especially later in the season. Expect to pay between 15% and 30% less off-season at most resorts, though that off-season period is shrinking.

FESTIVALS

Bahamas International Film Festival
FILM FESTIVALS | In early May, the Bahamas International Film Festival in Nassau celebrates cinema in paradise, with screenings, receptions, and movie-industry panels. ⊕ *www.bintlfilmfest.com.*

★ **Christmas Jollification**
FESTIVALS | FAMILY | This annual arts-and-crafts fair with Bahamian Christmas crafts, food, and music is held at The Retreat in Nassau the third weekend in November. ⊠ *Bahamas National Trust, Village Rd.* ⊕ *bnt.bs.*

★ **Junior Junkanoo Parade**
CULTURAL FESTIVALS | FAMILY | The island's schoolchildren compete for bragging rights in the Junior Junkanoo Parade in late January along Bay Street. The parade starts at 6 pm, and kids in preschool through high school dress up in crepe-paper costumes and put on an exciting show. ⊠ *Bay St.*

★ **Junkanoo**
CULTURAL FESTIVALS | FAMILY | Once Christmas dinner is over, the focus shifts to Junkanoo. The first major parade of the season starts just after midnight in downtown Nassau. There's a second parade on New Year's Day that starts just after 1 am. ⊠ *Bay St.*

Getting Here and Around

AIR
Lynden Pindling International Airport (NAS) is 8 miles west of Nassau. Many major U.S. airlines fly to Nassau from several different gateways offering a number of daily options. The nation's flag carrier, Bahamasair, flies to Nassau from four airports in Florida—Fort Lauderdale (FLL), Miami (MIA), Orlando (MCO), and West Palm Beach (PBI)—as well as Raleigh-Durham in North Carolina (RDU). Another local airline, Western Air, also has daily flights from Fort Lauderdale (FLL). Many smaller airlines depart from Nassau to the other islands of The Bahamas.

There is no public bus service from the airport to hotels. Major car-rental companies are represented at the airport. A taxi ride for two people from the airport to downtown Nassau costs $32; to Paradise Island, $38 (this includes the $2 bridge toll); and to Cable Beach, $22. Each additional passenger is $4, and excess baggage costs $2 a bag.

BOAT AND FERRY
Water taxis travel between Prince George Wharf and Paradise Island just west of the bridge that takes you to P. I. during daylight hours at half-hour intervals. The one-way cost is $6 per person, and the trip takes 12 minutes. Nassau is also the primary hub for Bahamas mail boats and ferries to The Family Islands.

BUS
The frequent jitneys are the cheapest choice on routes such as the #10 between Cable Beach and downtown Nassau. The fare is $1.50 each way, and exact change is required. Hail one at a bus stop, hotel, or public beach. In downtown Nassau, jitneys wait on Frederick Street and along the eastern end of Bay Street. Bus service runs throughout the day until 7 pm.

CAR

Rent a car if you plan to explore the whole island, and remember to keep to the left. Rentals run $55–$120 per day and are available at the airport, downtown, on Paradise Island, and at some resorts. Gasoline costs between $5 and $6 a gallon. Virgo Car Rental, a local company, doesn't have an airport rental desk, but it does offer a courtesy shuttle to and from its nearby office.

CONTACTS Avis Rent A Car. ⊠ *Lynden Pindling International Airport, Nassau* 📞 *242/377–7121* ⊕ *www.avisbahamas. com.* **Budget Rent-A-Car.** ⊠ *Lynden Pindling International Airport, Nassau* 📞 *242/377–9000* ⊕ *www.budget.com.* **Dollar Car Rental.** ⊠ *Lynden Pindling International Airport* 📞 *786/924-3802* ⊕ *www. dollar.com.* **Hertz Rent-A-Car.** ⊠ *Lynden Pindling International Airport, Nassau* 📞 *242/377–8684* ⊕ *www.hertzbahamas. com.* **Virgo Car Rental.** ⊠ *Airport Industrial Park, Western New Providence* 📞 *242/422-5040* ⊕ *www.virgocarrental. com.*

CRUISE SHIP

Cruise ships dock almost daily at the newly expanded and renovated Nassau Cruise Port, which has been transformed into a destination in and of itself. Taxi drivers who meet the ships may offer you a $2 "ride into town," but the historic government buildings and duty-free shops lie just steps from the dock area. Just outside the port entrance is an ATM that dispenses U.S. dollars.

Just beyond the new row of port shops, you will find a row of taxis and air-conditioned limousines. Fares are fixed by the government by zones. Unless you plan to jump all over the island, taxis are the most convenient way to get around. The fare is $9 plus a $2 bridge toll between downtown Nassau and Paradise Island, $20 from Cable Beach to Paradise Island (plus $2 toll), and $22 from Cable Beach

to Nassau. Fares are for two passengers; each additional passenger is $3. It's customary to tip taxi drivers 15%.

Water taxis travel between the western end of Prince George Wharf and Paradise Island during daylight hours at half-hour intervals. The one-way cost is $6 per person, and the trip takes roughly 10 minutes.

SCOOTER

Motor scooters that carry one or two people can be rented for about $85 for a half day or $150 for a full day.

TAXI

Unless you plan to explore the entire island, taxis are the most convenient way to get around. The fare between downtown Nassau and Paradise Island is $9 plus a $2 bridge toll, from Cable Beach to Paradise Island is $22 (plus $2 toll), and from Cable Beach to Nassau is $22. Fares are for two passengers; each additional passenger is $4. It's customary to tip taxi drivers 15%.

Hotels

If you want to meet locals and experience a little more of Bahamian culture, choose a hotel in downtown Nassau, whose beaches are not dazzling. Other reasons to stay in Nassau include proximity to shopping and affordability (although the cost of taxis to and from the better beaches and attractions can add up). If you want to be beachfront on a gorgeous white strand, stay on Cable Beach or Paradise Island's Cabbage Beach.

The plush Cable Beach and Paradise Island resorts are big and beautiful, glittering and splashy, and have the best beaches, but they can be overwhelming. In any case, these big, top-dollar properties generally have more amenities than you could possibly make use of, a selection of dining choices, and a full roster of sports and entertainment options. Stay in Cable Beach if you don't plan to visit Nassau or Paradise Island often; you need to take a cab or a jitney, and the costs add up.

Restaurants

Find everything from shabby shacks to elegant eateries. You'll recognize celebrity-chef names like Marcus Samuelsson, Jean-Georges Vongerichten, and Nobu Matsuhisa, all of whom have restaurants here. On a budget? Eat brunch at one of the myriad all-you-can-eat buffets at the larger hotels on Paradise Island and Cable Beach or grab a bite at one of the many food trucks that now pepper the island.

Note: A gratuity (15%) is often added to the bill automatically.

HOTEL AND RESTAURANT PRICES
⇨ *Restaurant prices are based on the median main course price at dinner, excluding gratuity (typically 15%) and VAT (10%), which are automatically added to the bill. Hotel prices are for two people in a standard double room in high season, excluding service and 6%–12% hotel tax plus 10% VAT. Restaurant and hotel reviews have been shortened. For full information, visit Fodors.com*

What It Costs in U.S. Dollars			
$	$$	$$$	$$$$
RESTAURANTS			
under $20	$20–$30	$31–$40	over $40
HOTELS			
under $200	$200–$300	$301–$400	over $400

Activities

BOATING
From Chub Cay—one of The Berry Islands, 35 miles north of New Providence—to Nassau, the sailing route goes across the mile-deep Tongue of the Ocean. The historic Paradise Island Lighthouse welcomes yachters to Nassau Harbour, which is open at both ends. The Nassau Cruise Port can handle the world's largest cruise liners; sometimes as many as eight tie up at one time. Two looming bridges bisect the harbor connecting Paradise Island to Nassau. Sailboats with masts taller than the high-water clearance of 72 feet must enter the harbor from the east end to reach marinas east of the bridges.

FISHING
The waters here are generally smooth and alive with many species of game fish, which is one of the reasons why The Bahamas has many fishing tournaments open to visitors every year. A favorite spot just west of Nassau is the Tongue of the Ocean, so called because it looks like that part of the body when viewed from the air. The channel stretches for 100 miles. For fishing charters, parties of two to six will pay $700 or so for a half day or $1,800 for a full day.

SCUBA DIVING AND SNORKELING
DIVE SITES
Coral Reef Sculpture Garden & Coral Nursery. Created by the Bahamas Reef Environment Educational Foundation (BREEF), this underwater art gallery is suitable for scuba divers and snorkelers. The highlight is the 17-foot-tall *Ocean Atlas* crouching on the ocean floor. The site is situated just off Clifton Heritage National Park on southwestern New Providence and is accessible from land or by boat. Be sure to take an underwater camera for a spectacular photographic souvenir.

Gambier Deep Reef. Off Gambier Village, about 15 minutes west of Cable Beach, Gambier Deep Reef goes to a depth of 80 feet.

Lost Ocean Hole. The elusive (and thus exclusive) Lost Ocean Hole (east of Nassau, 40–195 feet) is aptly named because it's difficult to find. The rim of the 80-foot opening in 40 feet of water is studded with coral heads and teeming with small fish—grunts, margates, and jacks—as well as larger pompanos, amberjacks, and sometimes nurse sharks. Divers will find a thermocline at 80 feet, a large cave at 100 feet, and a sand ledge at 185 feet that slopes down to 195 feet.

Lyford Cay Drop-Off. The Lyford Cay Drop-Off (west of Nassau, 40–200-plus feet) is a cliff that plummets from a 40-foot plateau almost straight into the inky blue mile-deep Tongue of the Ocean. The wall has endless varieties of sponges, black coral, and wire coral. Along the wall, grunts, grouper, hogfish, snapper, and rockfish abound. Off the wall are pelagic game fish such as tuna, bonito, wahoo, and kingfish.

Rose Island Reef. The series of shallow reefs along the 14 miles of Rose Island is known as Rose Island Reef (Nassau, 5–35 feet). The coral is varied, although the reefs are showing the effects of heavy traffic. Still, plenty of tropical fish live here, and the wreck of the steel-hulled ship *Mahoney* is just outside the harbor. On weekends be sure to look out for pleasure craft speeding along.

Sea Gardens. This site is off Love Beach on the northwestern shore beyond Gambier.

★ Stuart Cove's

SCUBA DIVING | Located on the island's south shore, this operator is considered by aficionados to be the island's leading dive shop. Although they're pros at teaching beginners (scuba instruction and guided snorkel tours are available), experienced thrill seekers flock to Stuart Cove's for the famous shark dives. The company runs dive trips to the south-shore reefs twice a day, weather permitting. The Snuba adventure, which requires no experience, is $165; snorkeling expeditions cost $118 for adults and $70 for kids 11 and under. The shark dives are $242 for a four-hour two-tank dive. Complimentary shuttle service from all major hotels is included. ⊠ *Coral Boulevard, Coral Harbour* ☎ *242/362–4171, 800/879–9832* ⊕ *stuartcove.com.*

DIVE OPERATORS

Stuart Cove's facilities are PADI-affiliated (Professional Association of Diving Instructors). Expect to pay about $185 for a two-tank dive or $218 for a Discover SCUBA beginner's course. Shark dives run $242, and certification costs $744 and up.

Beaches

New Providence is The Bahamas's most urban island, but that doesn't mean you won't find some beautiful beaches. Powdery white sand, aquamarine waves, and shade-bearing palm trees are easy to come by.

Cable Beach and the beaches near Atlantis are where you'll typically find loud music, bars serving tropical drinks, and vendors peddling everything from parasailing and Jet Ski rides to T-shirts and hair braiding. Downtown Nassau only has man-made beaches, the best being Junkanoo Beach just west of the The Pointe. Yet the capital city's beaches can't compare to the real thing. For a more relaxed environment, drive out of the main tourist areas. You'll likely find stretches of sand populated by locals only, or, more likely, no one at all. Another option is to take a charter or excursion to nearby Blue Lagoon Island or Rose Island.

Shopping

Most of Nassau's shops are on Bay Street between Rawson Square and the British Colonial Hotel and on some side streets leading off both sides of Bay Street. The new Nassau Cruise Port also has a section of colorful shack-style shops that sell only Bahamian-made souvenirs, home goods, and food items. Some stores are popping up on the main shopping thoroughfare's eastern end and just west of the Cable Beach strip. Bargains abound between Bay Street and the waterfront. Upscale stores can also be found in Marina Village, in the Crystal Court at Atlantis, and at Baha Mar on Cable Beach.

You'll find duty-free prices—sometimes as much as 25% to 50% less than U.S. prices—on imported items such as crystal, linens, watches, jewelry, leather goods, and perfumes, but you really need to know the prices before you buy. Not everything is a bargain.

Tours

DAY SAILS
Barefoot Sailing Cruises
BOAT TOURS | The company offers regularly scheduled half-day snorkeling trips, full-day sailing tours of New Providence, and sunset champagne cruises, not to mention private charters. ⊠ *Bayshore Marina, E. Bay St.* ☎ *242/393–5817* ⊕ *www.barefootsailingcruises.com* ⊠ *Half-day sail and snorkel $90; half-day sail, snorkel, and beach $115; full day $140. Prices are higher during peak season.*

Flying Cloud
CRUISE EXCURSIONS | This 57-foot catamaran based at the Paradise Island Ferry Terminal offers half-day sailing and snorkeling tours and full-day cruises with lunch included on Thursdays and Sundays, as well as romantic sunset sails. Private charters can also be arranged. Prices

include round-trip ground transportation from your hotel. ⊠ *Paradise Island Ferry Terminal, Paradise Island* ☎ *242/394–5067* ⊕ *flyingcloud.com* ⊠ *Half day (Mon.–Sat. but not Thurs.) $120; full day (Thurs. and Sun.) $160; evening cruise (Wed. and Fri.) $100.*

FAMILY (OUT) ISLANDS TRIPS
You can visit a number of islands and cays on a day trip by boat from Nassau. Bahamas Ferries does a day trip to Harbour Island: 2½ hours in an air-conditioned ferry (or with the ocean breeze blowing through your hair on the upper deck), with enough time onshore to explore the quaint island via golf cart, have lunch, and stroll the beautiful pink-sand beach. A number of operators offer daily powerboat trips to the upper cays in the Exuma chain, where you can see wild iguanas, stingrays, sharks, and of course the world-famous swimming pigs up close and enjoy their private islands for the day, and there are also excursions to Blue Lagoon Island or Rose Island—both a short boat ride away from Nassau.

★ **Powerboat Adventures**
CRUISE EXCURSIONS | **FAMILY** | The company offers speed-filled day trips to the Exuma Cays on two custom-made powerboats. You can feed wild iguanas and stingrays, go on a snorkeling safari where you are pushed along by the ocean currents, and watch the daily shark-feeding. They even have some swimming pigs. Enjoy an open bar, a filling Bahamian lunch, and conch salad made fresh on the beach. For a true adventure, book an overnight stay on the company's private island, Ship Channel Cay. ⊠ *Paradise Island* ☎ *242/363–2265* ⊕ *www.powerboatadventures.com* ⊠ *$260.*

SPECIAL-INTEREST TOURS
★ **Blue Lagoon Island**
ADVENTURE TOURS | **FAMILY** | Learn about dolphins, sea lions, stingrays, and sharks in their all-natural habitat at this American Humane Certified private-island attraction. Three of their dolphins starred in the

movie *Flipper,* and their sea lions played the lead in a number of Hollywood films. Ferry transportation is included with departure from the Paradise Island Ferry Terminal. All programs include beach access, loungers, and a grilled lunch. They also boast the largest inflatable aqua park in Nassau. Beach Day and adults-only VIP Beach Day packages are also available, as is a fun Segway Safari tour and a historic cultural excursion that combines a tour of downtown Nassau with a delicious curated and narrated local lunch accompanied by rum drinks and a bush-tea bar. ⊠ *Paradise Island* ☎ *242/363–1003, 866/448–9535 toll-free from the US* ⊕ *www.dolphinencounters. com* 🖃 *Dolphin Swim $220; Dolphin Encounter $150; Sea Lion Encounter $144; Beach Day $70; Segway Safari $115.*

★ Bowcar Bahamas

GUIDED TOURS | Rent an ATV, jeep, or buggy and head off on your own adventure, or sign up for one of their guided tours—you'll drive your own buggy while following a tour guide to Nassau's hot spots. Headsets are provided so you can listen along to the narrative. Hotel pickup is included from most major hotels on the island. ⊠ *Sands Road, Nassau* ✛ *off East Street* ☎ *242/557–2223, 800/558–1364* ⊕ *bowcarbahamas.com* 🖃 *ATV rentals starting at $211; 6-seater jeep rental starting at $300; ATV tour from $170; jeep tour starting at $138* ☞ *Drivers must be 21 years and older for ATV tours; 25 years and older for jeep and buggy tours.*

★ Sandy Toes

SPECIAL-INTEREST TOURS | **FAMILY** | Enjoy a day on the beach, in the ocean, at the bar, or frolicking with Nassau's very own swimming pigs at this private-island getaway. You'll enjoy a boat ride from Paradise Island to nearby Rose Island, where Sandy Toes has all the amenities you'll need for a fun day. The excursion includes time with the pigs, snorkeling,

and lunch. Drinks are available at two full-service bars at additional cost. If spending a couple of nights on a private island is a dream of yours, inquire about renting their luxury treetop villa—ideal for a romantic getaway or a weekend with friends or family. ⊠ *Nassau* ☎ *242/363–8637* ⊕ *www.sandytoesbahamas.com* 🖃 *Full-day excursion starting at $229.*

WALKING TOURS

★ Tru Bahamian Food Tours

SPECIAL-INTEREST TOURS | If you have three hours in Nassau, this is a great way to spend it. These ecofriendly walking tours combine the food, history, and culture of The Bahamas in a way that's sure to leave you satisfied. The five-tasting-stop Bites of Nassau tour includes some popular hot spots as well as some off-the-beaten-path gems. Adults may opt for the two- to three-hour-long Savor Old Nassau food and cocktail tour offered on Sunday. ⊠ *George St. and King St., Nassau* ✛ *Meet outside Christ Church Cathedral* ☎ *242/825–2759* ⊕ *www. trubahamianfoodtours.com* 🖃 *Food tour $75; Food and Cocktail tour $100* ☞ *Not suitable for visitors in wheelchairs; must be at least 18 to join cocktail tour.*

Visitor Information

The Ministry of Tourism operates a tourist information booth at the Nassau airport once you've completed the immigration process. The Ministry of Tourism's People-to-People Programme sets you up with a Bahamian family with similar interests to show you local culture firsthand.

CONTACTS Ministry of Tourism. ⊠ *Lynden Pindling International Airport* ☎ *242/302–2000* ⊕ *www.bahamas.com.* **People-to-People Programme.** ☎ *242/302-2000 ext 2716* ✉ *p2p@bahamas.com* ⊕ *www. bahamas.com/people-to-people.*

Nassau

Nassau's sheltered harbor bustles with cruise-ship activity, while a block away Bay Street's sidewalks are crowded with shoppers who duck into air-conditioned boutiques and a smattering of bars and restaurants. Shops angle for tourist dollars with fine imported goods at duty-free prices, yet you'll find a handful of stores overflowing with authentic Bahamian crafts, food supplies, and other delights.

With a more than $300 million overhaul and expansion of the Nassau Cruise Port now complete, Nassau is trying to recapture some of its past glamour. Nevertheless, modern influences are completely apparent: fancy restaurants and trendy coffeehouses have popped up everywhere. These changes have come partly in response to the growing number of upper-crust crowds that now supplement the spring breakers and cruise passengers who have traditionally flocked to Nassau. Of course, you can still find a rowdy bar, but you can also sip cappuccino while viewing contemporary Bahamian art or dine by candlelight beneath prints of old Nassau, serenaded by soft, island-inspired calypso music.

A trip to Nassau wouldn't be complete without a stop at some of the island's well-preserved historic buildings. The large, pink colonial-style edifices house Parliament and some of the courts, while others, like Fort Charlotte, date back to the days when pirates ruled the town. Take a tour via an electric replica vintage Model-T car with Snappa Tours (☎ 242/433–4004) to truly experience the modern and the historic elements of downtown Nassau.

Sights

Arawak Cay
RESTAURANT | Known to Nassau residents as "the Fish Fry," Arawak Cay is one of the best places to knock back a Kalik beer, chat with locals, watch or join in a fast-paced game of dominoes, or sample traditional Bahamian fare. The two-story Twin Brothers and Frankie Gone Bananas are two of the most popular places. Local fairs and crafts shows are often held in the adjacent field. ⊠ *W. Bay St. and Chippingham Rd.* ⌧ *Free.*

★ Ardastra Gardens & Wildlife Conservation Centre
GARDEN | FAMILY | Marching flamingos give a parading performance at Ardastra daily at 11, 1:30, and 3. Children can walk among the brilliant pink birds after the show. The zoo, with more than 5 acres of tropical greenery and ponds, also has an aviary of rare tropical birds, including the bright-green Bahama parrot, native Bahamian creatures such as rock iguanas, the little (harmless) Bahamian boa constrictors, and a global collection of small animals. ⊠ *Chippingham Rd. south of W. Bay St.* ☎ *242/323–5806* ⊕ *www.ardastra.com* ⌧ *Adults $30; children aged 4-12 $9; children 3 and under free.*

Balcony House
HISTORIC HOME | A delightful 18th-century landmark—a pink two-story house named aptly for its overhanging balcony—this is the oldest wooden residential structure in Nassau and its furnishings and design recapture the elegance of a bygone era. A mahogany staircase, believed to have been salvaged from a ship during the 19th century, is an interior highlight. A guided tour through this fascinating building is an hour well spent. ⊠ *Market St. and Trinity Pl., Nassau* ☎ *242/328–6036* ⊕ *ammcbahamas.org/museums/balcony-house* ⌧ *Donations accepted* ☉ *Closed Thurs. after 1pm, and Sat., Sun., and holidays.*

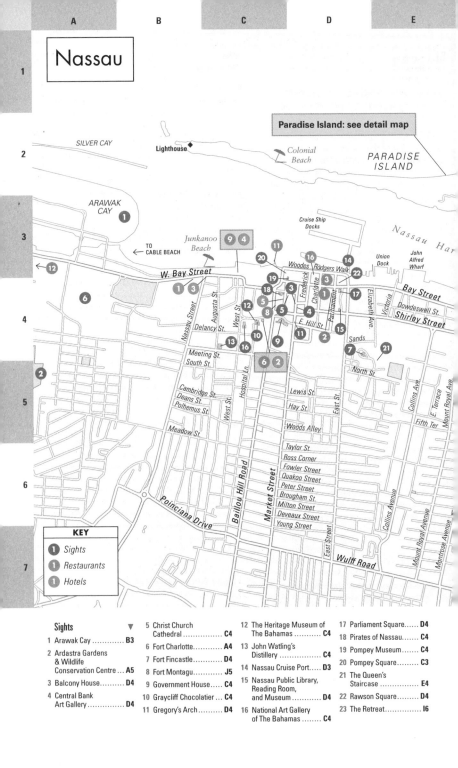

Nassau

Paradise Island: see detail map

SILVER CAY

Lighthouse

Colonial Beach

PARADISE ISLAND

ARAWAK CAY ①

Cruise Ship Docks

Nassau Har

← TO CABLE BEACH

Junkanoo Beach

⑨ ④

⑪

Woodes Rodgers Walk

⑯

⑭

Union Dock

John Alfred Wharf

W. Bay Street

⑳

① ③

⑫

⑥

⑲

⑱ ③

⑤

⑧ ⑤

⑩

⑬ ⑯

Nassau Street

Augusta St.

West St.

Delancy St.

Meeting St.
South St.

Cambridge St.
Deans St.
Polhemus St.

Meadow St.

Hospital Ln.

Frederick
Charlotte

Parliament

Woodes Rodgers Walk

③

① ⑰

Bay Street

Victoria

Dowdeswell St.

Shirley Street

E. Hill St.

⑪

②

⑮

Sands

⑦

North St.

② ⑨

⑥ ②

Elizabeth Ave.

Collins Ave.

E. Terrace

⑳

Lewis St.

Hay St.

Woods Alley

Taylor St.
Ross Corner
Fowler Street
Quakoo Street
Peter Street
Brougham St.
Milton Street
Deveaux Street
Young Street

East St.

Market Street

Fifth Ter.

Poinciana Drive

Baillou Hill Road

East Street

Collins Avenue

Mount Royal Avenue

Montrose Avenue

Wulff Road

KEY

① Sights
① Restaurants
① Hotels

Sights ▼

1 Arawak Cay **B3**
2 Ardastra Gardens
 & Wildlife
 Conservation Centre ... **A5**
3 Balcony House **D4**
4 Central Bank
 Art Gallery **D4**

5 Christ Church
 Cathedral **C4**
6 Fort Charlotte **A4**
7 Fort Fincastle **D4**
8 Fort Montagu **J5**
9 Government House **C4**
10 Graycliff Chocolatier ... **C4**
11 Gregory's Arch **D4**

12 The Heritage Museum of
 The Bahamas **C4**
13 John Watling's
 Distillery **C4**
14 Nassau Cruise Port..... **D3**
15 Nassau Public Library,
 Reading Room,
 and Museum **D4**
16 National Art Gallery
 of The Bahamas **C4**

17 Parliament Square...... **D4**
18 Pirates of Nassau **C4**
19 Pompey Museum **C4**
20 Pompey Square **C3**
21 The Queen's
 Staircase **E4**
22 Rawson Square......... **D4**
23 The Retreat **I6**

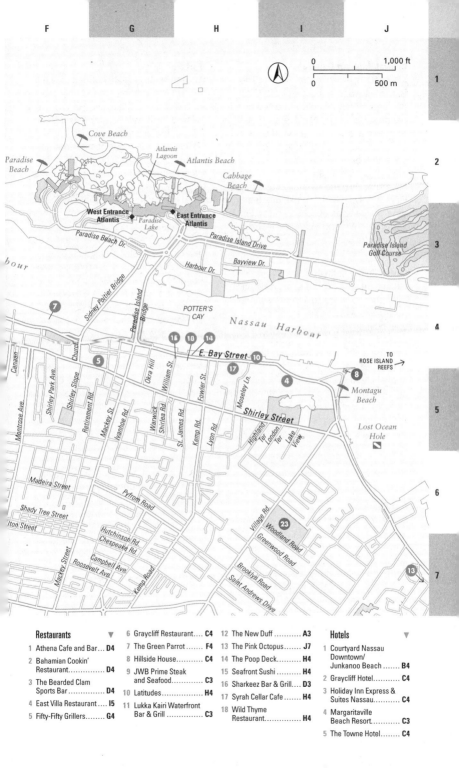

F	G	H	I	J

Restaurants ▼

1 Athena Cafe and Bar... **D4**
2 Bahamian Cookin'
   Restaurant............... **D4**
3 The Bearded Clam
   Sports Bar **D4**
4 East Villa Restaurant **I5**
5 Fifty-Fifty Grillers........ **G4**

6 Graycliff Restaurant.... **C4**
7 The Green Parrot **F4**
8 Hillside House........... **C4**
9 JWB Prime Steak
   and Seafood............. **C3**
10 Latitudes................. **H4**
11 Lukka Kairi Waterfront
   Bar & Grill **C3**

12 The New Duff **A3**
13 The Pink Octopus....... **J7**
14 The Poop Deck........... **H4**
15 Seafront Sushi **H4**
16 Sharkeez Bar & Grill.... **D3**
17 Syrah Cellar Cafe **H4**
18 Wild Thyme
   Restaurant............... **H4**

Hotels ▼

1 Courtyard Nassau
   Downtown/
   Junkanoo Beach **B4**
2 Graycliff Hotel........... **C4**
3 Holiday Inn Express &
   Suites Nassau........... **C4**
4 Margaritaville
   Beach Resort........... **C3**
5 The Towne Hotel........ **C4**

Central Bank Art Gallery

ART GALLERY | The Central Bank of The Bahamas was established in 1973 to oversee monetary policy in a newly independent Bahamas. Art lovers will delight to see that it has also evolved to protect and promote local art, with an extensive collection of more than 500 pieces of original Bahamian art. The bank's foyer is an impressive and carefully curated gallery with ever-changing exhibits featuring emerging and established artists. ⊠ *Market Street, Nassau* 🕾 *242/302–9849* ⊕ *artcentralbankbahamas.com* ☉ *Closed Sat. and Sun.*

Christ Church Cathedral

CHURCH | It's worth the short walk off the main thoroughfare to see the stained-glass windows of this cathedral, which was built in 1841, but only became a cathedral in 1861 when Nassau officially became a city. Don't miss the flower-filled Garden of Remembrance. Sunday Mass is held at 7:30 am, 9 am, 11:15 am, and 6 pm. Drop by the cathedral on Christmas Eve or New Year's Eve to see the glorious church at night and hear the music and choir. Call ahead to find out the time of the service. ⊠ *George and King Sts., Nassau* 🕾 *242/322–4186* ⊕ *www.christchurchcathedralbahamas. com* 🖾 *Free.*

Fort Charlotte

MILITARY SIGHT | FAMILY | Built in 1788, this imposing fort features a waterless moat, drawbridge, ramparts, and a dungeon with a torture device. Local guides bring the fort to life (tips are expected), and tours are suitable for children. Fort Charlotte was built by Lord Dunmore, who named the massive structure after George III's wife. The fort and its surrounding 100 acres offer a wonderful view of the cricket grounds, the beach, and the ocean beyond. ⊠ *W. Bay St. at Chippingham Rd.* ✢ *Opposite Arawak Cay* ⊕ *ammcbahamas.org/forts/fort-charlotte* 🖾 *Nonresidents $5.*

Fort Fincastle

MILITARY SIGHT | FAMILY | Shaped like the bow of a ship and perched near the top of the Queen's Staircase, Fort Fincastle—named for Royal Governor Lord Dunmore (Viscount Fincastle)—was completed in 1793 to be a lookout post for marauders trying to sneak into the harbor. It served as a lighthouse in the early 19th century. A 15- to 20-minute tour that brings this historic site to life costs just a few dollars and includes the nearby Queen's Staircase. The fort's 126-foot-tall water tower is more than 200 feet above sea level (and the island's highest point). Unfortunately the tower remains closed pending restoration. ⊠ *Top of Elizabeth Ave. hill, south of Shirley St., Nassau* ⊕ *ammcbahamas.org/forts/fort-fincastle* 🖾 *Nonresident adults $3.30; children five and under free.*

Fort Montagu

MILITARY SIGHT | The oldest of the island's three forts, Fort Montagu was built of local limestone in 1741 to repel Spanish invaders. The only action it saw was when it was occupied for two weeks by rebel American troops—among them a lieutenant named John Paul Jones—seeking arms and ammunition during the Revolutionary War. The small fortification is quite simple but displays a lovely elevated view of Nassau Harbour. The second level has a number of weathered cannons. A public beach looks out upon Montagu Bay, where many international yacht regattas and Bahamian sloop races are held. ⊠ *East of Bay. St. on Eastern Rd., Eastern Road, Nassau* ⊕ *www.bahamas.com/plan-your-trip/things-to-do/fort-montagu.*

Government House

GOVERNMENT BUILDING | The official residence of The Bahamas governor-general, the personal representative of the Queen since 1801, this imposing pink-and-white building on Duke Street is an excellent example of the mingling of Bahamian-British and American colonial architecture. ✉ *Duke and George Sts., Nassau* ⊕ *www.bahamas.com/plan-your-trip/things-to-do/government-house.*

★ Graycliff Chocolatier

FACTORY | Go behind the scenes at this boutique chocolate factory where you can make your own sweet souvenirs. The tour lasts about an hour, and after watching master chocolatiers in action and learning the history of chocolate production around the world, guests enter the chocolate classroom, where they get to design their own creations, including a signature Graycliff chocolate bar. There is also a chocolate and spirits pairing. ✉ *Graycliff Hotel, W. Hill St., Nassau* ☎ *242/302–9150* ⊕ *www.graycliff.com* ✆ *$10 for the tour; $54.95 for the chocolate making experience; $75 for the chocolates and spirits tour* ☞ *children must be at least 6 years old and accompanied by an adult.*

Gregory's Arch

HISTORIC SIGHT | Named for John Gregory (royal governor, 1849–54), this arch, at the intersection of Market and Duke streets, separates downtown from the "over-the-hill" neighborhood of Grant's Town, where much of Nassau's population lives. Grant's Town was laid out in the 1820s by Governor Lewis Grant as a settlement for freed slaves. Visitors once enjoyed late-night mingling with the locals in the small, dimly lit bars; nowadays you should exhibit the same caution you would if you were visiting the commercial areas of a large city. ✉ *Market St., Nassau* ⊕ *www.bahamas.com/vendor/gregorys-arch* ✆ *Free.*

The Heritage Museum of The Bahamas

HISTORY MUSEUM | **FAMILY** | So many artifacts are on display in this small but interesting museum nestled in historic Mountbatten House that you can easily spend an hour wandering. There is a 40-minute guided tour that covers Bahamian history from the days of pirates through the slavery era to the present.

One of the best exhibits is the life-size replica of the old Bay Street General Store. By a series of coincidences, the collection box from the country's oldest church ended up in this museum—right across the street from the remains of the very same church. ✉ *W. Hill St., Nassau* ☎ *242/302–9150* ⊕ *www.graycliff.com/heritage-and-history-at-graycliff* ✆ *$18.50 guided tour.*

★ John Watling's Distillery

DISTILLERY | The former Buena Vista Estate, which featured in the James Bond film *Casino Royale,* has been painstakingly transformed and returned to its glory days, emerging as the new home of John Watling's Distillery. Parts of the estate date back to 1789, and the line of John Watling's artisanal rums, gins, vodkas, and liquors are handmade, hand bottled, and hand labeled just as they would have been in that era. Take a self-guided tour through the grounds and working estate to learn the fascinating history of the home, and then walk out back to watch the rum production line from an overhead mezzanine. Sit in The Red Tavern with an internationally acclaimed Rum Dum or just a great mojito, and pick up a unique Bahamian souvenir in the on-site retail store. ✉ *17 Delancy St., Nassau* ☎ *242/322–2811* ⊕ *www.johnwatlings.com* ✆ *Free self-guided tour.*

★ Nassau Cruise Port

PROMENADE | Hundreds of millions of dollars have been pumped into expanding and overhauling the cruise port, and it shows. The space that cruise passengers encounter after they tumble off their ships is now a destination in and of itself, complete with exciting local restaurants, a gallery and wine bar, a gelato shop, a Junkanoo museum, an amphitheater with live entertainment, and myriad shops and shacks selling unique Bahamian-made goods. Up to a half-dozen gigantic cruise ships, including the largest in the world, call on Nassau Cruise Port at any one time, and megayachts too large to pull up to any of the island's marinas have a special pier all to themselves. While access to the ship piers is restricted, the new port has been designed to allow open access to all the retail and dining areas. ⊠ *Waterfront at Rawson Sq., Nassau* ☎ *242/608–1870* ⊕ *www.nassaucruiseport.com* 🎟 *Free.*

Nassau Public Library, Reading Room, and Museum

HISTORY MUSEUM | The octagonal building near Parliament Square was the Nassau Gaol (the old British spelling for jail), circa 1797. You're welcome to pop in and browse. The small prison cells are now lined with books. The museum has an interesting collection of historic prints and old colonial documents. ⊠ *Shirley St. between Parliament St. and Bank La., Nassau* ☎ *242/322–4907* ⊕ *https:// www.bahamas.com/plan-your-trip/ things-to-do/nassau-public-library-read-ing-room-and-museum* 🎟 *Free* ☉ *Closed Sun.*

★ **National Art Gallery of The Bahamas**

ART MUSEUM | FAMILY | The national gallery houses the works of esteemed Baha-mian artists such as John Cox, Amos Ferguson, Brent Malone, Antonius Roberts, and Max Taylor. The glorious Ital-ianate colonial mansion, built in 1860 and restored in the 1990s, has double-tiered verandas with elegant columns. It was the residence of Sir William Doyle, the first chief justice of The Bahamas. Don't miss the museum's gift shop, where you'll find books about The Bahamas as well as Bahamian quilts, prints, ceram-ics, jewelry, and crafts. ⊠ *West and W. Hill Sts., across from St. Francis Xavier Cathedral* ☎ *242/328–5800* ⊕ *nagb.org. bs* 🎟 *$10* ☉ *Closed Mon. and public holidays.*

Parliament Square

GOVERNMENT BUILDING | Nassau is the seat of the national government. The Bahami-an Parliament comprises two houses—a 16-member Senate (Upper House) and a 39-member House of Assembly (Lower

Pirates of The Bahamas

Pirates roamed the shallow waters of The Bahamas, hiding out in the 700 islands, but they especially liked New Providence Island. Edward Teach, or Blackbeard, even named himself governor of the island. He scared enemy and crew alike by weaving hemp into his hair and beard and setting it on fire.

House). If the House is in session, sit in to watch lawmakers debate. Parliament Square's pink, colonnaded government buildings were constructed in the late 1700s and early 1800s by Loyalists who came to The Bahamas from North Caro-lina. The square is dominated by a statue of a slim, young Queen Victoria that was erected on her birth date, May 24, in 1905. ⊠ *Bay St.* ☎ *242/322–2041* 🎟 *Free* ☉ *Closed weekends.*

Pirates of Nassau

OTHER ATTRACTION | FAMILY | Take a self-guided journey through Nassau's pirate days in this interactive museum devoted to such notorious members of the city's past as Blackbeard, Mary Read, and Anne Bonny. Board a pirate ship, see dioramas of intrigue on the high seas, hear historical narration, and experi-ence sound effects re-creating some of the gruesome highlights. It's a fun and educational (if slightly scary) family outing. ⊠ *George and King Sts., Nassau* ☎ *242/356–3759* ⊕ *www.piratesofnas-sau.com* 🎟 *$14 adults; $7 children.*

★ **Pompey Museum**

HISTORY MUSEUM | The building, where slave auctions were held in the 1700s, is named for an enslaved man who led a plantation rebellion on Exuma in 1830. The structure and historic artifacts inside were destroyed by fire in December 2011 but have been painstakingly re-created, and new exhibits have been acquired and produced. The exhibit *Struggle for Freedom in The Bahamas: From Slavery to Independence* is located on the ground floor, and a separate exhibit that changes from time to time and has its own admission charge is upstairs. A knowledgeable, enthusiastic young staff is on hand to answer questions. ⊠ *Bay and George Sts., Nassau* ☎ *242/356–0495* ⊕ *ammcbahamas.org/museums/pompey-museum* ⊠ *$5* ⊗ *Closed Sun. and Thurs. afternoons.*

Pompey Square

PLAZA/SQUARE | FAMILY | This open space at the western end of Bay Street overlooks busy Nassau Harbour and is the spot to catch local festivals and events, live music, and Bahamian crafts shows. With 24-hour security, public restrooms, an interactive water feature that delights kids of all ages, and a host of small restaurants and bars nearby, this square pays tribute to an enslaved man who fought for his freedom. ⊠ *Bay St., Nassau* ⊠ *Free.*

The Queen's Staircase

HISTORIC SIGHT | A popular early-morning exercise regime for locals, "the 66 Steps" (as Bahamians call them) are thought to have been carved out of a solid limestone cliff by enslaved people in the 1790s. The staircase was later named to honor Queen Victoria's reign. Pick up some souvenirs at the ad hoc straw market along the narrow road that leads to the site. ⊠ *Top of Elizabeth Ave. hill, south of Shirley St.* ⊕ *www.bahamas.com/natural-wonders/queens-staircase* ⊠ *Free.*

Rawson Square

PLAZA/SQUARE | This shady square connects Bay Street to Prince George Wharf and the Nassau Cruise Port. As you enter off Bay Street, note the statue of Sir Milo Butler, the first post-independence (and first native Bahamian) governor-general. The trees on either side of the bust are lignum vitae—the country's national tree.

The bright yellow flowers that line the sides of the square are the country's national flower, the yellow elder. Horse-drawn surreys wait for passengers to the east of the square (expect to pay about $30 for a half-hour ride through Nassau's streets). Often overlooked is the nearby Randolph W. Johnston bronze statue *Tribute to Bahamian Women,* situated at the entrance to the cruise port. ⊠ *Bay St., Nassau* ⊕ *www.bahamas.com/plan-your-trip/things-to-do/rawson-square* ⊠ *Free.*

The Retreat

GARDEN | Nearly 200 species of exotic palm trees grace the 11 verdant acres appropriately known as The Retreat, which is managed by The Bahamas National Trust. Stroll in blessed silence through the lush grounds of this protected national park, and be on the lookout for native birds. It's a perfect break on a steamy Nassau day. The Retreat hosts the Jollification—the island's unofficial start to the Christmas season—the third weekend in November. Carols, festive food and drinks, a kids' holiday craft center, and local artisans selling native and Christmas crafts make this a must-do event. ⊠ *Village Rd., Paradise Island* ☎ *242/393–1317* ⊕ *bnt.bs* ⊠ *$12* ⊗ *Closed weekends.*

⊕ Beaches

Junkanoo Beach

BEACH | Right in downtown Nassau, this beach is spring-break central from late February through April. The man-made beach isn't the prettiest on the island, but it's conveniently located if you only have a few quick hours to catch a tan. Food and drink shacks line the beach, and you can rent lounge chairs, umbrellas, and non-motorized water-sports equipment. **Amenities:** food and drink; parking (no fee); toilets; water sports. **Best for:** partiers; swimming. ⊠ *Immediately west of Margaritaville Beach Resort* ⊠ *Free.*

🍴 Restaurants

★ Athena Cafe and Bar

$$ | GREEK | You're greeted with a welcoming "Opa!" at this family-owned authentic Greek spot where they serve up tasty lunches at moderate prices. Sit on the second floor among Grecian statuary or on the balcony overlooking the action below. **Known for:** the best Greek salad around; flaming cheese; the cries of "Opa!" as guests walk in. $ *Average main: $28* ✉ *Bay St. at Charlotte St., Nassau* ☎ *242/326–1296* ⊕ *www. athenacafenassau.com* ⊗ *No dinner; closed Sun.*

★ Bahamian Cookin' Restaurant

$$ | BAHAMIAN | Three generations of Bahamian women treat patrons as if they were guests in their own home. And the Bahamian food whipped up in the kitchen is as close to homemade as you can get in a restaurant. **Known for:** home-style cooking; tasty conch fritters; friendly service. $ *Average main: $20* ✉ *Parliament St., Nassau* ☎ *242/328–0334* ⊕ *bahamiancookin.com* ⊗ *Closed Sun., No dinner.*

★ The Bearded Clam Sports Bar

$ | AMERICAN | Nestled in the middle of the International Arcade linking Bay Street and the wharf is this lively bar and restaurant serving up tasty appetizers and meals. Try the traditional Bahamian cracked conch or conch balls. **Known for:** potent drinks with cheeky names; tasty bar fare; lively atmosphere. $ *Average main: $15* ✉ *Nassau* ☎ *242/323–4455* ⊕ *www.facebook.com/BeardedClamNassau/* ⊗ *No dinner.*

East Villa Restaurant

$$$ | CHINESE | In a converted old Bahamian home, this is one of the most popular Chinese restaurants in town. The Chinese–continental menu includes entrées such as conch with black-bean sauce, *hung shew* (walnut chicken), and steak *kew* (cubed prime fillet served with baby corn, snow peas, water chestnuts, and vegetables). **Known for:** traditional Chinese cuisine; broiled NY strip steaks; huge portions. $ *Average main: $35* ✉ *near Nassau Yacht Club, E. Bay St., Nassau* ☎ *242/393–3377* ⊕ *www.eastvillabahamas.com* ⊗ *No lunch Sat. or public holidays.*

★ Fifty-Fifty Grillers

$ | BAHAMIAN | Follow the plume of smoke wafting onto Shirley Street to find this roadside spot with some of the best jerk chicken, pork, and slow-grilled ribs around. It's open Friday and Saturday for takeout only; meals come with a fresh baked roll as well as pasta salad or corn on the cob or cajun fries. **Known for:** best jerk pit around; great value for money; laid-back island vibe. $ *Average main: $14* ✉ *Opposite Ebenezer Methodist Church, Shirley St., Nassau* ☎ *242/677–2833* ⊕ *fiftyfiftygrillers.net* ⊗ *Closed Sun.–Thurs.*

★ Graycliff Restaurant

$$$$ | EUROPEAN | A meal at this hillside mansion's formal restaurant begins in the elegant parlor, where drinks are served over the sounds of a live piano. It's a rarefied world, where waiters wear tuxedos and Cuban cigars and cognac are served after dinner. **Known for:** only five-star rating in town; signature Kobe beef; third largest wine cellar in the world. $ *Average main: $55* ✉ *Graycliff, W. Hill St. at Cumberland Rd., across from Government House, Nassau* ☎ *242/302–9150* ⊕ *www.graycliff.com/dining/* 🏛 *Jacket required for dinner and no shorts permitted.*

★ The Green Parrot

$$ | AMERICAN | This often lively restaurant and bar is situated right along the harbor next to a marina. The large burgers are a favorite at the casual, all-outdoor locale. **Known for:** harbor views; simple but tasty American fare; large, lively bar. $ *Average main: $30* ✉ *E. Bay St. west of bridges to Paradise Island* ☎ *242/322–6900, 242/322–9248* ⊕ *www.greenparrotbar.com.*

Continued on page 78

JUNKANOO IN THE BAHAMAS

by Jessica Robertson

It's after midnight, and the only noise in downtown Nassau is a steady buzz of anticipation. Suddenly the streets erupt in a kaleidoscope of sights and sounds—Junkanoo groups are parading down Bay Street. Vibrant costumes sparkle in the light of the street lamps, and the revelers bang on goatskin drums and clang cowbells, hammering out a steady celebratory beat. It's Junkanoo time!

Junkanoo is an important part of The Bahamas' Christmas season. Parades begin after midnight and last until midday on Boxing Day (December 26), and there are more on New Year's Day. What appears to be a random, wild expression of joy is actually a well-choreographed event. Large groups (often as many as 500 to 1,000 people) compete for prize money and bragging rights. Teams choose a different theme each year and keep it a closely guarded secret until they hit Bay Street. They spend most of the year preparing for the big day at their "shacks," which are tucked away in neighborhoods across the island. They practice dance steps and music, and they design intricate costumes. During the parade, judges award prizes for best music, best costumes, and best overall presentation.

Junkanoo costume, Grand Bahama

JUNKANOO HISTORY

Junkanoo holds an important place in the history and culture of The Bahamas, but the origin of the word *junkanoo* remains a mystery. Many believe it comes from John Canoe, an African tribal chief who was brought to the West Indies as a slave and then fought for the right to celebrate with his people. Others believe the word stems from the French gens *inconnus*, which means "the unknown people"—significant because Junkanoo revelers wear costumes that mask their identities.

The origin of the festival itself is more certain. Though its roots can be traced back to West Africa, it began in The Bahamas during the 16th or 17th century when Bahamian slaves were given a few days off around Christmas to celebrate with their families. They left the plantations and had elaborate costume parties at which they danced and played homemade musical instruments. They wore large, often scary-looking masks, which gave them the freedom of anonymity, so they could let loose without inhibition.

Over the years, Junkanoo has evolved. Costumes once decorated with shredded newspaper are now elaborate, vibrant creations incorporating imported crepe paper, glitter, gemstones, and feathers.

MUSIC'S ROLE

There's something mesmerizing about the simple yet powerful beat of the goatskin drum. Couple that steady pounding with the "kalik-kalik" clanging of thousands of cowbells and a hundreds-strong brass band, and Junkanoo music becomes downright infectious.

Music is the foundation of Junkanoo. It provides a rhythm for both the costumed revelers and crowds of spectators who jump up and down on rickety bleacher seats. The heavy percussion sound is created by metal cowbells, whistles, and oil barrel drums with fiery sternos inside to keep the animal skin coverings pliant. In the late 1970s, Junkanoo music evolved with the addition of brass instruments, adding melodies from Christmas carols, sacred religious hymns, and contemporary hits.

If you're in Nassau anytime from September through the actual festival, stand out on your hotel balcony and listen carefully. Somewhere, someone is bound to be beating out a rhythm as groups practice for the big parade.

DRESS TO IMPRESS

Each year, talented artists and builders transform chicken wire, cardboard, Styrofoam, and crepe paper into magnificent costumes that are worn, pushed, or carried along the Junkanoo parade route. Dancers and musicians tend to wear elaborate headdresses or off-the-shoulder pieces and cardboard skirts

completely covered in finely fringed, brightly colored crepe paper—applied a single strip at a time until every inch is covered. Gemstones, referred to as "tricks" in the Junkanoo world, are painstakingly glued onto costumes to add sparkle. In recent years, feathers have been incorporated, giving the cardboard-covered creations an added level of movement and flair.

In order to wow the crowd, and more importantly, win the competition, every member of the group must be in full costume when they hit Bay Street. Even their shoes are completely decorated. Massive banner pieces so big they graze the power lines and take up the entire width of the street are carried along the route by men who take turns. Every element, from the smallest costume to the lead banner, as well as the entire color scheme, is meticulously planned out months in advance.

EXPERIENCE JUNKANOO

SECURE YOUR SEATS

■ Junkanoo bleacher seat tickets ($10–$50) can be hard to come by as the parade date approaches. Contact your hotel concierge ahead of time to arrange for tickets.

■ Rawson Square bleachers are the best seats. This is where groups perform the longest and put on their best show.

■ If you don't mind standing, make your way to Shirley Street or the eastern end of Bay Street, where the route is lined with barricades. Judges are positioned all along the way so you'll see a good performance no matter where you end up.

■ Junkanoo groups make two laps around the parade route. Each lap can take a few hours to complete, and there are many groups in the lineup, so most spectators stay only for the first round. Head to Bay Street just before dawn, and you'll be sure to score a vacant seat.

BEHIND THE SCENES

■ During the parade, head east along Bay Street and turn onto Elizabeth Avenue to the rest area. Groups take a break in the parking lot here before they start round two. Costume builders frantically repair any pieces damaged during the first "rush" (Bahamian slang for parading), revelers refuel at barbeque stands, goatskin drums are placed next to a giant bonfire to keep them supple, and in the midst of all the noise and hubbub,

you'll find any number of people taking a nap to ensure they make it through a long and physically demanding night.

■ If star-stalking is your thing, scour the crowds in the VIP section in Parliament Square or look across the street on the balcony of the Scotiabank building. This is where celebrities usually watch the parades.

■ When the parade ends, wander along the route and surrounding streets to score a one-of-a-kind souvenir. Despite the many hours Junkanoo participants spend slaving over their costumes, by the time they're done rushing the last thing they want to do is carry it home. Finders keepers.

■ If you're in Nassau in early December, watch the Junior Junkanoo parade. School groups compete for prizes in various age categories. The littlest ones are usually offbeat and egged on by teachers and parents, but are oh-so-cute in their costumes. The high school groups put on a show just as impressive as the groups in the senior parade.

JUNKANOO TRIVIA

■ Kalik beer, brewed in The Bahamas, gets its name from the sound of clanking cowbells.

■ An average costume requires 3,000 to 5,000 strips of fringed crepe paper to completely cover its cardboard frame.

■ During the height of sponge farming in The Bahamas, a major industry in the early 1900s, many Junkanoo participants used natural sponge to create their costumes.

Junkanoo parade in Nassau

JUNKANOO ON OTHER ISLANDS

Nassau's Junkanoo parade is by far the biggest and most elaborate, but most other islands hold their own celebrations on New Year's Day. Nassau's parades are strictly a spectator sport unless you are officially in a group, but Out Island parades are more relaxed and allow visitors to join the rush.

JUNKANOO YEAR-ROUND

Not satisfied with limiting Junkanoo to Christmastime, the Bahamas Ministry of Tourism hosts an annual **Junkanoo Summer Festival.** Smaller-scale parades are held on alternating weekends in June and July on most major islands, including Nassau. In addition to the traditional Junkanoo rush, these festivals offer arts and crafts demonstrations, conch cracking, crab catching, coconut-husking competitions, concerts featuring top Bahamian artists, and of course, lots of good Bahamian food. ☎ *242/302–2000.*

Marina Village on Paradise Island hosts **Junkanoo rushouts** on Wednesday and Saturday (9:30 pm). There are no big stand-alone pieces, but dancers and musicians wear color-coordinated costumes and headpieces. The parade is much less formal, so feel free to jump in and dance along.

The **Educulture Museum and Workshop** in Nassau gives a behind-the-scenes look at Junkanoo. Some of each year's best costumes are on display, as well as costumes from years gone by when newspaper and sponges were used as decoration. The diehard Junkanoo staff will help you make your own Junkanoo creations. Be sure to arrange your visit ahead of time. ☎ *242/328–3786.*

Hillside House

$ | BAHAMIAN | Tucked away in a courtyard off a busy street, you'll find this restaurant, bar, and art gallery all wrapped up in one. The gallery is housed in the 1840 back house—all that remains of an old Bahamian estate. **Known for:** cool, funky oasis; refreshing Bahamian cocktails; beautiful art gallery. $ Average main: $10 ⊠ 13 Cumberland Street, Nassau ☎ 242/322–7678 ⊕ www.hillside-housegallery.com ⊘ Closed Sun. and Mon. ⊂ Gallery admission $2.

★ JWB Prime Steak and Seafood

$$$$ | STEAKHOUSE | Part of the Jimmy Buffet Margaritaville Beach Resort complex, this steakhouse hits all the right marks when it comes to food, drinks, ambience, and service. Dine indoors or outside overlooking Nassau Harbour and the resort marina. **Known for:** steaks cooked to perfection; raw bar; sushi and cocktails happy hour. $ Average main: $50 ⊠ Margaritaville Beach Resort, W. Bay St., Nassau ☎ 242/603–8400 ⊕ www.margaritavilleresorts.com ⊘ No dinner Sun., Closed Mon.

Latitudes

$$$ | FUSION | Book one of Latitudes' teppanyaki tables for a delicious and entertaining dining experience. The chefs will cook your choice of a variety of meats and seafood on the hot grill as you look on in awe. **Known for:** only spot for teppanyaki; views of Nassau Harbour; international brunch on weekends. $ Average main: $35 ⊠ E. Bay St., Nassau ⊹ Opposite entrance to Harbour Bay Shopping Center ☎ 242/676–8025.

★ Lukka Kairi Waterfront Bar & Grill

$$$ | MEXICAN FUSION | For the best views of Nassau Harbour, dine at this quaint bar and restaurant. As you watch the cruise ships pulling in and out of the nearby port, you can sip on a frozen margarita and enjoy some of the best ceviche around. **Known for:** Mexican–Bahamian inspired menu; spectacular 180-degree harbor views; cool breezes

and spectacular sunsets. $ Average main: $35 ⊠ Boardwalk behind Señor Frogs, Woodes Rodgers Walk, Nassau ☎ 242/427–8886.

★ The New Duff

$ | FUSION | This funky little spot puts a unique Asian street-food twist on the guava duff, a traditional Bahamian dessert. Fluffy, handmade steamed *bao* buns filled with sticky sweet fillings like guava or caramelized coconut and smothered with traditional sauce are a must try, but they also serve savory *bao* buns filled with island flavors like jerk chicken, curried mutton, and ginger pork. **Known for:** delicious fusion street food; bao bun guava duff; variety of bush teas. $ Average main: $12 ⊠ W. Bay St., Nassau ⊹ 5 min. walk west of The Fish Fry ☎ 242/824–3000 ⊕ www.thenewduff.com.

The Pink Octopus

$$ | FUSION | One of the only restaurants on the far eastern end of the island, this cool spot is situated within a high-end gated community. The two-story, chic island-style building gets a cool ocean breeze from the beach just outside, and there's a bar situated poolside. **Known for:** upscale atmosphere on the far eastern end; amazing ocean breeze and views; wood-fired pizzas with crispy crust. $ Average main: $30 ⊠ Palm Cay, Yamacraw Rd., Nassau ☎ 242/698–0234 ⊕ palmcay.com/restaurant.

★ The Poop Deck

$$$ | BAHAMIAN | Just east of the bridges from Paradise Island and a quick cab ride from the center of town is this favorite local haunt that is always busy. Start with the conch fritters, then move on to the fish (it's usually served head-to-tail, so if you're squeamish, ask your waiter to have the head cut off before it comes out on your plate). **Known for:** pick-your-own fish; calypso coffee made with secret ingredients (alcoholic); marina and harbor views. $ Average main: $38 ⊠ E. Bay St. at Nassau Yacht Haven Marina ⊹ East of

bridges from Paradise Island ☎ *242/393–8175* 🌐 *thepoopdeck.com.*

Seafront Sushi

$$ | **SUSHI** | One of Nassau's hot spots, this simple restaurant has an extensive menu, including traditional rolls, sushi, and sashimi, as well as more innovative options that incorporate conch and other local delicacies. The volcano roll topped with their special conch sauce is a favorite. **Known for:** volcano roll; sushi worth waiting for; traditional tatami rooms. $ *Average main: $20* ✉ *E. Bay St., Nassau* ☎ *242/394–1706* 🌐 *www.facebook.com/seafrontsushi/* ⏲ *No lunch Sat.*

Sharkeez Bar & Grill

$$ | **BAHAMIAN** | You may have a hard time picking your drink from the extensive menu of frozen concoctions at this upstairs spot. The Sneaky Tiki, with seven types of rum, is a favorite, as are the Sharkeez Volcano (which is set ablaze) and the Nassau Iced Tea, a twist on the "Long Island" traditional. **Known for:** creative frozen concoctions; lively setting; theme nights. $ *Average main: $20* ✉ *Woodes Rodgers Walk, Nassau* ☎ *242/322–8519.*

★ **Syrah Cellar Cafe**

$$ | **ECLECTIC** | This intimate spot is usually packed with locals who reside on the eastern end of the island; be sure to call ahead to book a table. Dine surrounded by bottles of wine and, on some nights, live acoustic guitar. **Known for:** warm and friendly service and atmosphere; eclectic menu; impressive wine pairings. $ *Average main: $25* ✉ *Cotton Tree Traders Plaza, E. Bay St., Nassau* ☎ *242/676–0962* 🌐 *www.syrahvino.com* ⏲ *Closed Sun. and Mon.*

★ **Wild Thyme Restaurant**

$$$ | **ECLECTIC** | Dine inside or on the wraparound porches of a two-story traditional wooden Bahamian home. The menu is small, but there are lots of classic dishes to choose from, including golden beet and tomato salad with feta and goat cheese, or the loaded grilled short-rib grilled cheese sandwich. **Known for:** understated elegance; generous portions; classic and unique signature cocktails. $ *Average main: $40* ✉ *33 E. Bay St., east of Harbour Bay Shopping Plaza, Nassau* ☎ *242/393–4107* 🌐 *www.wildthyme-bahamas.com* ⏲ *Closed Sun.*

Hotels

Courtyard Nassau Downtown/Junkanoo Beach

$$ | **HOTEL** | Enjoy the hustle and bustle of downtown Nassau with a stay at this basic hotel with friendly staff and a nearby beach. **Pros:** easy access to downtown Nassau shops and restaurants; great service all around; great views of busy Nassau Harbour available. **Cons:** only basic breakfast and dinner restaurant on-site; located on a very busy street; beach is public access and extremely busy with cruise passengers. $ *Rooms from: $275* ✉ *Opposite Junkanoo Beach, W. Bay St., west of Nassau St., Nassau* ☎ *242/302–2975* 🌐 *www.marriott.com/hotels/travel/nascy-courtyard-nassau-downtown-junkanoo-beach* *118 rooms* *No Meals.*

Graycliff Hotel

$$$ | **HOTEL** | The old-world flavor of this Georgian colonial landmark—built in 1740 by ship captain John Howard Graysmith—has made it a perennial favorite among both the rich and the famous (past guests have included the Duke and Duchess of Windsor, Winston Churchill, Aristotle Onassis, and the Beatles). **Pros:** old-world charm; lush tropical gardens; cigar and chocolate factories on-site. **Cons:** near busy restaurant and bar area; not easily accessible for those with disabilities; no beach. $ *Rooms from: $400* ✉ *W. Hill St., Nassau* ☎ *242/302–9150* 🌐 *www.graycliff.com* *20 rooms* *Free Breakfast.*

The Graycliff Hotel.

Holiday Inn Express & Suites Nassau

$$ | **HOTEL** | This simple and quiet six-floor hotel is a welcome addition to the New Providence budget-lodging market. **Pros:** walking distance from downtown; breakfast included; friendly staff. **Cons:** on two busy streets; in need of some renovations; loud public beach across the street. 💲 *Rooms from: $235* ✉ *W. Bay St. and Nassau St., Nassau* ☎ *242/322-1515* ⊕ *www.ihg.com/holidayinnexpress* 🛏 *58 rooms* ❤️ *Free Breakfast.*

★ Margaritaville Beach Resort

$$ | **RESORT** | **FAMILY** | The newest resort addition to the downtown Nassau scene pays homage to the late Jimmy Buffett, the legendary musician whose song "Margaritaville" lent itself to the resort brand. **Pros:** sweeping ocean views in every room; 4th floor infinity pool overlooking Nassau Harbour; right in downtown historic Nassau. **Cons:** shared beach with public access; busy area; not a lot of space to spread out in pool area. 💲 *Rooms from: $260* ✉ *W. Bay St., Nassau* ☎ *242/603-8400, 855/410-2331*

⊕ *www.margaritavilleresorts.com/margaritaville-beach-resort-nassau* 🛏 *295 rooms* ❤️ *No Meals.*

The Towne Hotel

$ | **HOTEL** | For travelers hoping to do Nassau on a budget, this is one of the best options. **Pros:** cozy and quaint old Bahamian style; clean rooms; great location in historic downtown Nassau. **Cons:** only parking is public, street-side; dated decor; no additional amenities or activities. 💲 *Rooms from: $130* ✉ *40 George St., Nassau* ☎ *242/322-8450* ⊕ *www.townehotel.com* 🛏 *46 rooms* ❤️ *Free Breakfast.*

 Nightlife

BARS AND CLUBS

Club Waterloo

DANCE CLUBS | This legendary hot spot has had a complete revamp and offers indoor and outdoor bar and dining areas, accommodating up to 2,000 guests at a time. There's often live music, some of the island's top DJs, top-shelf drinks, and a delicious Sunday brunch. ⊠ *E. Bay St., Nassau* ☎ *242/393–5752* ⊕ *club-waterloo.com* ⊗ *Closed Mon.–Thurs.*

★ Tiki Bikini Hut

BARS | Day or night, you'll find a crowd of locals and tourists gathered around the largest beach bar on Junkanoo Beach. Pull up a bar stool or grab a table in the shaded dining area and enjoy views of Nassau Harbour and the sounds of live music. There are daily specials on drinks and shots, plus packages that include beach chairs, umbrellas, and snorkel gear. Group beach activities and Wi-Fi are free. ⊠ *Junkanoo Beach, W. Bay St., Nassau* ☎ *242/826–4053* ⊕ *bamboobeachtikibahamas.com.*

Shopping

CIGARS

Be aware that some merchants on Bay Street and elsewhere in the islands are selling counterfeit Cuban cigars—sometimes unwittingly. If the price seems too good to be true, chances are it is. Check the wrappers, and feel to ensure that there's a consistent fill before you make your purchase. Alternatively, try one of the locally made Graycliff cigars.

Graycliff Cigar Company

TOBACCO | Graycliff carries one of Nassau's finest selections of hand-rolled cigars, featuring leaves from throughout Central and South America. Graycliff's operation is so popular that it has been expanded by the hotel to include an entire cigar factory, which is open to the public for tours, purchases, and even a cigar-rolling lesson. More than a dozen Cuban men and women roll the cigars; they live on the premises and work here through a special arrangement with the Cuban government. True cigar buffs will seek out Graycliff's owner, Enrico Garzaroli. In addition to the shop in the hotel, there's another Graycliff boutique at Lynden Pindling International Airport, and you can also find their cigars and a cigar roller in their newest shop inside the Nassau Cruise Port. ⊠ *W. Hill St., Nassau* ☎ *242/302–9150* ⊕ *www.graycliff.com/graycliff-cigar-company/.*

CLOTHING AND ACCESSORIES

Brass & Leather

LEATHER GOODS | Here you can find leather goods for men and women, including bags, shoes, and belts. Pick up one of the unique soft-leather passport covers that come in an array of colors emblazoned with your country's coat of arms. ⊠ *Charlotte St., off Bay St., Nassau* ☎ *242/322–3806* ⊗ *Closed Sun.*

Cole's of Nassau

WOMEN'S CLOTHING | This is a top choice for everything from ball gowns and cocktail dresses to resort wear and bathing suits, with all the shoes and accessories for every look. Two additional boutiques can be found at The Coral at Atlantis and just outside the gates of Lyford Cay on the western end of the island. ⊠ *Parliament St, Nassau* ☎ *242/322–8393* ⊕ *colesofnassau.com.*

FOOD

★ Bahamas Rum Cake Factory

FOOD | At the Bahamas Rum Cake Factory, delicious Bahamian rum-soaked cakes are made and packaged in tins right on the premises (peek into the bakery) and make a great souvenir. Just make sure you take one home for yourself. ⊠ *602 E. Bay St., Nassau* ☎ *242/395–2109* ⊕ *www.thebahamasrumcakefactory.com.*

Da Bee Hive

FOOD | Beekeeping has taken off in The Bahamas, and this little shop in the Nassau Cruise Port features honey sourced from hives in The Exumas. You can take home amounts ranging from a 2-ounce jar to a gallon jug. The molasses-like amber honey is the most popular. There's a range of locally made beeswax candles as well. ⊠ *Nassau.*

Emporium de Coconut

FOOD | The Bahamas' only coconut-processing company takes every single fiber of a locally sourced coconut and transforms them into a dizzying array of organic coconut products—refreshing dairy-free ice cream, vegan Parmesan flakes, oil, flour, cake mixes, rum liquors, and even body products for you and your pets. You can also enjoy fresh coconut water right in the coconut. ✉ *Nassau* ☎ *242/801–6887* ⊕ *www.emporiumdeco-conut.com.*

★ Mortimer Candies

CANDY | Mortimer Candies whips up batches of uniquely Bahamian sweet treats daily. Pop in for a snow cone on a hot day, or buy some bags of benny cakes, coconut-cream candy, or their signature Paradise Sweets in a swirl of the Bahamian flag colors. ✉ *E. St. Hill, Nassau* ☎ *242/322–5230* ⊕ *www.face-book.com/mortimercandies.*

GIFTS

★ Bahama Handprints

MIXED CLOTHING | Bahama Handprints fabrics emphasize sophisticated tropical prints by local artists in an array of colors. Also look for leather handbags, a wide range of women's clothing, housewares, and bolts of fabric. Watch as the hand-made fabrics are designed right on-site. You can also find their outposts in Marina Village, at the Nassau Cruise Port, and at Baha Mar. ✉ *Harbour Bay Shopping Plaza, off East Bay Street, Nassau* ☎ *242/394–4111* ⊕ *bahamahandprints. com.*

★ The Craft Cottage

CRAFTS | This small shop situated in a traditional wooden structure is a great place to buy locally made souvenirs and gifts, including soaps and oils, hand-painted glassware, jewelry, straw bags, and textiles. The artists and artisans are often on-site. ✉ *20 Village Rd.* ☎ *242/446–7373* ⊕ *www.craftcottagebahamas.com.*

★ Down Home Bahamas

SOUVENIRS | Find some of the best locally made gifts, clothing, home goods, and food and drinks to take home with you in this consignment-based store. ✉ *Parliament Street, Nassau* ☎ *242/603–0733* ⊕ *downhomecollective.com.*

JEWELRY, WATCHES, AND CLOCKS

★ Coin of the Realm

JEWELRY & WATCHES | Coin of the Realm has Bahamian coins and stamps, native conch pearls, tanzanite, and semiprecious stone jewelry. ✉ *Charlotte St. off Bay St., Nassau* ☎ *242/322–4862* ⊕ *www.coinrealm.net.*

Colombian Emeralds International

JEWELRY & WATCHES | Colombian Emeralds International is the local branch of this well-known jeweler; its stores carry a variety of fine jewelry in addition to its signature gem. There are also branches in Marina Village and at the Atlantis Paradise Island Royal Towers and Beach Towers. ✉ *Bay St. near Rawson Sq., Nassau* ☎ *242/322–2230.*

★ John Bull

JEWELRY & WATCHES | Established in 1929 and magnificently decorated in its Bay Street incarnation behind a Georgian-style facade, John Bull fills its complex with wares from Tiffany & Co., Cartier, Mikimoto, Tori Burch, and Yves Saint Laurent. The company has seven locations throughout Nassau, including Atlantis and Baha Mar, and also operates a number of the better-known high-end boutique brand stores, including Gucci and Pandora. ✉ *284 Bay St., Nassau* ☎ *242/302–2800* ⊕ *www.johnbull.com.*

LIQUOR

★ Pirate Republic Brewing Company

WINE/SPIRITS | When you spot a pirate hanging out on Woodes Rogers Walk, you know you've found the home of this local craft brewery. Inside the shop is Pirate Republic beer to sample—Long John Pilsner, Gold and Haze of Piracy, and the Black Beer'd Stout—as well as live music most nights and a limited but tasty grub menu. For a look at how the brew is made, take one of the tours. ✉ *Woodes Rodgers Walk, Nassau* ☎ *242/328–0612* ⊕ *piraterepublicbahamas.com.*

MARKETS AND ARCADES
International Bazaar
SOUVENIRS | This collection of shops under a huge, spreading bougainvillea sells linens, jewelry, souvenirs, and offbeat items. There's often a small band playing all sorts of music along this funky shopping row. ✉ *Bay St. near N. Charlotte St., Nassau.*

Prince George Plaza
MALL | Prince George Plaza, which leads from Bay Street to Woodes Rogers Walk near the cruise-ship docks, just east of the International Bazaar, has about two dozen shops with varied wares. ✉ *Bay St., Nassau.*

PERFUMES AND COSMETICS
The Cosmetic Boutique
COSMETICS | Beauty experts are on hand to demonstrate the latest cosmetics offerings, including products from MAC, Clinique, Bobbi Brown, and La Mer. ✉ *Bay St. near Charlotte St., Nassau* ☎ *242/323–2731.*

The Perfume Bar
PERFUME | This shop carries the best-selling French fragrance Boucheron and the Clarins line of skin-care products, as well as scents by Chanel, Fendi, and other well-known designers. ✉ *Bay St., Nassau* ☎ *242/608–8550* ⊕ *www.facebook.com/theperfumebar/.*

Activities

BOATING
Bay Street Marina
BOATING | With 120 slips accommodating yachts up to 500 feet, this modern, centrally located marina on the Nassau side of the harbor has all the amenities you might need. The marina is within walking distance of Paradise Island as well as downtown Nassau and has a lively restaurant and bar, a hair and nail salon, and courtesy transportation to a nearby grocery store. ✉ *E. Bay St., Nassau* ☎ *242/676–7000* ⊕ *www.baystreet-marina.com.*

Brown's Boat Basin
BOATING | On the Nassau side, Brown's Boat Basin offers a place to tie up your boat, as well as on-site engine repairs. ✉ *E. Bay St., Nassau* ☎ *242/393–3331.*

Nassau Yacht Haven
BOATING | On the Nassau side of the harbor, the island's oldest marina, Nassau Yacht Haven, has 135 berths and also arranges fishing charters. ✉ *E. Bay St., Nassau* ☎ *242/393–8173* ⊕ *www.nassauyachthaven.com.*

Palm Cay Marina & Beach Club
BOATING | The easternmost marina on New Providence offers 194 slips and all the amenities, including a full restaurant, pool, and beach. ✉ *Palm Cay, Yamacraw Hill Rd., Nassau* ☎ *242/676–8554 Harbor Master contact, 242/822–3481 Sales Office* ⊕ *palmcay.com.*

FISHING
Born Free Charters
FISHING | This charter company has seven boats offering half- and full-day fishing charters around Nassau. They also offer snorkel and beach half-day and full-day tours around New Providence, or you can book a full-day tour to see the swimming pigs in The Exumas or at Eleuthera. ✉ *Paradise Island Ferry Terminal, Nassau* ☎ *242/376–9200, 954/526–2363 U.S. phone number* ⊕ *www.bornfreefishing.com* 🛥 *Half-day fishing or snorkeling tour from $700; full-day tour from $1,400; Exuma swimming pigs tour $399 per person; and Eleuthera swimming pigs tour $319 per person.*

Chubasco Charters
FISHING | This charter company has two boats for deep-sea and light-tackle sportfishing. Half- and full-day charters are available. Pickup is from Paradise Island

Ferry Terminal or Nassau Harbour in front of the Straw Market. They guarantee you'll catch something when you go out fishing with them for the full day or you'll get your money back. ⌧ *Paradise Island Ferry Terminal* ☎ *242/324–3474* ⊕ *www. chubascocharters.com.*

SPAS

Baha-Retreat Anti-Aging Spa

SPAS | This spa, situated in an old, wooden, two-story Bahamian home, is popular with locals and offers a full range of spa and salon services. Reservations are suggested, but walk-ins are welcome. Specialties include body-sugaring and threading for hair removal, but massages are also good here. Book a Couples Spa Day for a complete pampering treat. ⌧ *E. Bay St., Nassau* ☎ *242/323–6711* ⊕ *baha-retreat.com* ⊘ *Closed Sun.*

Windermere Day Spa and Salon at Harbour Bay

SPAS | This day spa offers a variety of spa treatments, including facials, massages, body scrubs, manicures, and pedicures, in addition to a full service hair salon. They also have a location in Caves Village in western New Providence. ⌧ *E. Bay St.* ☎ *242/393–8788 Harbour Bay location, 242/327–6135 Caves Village location* ⊕ *www.windermeredayspa.com* ⊘ *Closed Sun.*

TOURS

Bahama Barrels

SPECIAL-INTEREST TOURS | Right across the street from one of the world's largest wine collections is the country's only winery. Tour the space and enjoy samples in the tasting room, or try your hand at blending wine in a small group class. ⌧ *8–14 W. Hill St., Nassau* ☎ *242/302–9150* ⊕ *www.graycliff.com/bahama-barrels/* ⌧ *$55 per person.*

Paradise Island

Graceful, arched bridges ($2 round-trip toll for cars and motorbikes; free for bicyclists and pedestrians) lead to and from the extravagant world of Paradise Island. Until 1962 the island was largely undeveloped and known as Hog Island. A&P supermarket heir Huntington Hartford changed the name when he built the island's first resort complex. In 1994, South African developer Sol Kerzner transformed the existing high-rise hotel into the first phase of Atlantis. Many years, a number of new hotels, a water park, and more than $1 billion later, Atlantis has taken over the island. Home to multimillion-dollar homes and condominiums and a handful of independent resort properties, you can still find a quiet spot on Cabbage Beach or Paradise Beach, which is west of Atlantis.

Sights

★ Aquaventure

WATER PARK | FAMILY | From near-vertical slides that plunge through shark tanks to a quarter-mile-long lazy river ride, this 141-acre water park allows you to both unwind and get your adrenaline pumping. Spend the day going from ride to ride, or relax under an umbrella on the white sand of three unique beaches or by one of 14 swimming pools. Three pools are designed especially for the youngest of guests, including Poseidon's Playzone, a Maya-theme water playground. Day passes for non-resort guests are limited, so be sure to plan well ahead. ⌧ *Atlantis Paradise Island, Paradise Island* ☎ *242/363–3000* ⊕ *www.atlantisbahamas.com/things-to-do/aquaventure-water-park* ⌧ *Day pass $190.*

★ Atlantis Paradise Island

RESORT | FAMILY | With luxury shops, a glitzy casino, and seemingly unlimited choices for dining and drinks (40 restaurants, bars, and lounges), Atlantis

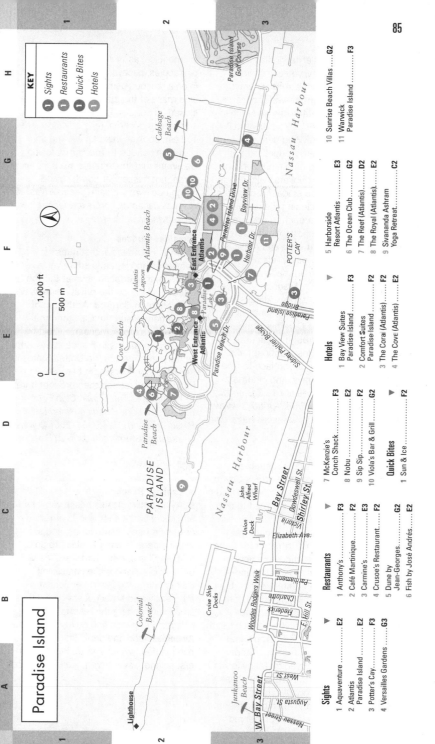

Paradise Island

KEY
- 🔴 Sights
- 🔴 Restaurants
- 🔴 Quick Bites
- 🔴 Hotels

0 _____ 1,000 ft
0 _____ 500 m

Sights ▶
1 Aquaventure E2
2 Atlantis
  Paradise Island E2
3 Potter's Cay F3
4 Versailles Gardens G3

Restaurants ▶
1 Anthony's F3
2 Café Martinique F2
3 Carmine's E3
4 Crusoe's Restaurant F2
5 Dune by
  Jean-Georges G2
6 Fish by José Andrés E2
7 McKenzie's
  Conch Shack F3
8 Nobu E2
9 Sip Sip F2
10 Viola's Bar & Grill G2

Quick Bites ▶
1 Sun & Ice F2

Hotels ▶
1 Bay View Suites
  Paradise Island F3
2 Comfort Suites
  Paradise Island F2
3 The Coral (Atlantis) F2
4 The Cove (Atlantis) E2
5 Harborside
  Resort Atlantis E3
6 The Ocean Club G2
7 The Reef (Atlantis) D2
8 The Royal (Atlantis) E2
9 Sivananda Ashram
  Yoga Retreat C2
10 Sunrise Beach Villas G2
11 Warwick
  Paradise Island F3

is as much a tourist attraction as a resort hotel. At Dolphin Cay, you can interact with dolphins, sea lions, and stingrays. The 63-acre Aquaventure water park provides thrilling waterslides and high-intensity rapids as well as a lazy-river tube ride through the sprawling grounds. Celebrity sightings are frequent at both Nobu restaurant and Aura nightclub. The on-site comedy club, Jokers Wild, brings top comedians to the stage. Many of the resort's facilities, including the restaurants and casino, are open to nonguests, but the leisure and sports facilities are open only to resort guests and those who purchase a day pass. Atlantis has the world's largest man-made marine habitat, consisting of 11 lagoons. To see it, take the guided Discover Atlantis tour, which begins near the main lobby at an exhibition called *The Dig.* This wonderful series of walk-through aquariums, themed around the lost continent and its re-created ruins, brings you face-to-face with sharks, manta rays, and innumerable forms of exotic sea life. ⊠ *Casino Dr., Paradise Island* ☎ *242/363–3000* ⊕ *www. atlantisbahamas.com* ⊠ *Aquaventure day pass $190. Rates vary.*

Potter's Cay

MARKET | Walk the road beneath the Paradise Island bridges to Potter's Cay to watch sloops bringing in and selling loads of fish and conch. Along the road to the cay are dozens of stands where you can watch the conch being extracted from its glistening pink shell, straight from the sea. If you don't have the know-how to handle the tasty conch's preparation—getting the diffident creature out of its shell requires boring a hole at the right spot to sever the muscle that keeps it entrenched—you can enjoy a conch salad on the spot, as fresh as it comes, and take notes for future attempts. Empty shells are sold as souvenirs. Many locals and hotel chefs come here to purchase the fresh catches; you can also find vegetables, herbs, and such condiments as fiery Bahamian peppers preserved

in lime juice, as well as locally grown pineapples, papayas, and bananas. Join in on a raucous game of dominoes outside many of the stalls. Some stalls are closed on Sunday. There's also a police station and dockmaster's office, where you can book an inexpensive trip on a mail boat headed to The Family Islands. Be aware that these boats are built for cargo, not passenger comfort, and it's a rough ride even on calm seas. ⊠ *Nassau* ⊕ *www.bahamas.com/experiences/potters-cay-nassau* ⊠ *Free.*

Versailles Gardens

GARDEN | Fountains and statues of luminaries and legends adorn Versailles Gardens, the terraced lawn at the The Ocean Club, once the private hideaway of Huntington Hartford. At the top of the gardens stand the Cloisters, the remains of a stone monastery built by Augustinian monks in France in the 13th century, imported to the United States in the 1920s by newspaper baron William Randolph Hearst and then brought here by Hartford. ⊠ *The Ocean Club Four Seasons Resort, Paradise Island Dr., Paradise Island* ☎ *242/363–2501* ⊕ *www. fourseasons.com/oceanclub* ⊠ *Free.*

Beaches

★ Cabbage Beach

BEACH | **FAMILY** | At this beach you'll find 3 miles of white sand lined with shady casuarina trees, sand dunes, and sun worshippers. This is the place to go to rent Jet Skis or get a bird's-eye view of Paradise Island while parasailing. Hair braiders and T-shirt vendors stroll the beach, and hotel guests crowd the areas surrounding the resorts, including Atlantis. For peace and quiet, stroll east. **Amenities:** food and drink; lifeguards; parking (fee); water sports. **Best for:** partiers; solitude; swimming; walking. ⊠ *Free*

🍴 Restaurants

Restaurants at Atlantis tend to close one or two nights a week (but not always the same nights each week), and their schedules and availability vary with the resort's occupancy levels. Check with the reservations desk at Atlantis or on their website. Reservations are essential at most of the upscale spots on Paradise Island and a good idea at all restaurants that accept them.

Anthony's
$$ | **AMERICAN** | This lively, casual spot is one of the most affordable places for breakfast, lunch, or dinner this side of Nassau Harbour, but that doesn't mean it's cheap. The baby back ribs with a homemade barbecue sauce are among the most popular on this Bahamian and American fare menu. **Known for:** one of few nonresort restaurants on P. I.; extensive menu; affordable (by P. I. standards) dining. [$] *Average main: $25* ✉ *Paradise Village Shopping Plaza, Paradise Island* ☎ *242/363–3152, 242/363–1682* 🌐 *www.anthonysparadiseisland.com.*

★ **Café Martinique**
$$$$ | **FRENCH** | The original restaurant, which was made famous in the 1965 James Bond film *Thunderball*, has long been bulldozed, but with the help of renowned international chef Jean-Georges Vongerichten and New York designer Adam Tihany, this resurrected classic remains one of the hottest tables at Atlantis. Nestled in the center of Marina Village on Paradise Island, Café Martinique is the height of sophistication in design, service, and cuisine. **Known for:** white-glove service; superior cuts of meat; the fluffy soufflé. [$] *Average main: $65* ✉ *Atlantis Paradise Island, Marina Village, Paradise Island* ☎ *242/363–3000* 🌐 *www.atlantisbahamas.com/dining/fine-dining/cafe-martinique* 💳 *No credit cards* ☞ *children under the age of 6 not permitted after 7pm.*

★ **Carmine's**
$$$$ | **ITALIAN** | **FAMILY** | This Italian restaurant is a great place to go with a small group. Appetizers, entrées, and desserts come in extra-large portions meant to feed a crowd and are served family-style, so the prices can be more affordable (by Paradise Island standards, at least) than they seem at first, especially if you share among several people. **Known for:** huge portions meant for sharing; Titanic (ice cream–laden chocolate torte); options for every member of the family. [$] *Average main: $55* ✉ *Atlantis Paradise Island, Marina Village, Marina Village, Paradise Island* ☎ *242/363–3000* 🌐 *www.atlantisbahamas.com/dining/casual-dining/carmines/menu* ⏲ *No lunch.*

★ **Crusoe's Restaurant**
$$ | **BAHAMIAN** | This hidden gem is worth a visit even if you are not staying at the Comfort Suites; the casual and family-friendly, alfresco restaurant has enticing menus. The lunch menu is available whenever the restaurant is open and offers a variety of sandwiches, wraps, and salads as well as delectable desserts. **Known for:** casual setting with great service; nice alternative to the larger, fancier Atlantis offerings; guava brioche bread pudding. [$] *Average main: $30* ✉ *Comfort Suites, Paradise Island* ☎ *242/363–3680* 🌐 *www.comfortsuites-pi.com/dining/cs-crusoe-restaurant.*

★ **Dune by Jean-Georges**
$$$$ | **MODERN FRENCH** | Feast on Jean-Georges Vongerichten's intricately prepared dishes while overlooking Cabbage Beach at the renowned Four Seasons Ocean Club. Go for breakfast or lunch for the most (relatively) reasonable prices. **Known for:** Chef Jean-Georges's signature dishes; fine dining overlooking the ocean; divine salted caramel banana cake. [$] *Average main: $60* ✉ *Four Seasons Ocean Club, Ocean Club Dr., Paradise Island* ☎ *242/363–2501* 🌐 *www.fourseasons.com/oceanclub/dining/restaurants/dune.*

Did You Know?

Marina Village, an open-air marketplace at Atlantis, is a popular tourist destination. The bazaar features a variety of restaurants, a crafts market, and upscale stores.

★ Fish by José Andrés

$$$$ | **SEAFOOD** | Celebrity chef and philanthropist José Andrés has added his name and global reputation to the restaurant offerings on Paradise Island. As you would expect from the name, seafood takes center stage on this restaurant's mouthwatering menu. **Known for:** fresh seafood; mouthwatering tasting menus; conch served many different ways. [$] *Average main: $55* ✉ *The Cove, Atlantis, Nassau* ☎ *242/363–3000* 🌐 *www.atlantisbahamas.com/dining/finedining/fish-by-jose-andres.*

★ McKenzie's Conch Shack

$ | **BAHAMIAN** | You no longer have to venture over the bridge to get a bowl of authentic conch salad—this takeout shack in Marina Village makes conch salad to order. Pull up a bar stool and watch the dizzying display of knife skills it takes to make this local delicacy. **Known for:** only fresh conch salad on Paradise Island; daiquiri bar; worth the long wait. [$] *Average main: $15* ✉ *Marina Village, Paradise Island* 🌐 *www.atlantisbahamas.com.*

★ Nobu

$$$$ | **SUSHI** | Sushi connoisseurs, celebrities, and tourists pack this Atlantis restaurant night after night. The rock shrimp tempura, yellowtail sashimi with jalapeño, and miso-glazed black cod are Nobu favorites, but this restaurant also takes advantage of fresh Bahamian seafood—try the lobster shiitake salad or the Nobu-style crack conch. **Known for:** traditional Japanese sushi; sake cellar; delicious miso-glazed black cod. [$] *Average main: $60* ✉ *Atlantis Paradise Island, Royal Towers, Paradise Island* ☎ *242/363–3000* 🌐 *www.atlantisbahamas.com/dining/finedining/nobu* ⏲ *No lunch.*

Sip Sip

$$ | **CARIBBEAN** | This famed Harbour Island staple has relocated to Marina Village on Paradise Island. Enjoy a variety of light bites featuring local ingredients, such as black bean hummus, conch chili nachos, or the delicious lobster quesadilla. **Known for:** authentic out-island style; light bites; fresh takes on seafood. [$] *Average main: $26* ✉ *Marina Village, Paradise Island* ☎ *242/363–2000* 🌐 *www.atlantisbahamas.com/dining//casualdining/sip-sip.*

★ Viola's Bar & Grill

$$ | **BAHAMIAN** | This unassuming bar and grill is a consistent Paradise Island favorite with locals and savvy visitors. Their menu is a simple but tasty mix of standard American basics like burgers, pizza, sandwiches, and salads as well as Bahamian classics like curry chicken and conch fritters. **Known for:** lively vibe; delicious Bahamian cooking; frequented by locals and "in the know" visitors. [$] *Average main: $25* ✉ *Casino Drive, Paradise Island* ☎ *242/363–3739* 🌐 *violasbarandgrill.com.*

Coffee and Quick Bites

★ Sun & Ice

$ | **BAHAMIAN** | **FAMILY** | Nothing beats ice cream to cool off after a hot day on the beach or by the pool. This local ice-cream shop serving unique Bahamian flavors is located in the heart of The Coral lobby in Atlantis and often has a long line, but it's worth the wait. **Known for:** locally made ice cream; worth waiting in line for; native fruit flavors like soursop and guava. [$] *Average main: $10* ✉ *The Coral lobby, Atlantis* ☎ *242/363–3000* 🌐 *www.atlantisbahamas.com/dining/cafesquickeats/sun-and-ice.*

Hotels

You'll find several hotels and apartment buildings on Paradise Island, but the sprawling Atlantis resort is the main attraction. It's a bustling fantasy world—at once a water park, entertainment complex, megaresort, and beach oasis. Other than the new Baha Mar resort complex in Cable Beach, it's the largest resort in the country. The public areas are lavish, with fountains, glass sculptures, and gleaming shopping arcades. There is plenty of nightlife on the premises; the casino, ringed by restaurants, is one of the largest in The Bahamas and the Caribbean. Some of these facilities can be visited by nonguests (restaurants, shops, the casino, and nightspots), but you will need to purchase a day pass to enjoy the famed Aquaventure water park as it is otherwise limited to guests of Atlantis and a handful of affiliated hotels as well as cruise passengers.

Bay View Suites Paradise Island

$ | HOTEL | FAMILY | This 4-acre condominium resort has a lush, intimate character, and guests can socialize around three pools that are surrounded by tropical plants, including several hibiscus and bougainvillea varieties. **Pros:** children 12 and under stay free; private "at-home" vibe; suites are huge. **Cons:** long walk from beach; no restaurant serving dinner on property; no organized activities on-site. [$] *Rooms from: $136* ✉ *Bay View Dr., Paradise Island* ☎ *242/363–2555, 800/757–1357* 🌐 *www.bayviewsuitesparadiseisland.com* 🛏 *25 rooms* 🍴 *No Meals.*

★ Comfort Suites Paradise Island

$$ | HOTEL | FAMILY | This all-suites hotel in the middle of Paradise Island is a great spot for families; guests have access to the features of nearby Atlantis, including the Aquaventure water park and the kids' club Atlantis Kids Adventures. **Pros:** use of all Atlantis amenities; near shops, restaurants, and Cabbage Beach; breakfast included. **Cons:** not on a beach; surrounded by busy traffic; activities are only at the Atlantis resort. [$] *Rooms from: $285* ✉ *Paradise Island Dr., Paradise Island* ☎ *242/363–3680, 855/603–1105* 🌐 *www.comfortsuitespi.com* 🛏 *223 suites* 🍴 *Free Breakfast.*

The Coral (Atlantis)

$$$ | RESORT | FAMILY | The family-friendly Coral is at the heart of the Atlantis resort, giving you good access to all the top amenities—including the casino and Aquaventure—at a moderate price point. **Pros:** on-site movie theater (included in resort fee); family-exclusive swimming pool; Marina Village steps away. **Cons:** always busy lobby area; guest rooms lack some of the pizazz you might expect at Atlantis; many kids running around. [$] *Rooms from: $305* ✉ *Atlantis Paradise Island, Paradise Island* ☎ *242/363–3000, 888/877–7525 reservations* 🌐 *www.atlantisbahamas.com/rooms/coraltowers* 🛏 *609 rooms* 🍴 *No Meals.*

★ The Cove (Atlantis)

$$$$ | RESORT | Worlds away from the other properties within the Atlantis resort in terms of overall look, experience, and sophistication, this high-rise overlooking two stunning white-sand beaches is a true grown-ups' getaway. **Pros:** highly exclusive adults-only pool; incredible private beaches; amenities of Atlantis, but separated from the hustle and bustle. **Cons:** a long walk to Atlantis amenities; limited dining and bar options on-site; pricey. [$] *Rooms from: $500* ✉ *Atlantis Paradise Island, Paradise Island* ☎ *242/363–3000, 888/877–7525 reservations* 🌐 *www.atlantisbahamas.com/rooms/thecoveatlantis* 🛏 *600 suites* 🍴 *No Meals.*

★ Harborside Resort Atlantis

$$$ | RESORT | FAMILY | It you want more space to stretch out during your Paradise Island vacation, consider these one-, two-, and three-bedroom town-house–style villas that can accommodate up to nine guests and are fully equipped with separate living/dining areas, kitchens, and private laundry facilities. **Pros:** lots of space to stretch out; pool area is less crowded than Aquaventure; right next door to Nassau water-taxi dock. **Cons:** Wi-Fi is extra; long walk to Atlantis restaurants and amenities; no room service.

Bond in The Bahamas

In *Casino Royale*, the 21st James Bond installment, Bond took on the bad guys at an embassy, which was, in reality, the lovely Buena Vista Restaurant and Hotel in Nassau, which closed shortly after filming and is now home to the John Watling's Distillery. Actor Daniel Craig also had the glamorous background of what is now the Ocean Club, a Four Seasons resort on Paradise Island, where another Bond, Pierce Brosnan, has been known to stay.

Bond and The Bahamas have a long relationship. Six Bond films have used The Bahamas as a backdrop, including *Thunderball*, filmed in 1965 with the original 007, Sean Connery. The late Connery loved The Bahamas so much he chose to live here year-round in the luxury gated community of Lyford Cay.

Thunderball was filmed at the original Café Martinique, which, after being closed for more than a decade, reopened at Atlantis resort on Paradise Island in 2006 albeit in a new location. Scenes were also shot at the Mediterranean Renaissance–style British Colonial, built in the 1920s.

You can swim and snorkel in Thunderball Cave in the Exumas, site of the pivotal chase scene in the 1965 Sean

Connery film. The ceiling of this huge, dome-shaped cave is about 30 feet above the water, which is filled with yellowtails, parrots, blue chromes, and yellow-and-black striped sergeant majors. Swimming into the cave is the easy part—the tide draws you in—but paddling back out can be strenuous, especially because if you stop moving, the tide will pull you back.

The Rock Point house on West Bay Street on New Providence island, better known to 007 fans as Palmyra, the villain Emilio Largo's estate, was another Bond location, and Bay Street, where Bond and his beautiful sidekick Domino attended a Junkanoo carnival, is still the location of Junkanoo twice a year. The *Thunderball* remake, *Never Say Never Again*, was also shot in The Bahamas, using many of the same locations as the original.

Underwater shots for many of the Bond flicks were filmed in The Bahamas, including Thunderball Grotto, while Nassau's offshore reefs were the underwater locations for the 1983 film *Never Say Never Again*, the 1967 film *You Only Live Twice*, the 1977 film *The Spy Who Loved Me*, and *For Your Eyes Only*, released in 1981.

—Cheryl Blackerby

$ *Rooms from: $330* ✉ *Paradise Beach Dr., Paradise Island* ☎ *242/363–3000* ⊕ *www.atlantisbahamas.com/rooms/harborsideresort* ⌁ *392 villas* ◎ *No Meals.*

★ **The Ocean Club**

$$$$ | **RESORT** | Once the private hideaway of A&P supermarket heir Huntington Hartford, this exclusive Four Seasons Resort on magnificent Cabbage Beach's quietest stretch provides the ultimate in understated—and decidedly posh—elegance. **Pros:** ultra-exclusive; lovely beach; top-rated amenities. **Cons:** not within walking distance of Atlantis; limited (and very expensive) on-site dining; Crescent Wing rooms have ocean views, but no pool nearby. $ *Rooms from: $1600* ✉ *Ocean Club Dr., Paradise Island* ☎ *242/363–2501, 800/819–5053 toll free from the U.S. and Canada* ⊕ *www.*

fourseasons.com/oceanclub � 107 rooms ◉ No Meals.

The Reef (Atlantis)
$$$$ | **RESORT** | **FAMILY** | This 497-suite tower has exquisitely outfitted studios or one- and two-bedroom condominium-style accommodations. **Pros:** units fully equipped with kitchens or kitchenettes; quiet; cost-effective option with Atlantis benefits. **Cons:** no restaurants or bars on property; long walk to Atlantis amenities; no grocery stores nearby. $ Rooms from: $550 ⊠ Atlantis Paradise Island, Paradise Island ☎ 242/363–3000, 888/877–7525 reservations ⊕ www.atlantisbahamas.com/rooms/thereefatlantis ➯ 497 apartments ◉ No Meals.

★ The Royal (Atlantis)
$$$$ | **RESORT** | **FAMILY** | At centrally located The Royal, spend your days riding the slides at Aquaventure and your nights in the casino and the nightclub. **Pros:** access to top amenities, including the spa and Aquaventure water park; larger rooms than The Coral; plenty of on-site activities. **Cons:** full balconies only in suites; noisy; pricey on-site dining, subpar fast-food options. $ Rooms from: $465 ⊠ Atlantis Paradise Island, Paradise Island ☎ 242/363–3000, 888/877–7525 reservations ⊕ www.atlantisbahamas.com/rooms/royaltowers ➯ 1201 rooms ◉ No Meals.

★ Sivananda Ashram Yoga Retreat
$$ | **B&B/INN** | Accessible only by boat, this resort features guest rooms in the main house and one-room bungalows overlooking a gorgeous white-sand beach in a 5-acre compound that stretches from Nassau Harbour to the ocean. **Pros:** ideal for peace and quiet; inexpensive accommodations; free shuttle to and from Nassau. **Cons:** two-night minimum stay year round; basic accommodations; no road access. $ Rooms from: $240 ⊠ Paradise Island ☎ 242/363–2902, 866/559–5167 ⊕ sivanandabahamas.org ➯ 190 rooms ◉ All-Inclusive ⌲ Two vegetarian buffet-style meals are included daily.

Sunrise Beach Villas
$$$$ | **HOTEL** | **FAMILY** | Lushly landscaped with crotons, coconut palms, bougainvillea, and hibiscus, this low-rise, family-run resort on Cabbage Beach has a tropical wonderland feel. **Pros:** on one of the best beaches on the island; lively bar on property; great for families. **Cons:** no activities; lots of walking to get to rooms; once-secluded spot on Cabbage Beach now busy due to an arrangement with the Warwick. $ Rooms from: $579 ⊠ Casino Dr., Paradise Island ☎ 242/698–7200, 800/451–6078 ⊕ sunrisebeachclub.com ➯ 28 suites ◉ No Meals ⌲ 1- or 2-bedroom condos sleep 4–6 people.

★ Warwick Paradise Island
$$$ | **ALL-INCLUSIVE** | Suitable for a friends getaway, a romantic weekend, or even a business trip, this 12-story, adults-only hotel overlooks Nassau Harbour. **Pros:** top-notch service; cocktails and dining options included in the rate; away from busy Atlantis. **Cons:** on-site beach is man-made; shuttle or walk to Cabbage Beach; not much by way of activities. $ Rooms from: $375 ⊠ Harbour Drive, Paradise Island ☎ 242/363–2560 ⊕ www.warwickhotels.com/warwick-paradise-island-bahamas ➯ 250 rooms ◉ All-Inclusive.

Nightlife

BARS AND CLUBS
Aura
DANCE CLUBS | Located upstairs from the Atlantis Casino, this nightclub is the place to see and be seen on Paradise Island, though many of the celebrities who frequent the club opt for the ultra-exclusive private lounge. Dancing goes on all night, and bartenders dazzle the crowd with their mixing techniques. The music varies from night to night. ⊠ Atlantis Paradise Island Royal Towers, Paradise Island ☎ 242/363–3000 ext 65734 ⊕ www.atlantisbahamas.com/things-to-do/entertainment/aura-nightclub.

★ The Dilly Club

BARS | You feel like you're stepping back in time inside this coffee shop by day, cocktail bar by night hot spot. The decor is vintage tropical, and the menu and the beverages are all very carefully crafted. The coffee is brewed from locally roasted beans, and the mochas and hot chocolates use locally crafted chocolate. There's also a small selection of food to accompany either your coffee or your cocktail. Take time to peruse the menu— the names and the descriptions are pure entertainment. ✉ *Marina Village, Paradise Island* ☎ *242/603–0266* ⊕ *thedillyclub. com.*

CASINOS

Atlantis Casino

THEMED ENTERTAINMENT | Featuring a spectacularly open and airy design, the 50,000-square-foot (100,000 if you include the dining and drinking areas) casino is ringed with restaurants and offers more than 1,100 slot machines, plus baccarat, blackjack, roulette, craps tables, and such local specialties as Caribbean stud poker. There's also a high-limit table area, and most of the eateries have additional games. The sports book with the massive video wall looks out over the luxury yachts in the marina. The casino is always open, with gaming tables available from 10 am to 4 am daily. ✉ *Atlantis Paradise Island Royal Towers, Paradise Island* ☎ *242/363–3000* ⊕ *www. atlantisbahamas.com/casino.*

Shopping

ARTS AND CRAFTS

The Bahamas Craft Centre

CRAFTS | The Bahamas Craft Centre offers some top-level Bahamian crafts, including a selection of authentic straw work. Dozens of vendors sell everything from baskets to shell collages inside this vibrantly colored building. You can catch a shuttle bus from Atlantis to the center. ✉ *Paradise Island Dr., Paradise Island*

Offshore Adventures

For a true beach getaway, head to one of the tiny islands just off the coast of Paradise Island. A 20-minute boat ride from Nassau, Blue Lagoon Island has a number of beaches, including one in a tranquil cove lined with hammocks suspended by palm trees. Enjoy a grilled lunch, and then rent a kayak or take the Segway tour if you're feeling ambitious.

⊕ *www.nassauparadiseisland.com/ experiences/bahama-crafts-center.*

★ The Plait Lady

OTHER SPECIALTY STORE | If you are looking for authentic Bahamian straw work, this is the place to find it. From bags in all shapes and sizes to floor mats and delightful Christmas ornaments, every piece is handcrafted. They also sell other locally handcrafted items made of conch shell and other shells. You can also buy yards of colorful Androsia fabric here. ✉ *Marina Village, Paradise Island* ☎ *242/363–1416* ⊕ *www.facebook.com/ profile.php?id=100057499786014.*

Activities

BOATING

Atlantis Marina

BOATING | The marina at Atlantis has 63 megayacht slips and room for yachts up to 240 feet. Stay here and you can enjoy all the amenities at Atlantis, including the Aquaventure water park. ✉ *Atlantis Paradise Island, Paradise Island* ☎ *242/363–6068* ⊕ *www.atlantisbahamas.com/ rooms/atlantis-marina.*

Hurricane Hole Superyacht Marina

BOATING | The newly expanded and overhauled Hurricane Hole Superyacht

Paradise Island's Ocean Club has a scenic golf course.

Marina is on the Paradise Island side of the harbor. It accommodates yachts up to 430 feet and offers all the amenities needed by guests and crew. ✉ *Paradise Island* ☎ *242/603–1950* ⊕ *hurricanehole-marina.com.*

FISHING
Live 2 Fish
BOAT TOURS | Hop on board a 38′ catamaran for a full- or half-day outing that includes light tackle fishing—perfect for kids or those who just want to throw a line over and see what's biting. If you do catch something, the crew will clean it and grill it up right there and then for you to enjoy. Tours also include snorkeling and beach activities. ✉ *Paradise Island Ferry Terminal, Paradise Island* ☎ *242/805–0700* ⊕ *live2.fish* ✉ *half-day tours $900; full day $1700 for up to 10 guests.*

GOLF
Ocean Club Golf Course
GOLF | Designed by Tom Weiskopf, the Ocean Club Golf Course is a championship course surrounded by the ocean on three sides, which means that the views are incredible but the winds can get stiff. Call to check on current availability and up-to-date prices. (Those not staying at Atlantis or The Ocean Club Four Seasons Resort can play at a higher rate at management's discretion.) The course is open daily from 6 am to sunset. ✉ *The Ocean Club, Paradise Island Dr.* ☎ *242/363–6682* ⊕ *oceanclubgolfcourse.com* ✉ *$230–$295 for 18 holes (discounted after 1 pm); club rentals $70* ⅃ *18 holes, 7100 yards, par 72.*

SPAS
Mandara Spa at Atlantis
SPAS | Located at Atlantis but open to the public, the expansive, multistory Indonesian-inspired Mandara Spa has treatments utilizing traditions from around the world. Plan to spend more time than your treatment or service requires to enjoy the unisex relaxation lounge, hot and cold plunge pools, and sauna and steam room. Use of the 15,000-square-foot fitness center is complimentary for a day when you spend more than $99

on spa or salon services. The full-service salon offers hair and nail treatments as well as tooth whitening, hair extensions, and waxing. Men can get the works at the barbershop. ⊠ *Atlantis Paradise Island Royal Towers, Casino Dr.* ☎ *242/363–3000* ⊕ *atlantisbahamas.com/things-to-do/spa.*

★ The Ocean Club Spa

SPAS | Paradise Island's Four Seasons Ocean Club has one of the island's most luxurious and indulgent spa retreats. For the ultimate relaxation, treat yourself to the signature Bahamas Rhythm Massage combining breathing techniques, percussive instruments, and deep tissue massage; finish it up with the Sea Lavender and Samphire Polish and Body Nectar Nourishing Wrap to replenish your skin. With just eight villas, it's a good idea to book well in advance, particularly during high season. You can also have the treatment in your hotel room. ⊠ *Four Seasons Resort, Paradise Island* ☎ *242/363–2501* ⊕ *www.fourseasons.com/oceanclub/spa.*

Cable Beach

From downtown Nassau, West Bay Street follows the coast west, past Arawak Cay to the Cable Beach strip. If you're not driving, catch the #10 jitney for a direct ride from downtown. This main drag runs the length of the sprawling Baha Mar resort development, separating the golf course and green space from the resorts and beach. Walk or drive west of the megaresort for a smattering of smaller restaurants and local neighborhoods.

 Sights

★ Baha Bay

WATER PARK | **FAMILY** | Whether you're up for an exhilarating rush down a near vertical waterslide or prefer to relax on a calm, lazy river loop, Baha Bay has something for everyone. The 15-acre water park includes a 20,000-square-foot wave

pool with intermittent waves reaching up to 5 feet as well as a three-lane surf simulator. There's also a pool area dedicated to younger guests with shallow pools and kid-sized slides. ⊠ *Cable Beach* ☎ *242/788–8000* ⊕ *bahabay.bahamar.com* ⊠ *$160 adults; $65 any guest under 48" tall.*

The Caves

CAVE | These large limestone caverns that the waves sculpted over the eons are said to have sheltered the early Arawak people. An oddity perched right beside the road, they're worth a glance—although in truth, there's not much to see as the dark interior doesn't lend itself to exploration. There's a funky chair outside for fun photo ops, and across the street is a concrete viewing platform overlooking the ocean. This has become a popular stop for the myriad jeep and ATV tours, so at any point a large crowd could descend. ⊠ *W. Bay St. and Blake Rd., Cable Beach* ⊠ *Free.*

 Beaches

Cable Beach

BEACH | Hotels, including the massive Baha Mar resort development and the new Goldwynn Resort & Residences, dot the length of this 3-mile beach, so don't expect isolation. Music from hotel pool decks wafts out onto the sand, Jet Skis race up and down the waves, and vendors sell everything from shell jewelry to coconut drinks right from the shell. Access via new hotels may be limited, but join the locals and park at the Goodman's Bay park on the eastern end of the beach. **Amenities:** parking (no fee); water sports. **Best for:** partiers; sunset; swimming; walking. ⊠ *Cable Beach.*

 Restaurants

Cafe Johnny Canoe

$$$ | **BAHAMIAN** | **FAMILY** | Years after this well-known restaurant was forced to close its doors, Cafe Johnny Canoe is

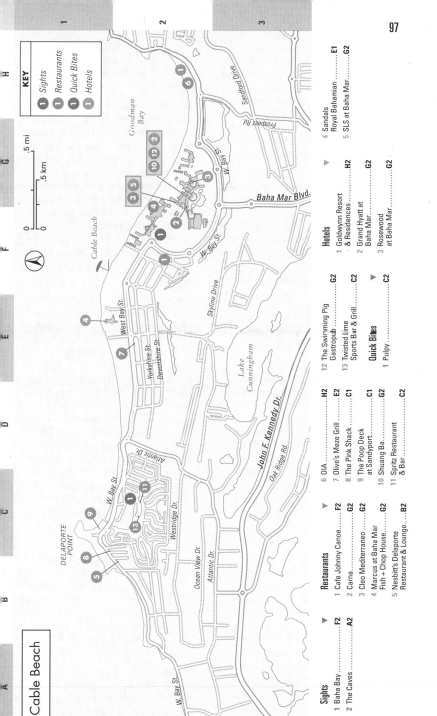

97

Cable Beach

KEY

- ⓵ Sights
- ⓵ Restaurants
- ⓵ Quick Bites
- ⓵ Hotels

Goodman Bay

Cable Beach

Lake Cunningham

DELAPORTE POINT

Sandford Drive

Prospect Rd.

Baha Mar Blvd.

Skyline Drive

John F. Kennedy Dr.

Oak Ridge Rd.

W. Bay St.

West Bay St.

Yorkshire St.

Devonshire St.

Westridge Dr.

Ocean View Dr.

Atlantic Dr.

Atlantic Dr.

W. Bay St.

0   .5 mi
0   .5 km

Sights ▶
1 Baha Bay **F2**
2 The Caves **A2**

Restaurants ▶
1 Cafe Johnny Canoe **F2**
2 Carna **G2**
3 Cleo Mediterraneo **G2**
4 Marcus at Baha Mar
   Fish + Chop House **G2**
5 Nesbit's Delaporte
   Restaurant & Lounge ... **B2**
6 OIA **H2**
7 Olive's Meze Grill **E2**
8 The Pink Shack **C1**
9 The Poop Deck
   at Sandyport **C1**
10 Shuang Ba **G2**
11 Spritz Restaurant
   & Bar **C2**
12 The Swimming Pig
   Gastropub **G2**
13 Twisted Lime
   Sports Bar & Grill **C2**

Quick Bites ▶
1 Pulpy **C2**

Hotels ▶
1 Goldwynn Resort
   & Residences **H2**
2 Grand Hyatt at
   Baha Mar **G2**
3 Rosewood
   at Baha Mar **G2**
4 Sandals
   Royal Bahamian **E1**
5 SLS at Baha Mar **G2**

back. With a focus on good local food, it showcases the best of The Bahamas in the heart of the Cable Beach scene. **Known for:** legendary status; conchy conch fritters; easier on the wallet than the resort spots. [$] *Average main: $35* ⊠ *W. Baha Mar Blvd., Cable Beach* ☎ *242/698–1171* ⊕ *cafejohnnycanoe.com.*

Carna

$$$$ | **STEAKHOUSE** | Legendary butcher Dario Cecchini brings his contemporary steak house to Baha Mar with Carna. Start off with charcuterie or something from the raw bar: fresh shucked oysters with classic mignonette or build your own seafood tower for a bit of the best the sea has to offer. **Known for:** best cuts of beef; fresh raw bar; extensive wine list. [$] *Average main: $90* ⊠ *Baha Mar near SLS, Cable Beach* ☎ *242/788–8200* ⊕ *bahamar.com/culinary* ☉ *Closed Mon.–Wed.*

★ **Cleo Mediterraneo**

$$$ | **MEDITERRANEAN** | Award-winning chef Danny Elmaleh's Cleo upholds the imaginative twists on Mediterranean cuisine for which his series of restaurants have gained acclaim. Order hummus and baba ghanoush for starters, followed by grilled octopus or *saganaki* Haloumi cheese, which is flambéed right at the table. **Known for:** Moroccan tagine menu; tasty artichoke hummus; the best Brussels sprouts you've ever had. [$] *Average main: $40* ⊠ *SLS, Baha Mar, Cable Beach* ☎ *242/788–8200* ⊕ *bahamar.com/culinary.*

★ **Marcus at Baha Mar Fish + Chop House**

$$$$ | **BAHAMIAN** | Celebrity chef and James Beard Award–winner Marcus Samuelsson is the mastermind behind this Baha Mar restaurant, which sources fresh local ingredients in its Bahamian dishes. The restaurant has a beachfront dining area and a rooftop cocktail bar, with a DJ from 9 p.m. on Friday and Saturday nights. **Known for:** raw bar; island favorites like conch fritters; sunset cocktails at the rooftop bar. [$] *Average*

main: $55 ⊠ *1 Baha Mar Blvd., Cable Beach* ☎ *242/788–7323* ⊕ *www.marcus-bahamar.com.*

Nesbitt's Delaporte Restaurant & Lounge

$$ | **BAHAMIAN** | The vibe in this hole-in-the-wall restaurant is set by whomever controls the jukebox, which has everything from current hits to old-school R&B to local Rake 'n' Scrape. The food is simple but hits the spot, and the lounge is a great place to meet some locals. **Known for:** late-night libations; authentic Bahamian fare; hangout for tourists and locals. [$] *Average main: $20* ⊠ *Cable Beach* ⊕ *West of BTC Delaporte phone tower* ☎ *242/327–6036* ⊕ *www.nesbitts-restaurant.com.*

OIA

$$$$ | **ASIAN FUSION** | Enjoy amazing views of the ocean from every seat at this Meditteranean–Japanese fusion restaurant inside the new Goldwynn Resort. Dishes are made for sharing—starting with the tapas, including the Gambas Pil Pil (shrimp tossed in their signature sauce), roasted cauliflower, and Korobuta pork belly. **Known for:** incredible ocean views from every table; unique Mediterr-Asian cuisine; food that looks as good as it tastes. [$] *Average main: $50* ⊠ *Goldwynn Resort, West Bay Street, Cable Beach* ☎ *242/605–3600* ⊕ *goldwynnresorts.com/restaurants/signature-restaurant-2/* ☉ *No lunch.*

Olive's Meze Grill

$$$ | **MEDITERRANEAN** | Hip and trendy, this restaurant puts a fresh twist on Mediterranean classics. The fare is simple, but locally grown greens and fish caught in nearby waters make the meals special. **Known for:** flaming cheese lit table-side; boozy brunches; late-night weekend hot spot. [$] *Average main: $35* ⊠ *W. Bay St., Cable Beach* ☎ *242/676–5396.*

★ **The Pink Shack**

$$ | **BAHAMIAN** | The name describes this vibrant and popular roadside eatery and bar perfectly. It's a wooden pink shack

on the roadside of busy West Bay Street. **Known for:** cool island vibe; juicy home-made burgers; fun spot to hang with locals. $ *Average main: $20* ⊠ *West Bay Street, Cable Beach* ☎ *242/676–8793, 242/455–6280.*

The Poop Deck at Sandyport

$$$ | **SEAFOOD** | A more upscale, albeit dated, version of the other Poop Deck in Nassau, this waterside restaurant has soaring ceilings and a dazzling view of the ocean. Seafood is the star on the menu here: shrimp, lobster, calamari, grouper, and, of course, conch. **Known for:** pick-your-own catch of the day; great ocean views; option to dine on the beach. $ *Average main: $38* ⊠ *W. Bay St., Cable Beach* ☎ *242/327–3325* ⊕ *www.thepoopdecksandyport.com* ⊘ *Closed Mon.*

★ Shuang Ba

$$$ | **CHINESE** | With a team of chefs flown in from China, this is as close as you can get to authentic Chinese cuisine on the island. The menu includes dim sum for starters and the impressive Pork Pyramid, which is made with one piece of braised pork belly that is sliced into thin strips and shaped into a pyramid with pickled Chinese mustard inside, served with a freshly steamed *bao* bun. **Known for:** Peking duck; authentic Chinese dining experience; Baijiu Chinese liquor selection. $ *Average main: $40* ⊠ *Baha Mar between Grand Hyatt and Rosewood, Cable Beach* ☎ *242/788–1234* ⊕ *bahamar.com/culinary.*

★ Spritz Restaurant & Bar

$$ | **NORTHERN ITALIAN** | **FAMILY** | This casual, open-air restaurant and bar overlooks the Sandyport Canal and the pedestrian-only streets of the Old Towne at Sandyport. Seating is limited, so reservations are recommended, especially for busy weekend nights. **Known for:** hand-tossed thin-crust pizzas; great spot for kids to run around; will cater to special dining needs. $ *Average main: $28* ⊠ *Sandyport Olde Towne Marina*

Plaza, Cable Beach ☎ *242/327–0762* ⊕ *www.facebook.com/p/Spritz-Restaurant-Bar-100036469075494/* ⊘ *No lunch Mon.*

The Swimming Pig Gastropub

$$ | **AMERICAN** | Paying homage to the world-famous swimming pigs with its name and a few small paintings, this bustling gastropub is one of the only spots in the resort where you can get late-night grub. The menu is mostly American-inspired—hearty burgers and flatbreads—with a few touches of English pub fare like the oxtail, Guinness pie, and fish-and-chips. **Known for:** a wide range of mostly local beers; 24-hour kitchen service; hearty American and English bar and pub fare. $ *Average main: $28* ⊠ *Baha Mar, Cable Beach* ☎ *242/788–7841.*

Twisted Lime Sports Bar & Grill

$$ | **AMERICAN** | There's something for everyone at this busy sports bar: indoors, the dining room and bar feature games on flat-screen TVs; outdoors, casual canal-front dining (think pub food like burgers and nachos) and drinks are available. The menu is quite extensive. **Known for:** dock and dine; sports fans' hangout; late-night food spot. $ *Average main: $30* ⊠ *Sandyport Marina Village, Cable Beach* ☎ *242/327–0061* ⊕ *www.twistedlimebar.com.*

☕ Coffee and Quick Bites

★ Pulpy

$ | **ICE CREAM** | **FAMILY** | There's no better way to take a break from the hot Bahamian sun than with a cool ice cream, and this new hot spot puts the cool in ice cream. Their signature dish is a cup or cone filled with premium rolled ice cream. **Known for:** rolled ice cream; locally grown unique ingredients; ice-cream taco. $ *Average main: $10* ⊠ *Sandyport, Cable Beach* ☎ *242/677–5227* ⊕ *www.facebook.com/pulpyfrozendesserts/.*

Cable Beach is the busiest island beach west of Nassau and Paradise Island. It's home to Baha Mar, as well as several other resorts.

Hotels

Goldwynn Resort & Residences
$$$$ | **HOTEL** | This boutique oceanfront 5-story hotel extends the Cable Beach strip eastward with an air of sophistication and relaxation. **Pros:** brand new; stunning views; 15-minute beach walk to Baha Mar. **Cons:** beach is not private; limited activities; small. [$] *Rooms from: $450* ✉ *West Bay Street, Cable Beach* ☎ *877/553–9966* 🌐 *goldwynnresorts.com* 🛏 *81 rooms* ☞ *daily room resort fee of $85 plus VAT is added.*

Grand Hyatt at Baha Mar
$$$$ | **RESORT** | The largest property within the Baha Mar resort is steps away from the ESPA spa and the Baha Mar Casino—the largest in the Caribbean—and offers guests access to an array of other amenities, even if it does lack some of the exclusivity of other hotels within the resort complex. **Pros:** plenty to do right on property; steps away from the casino, spa, and Baha Bay water park; resort-view rooms face the nightly fountain show. **Cons:** long walk to the beach; hard to get away from it all; no access to exclusive upscale SLS and Rosewood pool areas. [$] *Rooms from: $475* ✉ *Baha Mar Blvd., Cable Beach* ☎ *242/788–1234* 🌐 *bahamar.com/hotels/grand-hyatt* 🛏 *1800 rooms* 🍴 *No Meals* ☞ *a daily $65 resort fee will be added to your room rate.*

★ **Rosewood at Baha Mar**
$$$$ | **RESORT** | Luxurious touches abound at the most luxurious hotel within the sprawling Baha Mar resort complex. **Pros:** access to all the Baha Mar amenities, including new Baha Bay water park; situated on a stunning beach; luxurious accommodations. **Cons:** on the outer perimeter of the Baha Mar resort complex; a long walk to some of the prime restaurants and amenities; sometimes too quiet. [$] *Rooms from: $1095* ✉ *Baha Mar Blvd., Cable Beach* ☎ *242/788–8500* 🌐 *bahamar.com/hotels/rosewood* 🛏 *113 rooms, 87 suites* 🍴 *No Meals.*

★ **Sandals Royal Bahamian**

$$$$ | RESORT | Cable Beach's most expensive all-inclusive resort recently underwent a year-long, multimillion-dollar facelift; more than 200 rooms have been upgraded, and they've added trendy swim-up river suites that come with personal butler service. **Pros:** no children; lovely setting; private offshore cay. **Cons:** couples only; need car or taxi to go into town; convention center popular for local functions. $ *Rooms from: $1000* ✉ *W. Bay St., Cable Beach* ☎ *242/327–6400, 800/726–3257* ⊕ *www.sandals.com/royal-bahamian* ⇌ *404 rooms* �‖ *All-Inclusive* ☞ *Rates based on double occupancy.*

★ **SLS at Baha Mar**

$$$$ | RESORT | The first international property for the SLS brand—which emphasizes style, luxury, and service constantly reminds you that you are in The Bahamas, starting with the magnificent ocean-view lobby. **Pros:** access to top Baha Mar amenities; luxurious SLS style and service; a variety of exclusive day and night entertainment locations. **Cons:** ongoing construction on west side of hotel; long walk to rest of Baha Mar property; service and style come with a price. $ *Rooms from: $600* ✉ *Baha Mar Blvd., Cable Beach* ☎ *242/788–8200, 866/225–4561 reservations* ⊕ *bahamar.com/hotels/sls* ⇌ *299 rooms* �‖ *No Meals* ☞ *daily $65 resort fee additional.*

 Nightlife

BARS AND LOUNGES

Baha Mar Casino

COCKTAIL LOUNGES | With 100,000 square feet dedicated to gaming, this is the largest casino in the entire Caribbean. Out-of-the-ordinary, floor-to-ceiling windows keep gamers connected to the beautiful Bahamian ocean as they take a chance on 1,140 slot machines and 18 different table games or bet in the state-of-the-art Baha Mar Sports Book by William Hill. There's also the option of gaming in the exclusive high-limit slots area or one of five reserved high-roller gaming salons. ✉ *Baha Mar Resort, Baha Mar Blvd., Cable Beach* ☎ *888/788–8000* ⊕ *www.bahamar.com/casino.*

★ **Bon Vivants**

COCKTAIL LOUNGES | Tropical wallpaper and plush couches adorn this trendy hot spot, which takes its cocktails very seriously—we're talking 30-page-cocktail-menu seriously. They cover all the standards with a complete range of top-shelf liquors, but this is definitely the place to try something different. Take a drink from the absinthe fountain, build your own signature gin and tonic, or sip a cocktail out of a cute pig-shape cup in tribute to the country's famous swimming pigs. There's also an impressive mocktail menu and a small but tasty tapas menu for those who get peckish. Earlier in the day they serve delicious teas, coffees, and soft drinks. ✉ *Sandyport, 401 Sea Skye La., Cable Beach* ☎ *242/601–9463* ⊕ *bonvivantsbahamas.com.*

Bond

DANCE CLUBS | The only nightclub this side of the island is located inside Baha Mar and keeps the party going all night long. International celebrity DJs make sure the vibe is always on point, and the team of mixologists offer specialty handcrafted cocktails. ✉ *Baha Mar, Cable Beach* ☎ *242/788–8200* ⊕ *www.bahamar.com/bond.*

★ **Monkey Bar**

BARS | The SLS lobby comes to life at night as this lively spot heats up and takes over. The drinks flow from 11 am until midnight during the week and until 1 am on weekends, when there is also a DJ. This spot is popular with locals and hotel guests alike. ✉ *SLS, Baha Mar, Cable Beach* ☎ *242/788–8200* ⊕ *www.slshotels.com/bahamar/day-nightlife.*

Shopping

ART GALLERIES

★ The Current

ARTS CENTERS | FAMILY | In addition to the vast collection of Bahamian art that is showcased throughout the Grand Hyatt property in various rooms and spaces, there is this eclectic art gallery beneath the hotel's entrance. Exhibits change frequently, and the shop is a great place to pick up unique souvenirs. You can also sign up for one of the art classes—acrylic pour, leaf prints, and landscape painting are just a few of those available at the art center. ✉ *Baha Mar, Cable Beach* ☎ *242/788–8000* ⊕ *www.bahamar.com/art.*

Activities

GOLF

Mini Blue Golf

MINIATURE GOLF | FAMILY | This course is more miniature PGA than putt-putt, with its perfectly manicured greens that meander through lush greenery and natural hazards. It makes for a perfect outing for families or groups of friends looking for some fun competitive action. ✉ *Cable Beach* ⊕ *bahamar.com/experiences/mini-blue-golf* ⊠ *$30 per person* ⊘ *Closed Mon.–Wed. mornings.*

Royal Blue Golf Course

GOLF | At Baha Mar, you will get two different golf experiences in one golf course, which was created from the island's oldest course. Royal Blue has stunning ocean views on the front nine and a back nine taking players through a native forest all the way to the natural Lake Cunningham. Tee locations are placed each morning by the golf pros, ensuring a unique experience every time you hit the course. A bat cave on the course features a protected indigenous bat species, and more than 70 species of birds have been spotted on the course and surrounding lake. This course is challenging for players at all levels. Non–resort guests are welcome to book a tee time. Rates vary for guests and nonguests and on weekdays versus weekends. ✉ *Baha Mar Resort, Baha Mar Blvd., Cable Beach* ☎ *242/788–4653* ⊕ *www.bahamar.com/golf* ⊠ *$320 resort guests; $360 nonguests* ⅄ *18 holes, 7189 yards, par 72.*

SPAS

★ ESPA at Baha Mar

SPAS | Encompassing 30,000 square feet, the first ESPA flagship spa in the Caribbean is also one of the largest spas in the region. Indulge in massages, facials, and body treatments using a variety of local products designed to soothe and relax. Treatments are done in one of 24 rooms, two of which are designed to accommodate couples. Plan some extra time before and after to relax in the sauna and steam rooms—there are male- and female-specific as well as unisex areas—or in the serene Relax Lounge or social Chill Zone or on the outdoor ocean view terraces. ✉ *Baha Mar Casino & Hotel, Baha Mar Blvd., Cable Beach* ☎ *242/788–8000* ⊕ *www.bahamar.com/experiences/spa.*

Western New Providence

Immediately west of Cable Beach, the hotel strip gives way to residential neighborhoods interspersed with shops, restaurants, and cafés. Homes become more and more posh the farther west you go; Lyford Cay—the island's original gated community—was home to the original 007, Sean Connery. Hang a left at the Lyford Cay roundabout, and you'll eventually come across the historic Clifton Heritage National Park, the local brewery where Kalik and Heineken are brewed and bottled, an exclusive upscale second-home development whose financiers include golfers Ernie Els and Tiger Woods, and finally the sleepy settlement of Adelaide.

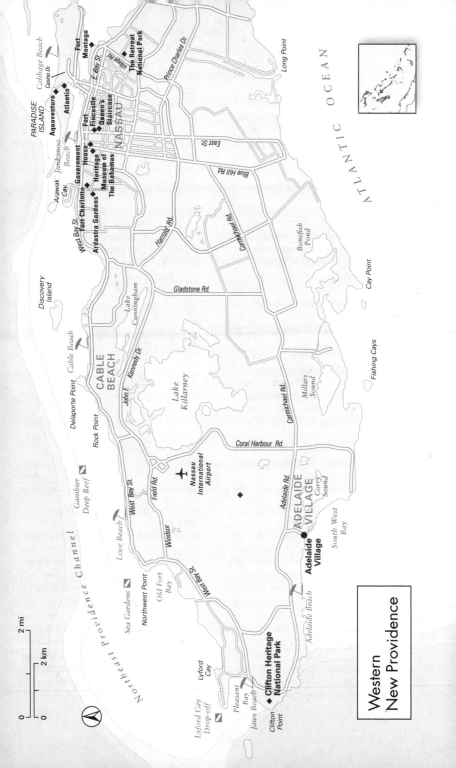

Western New Providence

PARADISE ISLAND

Cabbage Beach
Casino Dr.

Fort Montagu
E. Bay St.
Village Rd.
The Retreat National Park
Prince Charles Dr.
Long Point

Atlantis
Aquaventure
Fort Fincastle
Queen's Staircase
NASSAU
East St.
Arawak Cay
Junkanoo Beach
Government House
Fort Charlotte
Heritage Museum of The Bahamas
Ardastra Gardens
West Bay St.
Blue Hill Rd.
Harrold Rd.
Carmichael Rd.
Bonefish Pond
Cay Point

Discovery Island

Gladstone Rd.

Delaporte Point
Cable Beach
CABLE BEACH
Lake Cunningham
Fishing Cays

Rock Point
John F. Kennedy Dr.
Lake Killarney
Carmichael Rd.
Millars Sound

Gambier Deep Reef
West Bay St.
Field Rd.
Nassau International Airport
Coral Harbour Rd.
Adelaide Rd.
ADELAIDE VILLAGE
Corry Sound

Love Beach
Windsor
Adelaide Village
South West Bay

Sea Gardens
Old Fort Bay
West Bay St.

Northwest Point

Lyford Cay
Lyford Cay Drop-off
Pleasant Bay
Jaws Beach
Clifton Heritage National Park
Adelaide Beach
Clifton Point

Northeast Providence Channel

ATLANTIC OCEAN

0   2 mi
0   2 km

The loop around the island's west and south coasts can be done in a couple of hours by car or scooter, but take some time for lunch and a swim along the way. Unless you're being taken around by a taxi or local, it's best to return along the same route, as internal roads can get confusing.

Sights

Adelaide Village

SCENIC DRIVE | The small community on New Providence's southwestern coast sits placidly, like a remnant of another era, between Adelaide Road and the ocean. It was first settled during the early 1830s by Africans who had been captured and loaded aboard slave ships bound for the New World. They were rescued on the high seas by the British Royal Navy, and the first group of liberated slaves reached Nassau in 1832. Today, there are two sides to Adelaide—the few dozen families who grow vegetables, raise chickens, and inhabit well-worn, pastel-painted wooden houses, shaded by casuarina, mahogany, and palm trees; and the more upscale beach cottages that are mostly used as weekend getaways. The village has a primary school, a few small grocery stores, and a few restaurants serving native foods. ⊠ *Adelaide* ⌑ *Free.*

Clifton Heritage National Park

NATIONAL PARK | FAMILY | It's quite a distance from just about any hotel you could stay at, but for history and nature buffs, this national park, rescued from the hands of developers, is worth the drive. Situated on the site of a Lucayan village dating back to AD 1000–1500, Clifton Heritage National Park allows you to walk through the ruins of slave quarters from an 18th-century plantation. The site can claim ties to pop culture as well because a number of hit movies have been filmed here on land and sea. Book one of the land or sea tours ahead of time—they offer snorkeling out to the Coral Reef Sculpture Garden and a heritage tour for history buffs. Be sure to walk the path from the main parking lot toward the west, where you can enjoy the peace and quiet of the Sacred Space and admire the African women carved out of casuarina wood by local artist Antonius Roberts. Naturalists will enjoy walking along the paths lined with native flora and fauna that lead to wooden decks overlooking mangrove swamps. ⊠ *Clifton Pier, W. Bay St., Clifton* ☏ *242/362–9312, 242/477–0978* ⊕ *tourcliftonheritage.com* ⌑ *entrance $16.50 adults and $3.30 children 3-11; heritage tour $22 adults and $5.50 children; snorkeling tour $48.40.*

Beaches

Adelaide Beach

BEACH | FAMILY | Time your visit to this far-flung beach on the island's southwestern shore to catch low tide, when the ocean recedes, leaving behind sandbanks and seashells. It's a perfect place to take the kids for a shallow-water dip in the sea or to sneak away for a truly private rendezvous. Popular with locals, you'll likely have the miles-long stretch all to yourself unless it's a public holiday. **Amenities:** none. **Best for:** solitude; swimming; walking. ⊠ *Adelaide* ⌑ *Free.*

Jaws Beach

BEACH | FAMILY | This beach got its name after scenes of one of the Jaws movies was filmed on-site. Usually quiet and calm, Jaws Beach is a favorite with local families. On holiday weekends expect larger crowds, who set up grills and loudspeakers. Look out to the right for a glimpse of the glitzy homes that line Clifton Bay within the exclusive Lyford Cay neighborhood. **Amenities:** none. **Best for:** solitude; snorkeling; sunbathing. ⊠ *Western Road, Western New Providence.*

Love Beach

BEACH | If you're looking for great snorkeling and some privacy, drive about 20 minutes west of Cable Beach. White sand shimmers in the sun, and the azure waves gently roll ashore. About a mile offshore are 40 acres of coral reef known as the Sea Gardens. Access is not marked; just look for a vacant lot. **Amenities:** none. **Best for:** solitude; snorkeling; sunset. ✉ *Gambier Village.*

🍴 Restaurants

★ Avery's

$$ | BAHAMIAN | A longtime staple in the historic village of Adelaide, the original restaurant closed years ago, but the owner's daughter and son-in-law have brought it back to life. They serve traditional Bahamian fare, but elevate the ingredients with an upscale flair. **Known for:** weekend brunch; upscale Bahamian fare; live music. $ *Average main: $25* ✉ *49 Adelaide Village, Adelaide* ☎ 242/677–5016 ☾ *No breakfast or brunch except Sun.*

★ Dino's Gourmet Conch Salad

$ | BAHAMIAN | Conch salad is the draw at this popular roadside joint; it might take half an hour or longer to get your made-to-order food, but you can grab a stool and order a refreshing (and intoxicating) gin and coconut water while you wait. If you're in a hurry, call ahead to place your order. **Known for:** cash only; great photo-op spot; signature tropical conch salad. $ *Average main: $12* ✉ *W. Bay St., Gambier Village* ☎ 242/677–7798 ⊕ *dinos-gourmet-conch-salad.business.site.*

★ Shima

$$$ | ASIAN FUSION | Enjoy authentic Southeast Asian–inspired cuisine at this popular restaurant and bar. The little fire symbols peppered throughout the menu indicate their propensity for spice, but they're happy to tone things down if you ask. **Known for:** authentic Asian cuisine; happening weekend brunch; extremely spicy food. $ *Average main: $38* ✉ *Upstairs at the Island House, Lyford Cay* ☎ 242/698–6300 ⊕ *www.the-island-house.com/dining/shima/* ☾ *Closed Mon.*

★ Studio Cafe

$$ | ECLECTIC | This cozy upstairs restaurant pays homage to its former life as Compass Point Studio, where Bob Marley, the Rolling Stones, and James Brown used to record. In addition to Asian-fusion cuisine, they have a burger named after the B52s, live music or karaoke most Fridays, an acoustic brunch on Sunday, and rich desserts. **Known for:** authentic guava duff; laid-back delicious brunch; theme nights. $ *Average main: $20* ✉ *W. Bay St., Western New Providence* ☎ 242/677–3991 ⊕ *www.studiocafebahamas.com.*

★ Zen Asian Fusion

$$ | ASIAN FUSION | There's an array of tasty Chinese dishes on one side of the menu and an extensive selection of sushi on the other at Zen Asian Fusion. This is the only spot on the island where you can get Peking duck without placing an order the day before. **Known for:** crispy Peking duck; peanut butter and pork dumplings; full sushi menu. $ *Average main: $30* ✉ *Windsor Field Rd., Western New Providence* ☎ 242/826–4000 ⊕ *www.asianzen242.com* ☾ *Closed Sun.*

☕ Coffee and Quick Bites

★ Mudda Freeze x Bakehouse

$ | DESSERTS | She bakes, and he makes ice cream. Together this husband-and-wife team created a unique ice-cream parlor and bakery where everything is whipped up by hand on-site. **Known for:** artisanal hand-crafted ice cream; fluffy doughnuts; delicious baked goods. $ *Average main: $10* ✉ *Old Fort Plaza, Windsor Field Road, Western New Providence* ⊕ *www.facebook.com/p/Mudda-Freeze-100083272566259/* ☾ *Closed Mon.*

Hotels

★ The Island House

$$$$ | **HOTEL** | The antithesis of the big resorts typically found in New Providence, The Island House delivers casual sophistication with high-end yet understated amenities and features at every turn. **Pros:** tranquil and private; near the airport; variety of amenities for sports and wellness enthusiasts. **Cons:** far from main attractions; must take a shuttle to the beach; caters primarily to fitness-lovers. $ *Rooms from: $495 ⊠ Mahogany Hill, Western Rd., Western New Providence ☎ 242/698–6300 ⊕ www.the-island-house.com 30 suites ¡◯¡ No Meals.*

Orange Hill Beach Inn

$ | **B&B/INN** | If you prefer down-home coziness over slick glamour, then this basic hotel—on the site of a former orange plantation perched on a hilltop overlooking the ocean—is the place to stay. **Pros:** close to beach; family-friendly; honor bar with best prices on the island. **Cons:** long distance from town; not many activities; basic accommodations. $ *Rooms from: $166 ⊠ W. Bay St., Gambier Village ☎ 242/327–7157 ⊕ orangehill.com 32 rooms ¡◯¡ No Meals.*

A Stone's Throw Away

$$ | **B&B/INN** | Featuring seaside comfort in cozy surroundings, this hotel advertised as a bed-and-breakfast is a three-story colonial-style inn with wraparound verandas, perched on a limestone cliff overlooking the beach, 13 miles west of Nassau. **Pros:** serene; secluded public-beach access; friendly staff. **Cons:** in flight path; long distance from anything else; hotel access up a steep staircase cut out of the limestone hill. $ *Rooms from: $299 ⊠ Tropical Garden Rd. and W. Bay St., Gambier Village ☎ 242/327–7030 ⊕ www.astonesthrowaway.com 10 rooms ¡◯¡ Free Breakfast.*

 Activities

BOATING

Lyford Cay

BOATING | At the western end of New Providence, Lyford Cay, a posh, private home development for the rich and famous, has an excellent 74-slip marina and a golf course, but there is limited availability for the humble masses. ☎ *242/362–4261.*

Chapter 4

GRAND BAHAMA ISLAND

4

Updated by
Jessica Robertson

 Sights
★★★★☆

🍴 Restaurants
★★★☆☆

🛏 Hotels
★★☆☆☆

🛍 Shopping
★★☆☆☆

🌙 Nightlife
★☆☆☆☆

WELCOME TO
GRAND BAHAMA ISLAND

TOP REASONS TO GO

★ **Take endless strolls on your own private beach.** Sprawling, reef-protected shoreline and cays offer more than 50 miles of secluded white-sand beaches along the southern shore.

★ **Go down under.** Between the shipwrecks, caves, coral reefs, and abundant marine life, there's no end to the country's varied and vivid snorkeling and diving.

★ **Get your green on.** Learn about the island's ecology underwater and among the mangroves, where you can feed stingrays or catch sight of spotted dolphins and their calves.

★ **Party at the weekly fish fry or a beach bonfire.** Head to Smith's Point to feast and party with locals.

★ **Swim with the dolphins or feed the sharks.** Several professional dive shops stand ready to introduce you to some of the ocean's most interesting characters.

Only 52 miles off Palm Beach, Florida, 96-mile-long Grand Bahama is one of the chain's northernmost islands. Freeport and Lucaya are its main cities, comprising the second-largest metropolitan area in The Bahamas. Lucaya sees the most action, as Freeport struggles to regain ground lost in the hurricanes and financial setbacks of the last decade. The town of West End, once a quiet, colorful fishing village, was nearly decimated during Hurricane Matthew in October 2016 but thankfully was spared the worst that Hurricane Dorian had to offer in 2019. The residents have pulled together to reconstruct their homes, and the conch shacks that lined the road along the coastline are slowly being rebuilt. Its upscale Old Bahama Bay Resort and marina are the extent of tourism on this end of the island. The area east of Freeport and Lucaya was leveled by Hurricane Dorian. Small fishing settlements experienced extensive damage, and all the rustic bars, restaurants, and hotels were destroyed,

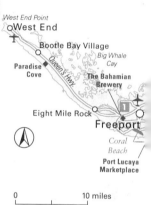

with few having made a comeback. Secluded beaches and undeveloped forest stretching for 60 miles were all impacted by the hurricane, and little was left, so if you do venture east, be sure to pack all that you will need for the day.

1 Freeport. The working end of Grand Bahama, Freeport is convenient to the airport and harbor for

visitors in transit. The Rand Nature Centre and The Bahamian Brewery make the area worth a visit, although downtown looks depressed and forlorn as developers await economic recovery.

2 Port Lucaya. Freeport's beachfront counterpart is dominated by two of the island's largest hotels and resorts and the Port Lucaya Marketplace (the island's best shopping).

3 Greater Lucaya. Lucayan Beach along Port Lucaya can get crowded (by Grand Bahama standards), but Taino Beach, Coral Beach, and Fortune Beach are nearby for those who prefer even more space and solitude; you'll find additional hotels and restaurants here as well.

4 Greater Grand Bahama. The bulk of the island lies on either side of the neighboring metropolitan duo of Freeport and Lucaya. Escaping town means discovering treasures such as Paradise Cove and Lucayan National Park, in addition to remote beaches, time-stilled fishing villages, and wooded land the locals refer to as the "bush."

LUCAYAN NATIONAL PARK

Views of Lucayan National Park.

In this extraordinary 40-acre land preserve, trails and elevated walkways wind through a natural forest of wild tamarind and gumbo-limbo trees, past an observation platform, over a mangrove swamp, along a postcard-worthy beach, and in and around one of the world's largest explored underwater cave systems (more than 6 miles long).

Twenty-five miles east of Lucaya, the park contains examples of the island's five ecosystems: beach, hardwood forest, mangroves, rocky coppice, and pine forest. From the designated parking lot, you can enter the caves at two access points; one is closed in June and July for bat-nursing season.

Across the highway from the caves, two trails form a loop. Creek Trail's boardwalk showcases impressive interpretive signage, crossing a mangrove-clotted tidal creek to Gold Rock Beach, claimed by Grand Bahama's Ministry of Tourism to be the island's "welcome mat." A narrow strand of white sand at high tide and an expansive white-sand playground at low tide, this lightly visited beach is edged by some of the island's highest dunes and a picturesque jewel-tone sea.

Visitors will find subtle treasures no matter what time of year they explore. Summer can be overbearingly hot for walking. However, that's also when certain orchids and other plants flower. Migrating birds and cooler temperatures make October–April optimal, especially mornings and at low tide, when birds are most plentiful.

BEST WAYS TO EXPLORE

By kayak. A kayak launch, near a beach where parts of the *Pirates of the Caribbean* movies were filmed, lies just east of the park's parking lot on the south side. From here paddlers can work their way through mangrove forest to the beach and Gold Rock Creek.

Underwater. Snorkeling is popular around Gold Rock Beach and its eponymous offshore Gold Rock. Certified cave divers can explore the intricate underwater network with the Underwater Explorers Society (UNEXSO).

On foot. Trails come in two parts. On the north side of the highway at the parking lot, one trail takes you into Ben's Cave and the Burial Mound Cave, where ancient Lucayan remains and artifacts have been discovered. A tricky spiral staircase descends into the dark depths of the former, an easier wooden staircase to the latter. At both, observation platforms accommodate visitors who want to peer into the caves' clear depths. Across the highway, two flat, easy trails form a loop to the beach. Creek Trail (0.2 mile) is the easiest because its boardwalk is newer and more elevated. Birds are more

Ben's Cavern on Grand Bahama Island.

abundant here in the tidal creek with its low forest of mangroves at your feet. Mangrove Swamp Trail (0.3 mile) tends to be wet at high tide and its boardwalk more difficult to negotiate (especially for small feet). Take one to the beach and the other to return to see the full range of environment here.

Exploring the park by kayak is one of the best ways to see it.

Natural beauty conspires with resort vitality to make Grand Bahama Island one of The Bahamas's most diverse destinations. In its two main towns, Freeport and Lucaya, visitors can find what the more bustling Nassau has to offer, but at a much slower pace: hotels, a variety of restaurants, golfing, and duty-free shopping. But unlike New Providence, the touristy spots take up only a small portion of an island that, on the whole, consists of uninhabited stretches of sand and forest.

Prior to the development of Freeport, West End (the capital of Grand Bahama Island) was the epicenter of The Bahamas's logging industry and a playground for the wealthy in the 1920s. The fate of Grand Bahama changed in the 1950s when American financier Wallace Groves envisioned Grand Bahama's grandiose future as a tax-free shipping port. The Bahamian government signed an agreement that set in motion the development of a planned city, an airport, roads, waterways, and utilities as well as the port. From that agreement, the city of Freeport—and later, Lucaya—evolved. The past decade's hurricanes and resulting economic downfall have demolished Freeport's resort glamour entirely and have left Lucaya struggling to stay afloat. That said, there are lots of gems, particularly for someone looking for relaxation on spectacular beaches or opportunities to explore nature.

Not much else on the island has changed since the early days, however. Outside of the Freeport–Lucaya commercial and resort area, fishing settlements remain, albeit now with electricity and paved roads. The East End is Grand Bahama's "back-to-nature" side, where Caribbean yellow pine and palmetto forest stretches for 60 miles, interrupted by the occasional small settlement. Unfortunately, most of these settlements were destroyed by Hurricane Dorian in 2019, leaving little to see aside from the natural features, and even those have been altered by the storm. Little seaside villages with white churches and concrete-block houses painted in bright pastels once filled in the landscape between Freeport and West End, but storms have nearly wiped them all out, and with the poor economy, rebuilding has been slow. Many of these settlements are more than 100 years old.

Planning

When to Go

As one of the northernmost Bahamas islands, Grand Bahama is also one of the coolest during the winter. Temperatures dip into the 60s with highs in the mid-70s in January and February, so you may need a jacket and wet suit. On the upside, the migrant bird population swells and diversifies during that time of year. High tourist season (which means seasonal crowds and increased room rates) runs from the holidays to Easter, peaking during spring break (late February to mid-April), when the weather is the most agreeable. October through mid-December can also exhibit good weather, so long as there hasn't been a particularly active hurricane season. Almost daily isolated thunderstorms never last more than a half hour, and the average temperatures steadily decrease from the high 80s at the beginning of October to the high 70s by mid-December.

Summers can get oppressively hot (into the mid- and high 90s) and muggy; unless you're planning on doing a lot of snorkeling, diving, and other water sports, you may want to schedule your trip for cooler months. Afternoon thunderstorms and occasional tropical storms and hurricanes are also common in late summer. The island averages around 20 days of rain per month from June to September, but it usually falls briefly in the afternoon. The good news is that hotel rates plummet and diving and fishing conditions are great.

FESTIVALS

Conchman Triathlon

LOCAL SPORTS | The annual Conchman Triathlon at Taino Beach the first weekend in November is a swimming-bicycling-running competition for amateurs of all ages that raises funds for local charities. International applicants are welcome. ⊠ *Taino Beach, Lucaya* ⊕ *conchmantriathlon.com.*

★ Festival Noel

ARTS FESTIVALS | Since 1993, Festival Noel has marked the official start to the Christmas season. Traditionally held the first Friday evening in December at the Rand Nature Centre, this wine- and food-tasting event and art show displays local talent. Proceeds aid the Bahamas National Trust for the development and restoration of national parks on Grand Bahama Island. ⊠ *Rand Nature Centre, East Settler's Way, Freeport* ⊕ *Across street from Sir Jack Hayward Junior High School* ☎ *242/352–5438* ⊕ *bnt.bs* ☎ *$55.*

New Year's Day Junkanoo Parade

CULTURAL FESTIVALS | **FAMILY** | Junkanoo is the national festival of The Bahamas, named after an African tribal chief named "John Canoe," who demanded the right to celebrate with his people after being brought to the West Indies in slavery. Starting in the evening on January 1 and running into the early morning hours, the downtown streets of Freeport come alive with larger-than-life costumed dancers jumping to the sounds of drums, whistles, and cowbells. At the end of January, watch local primary and secondary students take to the streets in the same colorful, cultural garb for Junior Junkanoo. ⊠ *Freeport.*

Pelican Point Coconut Festival

CULTURAL FESTIVALS | This homecoming celebration on the East End of the island held annually on Easter Monday features live music, coconut food sampling, coconut crafts, coconut bowling, and more.

Getting Here and Around

AIR

Grand Bahama International Airport (FPO) is about a six-minute drive from downtown Freeport and about 10 minutes from Port Lucaya. Several international carriers offer direct service to Grand Bahama from various U.S. gateways, but you can also connect in Nassau on regional carriers, including Bahamasair. No bus service is available between the airport and hotels. Metered taxis meet all incoming flights, although most of the resorts can make arrangements ahead of time for you, for a fee. Rides cost about $15 for two to Freeport, or $22 to Lucaya; see posted signs for fixed rates. The · price drops to $4 per person with larger groups. There's also an airport in West End (WTD), but it's strictly for private planes and charters.

BOAT AND FERRY

Baleària Caribbean sails from Fort Lauderdale's Port Everglades three times a week and provides fast-ferry service, making a day trip possible, while Margaritaville at Sea sails overnight from West Palm Beach, offering a more traditional three-day, two-night cruise-ship experience, with Grand Bahama hotel packages available for an additional two or four nights. Taxis meet all ships.

BUS

Buses (usually minivans) are an inexpensive way to travel the 4 miles between downtown Freeport and the Port Lucaya Marketplace daily until 8 pm. The fare is $1.50. Buses from Freeport to the West End cost $5 each way; to the East End, $15. Exact change is required. It should be noted that although this is a good way for the budget-conscious traveler to get around, these buses are independent operators, don't run on an exact schedule, and are often not in prime mechanical condition.

CAR

If you plan to drive around the island, it's cheaper and easier to rent a car than to hire a taxi. You can rent vehicles from local and major U.S. agencies at the airport. Calling ahead to reserve a car is recommended, especially during high season. Some require minimum-day rentals if the island is busy. Cars can range

from $60/day to $150/day depending on the agency and length of rental.

CONTACTS Avis. ⊠ *Grand Bahama International Airport, Freeport* ☎ *242/351–2847 airport, 242/352–7666 cruise port* ⊕ *avis.com.* **Brad's Car Rental.** ⊠ *Grand Bahama International Airport, Freeport* ☎ *242/352–7930, 954/735–5676* ⊕ *bradscarrental.com.* **Hertz Rent-a-Car.** ⊠ *Grand Bahama International Airport, Freeport* ☎ *242/352–3297* ⊕ *hertz.com.* **KSR Car Rental.** ⊠ *Queen's Highway, Freeport* ☎ *242/351–5737, 954/703-5819* ⊕ *ksrrentacar.biz.*

CRUISE SHIP

Cruise-ship passengers arrive at Freeport Harbour, which has a Bahamian-style look, extensive cruise-passenger terminal facilities, and an entertainment-shopping village with various bars and restaurants. The harbor lies about 10 minutes west of Freeport and about 20 minutes from Port Lucaya Marketplace. Taxis, limos, and tour operators meet all cruise ships. For two passengers, the cost is $20 to Freeport and $27 to Lucaya. The fare is $30 to Taino Beach. The price per person drops $5 for larger groups. It's customary to tip taxi drivers 15%.

Grand Bahama's flat terrain and straight, well-paved roads can make for good scooter riding. Helmets are required and provided. It's cheaper to rent a car than to hire a taxi. Automobiles, Jeeps, and vans can be rented at the Grand Bahama International Airport. Some agencies provide free pickup and delivery service to the cruise-ship port and Freeport and Lucaya. Keep in mind that drivers drive on the left side of the road in The Bahamas, so remember to always look right before pulling into traffic.

SCOOTER

CONTACTS Island Jeep and Car Rentals. ⊠ *Freeport* ☎ *242/351-7333, 954/237-6660 US calls* ⊕ *islandjeepcarrental.com.*

TAXI

Taxi fares are fixed (generally you're charged a flat fee for routine trips; see posted trip fares at the airport) at $3 for the first ¼ mile and 40¢ for each additional ¼ mile. After two people, additional passengers are $3 each. Taxis are available outside the big resorts, the airport, and the cruise terminal, or you can call the Grand Bahama Taxi Union for pickup.

CONTACTS Grand Bahama Taxi Union.
✉ *Freeport* ☎ *242/352–7101.*

Hotels

Grand Bahama accommodations remain some of The Bahamas's most affordable, especially those away from the beach. The majority of these provide free shuttle service to the nearest stretch of sand. With the exception of Pelican Bay, the island's more expensive hotels are beachfront. These include the all-inclusive Lighthouse Pointe at Grand Lucayan; Viva Wyndham Fortuna Beach, an all-inclusive east of Port Lucaya; and West End's elegant Old Bahama Bay Resort & Yacht Harbour. Small apartment complexes, rental homes, and time-share rentals are economical alternatives, especially if you're planning to stay for more than a few days.

Rates post-Easter through December 14 tend to be 25%–30% lower than those charged during the rest of the year.

Restaurants

The Grand Bahama dining scene stretches well beyond traditional Bahamian cuisine. The resorts and shopping plazas have eateries that serve everything from incredible curries and sushi to fine continental and creative Pacific Rim specialties. For a true Bahamian dining experience, look for restaurants named after the owner or cook—such as Tony Macaroni's, Tanya's, or Bishop's.

A native fish fry takes place every Wednesday evening at Smith's Point, east of Port Lucaya (taxi drivers know the way). Here you can sample fresh fish, sweet-potato bread, conch salad made to order, and all the fixings cooked outdoors at the beach. It's a great opportunity to meet local residents and taste real Bahamian cuisine—and there's no better place than seaside under the pines and palms.

⇨ *Note: A gratuity or "service charge" (15%) is often added to the bill automatically; be sure to check your total before adding an additional tip. Restaurant prices are based on the median main course price at dinner, excluding gratuity, typically 15% and 10% VAT, which is often automatically added to the bill. Hotel prices are for two people in a standard double room in high season, excluding service and 6%–12% of various taxes. Restaurant and hotel reviews have been shortened. For full information, visit Fodors.com.*

What It Costs in U.S. Dollars			
$	$$	$$$	$$$$
RESTAURANTS			
under $20	$20–$30	$31–$40	over $40
HOTELS			
under $200	$200–$300	$301–$400	over $400

Activities

BOATING CHARTERS

Private boat charters for up to four people average about $100 per person and up for half a day. Bahamian law limits the catching of game fish to a combination of up to 18 total dolphinfish, kingfish, tuna, or wahoo per vessel.

Bonefish Folley & Sons at Old Bahama Bay

FISHING | Committed to giving you the best fishing experience possible, Bonefish Folley & Sons will take you deep-sea fishing or through the flats for bonefish and permit. The late "Bonefish Folley" is a legend here, who delighted in taking people on bonefish tours for more than 60 years. He passed away in 2012 at the age of 91, but his son and grandson, Tommy Sr. and Tommy Jr., are continuing on in his footsteps. They offer a series of different packages, from fishing and snorkeling to romantic sunset cruises. ⊠ *Old Bahama Bay, West End* ☎ *242/646–9504, 242/813-3251* ⌨ *bonefishing from $550; reef fishing 1/2 day from $750 and full day $950-$1150.*

H2O Bonefishing

BOATING | Clients of this professional saltwater fly-fishing outfitter book well ahead of their arrival on island. H2O's fleet of flats boats and professional guides are available as part of a prearranged multiday package that typically includes two to six days of fishing. They cater exclusively to their anglers both on and off the water for the length of their stay, including waterfront lodging at one of Grand Bahama's finest hotels. Fish year-round for trophy-sized bonefish and permit as well as seasonal tarpon, or fish offshore for yellowfin tuna and mahimahi from spring through summer. Light tackle and conventional fishing is also available. Check out their trendy clubhouse, Bones Bar. ⊠ *Lucaya* ☎ *954/364–7590* ⊕ *h2obonefishing.com* ⌨ *Packages from $1695 for 3 night 2 day fishing and room based on double occupancy.*

★ West End Ecology Tours

WILDLIFE-WATCHING | FAMILY | You'll have fun while learning a lot about the marine life of The Bahamas when you take one of these ecotours run by Keith Cooper, whose family has lived in West End for generations. He provides educational fishing experiences focused on Grand Bahama's historical West End and the conservation and preservation of the area and its marine life. The private small-group tours include deep-sea fishing, coral reef snorkeling, and the popular wild stingray interaction on beautiful Sandy Cay. Pricing is per tour for up to six people. ⊠ *West End* ☎ *242/727–1156* ⊕ *www.westendecologytours.com* ⌨ *Tours from $350 per person with discounted rates for additional guests.*

KAYAKING TOURS

★ Calabash Eco Adventures

ADVENTURE TOURS | FAMILY | Run by Grand Bahama local and avid diver Shamie Rolle, this tour company offers a variety of eco-excursions to areas all over Grand Bahama for sport, history, and education. Options include kayaking, snorkeling, birding, bicycling, and cavern diving into some of the island's famous inland blue holes. All tours include pickup and drop-off at your lodging. ⊠ *Lucaya* ☎ *242/829-7400* ⊕ *calabashecoadventures.com* ⌨ *Tours from $89.*

★ Grand Bahama Nature Tours

ECOTOURISM | Operating on the island for more than 20 years, Grand Bahama Nature Tours is continually updating and adding to their wide variety of excursions, run mostly by Grand Bahama natives, who are both entertaining and full of island insight. Popular adventures include kayaking through the mangroves at Lucayan National Park, Jeep safaris, off-road ATV tours, and birding through the Garden of the Groves. Tours start and end at the Garden of the Groves. ⊠ *Garden of the Groves, Lucaya* ☎ *242/373–2485* ⊕ *www.gbntours.com* ⌨ *Tours $99 per person.*

MARINAS

Blue Marlin Cove Marina

FISHING | This privately owned marina caters to fishermen with 30 slips, a 300-foot straight-line dock, a covered fish-cleaning station, and a commercial ice house. You can drop a line in 1,000 feet of water a mile from the dock and grill your catch on-site the same day. In addition, they have 30 apartment rental units in a gated community "designed for fishermen, by fishermen." ⊠ *Blue Marlin Cove Resort & Marina, Bootle Bay, West End* ☎ *772/485–0040, 242/349–4101* ⊕ *bluemarlincove.com.*

SCUBA DIVING SITES

An extensive reef system runs along Little Bahama Bank's edge; sea gardens, caves, and colorful reefs rim the bank all the way from West End to Freeport–Lucaya and beyond. The variety of dive sites suits everyone from the novice to the advanced diver and ranges from 10 to 100-plus feet deep. Many dive operators offer a "discover" or "resort" course where first-timers can try out open-water scuba diving with a short pool course and an instructor at their side.

A horseshoe-shape ledge overlooks **Ben's Blue Hole,** which lies in 40–60 feet of water. Certified cavern divers can further explore the depths of the cave with guided groups from UNEXSO or Calabash Eco Adventures. Otherwise, interested visitors can view it aboveground when visiting Lucayan National Park.

For moderately experienced divers, **Pygmy Caves** provides a formation of overgrown ledges that cut into the reef. The high-profile corals here form small caves.

One of Grand Bahama Island's signature dive sites, made famous by the UNEXSO dive operation, **Shark Junction** is a 45-foot dive to where 4- to 6-foot reef sharks hang out, along with moray eels, stingrays, nurse sharks, and grouper. UNEXSO provides orientation and a shark feeding with its dives here.

SPID City has an aircraft wreck, dramatic coral formations, blue parrotfish, and an occasional shark. You'll dive about 40 to 60 feet down.

For divers with some experience, **Theo's Wreck,** a 228-foot cement hauler, was sunk in 1982 in 100 feet of water. This was the site for the 1993 IMAX film *Flight of the Aquanaut.*

Nightlife

For evening and late-night entertainment, Port Lucaya is filled with restaurants and bars. From time to time you'll find live entertainment in the middle square; the best nights are Friday and Saturday. Other options include the Wednesday-night fish fry at Smith's Point or taking a sunset cruise through the canals.

Shopping

In the stores, shops, and boutiques in the Port Lucaya Marketplace you can find duty-free goods costing less than what you might pay back home. At the numerous perfume shops, fragrances are often sold at a sweet-smelling 25% below U.S. prices. Be sure to limit your haggling to the straw markets.

Shops in Lucaya are mostly open Monday–Saturday from 9 am to 5 pm. Stores may stay open later at the Port Lucaya Marketplace. Straw markets, grocery stores, some boutiques, and drugstores are open on Sunday.

Visitor Information

Tourist information centers are open weekdays at the Grand Bahama International Airport (9–5), Freeport Harbour (when ships are in port), and the Port Lucaya Marketplace (10–6). The People-to-People program matches your family with hospitable locals who share like interests.

CONTACTS Ministry of Tourism Grand Bahama Office. ⊠ *Fidelity Financial Center, Poinciana Dr., 1st fl., Freeport* ☎ *242/350–8600* ⊕ *bahamas.com.* **People-to-People Program.** ⊠ *Freeport* ☎ *242/302–2000* ⊕ *www.bahamas.com/ people-to-people.*

Freeport

Freeport, once an attractive, planned city of modern shopping centers, resorts, and other convenient tourist facilities, took a bad hit from hurricanes in the past two decades and the resulting economic downturn; its main resort and casino have yet to reopen. An Irish firm purchased the former Royal Oasis Resort & Casino ages ago, but no plans have been made to rebuild or renovate. The International Bazaar next door is now a burnt-out shell and the iconic torii gate is no more. Despite all this, Freeport's native restaurants, Rand Nature Centre, The Bahamian Brewery, and beaches make it worth the visit. It's close to Lucaya (a 15-minute drive), and the airport and harbor are just a few minutes from downtown.

 ## Sights

The Bahamian Brewery

BREWERY | One hundred percent Bahamian-owned, this 20-acre brewery opened in 2007, bringing to the Bahamian islands five new beers, including Sands, High Rock Lager, Bush Crack, and Strong Back Stout. They now offer nine products, including the popular refreshing pink grapefruit and passionfruit/guava radlers, plus a nonalcoholic option. The brewery does everything on-site, including bottling and labeling, and offers 45-minute to hour-long tours on weekdays that take you along each step in the brewing process. The tour ends in the tasting room, where you can belly up to the bar or cocktail tables to sample each beer. Walk-ins are accepted. Beer, wine, and liquor can be purchased in the retail store; The Bahamian Brewery souvenirs are available in the gift shop. ⌧ *Just off Queen's Hwy., east of turn to West End* ☎ *242/688–2337* ⊕ *bahamianbrewery. com* ⌧ *$15 for tours* ⊙ *No tours on weekends, but liquor store open Sat. Closed Sun.*

Rand Nature Centre

NATIONAL PARK | Established in 1939 on 100 acres just minutes from downtown Freeport, a half mile of self-guided botanical trails shows off 130 types of native plants, including many plants known for their use in bush medicine. The remaining tracts of land are left natural and undisturbed to serve as wildlife habitat. Acquired by the Bahamas National Trust in 1992, the center is also one of the island's birding hot spots, where you might spy a red-tailed hawk or a Cuban emerald hummingbird. Visit Donni, the one-eyed Bahama parrot the center has adopted, and the two Bahamian boas, a species that inhabits most Bahamian islands, but not Grand Bahama. The visitor center also hosts changing local art exhibits. The center survives on admissions, gift shop purchases, and donations alone but has plans for a future facelift and new exhibits. ⌧ *E. Settlers Way* ☎ *242/352–5438* ⊕ *bnt.bs/explore/ grand-bahama/rand-nature-centre/* ⌧ *$12* ⊙ *Closed weekends and after 1 pm weekdays.*

 ## Beaches

Lucayan Beach and Coral Beach

BEACH | This stretch of sand divides into separately named beaches at the intersection of Sea Horse Road and Royal Palm Way. The eastern end is Lucayan Beach, monopolized by the broad spread of Lighthouse Pointe at the Grand Lucaya resort, where nonguests can purchase day passes from the hotel, which include the use of pools and nonmotorized water equipment, as well as access to restaurants. Feed jackfish, snorkel at Rainbow Reef, parasail, or take a WaveRunner tour. Near the long-standing Ocean Motion water-sports operation, there is no admission fee for the beach. Go west from here along Coral Beach, where the shore widens for easier strolling and the crowds thin considerably on the way to the Coral Reef Beach

More than 300 bird species call The Bahamas home, including this bananaquit.

Bar. **Amenities:** food and drink; lifeguards; parking (no fee); water sports. **Best for:** partiers; snorkeling; sunrise; swimming; walking. ⊠ *Sea Horse Dr., Royal Palm Way, behind Grand Lucayan, and Coral Beach Bar, Freeport.*

William's Town Beach

BEACH | When the tide is high, this 1.9-mile slice of relatively hidden beach (from East Sunrise Highway, take Coral Road south, turn right onto Bahama Reef Boulevard, then left on Beachway Drive) can get a little narrow, but there's a wide area at its east end on Silver Point Beach near Island Seas Resort. Just west of here, a sidewalk runs the length of the beach along the road, and at low tide the beach expands far and wide for easy walking on the shore. Island Seas Resort has its own modern interpretation of the local beach shack, called Coconuts. **Amenities:** food and drink; parking (no fee); water sports. **Best for:** solitude; swimming; walking. ⊠ *Next to Island Seas Resort, Silver Point Dr. at Beachway Dr., Freeport.*

Xanadu Beach

BEACH | The old Xanadu Resort of Howard Hughes fame has been abandoned and is all but crumbling, and even the surrounding buildings look depressed, but there is local talk that the day will come when the area will be restored and renovated. There are no longer amenities nor flocks of tourists on this beach. However, the mile-long stretch of sand is still serene and worth a walk at sunset, especially when cruise ships depart into the twilight. **Amenities:** parking (no fee). **Best for:** solitude; sunset; walking. ⊠ *Freeport.*

🍴 Restaurants

★ Merport Bistro

$$ | **FRENCH FUSION** | Offering French cuisine with a strong Bahamian influence, Merport Bistro is the spot in downtown Freeport for the local business crowd. Their weekly specials are worth checking out, and although the menu changes constantly, there is something for everyone, from wraps and sandwiches and a variety of soups, to seafood or

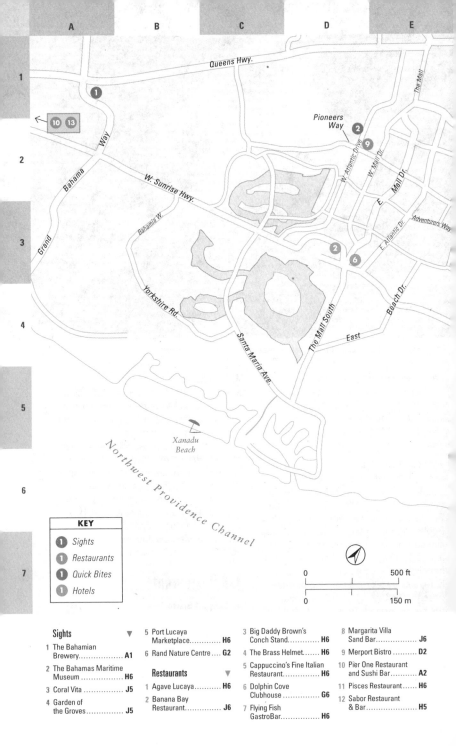

KEY

- **1** Sights
- **1** Restaurants
- **1** Quick Bites
- **1** Hotels

Xanadu Beach

Northwest Providence Channel

| 0 | | 500 ft |
| 0 | | 150 m |

Sights ▼

1 The Bahamian
   Brewery................. **A1**

2 The Bahamas Maritime
   Museum **H6**

3 Coral Vita **J5**

4 Garden of
   the Groves............. **J5**

5 Port Lucaya
   Marketplace............. **H6**

6 Rand Nature Centre **G2**

Restaurants ▼

1 Agave Lucaya........... **H6**

2 Banana Bay
   Restaurant.............. **J6**

3 Big Daddy Brown's
   Conch Stand............. **H6**

4 The Brass Helmet....... **H6**

5 Cappuccino's Fine Italian
   Restaurant.............. **H6**

6 Dolphin Cove
   Clubhouse **G6**

7 Flying Fish
   GastroBar............... **H6**

8 Margarita Villa
   Sand Bar................ **J6**

9 Merport Bistro **D2**

10 Pier One Restaurant
   and Sushi Bar........... **A2**

11 Pisces Restaurant...... **H6**

12 Sabor Restaurant
   & Bar.................... **H5**

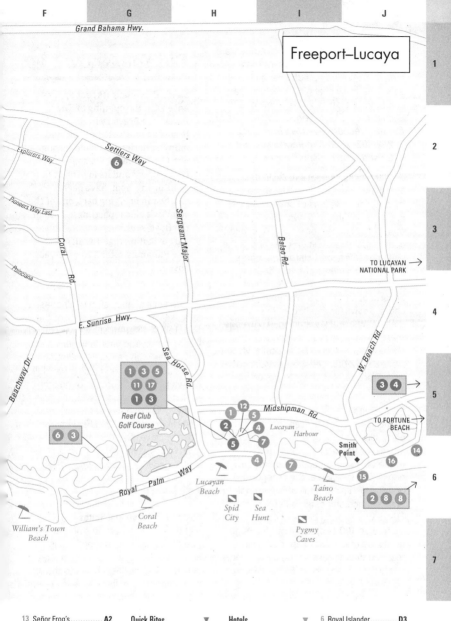

Freeport–Lucaya

F G H I J

Grand Bahama Hwy.

Explorers Way

Settlers Way

Pioneers Way East

Coral Rd.

Poinciana

Sergeant Major

Balao Rd.

TO LUCAYAN
NATIONAL PARK →

E. Sunrise Hwy.

Beachway Dr.

Sea Horse Rd.

W. Beach Rd.

Reef Club
Golf Course

Midshipman Rd.

Lucayan
Harbour

TO FORTUNE
BEACH →

Smith
Point

Royal Palm Way

Lucayan
Beach

Taíno
Beach

Coral
Beach

Spid
City

Sea
Hunt

Pygmy
Caves

William's Town
Beach

1

2

3

4

5

6

7

chicken vol-au-vent, juicy stacked burgers or hearty steaks. **Known for:** amazing breakfasts, including fluffy banana pancakes; daily changing specials; warm and friendly staff. $ *Average main: $20* ✉ *3 Merport Bldg., Pioneer's Way, 1 Town Center, Freeport* ✚ *Across from BTC* ☎ *242/602–7506* ⊕ *merportbistro.net* ⊗ *Closed weekends, no dinner.*

★ Pier One Restaurant and Sushi Bar

$$ | SUSHI | Pier One has one of the most unique settings of any restaurant in Grand Bahama and two different menus to choose from: sushi or cooked continental fare. Built on stilts above the ocean near Freeport Harbour, it offers one-of-a-kind views of magnificent sunsets, larger-than-life cruise ships departing, and sharks swimming for chum. **Known for:** fresh, quality sushi; great views; shark-watching. $ *Average main: $25* ✉ *Next to Freeport Harbour, and a 2nd location in Port Lucaya Marketplace* ☎ *242/602–0984* ⊕ *www.facebook. com/PierOneRestaurant* ⊗ *No lunch weekends.*

Señor Frog's

$ | MEXICAN | This Mexican-themed party place fills with cruise-ship passengers in port for the day and sends them back to the boat happy, fed, and full of rum drinks. The location at the Freeport Harbour is open-air and full of life, complete with a dance stage, large flat-screen TVs, a wraparound bar, and seating for more than 100 people. **Known for:** huge portions of tasty Mexican food; waiters roaming with tequila shots; party atmosphere. $ *Average main: $17* ✉ *Freeport Harbour, Freeport* ☎ *242/351–3764* ⊕ *senorfrogs.com/what-to-do-in-freeport* ⊗ *Closed when there are no docked cruise ships.*

Coffee and Quick Bites

Livity Vegetarian Take-Out & Juice Bar

$ | VEGETARIAN | Offering the healthiest food option on the island, this little shop

Did You Know?

Sands Beer made its first appearance with the opening of The Bahamian Brewery in 2007 and is now a favorite local brew with many varieties, available throughout The Bahamas. Subsequently, the brewery, and its logo of a man sculling in a boat, have been a catalyst in bringing back one of the country's oldest pastimes: "Man in the Boat" sculling races are now part of sailing regattas all over The Bahamas, after a 20-plus-year absence.

(located in a shabby strip mall) doesn't look like much, but the quality of the food tells a different story. Livity blends up fresh fruit and vegetable juices and smoothies with names like Flu Shot, Pressure Reliever, and Incredible Hulk. **Known for:** hearty portions of healthful food; fantastic burgers, with multiple fish and vegetarian options; friendly staff. $ *Average main: $10* ✉ *RayVin Mall, East Atlantic Drive, Freeport* ☎ *242/804–5483* ⊕ *facebook.com/LivityVegetarianTake-OutJuiceBar* ⊗ *Closed Sun.*

🛏 Hotels

Castaways Resort and Suites

$ | HOTEL | In Freeport, this property is one of the nicer budget options in the area. **Pros:** basic but clean; nice array of services and facilities; close to the airport. **Cons:** the neighborhood is currently in a slump; lacking character; not much nearby. $ *Rooms from: $115* ✉ *E. Mall Dr., Freeport* ☎ *242/352–6682* ⊕ *castawaysresort.xyz* ⇥ *118 rooms* ⦿ *No Meals.*

Royal Islander

$ | HOTEL | Amenities without the sticker shock: this two-story, tin-roof, motel-style property offers simple rooms with

Pinetree Stables can take you horseback riding on the beach.

light-wood and rattan furnishings, lively tropical fabrics, framed pastel prints, and tile floors on the lower level. **Pros:** affordable; convenient to airport; basic but comfortable. **Cons:** not on the beach; low on character; nothing much nearby. $ *Rooms from: $90* ✉ *E. Mall Dr., Freeport* ☎ *242/351–6000* ⊕ *royalislanderhotel.com-bahamas.com/en/* ⇗ *100 rooms* ⦿ *No Meals* ⚲ *$50 security deposit charged at check in.*

 Activities

HORSEBACK RIDING
★ Pinetree Stables
HORSEBACK RIDING | Horseback rides are offered on ecotrails and the beach twice a day, starting at 9 am. All two-hour rides are accompanied by a guide—no previous riding experience is necessary, but riders must be at least eight years old. Plan to bring a waterproof camera because you will get wet. Reservations are essential, and drinks are available for purchase. Pinetree Stables offers free shuttles from hotels and the harbor.

✉ *Beachway Dr., Freeport* ☎ *242/727– 0089* ⊕ *pinetree-stables.com* ⚲ *$185 for 2-hr ride.*

SPAS
Love's Healing Touch
SPAS | This small but charming luxury day spa offers top-of-the-line treatments and specialty services such as gel manicures and pedicures, advanced facials and enzyme peels, reflexology, and hot stone massages. The technicians are knowledgeable and friendly, and you can relax with provided refreshments to the sounds of trickling water and meditative music. ✉ *W. Atlantic Blvd., Freeport* ☎ *242/351–3565, 242/478–6402* ⊕ *www. loveshealingtouchbahamas.com* ⚲ *1 hr massage from $100* ⊙ *Closed Sun.*

Renu Day Spa
SPAS | This simple yet elegant spa situated in the bright blue, statuesque Millenium House offers many general spa services, including nail treatments, waxing, facials, body wraps and scrubs, massage, and Reiki. They use Essie and OPI nail products and Guinot skin

products, in addition to several other organic lines. ✉ *Millenium House, E. Mall Dr., Freeport* ☎ *242/727-9928* ⊕ *renuday-spabahamas.com* 🗇 *50-minute massage from $104* 🕙 *Closed all day Sun. and Mon. afternoons except by appointment.*

Port Lucaya

On the beach and harbor of Grand Bahama's southern coast is resort center Lucaya, developed after its neighbor Freeport. The colorful Port Lucaya Marketplace grew up along the safe harbor, known for its duty-free shops, bars, restaurants, straw market, and outdoor bandstand. This is also the home of UNEXSO, the island's famous diving and dolphin-encounter attraction. Surrounding the port are the island's biggest hotels: Lighthouse Pointe at Grand Lucayan, and Pelican Bay.

This quaint harborside shopping, dining, and entertainment village is one of the liveliest locales on the island, although lately it hasn't seen as much action as in years gone by. You can hop from bar to bar, find a variety of restaurants for breakfast, lunch, and dinner, and there is also a local chocolate factory and coffee shop. There's an extensive straw market and 20-plus local crafts vendors. Live music and entertainment bring the center bandstand to life some weekend nights, and additional entertainment is provided on busy cruise-ship days. A few steps to the east and across the street, you'll find more hotels and restaurants within walking distance.

◉ Sights

★ The Bahamas Maritime Museum
HISTORY MUSEUM | FAMILY | Learn about The Bahamas' fascinating maritime history at this new museum that houses exhibits and valuable artifacts from one of the country's most famous wrecks: *Nuestra Señora de las Maravillas,* which

sank on the Bahama Banks in 1656. The museum also features exhibits about the indigenous people of The Bahamas, the Lucayans, as well as the transatlantic slave trade. ✉ *Port Lucaya Marketplace, Port Lucaya Marketplace* ☎ *242/602–0985* ⊕ *www.bahamasmaritimemuseum. com* 🗇 *$12 adults; $6 children 5-12; children under 5 free* 🕙 *closed Sun.*

★ Coral Vita
NATURE SIGHT | Visit this first of its kind, revolutionary land-based coral farm to learn about this important marine animal and how Coral Vita is working to save endangered coral reefs using microfragmenting technology. They have 30 tanks and expect to grow more than 10,000 pieces of 20 different coral species each year. Kids of all ages will enjoy hands-on learning with the touch tank. Tours last one hour and are available on Monday and Thursday at 10 am. ✉ *near the abandoned Arawak Hotel, Topgallant Drive off Magellan Street, Greater Lucaya* ⊕ *coralvita.co.*

Port Lucaya Marketplace
MARKET | Lucaya's large and lively shopping complex is on the waterfront across the street from the Grand Lucayan hotel and right in front of the Pelican Bay hotel. Wander walkways lined with hibiscus, bougainvillea, and croton to discover a wealth of brightly painted waterfront restaurants and bars, water-sports operators, and shops selling clothing, silver, jewelry, perfumes, and local arts and crafts. The marketplace's centerpiece is Count Basie Square, where live entertainment featuring Bahamian bands appeals to joyful nighttime crowds most weekends. Lively outdoor watering holes line the square. ✉ *Across from Grand Lucayan, Sea Horse Rd., Port Lucaya Marketplace* ☎ *242/373–8446* ⊕ *portlucaya.com.*

These handwoven souvenirs can be purchased at the Port Lucaya Marketplace.

Restaurants

Most of the dining in Lucaya is in or around the Port Lucaya Marina or the Port Lucaya Marketplace, which means that nearly all the restaurants are within walking distance of each other and the hotels in the immediate vicinity.

★ Agave Lucaya

$$ | MEXICAN FUSION | This Port Lucaya Marketplace spot offers Mexican staples with a unique Caribbean and Bahamian blend. The Caribbean Jerk Burrito is packed with chicken or shrimp, black beans, rice, roasted corn, bell pepper, and their signature creamy jerk sauce. **Known for:** fusion lychee-tini and various margaritas, mojitos, and martinis; great Chinese menu on Wednesday; two daily happy hours (11 am – 2 pm and 4 – 7 pm). $ *Average main: $30* ✉ *Port Lucaya Marketplace, Lucaya* ☎ *242/374–4887* ⊕ *agavebahamas.com.*

★ Big Daddy Brown's Conch Stand

$ | BAHAMIAN | Located in the Port Lucaya Marketplace along the water, Big Daddy

Brown's offers fresh conch salad and authentic Bahamian staples. Watch this family team put on a show as they prepare the salad right in front of you; they also serve conch fritters, fried fish, and fried lobster in this little, brightly painted shack. **Known for:** special of grouper, conch fritters, and fried shrimp; generous portions of the freshest seafood; fun owner and friendly service. $ *Average main: $15* ✉ *Port Lucaya Marketplace, Lucaya* ▭ *No credit cards.*

The Brass Helmet

$$ | BAHAMIAN | FAMILY | This relaxing outdoor poolside bar and grill at UNEXSO is great for lunch and weekend brunch, with delicious and creative menu items. Kids and adults alike can splash in the pool (which has underwater windows to the marina, so bring goggles) while adults sip spicy Bloody Marys and tropical drinks. **Known for:** tasty jerk pork plates; friendly service; patrons can use the pool. $ *Average main: $20* ✉ *UNEXSO, Lucaya* ⊹ *Next to Pelican Bay Hotel*

☎ 242/373–1244 🌐 *unexso.com* ⏲ *closed Sunday through Wednesday nights.*

★ **Cappuccino's Fine Italian Restaurant**
$$ | **ITALIAN** | This family-run cozy Italian restaurant offers consistently good food and great service. Traditional comfort pasta dishes adorn the menu, like pesto gnocchi and seafood linguine, in addition to steaks and daily fresh fish specials. **Known for:** speciality pastas like pappardelle with truffle oil; warm owner and attentive staff; delicious desserts. [$] *Average main: $25* ✉ *Port Lucaya Marketplace, Sea Horse Rd., Lucaya* ☎ *242/373–1584.*

★ **Flying Fish GastroBar**
$$$ | **ECLECTIC** | One of the finest culinary experiences in the Caribbean, Flying Fish serves an eclectic collection of seafood and Bahamian favorites, made with only the best, sustainable ingredients. The owners, originally from Canada, are local couple Tim and Rebecca Tibbits—Tim being the genius behind the food, Rebecca the genius behind the wine. **Known for:** happy hour 5–7 pm; casual Sunday evenings with live music. [$] *Average main: $38* ✉ *1 Sea Horse Rd., Lucaya* ✣ *Next to Pelican Bay Hotel* ☎ *242/801–5052* 🌐 *flyingfishbahamas.com* ☞ *Docking facilities for boaters.*

★ **Pisces Restaurant**
$$ | **ECLECTIC** | This well-established restaurant has changed location but offers the same reliable quality. The extensive pizza menu offers five sizes and a multitude of topping combinations, including the popular and unique Alfredo pizzas (with a rich Alfredo sauce instead of the typical tomato sauce). **Known for:** late-night eats, open until midnight; seafood pizzas, such as fish, shrimp, lobster, or conch; family-friendly atmosphere. [$] *Average main: $20* ✉ *Grand Bahama Yacht Club, Midshipman Road, Lucaya* ☎ *242/373–5192* ⏲ *Closed Weds.*

Conching Out 🍴

Conch harvesting is illegal in the United States and closely regulated in other tropical locations to guard against overfishing. In The Bahamas, conch harvesting is currently limited to six per vessel and of a certain size, but populations, while still plentiful, are slowly becoming depleted. The Bahamas National Trust launched a "Conchservation" campaign in an effort to educate and preserve queen conch fishing in The Bahamas. Read more about it at 🌐 *bnt.bs/support/conchservation.*

★ **Sabor Restaurant & Bar**
$$ | **ECLECTIC** | This is the perfect spot to enjoy a delicious cocktail while looking out over the Port Lucaya Marina or nestled among the twinkling lights and palm trees around the pool deck. The lunch and dinner menu is a fun fusion of Bahamian and American favorites. **Known for:** unique twist on the usual island cuisine, such as O.M.G. jalapeño shrimp; nightly happy hour from 5 to 7; pleasant, intimate atmosphere. [$] *Average main: $28* ✉ *Harborside, Pelican Bay Hotel, Lucaya* ☎ *242/373–5588* 🌐 *sabor-bahamas.com.*

★ **Zorba's Greek Cuisine**
$ | **GREEK** | Besides Greek favorites, this longtime Port Lucaya restaurant serves popular Bahamian dishes. Join the port's yacht-in clientele, shoppers, and locals for breakfast, lunch, or dinner on the white-and-blue-trimmed sidewalk porch. Specialties include gyros, moussaka, Greek salad, pizza, conch fritters, fried snapper, and roasted leg of lamb. **Known for:** tasty grilled seafood platters; stewed fish with grits and johnny cakes; great value, with daily specials. [$] *Average main: $17* ✉ *Port Lucaya Marketplace, Lucaya* ☎ *242/373–6137.*

Coffee and Quick Bites

★ Bootleg Chocolates

$ | **CAFÉ** | This cozy little café offers strong gourmet coffees, delicious pastries, and creative and delicious chocolates, handcrafted in-store. It's also a great spot to cool off with handmade ice-cream treats. **Known for:** an ever-changing menu of chocolate flavors; "concochinno" frappés; ice-cream sandwiches made on-site. [$] *Average main: $10* ✉ *Port Lucaya Marketplace, on waterfront near main parking lot, Port Lucaya Marketplace* ☎ *242/373–6303* 🌐 *bootlegchocolates.com.*

★ Zorba's Cafe & Pastries

$ | **CAFÉ** | Enjoy a great cup of coffee or specialty *boba* tea any time of day or night at this quaint café immediately adjacent to Zorba's Greek Restaurant. Try fresh-baked croissants, chocolate eclairs, and tiramisu, as well as a variety of other sweet and savory treats. **Known for:** delicious creamy conch chowder; traditional Greek cookies and cakes; fun, friendly atmosphere. [$] *Average main: $6* ✉ *Lucaya* ☎ *242/373-6137* 🌐 *facebook.com/zorbaspastries.*

Hotels

Lighthouse Pointe at Grand Lucayan

$$ | **RESORT** | **FAMILY** | This two-story all-inclusive property replicates Caribbean-style plantation manors with quiet ocean-view rooms and suites. **Pros:** across the street from the Port Lucaya Marketplace; great beachfront activities; welcoming, family feel. **Cons:** service can be spotty; all-inclusive meals can be repetitive and lack choice; much of the sprawling resort complex remains closed. [$] *Rooms from: $210* ✉ *Sea Horse Rd., Lucaya* ☎ *242/373–1333, 800/252–9079* 🌐 *www.grandlucayan.com/accomodations/lighthouse-pointe/* 💳 *No credit cards* 🛏 *196 rooms* 🍴 *All-Inclusive.*

★ Pelican Bay Hotel

$ | **RESORT** | Close to the beach, with rooms overlooking the Port Lucaya Marina or the waterfront along the canal, Pelican Bay has a funky modern appeal, and suites overflow with character and decorative elements collected from around the world. **Pros:** stylish and comfortable; water views; warm and welcoming staff. **Cons:** no beach; poolside/marina-front rooms can be noisy; no elevators to upper-level rooms. [$] *Rooms from: $154* ✉ *Sea Horse Rd., Port Lucaya, Lucaya* ☎ *242/373–9550, 800/852–3702* 🌐 *pelicanbayhotel.com* 🛏 *183 rooms* 🍴 *No Meals.*

Nightlife

BARS

★ Bones Bar

BARS | This trendy spot on the waterfront at Pelican Bay Hotel is a popular evening and late-night watering hole with the local expat crowd, with swim-up seating at the adjacent pool. Sip high-end tasting rums or fresh-squeezed cocktails like the Silver Fox (lime juice, homemade simple syrup, and vodka). The only food option is their delicious homemade savory meat pies. Call ahead to place your order as they tend to run out early. ✉ *Pelican Bay Hotel, Sea Horse Rd., on the canal next to Flying Fish GastroBar, Lucaya* ☎ *242/602–2663* 🌐 *www.bones-bar.com.*

★ Rum Runners

BARS | This busy bar on the corner of Count Basie Square specializes in keeping bar hoppers young and old supplied with free Wi-Fi, tropical frozen drinks and punches, and piña coladas served in coconuts. Sit outside for people-watching or inside for cool air-conditioning and TVs broadcasting sports events. The kitchen serves up basic American and Bahamian bar food. Happy hour is daily from 5 to 7. ✉ *Port Lucaya Marketplace, Lucaya* ☎ *242/373–7233* 🌐 *rumrunnersgbi.com* 🕒 *closed Weds.*

Shopping

ART

★ Glassblower Shop

CRAFTS | Master artisan Sidney Pratt creates his incredibly beautiful blown-glass masterpieces inside this small freestanding shop. Order your name in glass or ask him to make whatever it is you want if you don't see it in the store. ⊠ *Port Lucaya Marketplace, Lucaya* ☎ *242/442–3798.*

IIWII (It Is What It Is)

ART GALLERIES | This gallery showcases owner Matthew Wildgoose's paintings as well as the works of other local artists. It's also a spot to embrace your own inner Picasso under the guidance of Wildgoose by taking an art class, workshop, or a fun sip-and-paint session. ⊠ *Two doors down from Bahama Mama's, Lucaya* ☎ *242/426-0329* ⊙ *closed Saturday.*

Leo's Art Gallery

ART GALLERIES | This storefront serves as both studio and showroom for famed local artist Leo Brown. Each of his expressive Haitian-style paintings and colorful Bahamian impressionist pieces has its own story. This place is worth a visit just to meet the charming Leo and witness his inspiring work and creativity. ⊠ *Port Lucaya Marketplace, across from Zorba's, Lucaya* ☎ *242/373–1758* ⊙ *closed Sat.*

FASHION

Bandolera

WOMEN'S CLOTHING | Bandolera sells European-style women's fashions and accessories from designers such as Joseph Ribkoff. Find that perfect little chic dress and everything from casual wear to gowns. ⊠ *Port Lucaya Marketplace, Lucaya* ☎ *242/373–7691, 242/457-5140.*

JEWELRY AND WATCHES

Colombian Emeralds International

JEWELRY & WATCHES | Shop here for beautiful Colombian emeralds and other precious gemstone jewelry. They also stock a selection of crystal items. ⊠ *Port Lucaya Marketplace, Lucaya* ☎ *242/373–8400.*

Freeport Jewellers

JEWELRY & WATCHES | This jeweler caters to locals and visitors alike with watches, heavy gold and silver chains, pretty larimar stone pieces, and unique sea charms like conch shell jewelry. It also sells cigars, crystal, and Swiss-brand watches. ⊠ *Port Lucaya Marketplace, Lucaya* ☎ *242/373–2776* ⊕ *www.facebook.com/freeportjewellers* ⊙ *Closed after 3 pm on Sun.*

MARKETS AND ARCADES

Arawak Crafts Centre

CRAFTS | This collection of 27 small shops and booths on the west side of the Port Lucaya Marketplace is comprised of individual Bahamian artisans, each selling unique arts and homemade handicrafts, many customized on request. Items for sale include seashell ornaments, candles, soaps, straw goods, dolls, and more. ⊠ *Port Lucaya Marketplace, across from Dominos Pizza, Lucaya* ⊕ *portlucaya.com.*

Port Lucaya Straw Markets

CRAFTS | Come to this collection of wooden stalls at the Port Lucaya Marketplace's east and west ends to bargain for straw goods, T-shirts, and souvenirs. ⊠ *Port Lucaya Marketplace, Sea Horse Rd., Lucaya* ⊕ *portlucaya.com.*

MISCELLANEOUS

Photo Specialist

CAMERAS & PHOTOGRAPHY | Head here for photo and video equipment, memory cards, rechargeable batteries, cell-phone chargers, and any other electronic accessory you may have forgotten to bring with you. ⊠ *Port Lucaya Marketplace, Lucaya* ☎ *242/373–7858.*

★ Sun & Sea Outfitters at UNEXSO

MIXED CLOTHING | This retail shop at UNEXSO offers the biggest shopping selection in Lucaya. Here you'll find watersports equipment, toys, jewelry and

This boat sails in front of the Grand Lucayan.

accessories, home decor, brand-name apparel, and swimsuits for both men and women. Walk along the marina to enter poolside or at the front of the UNEXSO building. ✉ *UNEXSO, next to Pelican Bay Hotel, Lucaya* ☎ *242/373–1244, 800/992–3483* ⊕ *unexso.com/retail-store/.*

🏃 Activities

BIKING

By virtue of its flat terrain, broad avenues, and long straight stretches of highway, Grand Bahama is perfect for bicycling. There's a designated biking lane on Midshipman Road.

Inexpensive bicycle rentals are available from some resorts, and the Viva Wyndham Fortuna Beach allows guests free use of bicycles. In addition to its other ecotouring options, Grand Bahama Nature Tours offers 10-mile biking excursions that include a visit to a native settlement and the Garden of the Groves.

★ CocoNutz Cruisers

BIKING | CocoNutz is locally owned and operated and offers the only motorized (electric) bicycle experience on the island. Alfredo Bridgewater or one of his knowledgeable guides takes tourists along the southern shores of the island, offering island history and stops along the way for unique Grand Bahamian experiences. The 5½-hour ride can take up to 12 bikers and includes bottled water and lunch. The guides even take photos along the way to send to you later. Find them behind the Port Lucaya Marketplace parking lot at the water's edge. If you're staying farther away, they'll arrange hotel pickup and drop-off at no additional charge. ✉ *Port Lucaya Marketplace, Lucaya* ☎ *242/808–7292, 954/354–6889* ⊕ *facebook.com/ CocoNutzCruisers* 🎟 *$125 per person.*

DIVE OPERATORS

★ UNEXSO

(*Underwater Explorers Society*)
SCUBA DIVING | This world-renowned scuba-diving facility provides rental equipment, guides, and boats. Facilities include a 17-foot-deep training pool with windows that look out on the harbor, changing rooms and showers, docks, an outdoor bar and grill, and an air-tank filling station. Daily dive offerings range from one-day discovery courses and dives to specialty shark, dolphin, and cave-diving excursions. Both the facility and its dive masters have been featured in international and U.S. magazines for their work with sharks and cave exploration. UNEXSO and its sister company, The Dolphin Experience, are known for their work with Atlantic bottlenose dolphins. ⊠ *Port Lucaya, Lucaya* ⊹ *Next to Pelican Bay Hotel* ☎ *242/373–1244, 800/992–3483* ⊕ *unexso.com* ⌨ *One-tank reef dives $59, Discover Scuba course $129, night dives $79, dolphin dives $219, shark dives $109.*

SPAS

Dermalogica Skin Centre

SPAS | After analyzing your skin, experienced Dermalogica-trained aestheticians deliver beautiful, personalized facials and product recommendations. This small, clinical day spa also offers microneedling, Swedish massages, face and body waxing, and brow and lash tinting. ⊠ *Port Lucaya Marketplace, Port Lucaya Marketplace* ☎ *242/373–7546* ⊕ *www.dermalogicaskincentre.com/freeport* ⌨ *Facials from $95, massages from $75* ⊙ *Closed Sun. and Mon.*

Senses Spa at Grand Lucayan

SPAS | This spa offers a variety of luxury services, including body wraps and scrubs, facials, various massage techniques, and manicures and pedicures, in addition to a full-service salon. Senses is open to nonguests as well, and a daily fee includes use of the locker room, lap pool, hot tubs, and sauna facilities.

All spa services are by appointment. ⊠ *Grand Lucayan, Lighthouse Point, Lucaya* ☎ *242/350–5466* ⊕ *www.grandlucayan.com/wellness/the-spa/.*

Greater Lucaya

The lion's share of restaurants and resorts in Lucaya is located around Port Lucaya, but if you venture a bit farther, you'll find a handful of attractions, eateries, and places to stay that are worth the extra effort to get to.

Sights

★ Garden of the Groves

GARDEN | **FAMILY** | This vibrant, 12-acre garden and certified wildlife habitat, with a trademark chapel and waterfalls, is filled with native Bahamian flora, butterflies, birds, and turtles. Interpretive signage identifies plant and animal species. First opened in 1973, the park was renovated and reopened in 2008; additions include a labyrinth modeled after the one at France's Chartres Cathedral, colorful shops and galleries with local arts and crafts, a playground, and a multideck indoor and outdoor café and bar. Explore on your own, or take a half-hour guided tour at 10 am (Monday–Saturday). ⊠ *Midshipman Rd. and Magellan Dr.* ☎ *242/374–7778, 242/374–7779 café* ⊕ *thegardenofthegroves.com* ⌨ *$17.*

Beaches

★ Fortune Beach

BEACH | **FAMILY** | Fortune Beach lies between two canal channels, and in the middle sits the Viva Wyndham Fortuna all-inclusive resort, where visitors can purchase day passes to use water-sports equipment and resort facilities. Steps from the resort, the secluded beach offers exceptional strolling, off-shore snorkeling, and swimming. The western end backs the Margarita Villa Sand Bar and the private homes along Spanish Main Drive, known as "Millionaire Row." The eastern end is home to Banana Bay Restaurant, where at low tide a shallow lagoon forms alongside a drawn-out sandbar, allowing you to walk yards out to sea with cold drink in hand. **Amenities:** food and drink; parking, near east end only (no fee). **Best for:** solitude; snorkeling; sunrise; swimming; walking. ✉ *Fortune Bay Dr., Greater Lucaya.*

Taino Beach

BEACH | **FAMILY** | Along this beautiful stretch of beach, you'll find the famed restaurant The Stoned Crab and their photo-worthy swings over the shallow sea. A few steps farther is Outriggers Beach Club, home to the popular fish fry held every Wednesday night. This is also where you'll find the legendary Tony Macaroni's beach shack; be sure to give his roast conch a try. Plenty of green space edges the beach, and there's also a playground. **Amenities:** food and drink; parking (no fee); toilets; water sports. **Best for:** partiers; sunset; swimming; walking. ✉ *W. Beach Rd., near Smith's Point, Greater Lucaya.*

🍴 Restaurants

★ Banana Bay Restaurant

$ | **BAHAMIAN** | **FAMILY** | Directly on Fortune Beach, Banana Bay is a great place for lunch or daytime cocktails, whether you sit on the restaurant's shaded deck or on a lounger in the sand. In addition to daily fresh fish specials, the kitchen serves up homemade warm loaves of banana bread along with salads, sandwiches, wraps, and seafood appetizers like conch fritters and crab cakes. **Known for:** daily fresh fish specials; tasty daiquiris and generously poured cocktails; warm homemade banana bread. [$] *Average main: $18* ✉ *Fortune Beach, Fortune Bay Dr.* ☎ *242/373–2960* 🕒 *Closed after 5 pm except Fri.*

> ### Did You Know? 👁
>
> The term "Lucayan" is derived from the Arawak word *Lukka-Kairi*, meaning "Island People." The early indigenous people gave The Bahamas its first name, the Lucayas.

★ Dolphin Cove Clubhouse

$$$$ | **ECLECTIC** | Each seat in this small but sophisticated old Bahamian manor home-styled dining room has a view into the open kitchen. With just 30 diners at a time, it's like the chef and his team are cooking dinner for an intimate group of friends as they watch. **Known for:** upscale island dining experience; warm and friendly service; divine molten three-cheese mac and cheese. [$] *Average main: $40* ✉ *14 Swans Drive, Greater Lucaya* ☎ *242/602–4964 5 pm–10 pm, 242/602–3346 8 am–5 pm* 🌐 *www.dolphincovebahamas.com/restaurant* 🕒 *Closed Sun.* 👔 *no tshirts, tank tops, flip flops or caps allowed* ☞ *children under 16 not allowed.*

★ Margarita Villa Sand Bar

$ | **AMERICAN** | At this cozy, toes-in-the-sand bar, the bartender treats you like an old friend. Party photos adorn the walls along with velvet paintings of Elvis. **Known for:** variety of delicious conch dishes; free Wi-Fi; party atmosphere, often with live music. [$] *Average main: $15* ✉ *Fortune Beach, off Spanish Main Rd., Mather Town, Lucaya* ☎ *242/813–3525* 🌐 *sandbarbahamas.net.*

★ Smith's Point Fish Fry

$ | **BAHAMIAN** | For the most authentic Bahamian food, head to Smith's Point for the famous weekly fish fry. Every Wednesday night, this little settlement by Taino Beach comes to life when the open-air beach shacks along the street serve fried fish (with the head and tail still on), cracked conch (pounded and fried), lobster tail, fried grouper, and barbecue chicken down-home style. **Known for:** traditional Bahamian food; party atmosphere with occasional beach bonfires; great place to rub shoulders with locals. $ *Average main: $10* ✉ *Smith's Point, Off W. Beach Rd., Lucaya* ✛ *Next to Taino Beach* ☒ *No credit cards.*

★ **The Stoned Crab**

$$$ | ECLECTIC | The Stoned Crab is a place to see and be seen. Open glass walls all around provide every seat with a view of the ocean off Taino Beach, and vaulted white wooden ceilings that rise into the spectacular dual triangular peaked roof make it feel larger than it is. **Known for:** generous portions of exceptional seafood; sophisticated beachy atmosphere; you can spend all day eating and drinking here. $ *Average main: $38* ✉ *Taino Beach West, Greater Lucaya* ☎ *242/602–1010* ⊕ *www.facebook.com/ stonedcrabfreeport.*

★ **Tony Macaroni's Conch Experience**

$ | BAHAMIAN | FAMILY | For a taste of the local beach scene, follow the music to this weathered, thatch-roof shack at Taino Beach and get your fill of mouthwatering roast conch, the specialty of the "house." Operated by local personality Anthony "Tony Macaroni" Hanna, the popular eatery also sells conch salad, roast lobster and shrimp, and Gully Wash cocktails (fresh coconut water, sweetened condensed milk, a healthy dose of gin, and a sprinkle of nutmeg) for noshing alfresco on a stilted deck overlooking pristine sands and sea. **Known for:** fresh conch served many ways; incredible ocean views; memorable chats with Tony Macaroni. $ *Average main: $12* ✉ *Taino Beach, Lucaya* ☎ *242/533–6766* ☒ *No credit cards.*

Hotels

Bell Channel Inn

$ | HOTEL | Right on the water and a short walk from the Port Lucaya Marketplace, this charming family-run (through three generations) inn with simple-yet-spacious rooms has quick and easy access to the island's best underwater sites, making it perfect for scuba-oriented and budget-minded travelers. **Pros:** friendly, longtime staff; clean, simple rooms with refrigerators, free Wi-Fi, and canal views; bar/restaurant on-site. **Cons:** no beach but on the canal; 10-minute walk from shopping and restaurant scene; rooms are not fancy. $ *Rooms from: $105* ✉ *Kings Rd., just off Midshipman, Lucaya* ☎ *242/373– 1053* ⊕ *bellchannelinn.com* ⤶ *32 rooms* ⦾ *No Meals.*

★ **Dolphin Cove**

$ | HOTEL | This adults-only apartment-style resort situated on the Grand Bahama canals offers a quiet getaway perfect for a long weekend or an extended stay. **Pros:** deluxe units have a washer and dryer; one of the island's best restaurants on-property; friendly, personal service. **Cons:** not on the beach; limited amenities; shopping, entertainment, and other restaurants not within walking distance. $ *Rooms from: $175* ✉ *14 Swans Dr., Greater Lucaya* ☎ *242/602–3346* ⊕ *www. dolphincovebahamas.com* ⤶ *36 rooms* ⦾ *No Meals.*

Taino Beach Resort & Clubs

$$ | RESORT | FAMILY | Studio and one- and two-bedroom contemporary self-functioning suites, most with garden views, surrounding a large pool with a lazy river and waterslide, make this timeshare resort a haven for families. **Pros:** easy walk to Smith's Point for Wednesday night Fish Fry; on-site restaurant and swim-up bar; offers grocery-run service for a small fee three days a week. **Cons:** no beachfront rooms; need a car, ferry, or taxi to get to main shopping and restaurant spots; Wi-Fi not available in rooms.

$ Rooms from: $208 ⊠ Jolly Roger Dr., Greater Lucaya ☎ 242/350–2200 ⊕ tainobeach.com ⤴ 157 rooms ❖ No Meals.

Viva Wyndham Fortuna Beach
$$ | **RESORT** | **FAMILY** | Popular with couples, families, and spring breakers, this secluded resort provides a casual, all-inclusive getaway where one price covers meals, drinks, tips, nonmotorized water sports, and nightly entertainment. **Pros:** kids' club and pool, plus family-friendly shows; trapeze lessons from professional circus performers; warm, friendly atmosphere. **Cons:** need a car or taxi to Port Lucaya or any other part of the island; rooms are in need of an update; resort bustles with spring breakers. $ Rooms from: $220 ⊠ Churchill Dr. at Doubloon Rd., Lucaya ☎ 242/373–4000, 888/774–0040 in U.S. ⊕ vivafortunaresort.com ⤴ 276 rooms ❖ All-Inclusive.

 Activities

GOLF
Reef Club Golf Course
GOLF | The Reef Course is a par-72, 6,930-yard links-style course. Designed by Robert Trent Jones Jr., it features lots of water (on 13 of the holes), wide fairways flanked by strategically placed bunkers, and a tricky dogleg left on the 18th. While it is the most expensive and most pristine golf course on the island, budget constraints have left it comparable to an average municipal course in the States. Club rentals are available. Guests staying at Lighthouse Pointe have unlimited golf included in their stay. ⊠ Sea Horse Rd. ☎ 242/373–1333, 855/350-4653 ⊕ www.grandlucayan.com/reef-club/ ⛳ High season and summer weekends $71.20; summer weekdays $39.30. 🏌 18 holes, 6930 yards, par 72 ⊗ Closed Tues.

DIVE OPERATORS
Sunn Odyssey Divers
SCUBA DIVING | This family-run shop has been on the island for more than 20 years. You'll dive with Nick Rolle, the owner himself, who caters to smaller dive groups for a more personalized experience. Full PADI certifications available. ⊠ Beach Way Dr., Williams Town ✚ Near Island Seas Resort and Williams Town Beach ☎ 866/652–3483, 242/373–4014 ⊕ sunnodysseydivers.com ⛵ 2 tank dive $110; night dive $85; snorkel or passenger $50; Discover SCUBA $175.

Viva Dive Shop, a Reef Oasis Diving Center
SCUBA DIVING | Part of the Reef Oasis Dive Club, this shop offers daily dives and snorkels to various reefs and wrecks. Their large boat seats 21 and leaves from Fortune Beach at Viva Wyndham Fortuna Resort. This professional PADI-licensed shop also offers certifications for all levels (all equipment is included). ⊠ Viva Wyndham Fortuna Resort, Churchill and Doubloon Rd., Lucaya ☎ 242/441–6254, 242/350–2023 ⊕ www.reefoasisdiveclub.com ⛵ Dives from $58; night dives from $103; shark dives from $130.

WATER SPORTS
Lil B Fishing
FISHING | Whether you're looking to go reef fishing, night fishing, or snorkeling or want to take a sunset harbor tour, this family-friendly outfitter has you covered. ⊠ Coral Beach Marina, Bahama Reef Boulevard, Greater Lucaya ☎ 242/351-6917 ⊕ lilbfishingbahamas.com ⛵ Fishing from $75pp with 2 person minimum; sunset harbor tour $50 adults, $35 children.

Lucaya Watersports and Tours
WATER SPORTS | Book a range of watersports activities and tours at either of their two locations: Port Lucaya or Flamingo Bay Hotel. Choose from three daily snorkeling or glass-bottom boat excursions, rent a WaveRunner, or sign up for a WaveRunner tour. They also rent snorkel gear, kayaks, and paddleboards. ⊠ Port Lucaya Marketplace ☎ 242/819-9888, 242/350-2219 ⊕ www.lucayawatersports.com ⛵ Tours from $55.

Did You Know?

Most dive operations in The Bahamas offer certification programs. If you are simply looking to try scuba on your vacation, opt for a resort course that provides enough instruction to get you into the water with equipment. If you find scuba is your new favorite adventure, get a full open-water certification. Initial certification in The Bahamas costs about $600. To save valuable vacation and bottom time, you can often begin your instruction at home or online.

Greater Grand Bahama

Farther out on either side of the Free-port–Lucaya development, the island reverts to natural pine forest, fishing settlements, and quiet secluded beaches. Heading west from Freeport, travelers pass the harbor area, a cluster of shacks selling fresh conch and seafood at Fishing Hole, a series of small villages, and Deadman's Reef at Paradise Cove before reaching the historic fishing town of West End and its upscale resort at the very tip of the island. East of Lucaya lie long stretches of forest interrupted by the occasional small village, Lucayan National Park, and myriad bonefishing flats along the eastern end. In 2019, Hurricane Dorian left extensive damage along the eastern end of the island, so apart from the beaches there is not much to see or do, but things are gradually making a comeback.

Sights

Celebrity Eco Adventures

ECOTOURISM | FAMILY | Grand Bahama has its own swimming pigs on Crystal Beach. The only way to swim with these swine is to book a tour. Other activities include snorkeling, ocean kayaking, and beach volleyball. You can also just grab a beach chair or hammock and relax. There's an on-site bar and restaurant serving local cuisine. ⊠ *West End* ☎ *242/727–4958* ⊕ *celebecotours.com* ⊠ *Swimming pig adventure $60; kayak rental $20 and $25 per hour; snorkel equipment rental $25 per hour.*

Eight Mile Rock

TOWN | You have to get off the main road to get to what was once a real example of the heart and soul of Grand Bahama Island. This settlement is only 10 miles from Freeport Harbour but now offers little to the tourist except for a few churches and the occasional conch stand. Much of its former glory has been

Here's Where

The last time locals spotted pirates on Grand Bahama Island was in 2005, when Johnny Depp, aka Captain Jack Sparrow, and his crew were filming the second and third installments of the *Pirates of the Caribbean* series. They used a special device in Gold Rock Creek at one of the world's largest open-water filming tanks to give the illusion that the pirate ship was pitching and yawing.

destroyed by hurricanes over the past decade. Driving north through Eight Mile Rock will lead you to West End, home to the Paradise Cove and Old Bahama Bay resorts. ⊠ *Western Grand Bahama.*

High Rock

BEACH | About 45 miles east of Lucaya and 8 miles from Lucayan National Park, it's worth the extra drive to visit an authentic, old-time island settlement affected only lightly by tourism. Its beach spreads a lovely white blanket of plump sand, with stunning views in either direction. Time spent at the bar at Bishop's Beach Club on the waterfront with Bishop himself (aka Ruban "Bishop" Roberts) and his dog will make you feel like a local. Take a walk along the beach and its parallel road (rock outcroppings interrupt the sand in places) past the cemetery to the remains of a concrete lighthouse that shows the intensity of Hurricane Dorian, which completely changed the landscape of this and other settlements in 2019. ⊠ *Eastern Grand Bahama.*

★ Lucayan National Park

NATIONAL PARK | FAMILY | Considered the crown jewel of the four national parks on Grand Bahama, Lucayan National Park is the only place to find all six Bahamian ecosystems in a single, 40-acre expanse of land: pine forest, blackland coppice

Did You Know?

Grand Bahama is one of the most eco-oriented islands in The Bahamas. Kayaks are readily available across the island.

(ferns, bromeliads, orchids), rocky coppice (hardwoods), mangrove swamp, whiteland coppice (rich plant life, poisonwood), and beach/shoreline. Because it is 25 miles east of Lucaya, booking a tour or renting a car is necessary in order to experience all the park has to offer. Explore two caves, hike along the nature trails, bird-watch across the raised boardwalks through the mangroves, or stroll along spectacular Gold Rock Beach during low tide as the shoreline sets out its "welcome mat"—sand ripples created by tidal pools as the water recedes. ⊠ *Grand Bahama Hwy., Freetown* ☎ *242/352–5438* ⊕ *bnt.bs/explore/grand-bahama/lucayan-national-park/* ⊠ *$12* ⊙ *Closed weekdays*.

Owl's Hole

CAVE | Named for the mama owl who nests here every year, this vertical freshwater cave (a limestone sinkhole formed by the collapse of a section of a cavern's roof) is a popular local swimming hole. It's rimmed by a 24-foot cliff if you're up for taking a plunge. The less adventuresome can climb down a ladder into the cool but refreshing water. Take snorkel gear down with you to experience the beauty at its full potential, and if you're a certified cavern diver, you can join local scuba-diving excursions to explore even deeper. If your timing is right, you will see a nest full of fuzzy owlets (April and May) tucked under the ledge as you descend the ladder. The drive here feels a bit like a ride on a Bahamian bush roller coaster, but it's worth it—finding the hole is half the adventure. ⊠ *Off Grand Bahama Hwy.* ✛ *From Grand Bahama Hwy., turn right on last dirt road before "Dangerous Curve" sign (before Lucayan National Park). Drive 1.6 miles to tiny parking area on left. You've gone too far if you reach beach.*

West End

TOWN | Once a rowdy, good-time resort area, West End was nearly leveled by Hurricane Matthew in 2016 and is still

Island Dogs

Island dogs, known as "potcakes"—a reference to the bottom of the peas and rice pans they clean up—run wild, so be careful when driving. Efforts in recent years by the active Humane Society of Grand Bahama have raised awareness of the need for neutering and spaying.

rebuilding. It still attracts small crowds on Sunday evening for friendly, casual street gatherings and on weekend afternoons for small fish-fry shacks offering up some of the island's best traditional Bahamian fare. Today's visitors stop at Paradise Cove for snorkeling and farther west at the bay-front conch shacks for conch salad straight from the shell (try Tanya's) or at other tiny eateries along the way, like Chicken's Nest, known for having the best conch fritters on island. Overnighters stay at Old Bahama Bay Resort & Yacht Harbour, an upscale gated resort. Nonguests are welcome at the hotel's beachside Teaser's Tiki Bar for breakfast and lunch, or at the Dockside Bar & Grill for dinner. ⊠ *Western Grand Bahama, West End.*

🌀 Beaches

★ Gold Rock Beach

BEACH | FAMILY | Located just off the Grand Bahama Highway, 26 miles outside town, this secluded beach, extending for yards into the sea when the tide is low, is accessible via a lovely 10-minute walk through Lucayan National Park. The turquoise water is exceptionally clear, calm, and shallow. Occasional cruise-ship tours visit for a couple of hours around midday, but there is enough space that you will never feel crowded. The beach is almost nonexistent when the tide is high, and shade is sparse, but when the tide rolls out, it's one of the most

Greater Grand Bahama

Key

Beaches

Dive Sites

Water Depths

-25ft deep

-50ft deep

-100ft deep

LITTLE BAHAMA BANK

Hawksbill Cays

Fish Cays

Upper Cay

Fox Town

LITTLE ABACO ISLAND

Sponge Cay

Little Cave Cay

Cross Cays

Great Sale Cay

Mangrove Cay

Mangrove Rocks

Noss Mangrove

Sandy Harbour

Sandy Cay

Little Water Cay

Water Cay

Water Cay

Dover Sound

GRAND BAHAMA ISLAND

Lucayan National Park

Dwt's Hole

Smith's Point

Theo's Wreck

Ben's Blue Hole

Fortune Beach

Gold Rock Beach

Old Freetown Beach

Freetown

Bevans Town

High Rock

Grand Bahama Hwy.

Riding Point

Halls Point

Rocky Creek

Pelican Point

Deep Water Cay

August Cay

McLean's Town

Sweeting's Cay

Sweetings

Lighthouse Cay

Big Cross Cay

Michael's Cay

Long Cay

Northwest Providence Channel

Grand Bahama International Airport

Lucaya

Freeport-Lucaya see detail map

Freeport

William's Town

Midshipman Rd.

Shark Junction

Sea Horse Rd.

Lucayan Beach

Taino Beach

Coral Beach

William's Town Beach

Xanadu Beach

Freeport Harbour

Lover's Beach

Eight Mile Rock

Queen's Hwy.

Bootle Bay Village

West End

West End Point

Paradise Cove Beach

Deadman's Reef

Crystal Beach

Celebrity Eco Adventures

Big Whale Cay

LITTLE BAHAMA BANK

10 mi

10 km

0

0

spectacular beaches around, so time your visit accordingly. **Amenities:** none. **Best for:** solitude; swimming; walking. ✉ *Grand Bahama Hwy., Freetown.*

Lover's Beach

BEACH | This beach on the island's west side is relatively unknown and rarely visited by tourists, with sand that's far less fine and powdery than what's found along the southern shores. However, it's the only spot on Grand Bahama to find sea glass. Adding to its uniqueness are its view of the large tanker and container ships anchored at sea for the island's industrial businesses and the pastel-painted heavy-equipment tires planted in the sand for seating. **Amenities:** parking (no fee). **Best for:** walking. ✉ *Hepburn Town, across the channel from Freeport Harbour, West End.*

Old Freetown Beach

BEACH | This lightly visited beach will take you far from the tourist crowds and resorts. Considered one of the prettiest beaches on the island, with a wide scattering of sea biscuits, blinding white sand, and shallow turquoise water, you will most likely have the whole stretch of sand to yourself. **Amenities:** none. **Best for:** solitude; swimming; walking. ✉ *Off Grand Bahama Hwy., just west of Ol' Freetown Farm* ✣ *Turn south on dirt road that lies just east of Grand Bahama Hwy.'s "Dangerous Curve" sign. Road to Owl's Hole will also land you at this beach.*

★ Paradise Cove Beach

BEACH | **FAMILY** | A 20-minute drive from Freeport, this beach's spectacular swim-to reef (called Deadman's Reef) is its best asset. Close to shore, you'll also find the longest man-made reef (composed of a long line of concrete reef balls) in The Bahamas, with spectacular marine life that includes various rays, sea turtles, and barracudas. Paradise Cove is a small native-owned resort with many different adventure packages, which all include return transportation from Freeport and Lucaya. The beach is short but wide, with scrubby vegetation and swaying palm trees. Snorkel equipment and kayaks are available to rent, and refreshments flow at The Red Bar. Beaches are public access up to the high-water mark in The Bahamas, so you can go and explore, but if you want to use any amenities, you must pay a small fee at the bar. **Amenities:** food and drink; parking (no fee); showers; toilets; water sports. **Best for:** snorkeling. ✉ *Warren J. Levarity Hwy., between Eight Mile Rock and West End, West End* ☎ *242/727–5339 Paradise Cove tour reservations number* 🌐 *deadmansreef.com.*

🍴 Restaurants

★ Bishop's Beach Club Restaurant & Bar

$ | **BAHAMIAN** | A longtime favorite of locals and visitors who venture out to Lucayan National Park (about 6 miles away) and into the east end's settlements, Bishop's serves all the fried Bahamian favorites with a view of the sea. The beach bar itself doesn't sell food, so you'll have to make the short walk across the parking lot to order in the restaurant and they will bring it out to you. **Known for:** ice-cold beer and tender cracked conch; great vibe with plenty of local color; tasty burgers. [$] *Average main: $12* ✉ *High Rock* ☎ *242/808-7949.*

🛏 Hotels

Grand Bahama has a selection of time-shares in addition to regular hotels and resorts. For more information about time-share houses, apartments, and condominiums, contact the Ministry of Tourism's Grand Bahama office (☎ *800/224–2627 bahamas.com*).

★ Old Bahama Bay Resort & Yacht Harbour

$$ | **RESORT** | **FAMILY** | Fishing enthusiasts, yachters, and families can relax in relative seclusion at this West End resort, made up of colorful beachfront and poolside suites individually decorated with island charm. **Pros:** top-shelf marina, tennis and basketball courts; quiet and secluded; complimentary use of bicycles, kayaks, paddleboards, and snorkeling equipment. **Cons:** limited dining choices; far from main airport, shopping, and other restaurants; need a car to explore the rest of the island. $ *Rooms from: $210* ⊠ *West End* ☎ *242/602–5171, 800/329–0068* ⊕ *www.oldbahamabayresorts.com* ⚓ *76 rooms* ❍❍ *No Meals.*

Paradise Cove

$ | **HOTEL** | **FAMILY** | Devoted snorkelers and peace-lovers will like this offbeat location (owned and operated by a local family), offering two two-bedroom stilted cottages overlooking the beach. **Pros:** accommodating and friendly staff; superb snorkeling just off the beach; quiet in the off-hours. **Cons:** far from restaurant options, nightlife, and shopping; sometimes swarmed with bused-in visitors during the day; fee to rent snorkeling gear and kayaks. $ *Rooms from: $175* ⊠ *Warren J. Levarity Hwy., 8 miles east of West End turnoff, West End* ☎ *242/602–5180, 242/727-5339* ⊕ *deadmansreef.com* ⚓ *2 cottages* ❍❍ *No Meals.*

⚡ Activities

TOURS
Blue Green Outdoors

ECOTOURISM | Lead guide Rudy Sawyer knows pretty much everything there is to know about the flora and fauna of Grand Bahama Island as well as all the most special spots to see. Choose between tours that take you kayaking, snorkeling, exploring blue holes, learning about mangroves, visiting local settlements, or even bird-watching. ⊠ *Queen's Highway, McClean's Town* ☎ *242/727-6161* ⊕ *bluegreenoutdoors.biz* ▦ *Tours from $95.*

H. Forbes Charter Services

ADVENTURE TOURS | This full-service tour operator can arrange a variety of tours for you, including swimming with pigs, van tours of the island, or other experiences like sunset cruises or beach bonfire nights. ⊠ *Queen's Highway, Freeport* ☎ *242/352–9311* ⊕ *forbescharter.com* ▦ *Tours from $35.*

★ West End Ecology Tours

ECOTOURISM | Join renowned stingray whisperer Keith Cooper on an amazing trip by boat to the shallow banks of nearby Sandy Cay, where he summons wild stingrays and lemon sharks for an up-close encounter. Your guide is a wealth of knowledge on these majestic sea creatures and has developed an incredible relationship with them. Add on a coral reef snorkeling or reef-fishing experience. ⊠ *West End* ☎ *242/727-1156* ⊕ *www.westendecologytours.com* ▦ *Tours start at $350.*

Chapter 5

THE ABACOS

Updated by
Jessica Robertson

◉ Sights	🍴 Restaurants	🛏 Hotels	🛍 Shopping	🍸 Nightlife
★★★☆☆	★★★☆☆	★★☆☆☆	★★☆☆☆	★☆☆☆☆

WELCOME TO THE ABACOS

TOP REASONS TO GO

★ **Bonefish the Marls:**
One of the most spectacular bonefishing flats anywhere, the Marls is an endless maze of lush mangrove creeks, hidden bays, and sandy cays. Hire a professional guide to show you the best spots.

★ **Cay-hop:** Rent a boat and spend a day (or more) skipping among 150 cays. Settle onto your own private strip of beach and enjoy.

★ **Beach bash:** Stop in at Miss Emily's Blue Bee Bar in historic New Plymouth on Green Turtle Cay for a mind-altering rum, pineapple juice, and apricot brandy Goombay Smash; it's where the popular drink was born. When the weather is calm, hit Tahiti Beach on the end of Elbow Cay and wade out to The Thirsty Cuda—a funky floating bar and food truck.

★ **Swim with the fishes:**
With clear shallow waters and a series of colorful coral reefs extending for miles, The Abacos provide both the novice and the experienced underwater explorer plenty of visual stimulation.

1 Marsh Harbour. The third largest city in The Bahamas was the commercial center of the Abaco chain and home to a large sheltered harbor with a few marinas. Efforts to recover following Hurricane Dorian continue slowly, but it remains a far cry from the bustling town it was before the storm. Marsh Harbour serves as a hub for travel between the smaller cays and is where the largest international airport is situated.

2 Treasure Cay. Despite its name, Treasure Cay is part of the mainland. Within this sprawling gated residential and resort community, you will find one of the most famous beaches in all of The Bahamas. The main resort was destroyed by the storm, but gradually, homes are being restored.

3 South of Marsh Harbour. First up is Little Harbour, an idyllic spot home to the classic Pete's Pub and the country's only bronze foundry. Farther south is the modern second-home and vacation community of Schooner Bay. Beyond that are a few remote communities and protected Abaco National Park.

4 Elbow Cay. Home of the famous candy cane–striped Hope Town Lighthouse, this cay balances a historic getaway with modern conveniences. Hope Town, the main settlement, is known for neat clapboard cottages painted in pastel hues.

5 Man-O-War Cay. Proud of its stance as a traditionally dry island, this community holds fast to its history. It's famous for its boatbuilding, which can still be seen here daily on the waterfront, where people work by hand.

6 Great Guana Cay. A real getaway island, here you'll find modern luxuries and empty beaches. Guana also has Grabbers and Nippers, fun restaurant–bars with happening party scenes.

7 Green Turtle Cay. This idyllic island, with homes still built with Loyalist architecture and painted in pastels, is a great spot to wander on foot or by golf cart. A short drive outside historic New Plymouth is where you will find most of the hotels.

8 Spanish Cay. This private cay has a marina and an airstrip. It's a good fuel stop when arriving by boat or an even better secluded getaway.

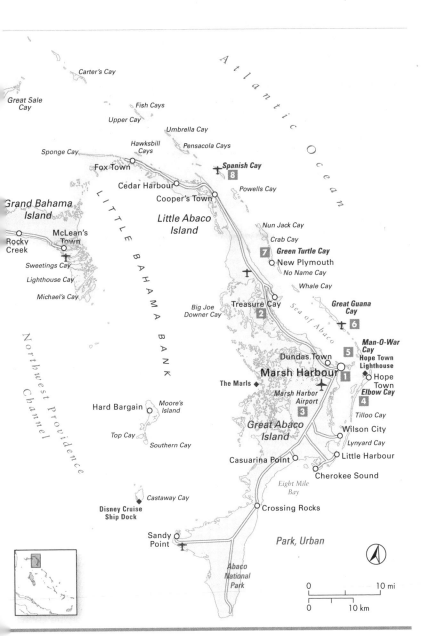

ABACO NATIONAL PARK

Abaco National Park was established in 1994 as a sanctuary for the endangered Bahama parrot, of which there are now nearly 9,000. Many other birds call the park home, including the pine warbler and the Bahama yellowthroat.

A 15-mile dirt track passes through the 20,500 protected acres, ending at the Hole in the Wall Lighthouse, a starkly beautiful and desolate location overlooking the ocean. The drive from the paved highway all the way to the lighthouse takes about 1½ hours and can only be done in a 4x4 vehicle. The lighthouse is not technically open to visitors, but people still do climb the rickety stairs to the top, where views of the island and the sea are mesmerizing. ✢ *South end of Great Abaco Island, before you make the final turn on the main road leading to Sandy Point.*

BEST TIME TO GO

In the fall and spring, berries ripen and the parrots become active. The best time to spot the birds is early morning, when they move out of the forest to feed. Temperatures then are also ideal, in the 70s and 80s. The annual bird counts in north and south Abaco held at the beginning of each year are a good opportunity to work with other bird-watchers to gather information on the parrots, which is shared with the Audubon Society.

BEST WAYS TO EXPLORE

By car on your own. Take the 15-mile, 1½-hour drive along a dirt trail out to the lighthouse. This is the only part of the park you can drive. This lighthouse has spectacular views of the coast. Take a packed lunch and have a picnic on a ledge overlooking the ocean.

By guided tour. For the best experience, arrange a guided tour with the tourist office. A knowledgeable guide will walk or drive you through the park, pointing out plant and animal species. If you're an early riser, join a bird-watching tour to find the endangered Bahama parrot, as well as other avian beauties that reside here. Walking the park alone is not recommended as poisonous wood saplings are a problem if you don't know how to identify them.

Friends of the Environment (☎ 242/801–0235) is a local education organization that offers more information on the park and the parrots.

FUN FACT
The park's pine forest is prone to summer-lightning fires, but the Abaco pine is extremely resistant and actually depends on the fires to remove dense underbrush that would otherwise smother it. The Bahama parrots nest in holes in the limestone floor to escape the flames. Unfortunately, this makes them vulnerable to raccoons and feral cats that threaten their population.

Hole in the Wall Lighthouse

The parks are sanctuaries for many bird species.

FOWL CAYS NATIONAL PARK
This quarter-mile reef located on the ocean side of Fowl Cay is a great snorkeling and dive spot. It's well known among divers for its tunnels and wide variety of fish. On the opposite side of Fowl Cay is a small sand spit, which makes a great spot to reconvene for a sun-soaked picnic.

PELICAN CAYS LAND AND SEA PARK
This 2,000-acre land and marine park is protected and maintained by the Bahamas National Trust. The park's preserved reef is only 25 feet underwater, making it an easy snorkel excursion. It's also a great dive site as the variety of life here is astounding. Nearby is an incredibly soft beach, great for a post-swim picnic.

The Abacos, 200 miles east of Palm Beach, Florida, are the northernmost chain of cays in The Bahamas. Covering 120 miles, this mini-archipelago offers both historic settlements and uninhabited islands. Ecotourism is popular here, and aficionados have revitalized exploration of these island's Caribbean pine forests, which are home to boars, parrots, and more. Hiking and biking through these forests and along abandoned beaches provides a rewarding sense of adventure.

The resilience of the islanders who call Abaco home is evident in the amount of rebuilding that has happened since Hurricane Dorian demolished much of what was there in 2019. While some areas are still struggling to make a comeback, other islands and communities have banded together, worked hard, taken advantage of government concessions, and rebuilt much of what was destroyed.

One of the region's best assets is the water; snorkeling and diving have long been staple activities for visitors. Abaconians are proud of their marine environment and have worked with the government to protect some of the more vibrant reefs. The islands' calm, naturally protected waters, long admired for their beauty, have also helped the area become The Bahamas's sailing capital. Man-O-War Cay remains The Bahamas's boatbuilding center; its residents turn out traditionally crafted wood dinghies as well as high-tech fiberglass craft. The Abacos play host annually to internationally famous regattas and to a half dozen game-fish tournaments.

MAJOR REGIONS

Great Abaco Island is The Abacos' commercial center and boasts fishing and farming communities, blue holes, caves, wild parrots, and pine forests.

Marsh Harbour, the island's main hub, was hit hard by Hurricane Dorian and continues to limp back to life.

Treasure Cay lost most of its resorts and restaurants to the storm, but the world-famous beach remains and long-time second-home owners are gradually bringing life back to this spot.

Other communities **south of Marsh Harbour** are quiet and tucked away, each with its own personality, making them worthy day trips.

Planning

When to Go

June, July, and early August are the best months for sailing, boating, and swimming, precisely why the most popular regattas and fishing tournaments are held during this time. Afternoon thunderstorms are common but usually clear quickly. Temperatures often reach the 90s.

December through May is a pleasant time to visit, with temperatures in the 70s and 80s, though sometimes dropping into the 50s at night when cold fronts blow through. Fishing, particularly deep-sea fishing, is good during this time of year.

From mid-August to late October, typically the peak of hurricane season, visitors drop to a trickle, and many hotels, restaurants, and stores shut down for up to three months. If you're willing to take a chance on getting hit by a storm, this can still be a great time to explore, with discounts of as much as 50% at the hotels that remain open.

FESTIVALS

Goombay Summer Festival

FESTIVALS | Goombay Summer Festival—traditional summertime parties with dance troupes, musical groups, and lots of local food and crafts—takes place in Marsh Harbour. ✉ *Marsh Harbour.*

Hope Town Music and Rum Festival

MUSIC FESTIVALS | Early to mid-February, Elbow Cay comes alive with the sound of music during this week-long festival. Leading songwriters from around the world perform original songs at venues across the island. ✉ *Elbow Cay* ☏ 242/557-7677 ⊕ *hopetownmusicandrumfestival.com.*

Junkanoo

CULTURAL FESTIVALS | Many Abaco communities have their own Junkanoo celebrations; Hope Town has a New Year's Eve children's rush-out for locals and visitors to join in. Parades in The Abacos are much smaller and more intimate than in Nassau—and far less competitive. ✉ *Hope Town.*

Regatta Time

FESTIVALS | Regattas in The Abacos is a fun-filled 10-day event held in late June or early July, stretching over several islands, with races and plenty of onshore parties. ✉ *Green Turtle Cay* ☏ 242/359-6046 ⊕ *regattasintheabacos.com.*

Getting Here and Around

AIR

Most flights land at **Leonard M. Thompson International Airport (MHH)** in Marsh Harbour. Taxi fare to most places in Marsh Harbour or the ferry dock to the cays is between $15 and $30 for the first two passengers and $3 for each additional person. Cab fare between Marsh Harbour and Treasure Cay or the ferry dock is $85 each way.

CONTACTS Marsh Harbour Airport. ✉ *Marsh Harbour* ☏ 242/367–5500.

BOAT AND FERRY

The *Legacy* mail boat leaves Potter's Cay in Nassau on Tuesday evening, arriving in Marsh Harbour Wednesday morning, and departing late afternoon on Thursday for a Friday morning arrival in Nassau. Each one-way journey takes about 10 hours. The *Sealink* ferry takes 13 hours from Abaco to Nassau, leaving from Marsh Harbour Sunday at 1pm and arriving in Nassau at 1 am the following day. The reverse trip leaves from Nassau at 7 pm on Saturday, arriving in Marsh Harbour at 7 am on the following day. For details and updated schedules, call the **Dockmaster's Office.** A good system of public ferries allows you to reach even the most remote cays. ⇨ *See Getting Here and Around within the island sections for more information.*

You can also rent a boat at Marsh Harbour, Hope Town, and Green Turtle Cay.

CONTACTS Dockmaster's Office. ✉ *Nassau* ☎ *242/393–1064.*

CAR

On Great Abaco, renting a car is the best option if you plan on exploring outside Marsh Harbour or Treasure Cay, and it is best to make arrangements ahead of your arrival on the island. Rentals start at $70 a day, and gasoline costs about $6 per gallon. Cars are not necessary on most of the smaller cays in The Abacos; in fact, rental cars aren't even available in most locations.

CONTACTS A & P Auto Rentals. ✉ *Marsh Harbour* ☎ *242/577–0748.* **Cornish Car Rentals.** ✉ *Treasure Cay* ☎ *242/357–6714.* **Rental Wheels of Abaco.** ✉ *Marsh Harbour* ☎ *242/367–4643* ⊕ *rentalwheels.com.*

GOLF CART

Golf carts are the vehicle of choice on the majority of the smaller cays, including Elbow Cay, Green Turtle Cay, Great Guana Cay, and Man-O-War Cay, as well as in Treasure Cay on Great Abaco. Rates are $60 per day or $350–$400 per week. Reservations are essential. See sections on specific islands for rental recommendations.

TAXI

Taxi service is available on Great Abaco in Marsh Harbour and in Treasure Cay. Hotels will arrange for taxis to take you on short trips and to the airport. Fares are generally $1.50 per mile. Expect to pay about $85 for a one-way ride from Thompson International Airport to Treasure Cay. A 15% tip is customary.

Hotels

Intimate hotels, cottage-style resorts, and rental homes are the rule in The Abacos. There are a few full-scale resorts in Marsh Harbour, on Green Turtle Cay, and in Hope Town—with multiple restaurants, bars, pools, and activities—but most accommodations are more homey. What you might give up in modern amenities, you'll gain in privacy and beauty. Many hotels have water views, and with a cottage or private house, you may even get your own stretch of beach. Air-conditioning is a standard feature, and most places have added luxuries like cable TV and Wi-Fi. Small and remote doesn't equate with inexpensive, though; it's almost impossible to find lodging for less than $100 a night and not uncommon to pay more than $300 a night for beachside accommodations with all the conveniences. Both restaurant meals and hotel rooms—as well as just about every other good or service you purchase—also now incur an additional 10% government VAT (down from 12%, effective January 2022).

Restaurants

Fish, conch, and lobster—called crawfish by the locals—have long been the bedrock of local cuisine. Although a few menus, mostly in upscale resorts, feature dishes with international influences, most restaurants in The Abacos still serve simple Bahamian fare, with a few nods to American tastes. There are some fancier restaurants in Marsh Harbour and Hope Town as well as on Green Turtle Cay, but most restaurants are relaxed about attire and reasonably priced. Some offer live music, shaping the nightlife scene on weekends.

⇨ *Restaurant prices are based on the median main course price at dinner, excluding gratuity. Many Abaco restaurants do not add the customary 15% gratuity, leaving it up to the customer. Hotel prices are for two people in a standard double room in high season, excluding service and 10% VAT tax plus other government taxes. Restaurant and hotel reviews have been shortened. For full information, visit Fodors.com.*

Did You Know?

Bahamian currency includes a $3 bill. There's also a half-dollar bill and a 15-cent piece, which is square with rounded corners and decorated with a hibiscus. These three currencies are not frequently seen today and can make a great souvenir if you come across one.

What It Costs in U.S. Dollars

	$	$$	$$$	$$$$
RESTAURANTS				
	under $20	$20–$30	$31–$40	over $40
HOTELS				
	under $200	$200–$300	$301–$400	over $400

Great Abaco Island

If arriving by air, your trip will begin on Great Abaco, the main island. It's bordered on its eastern side by a chain of cays that extend from the north to about midway down the island and on the western side by a fishing flat called the Marls, a shallow-water area of mangrove creeks and islands. Great Abaco was once logged for its pine trees, and traveling by car allows you to access many old logging trails that will lead you to secluded beaches along the coast. The island is home to cows and boars, as well the endangered Bahama parrots, who make their homes in the pine forests.

Marsh Harbour is the main hub of activity on the island and continues to be rebuilt after 2019's Hurricane Dorian destroyed many homes and businesses. Heading north on S. C. Bootle Highway will take you to **Treasure Cay** peninsula, a

second-home community development. There's another, smaller, airport here that is currently open to private flights only. Farther north are **Cooper's Town** and the small communities of **Little Abaco,** which don't provide much for visitors aside from near-total seclusion. South of Marsh Harbour off Ernest Dean Highway are artists' retreat **Little Harbour** and **Cherokee Sound** and **Sandy Point,** both small fishing communities. There is also the quaint yet upscale second-home and vacation community of **Schooner Bay.**

GETTING HERE AND AROUND

To travel around Great Abaco, you'll need a vehicle. Renting a car is the most convenient and economical option, but if you plan on spending most of your vacation in one town, hiring a taxi is also viable. Taxis are available all over the island, but the farther you travel from Marsh Harbour, the more extreme rates get, sometimes well in excess of $100. The closest settlement worth a visit out of Marsh Harbour is Little Harbour, about 30 minutes away.

From Marsh Harbour, you can travel by boat to Little Harbour and Cherokee Sound to the south and Treasure Cay in the north. Golf carts are used to travel locally within Treasure Cay and Cherokee Sound.

Marsh Harbour

Most visitors to The Abacos make their first stop in Marsh Harbour; however, post–Hurricane Dorian, there's not nearly as much to see or do. What was once the epicenter of The Abacos and the country's third largest city center is now not much more than a central jumping off point for exploring the surrounding cays and the rest of the mainland. The island grouping's largest international airport is situated here, and there are a few nice hotels, restaurants, and marinas that have made a comeback.

Marsh Harbour has the largest grocery store, Maxwell's Supermarket, and one of the larger liquor stores, and it is customary for most visitors to stock up on supplies on the way to other settlements or islands. If you need cash, this is the place to get it; banks here are open every day and have ATMs, neither of which you will find with the smaller, more remote settlements or cays.

🍴 Restaurants

★ The Bistro
$$$$ | **ECLECTIC** | Dine on a rib eye with smashed potatoes or a broiled lobster tail while overlooking gleaming rows of yachts moored in the Boat Harbour Marina at Abaco Beach Resort. For fresh seafood, the seared snapper and lobster ravioli are particularly good. **Known for:** tasty Bahamian lobster rolls and cracked shrimp tacos; casual elegance; island-style fine dining. [$] *Average main: $50* ✉ *Abaco Beach Resort, off Bay St., Marsh Harbour* ☎ *242/367–2158* 🌐 *www.abacobeachresort.com/bahamas-dining* 🕒 *Closed Monday through Tuesday.*

★ Colors
$$ | **BAHAMIAN** | This brightly painted restaurant is perched on a wooden dock over the southwestern side of the harbor. The Bahamian food menu is simple, but everything is delicious. **Known for:** best sunset view in Marsh Harbour; a DJ spins tunes on Friday and Saturday nights; conch tacos on Taco Tuesday. [$] *Average main: $28* ✉ *Marsh Harbour* ☎ *242/699–3294* 🌐 *www.facebook.com/colorsbythesea242.*

★ Jib Room Restaurant
$$ | **BAHAMIAN** | Expect casual lunches and dinners of hot wings, conch burgers, fish nuggets, and steak wraps in this harbor-view restaurant and bar, located inside the Marsh Harbour Marina. If you're dying for a steak after a steady fish diet, these are the best in The Abacos. **Known for:** barbecue ribs on Wednesday night, barbecue steaks on Saturday night; delicious grouper Reuben sandwiches; live local music and entertainment. [$] *Average main: $25* ✉ *Pelican Shores, Marsh Harbour* ☎ *242/802–1257* 🌐 *www.jibroom.com/restaurant/* 🕒 *Closed Sun.–Tues.*

★ Snappas Bar and Grill
$$ | **BAHAMIAN** | They've got a new location (just up the road at The Conch Inn), but it's the same good food, great drinks, and lively atmosphere that has made Snappas a longtime must-stop restaurant and bar. The food is a mix of American and Bahamian fare—tacos, burgers, steaks, fish, and conch. **Known for:** live music most Saturday nights; potent cocktails such as the signature guava duff daiquiri; lively, fun atmosphere. [$] *Average main: $30* ✉ *located at the Conch Inn, Marsh Harbour* ☎ *242/807-6501* 🌐 *snappasbar.com* 🕒 *closed Tues.*

Wally's Fine Dining
$$ | **BAHAMIAN** | Grab a seat on the large porch and enjoy cocktails and sunset before dinner, or escape the heat with an indoors lunch at this top Marsh Harbour spot. Burgers, wraps, pasta dishes, and nightly specials draw a crowd. **Known for:** fun, friendly staff; delicious signature cocktails; decadent desserts, including a must-try fried cheesecake. [$] *Average main: $30* ✉ *Marsh Harbour* ☎ *242/551–5476* 🌐 *www.facebook.com/wallysabaco*

Abaco Beach Resort spans 40 acres of beach in Marsh Harbour.

🕒 *closed Sun. through Weds. and September through October.*

Coffee and Quick Bites

Calypso Coffee House

$ | **CAFÉ** | Start your day off right with a hot Starbucks coffee or an iced frappé and a breakfast sandwich or one of the day's special offerings. Lunch is a variety of soups, salads, wraps, and pasta dishes. **Known for:** best coffee in Marsh Harbour; spot to catch a bit of the local sip sip (gossip); yummy grab-and-go lunch options. [$] *Average main: $15* ✉ *Inside Premier Importers, Marsh Harbour* ☎ *242/699-1407, 242242242/817–8136* 🕒 *Closed weekends.*

Hotels

★ **Abaco Beach Resort and Boat Harbour Marina**

$$$ | **RESORT** | **FAMILY** | The largest hotel in Marsh Harbour has a fresh look and feel following a major post–Hurricane Dorian overhaul. **Pros:** ideal location for all water-related activities; only hotel in Marsh Harbour with a private beach; one of the best marinas in The Abacos. **Cons:** can be crowded and noisy during fishing tournaments; pricey accommodations; long walk from car to rooms (call front desk for golf cart pickup). [$] *Rooms from: $395* ✉ *East of Conch Sound Marina, Marsh Harbour* ☎ *242/367–2158, 877/533–4799* 🌐 *abacobeachresort.com* 🔑 *88 rooms* 🍴 *No Meals.*

Abaco Suites

$$ | **MOTEL** | There's nothing fancy about this all-suites motel, but its rooms are clean and spacious. **Pros:** ideal for longer stays; near the current heart of Marsh Harbour; one of the few lodging options in the city. **Cons:** in the heart of downtown; no amenities; not walking distance from the ocean or beach. [$] *Rooms from: $220* ✉ *Don Mackay Blvd., Marsh Harbour* ☎ *242/699–1130* 🌐 *abacosuites.com* 🔑 *10 suites* 🍴 *No Meals.*

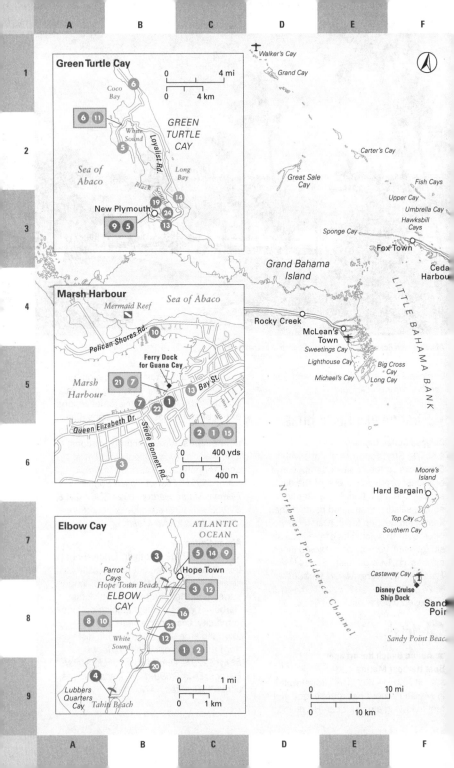

The Abacos

ATLANTIC OCEAN

Pensacola Cays

Spanish Cay

Cooper's Town
Powells Cay

Little Abaco Island

Nun Jack Cay

Crab Cay

New Plymouth

No Name Cay
Treasure Cay Beach
Whale Cay

Green Turtle Cay
see inset map

Great Guana Cay

Big Joe Downer Cay

Treasure Cay

THE MARLS

Sea of Abaco

Dundas Town

Marsh Harbour
see inset map

Marsh Harbor Airport

Great Abaco Island

Mastic Point

Fowl Cay Nat'l Reserve
Man-O-War Cay

Hope Town

Tilloo Cay

Pelican Cay Beach

Elbow Cay
see inset map

Wilson City

Little Harbour
Lynyard Cay

Casuarina Point

Cornwall Point
Cherokee Sound

Abaco Club on Winding Bay

Eight Mile Bay

Crossing Rocks

Saw Mill Sink Blue Hole

KEY

- Sights
- Restaurants
- Quick Bites
- Hotels

Sights ▼

1 Abaco National Park ... **G8**
2 Carleton Settlement Dunes **H5**
3 Elbow Reef Lightstation **B7**
4 Gifts from the Sea Museum **I7**
5 Hero's Wall **I6**
6 Hole in the Wall Lighthouse **G9**
7 The Johnston Art Foundry and Gallery **I7**
8 The Long Dock **I7**
9 Loyalist Memorial Sculpture Garden ... **B3**
10 Man-O-War Heritage Museum **I6**
11 Sawmill Sink Blue Hole **H7**
12 Treasure Cay Blue Hole **G5**

Restaurants ▼

1 Abaco Inn Restaurant **B8**
2 The Bistro **C5**
3 Bridget's Rum Bar **B8**
4 Café La Florence **H5**
5 Cap'n Jack's Restaurant and Bar..... **B7**
6 The Club Restaurant at Green Turtle Club Resort **B2**
7 Colors **B5**
8 Firefly Bar & Grill....... **B8**
9 Grabbers Bed, Bar, Dock & Grille **B8**
10 Jib Room Restaurant ... **B4**
11 Kidd's Cove Seafood Bar & Grill **I5**
12 Mackey's Takeout **B8**
13 McIntosh Restaurant & Bakery **B3**
14 Munchies **B7**
15 Nippers Beach Bar & Grill **I5**
16 On Da Beach Bar & Grill **B8**
17 The Pavilion **H5**
18 Pete's Pub **I7**
19 Pineapples Bar & Grill **B3**
20 Sea Spray Resort & Marina **B9**
21 Snappas Bar and Grill **B5**
22 Wally's Fine Dining **B5**
23 Willie's Kitchen & Bar .. **B8**
24 The Wrecking Tree **B3**

Quick Bites ▼

1 Calypso Coffee House **B5**
2 Mama's Restaurant & Bar **I5**
3 Man-O-War Heritage Museum Coffee Shop **I6**
4 Thirsty Cuda **A9**
5 Turtle Crawl Cafe **B3**

Hotels ▼

1 Abaco Beach Resort and Boat Harbour Marina ... **C5**
2 Abaco Inn **B8**
3 Abaco Suites **B6**
4 Bahama Beach Club ... **H5**
5 Bluff House Beach Resort & Marina **B2**
6 Cocobay Cottages **B1**
7 The Conch Inn & Marina **B5**
8 The Delphi Club **H7**
9 Elbow Cay Properties **B7**
10 Firefly Sunset Resort **B8**
11 Green Turtle Club Resort & Marina **B2**
12 Hope Town Inn & Marina **B8**
13 Island Breezes Hotel **C5**
14 Linton's Beach and Harbour Cottages **C3**
15 The Residences at Abaco Beach Resort.... **C5**
16 Sandpiper Inn & Cottages **H8**
17 Schooner Bay **H8**
18 Spanish Cay Resort and Marina **G3**

G   H   I

★ The Conch Inn & Marina

$$ | **HOTEL** | Completely rebuilt and expanded after Hurricane Dorian, this 17-room three-story marina hotel is a great choice for tourists and business travelers alike. **Pros:** centrally located; easy to arrange boat rentals and diving; good value for comfortable rooms. **Cons:** far from beaches; small pool area; basic amenities only. $ *Rooms from: $252* ✉ *E. Bay St., Marsh Harbour* ☎ *242/577–7000* ⊕ *conchinn.com* 🛏 *17 rooms* ⦿ *No Meals.*

Island Breezes Hotel

$ | **HOTEL** | This simple, no-frills motel is ideal if you plan to spend your days exploring the mainland by car or the surrounding cays by ferry or boat and just need a place for a shower and a good sleep before starting all over the next day. **Pros:** lowest rates in Marsh Harbour; warm and friendly staff; one of the only hotels for short-term stays. **Cons:** very simple accommodations; no indoor common areas; no pool. $ *Rooms from: $175* ✉ *Bay St., Marsh Harbour* ☎ *242/577–0427, 242/367–3776* ⊕ *islandbreezeshotel.com* 🛏 *8 rooms* ⦿ *No Meals.*

★ The Residences at Abaco Beach Resort

$$$$ | **RESORT** | **FAMILY** | Lots of room, contemporary upscale island decor, and large balconies where you can sit and enjoy amazing views of the Sea of Abaco make these two- and three-bedroom condos a popular choice. **Pros:** lots of room for families; upscale accommodations; offers chef and butler service. **Cons:** extremely pricey; noise from marina below; beach is a far walk from rooms. $ *Rooms from: $1345* ✉ *Abaco Beach Resort & Marina, Bay St., Marsh Harbour* ☎ *242/367–2158, 877/533–4799* ⊕ *abacobeachresort.com* 🛏 *9 condos* ⦿ *No Meals.*

Shopping

SPECIALTY STORES

★ Abaco Ceramics

CERAMICS | This shop offers the signature Abaco Ceramics white-clay pottery with a variety of island- and sea-inspired designs. The Funky Fish pattern remains a favorite. You can also pick up some fun and funky painted wooden signs and handmade quilts made with hand-dyed fabrics from sister company Bahama Dawn Designs. ✉ *Don Mackay Blvd., Marsh Harbour* ⊹ *three buildings south of the Marsh Harbour traffic light* ☎ *242/375–8774* ⊕ *abaco-ceramics.com* ⊙ *Closed Sun.*

Abaco Neem

OTHER SPECIALTY STORE | More than 30 different products are derived from locally grown neem trees at this shop and production plant. Salves, soaps, and lotions are organic and in many cases claim to offer medicinal benefits against skin conditions, arthritis, and even hypertension. Abaco Neem also produces an entire range of pet products. Call or e-mail in advance to arrange a tour of the production facility and nearby farm. ✉ *Ernest Dean Highway, Marsh Harbour* ☎ *242/357–5255, 242/375–8053* ⊕ *abaconeem.com.*

Activities

BIKING

Rental Wheels of Abaco

BIKING | Rent single-speed beach cruisers with baskets to cruise around the island from this outfitter that also offers car rentals. ✉ *E. Bay St., Marsh Harbour* ☎ *242/367–4643* ⊕ *rentalwheels.com* 🚲 *Rentals $35 a day or $100 per week.*

BOAT RENTALS

The best way to explore The Abacos is by renting a small boat from one of the rental companies in Marsh Harbour.

The Abacos are the sailing capital of The Bahamas.

Bluewave Boat Rentals

BOATING | Boats range from 21 to 33 feet. Bookings should be made well in advance, and rentals are for a minimum of three days. ✉ Bay St., Marsh Harbour 📞 242/699–1476 ⊕ www.bluewaverentals.com ✉ 3-day rentals start at $880 off season and $1100 high season.

Cruise Abaco

BOATING | Choose your sailboat or catamaran—they have boats that comfortably sleep eight adults in four double cabins. Then choose whether you want to captain your own vessel or opt to have a captain by day to take you around The Abacos and safely get you docked or moored, leaving you alone until the following morning when it's time to go exploring again. Four- or seven-day charters as well as single-day rentals are available. ✉ Abaco Beach Resort, Bay St., Marsh Harbour 📞 321/830–9412 ⊕ www.cruiseabaco.com ✉ Day trips from $1,700, week-long captained excursions from $7,275.

Dream Yacht

BOATING | Choose from six catamarans or a monohull sailboat—including a 42-foot boat that sleeps nine and a 45-foot boat that sleeps 12—to sail from island to island, beach to beach. You can take the helm or have the charter skippered or even have a full crew at your beck and call. ✉ E. Bay St., Marsh Harbour 📞 855/650–8902 ⊕ dreamyachtcharter.com ✉ 4-day charters from $1335 bareboat and $2275 skippered. Max 6 passengers.

BOATING

Abaco Beach Resort and Boat Harbour Marina

BOATING | The marina has 200 fully protected slips and a slew of amenities, including on-site customs and immigration clearance and accommodations at the resort. This marina can accommodate vessels up to 200 feet. There is also a helipad for use by guests booked in at the marina or the resort. ✉ Bay St., Marsh Harbour 📞 242/367–2158, 877/533-4799 ⊕ abacobeachresort.com.

The Conch Inn Marina

BOATING | This is one of the busiest marinas and has 72 slips and full amenities, with accommodations available at The Conch Inn. ⊠ *Bay St., Marsh Harbour* ☎ *242/577–7000* ⊕ *www.conchinn.com.*

Marsh Harbour Marina

BOATING | Marsh Harbour Marina has 38 slips and is the only full-service marina on the far side of the harbor, near Pelican Shores. It is a 10-minute drive from most shops and restaurants. ⊠ *Marsh Harbour* ☎ *242/802–1257* ⊕ *www.jibroom.com/marina/.*

FISHING

You can find bonefish on the flats, yellowtail and grouper on the reefs, or marlin and tuna in the deep waters of The Abacos. For the best experience, hire a local guide who knows the prime spots.

Justin Sands Bonefishing

FISHING | Premier fly-fishing guide Justin Sands works out of a state-of-the-art Hell's Bay flats skiff that will put you in the shallowest of water. Justin was The Abacos bonefish champ for two years running, and he will guide you in the Marls or around Snake Cay, Little Harbour, and Cherokee Sound. Advance reservations are a must. ⊠ *Marsh Harbour* ☎ *242/359–6890* ⊕ *justfishjs.com* 🍴 *$500 for half-day fishing; $600 for full day.*

Pinder's Bonefishing

FISHING | Buddy Pinder has decades of experience in the local waters, and Pinder's Professional Bonefishing provides year-round excursions in the Marls, a maze of mangroves and flats on the western side of Abaco. Advance reservations are essential. ⊠ *Marsh Harbour* ☎ *242/577–7612.*

SCUBA DIVING AND SNORKELING

There's excellent diving throughout The Abacos. Many sites are clustered around Marsh Harbour, including the reef behind **Guana Cay,** which is filled with small cavelike catacombs, and **Fowl**

Play the Tides

If you're going bonefishing, tide pooling, or snorkeling, you'll want up-to-date tide information for the best results. A low incoming tide is usually best for bonefishing, though the last of the falling is good, too. Low tides are best for beachcombing and tide pools, although higher tides can give better coverage to your favorite reef. Ask at your hotel or a local dive shop for current tide information.

Cays National Park, which contains wide tunnels and a variety of fish. **Pelican Cays Land and Sea Park** is a popular dive area south of Marsh Harbour. This shallow, 25-foot dive is filled with sea life; turtles are often sighted, as are spotted eagle rays and tarpon. The park is a 2,000-acre national park protected and maintained by the Bahamas National Trust. Hook up your own boat to one of the moorings, or check with the local dive shops to see when trips to the park are scheduled. All these sights can be easily snorkeled. Snorkelers will also want to visit **Mermaid Beach,** just off Pelican Shores Road in Marsh Harbour, where beautiful live reefs and green moray eels make for some of The Abacos' best snorkeling.

TOURS

★ Brendal's Dive Center

SCUBA DIVING | Whether you're looking for a close encounter with a shark, dolphin, turtle, or swimming pig, this dive operator has a tour designed just for you. They also offer scuba courses, island-hopping adventures, and sunset cruises. ⊠ *Green Turtle Cay* ☎ *242/365–4411, 242/458–7868* ⊕ *brendal.com* 🍴 *2-tank dives $175; half-day adventure tours from $55; full-day adventure tours from $165.*

Treasure Cay

Twenty miles north of Marsh Harbour is Treasure Cay, technically not an island but a large peninsula connected to Great Abaco by a narrow spit of land. This was once the site of the first Loyalist settlement in Abaco, called Carleton.

The area's main resort, restaurants, bars, and marina were completely destroyed by Hurricane Dorian in 2019, and its future development remains uncertain. This loss changed the landscape and the island vibe, but gradually the longtime local and expatriate homeowners are repairing and rebuilding their homes, and a much needed sense of community and life is slowly returning.

Much of Treasure Cay's commercial center was also wiped out, but one row of shops has been brought back to life, and some amenities have returned.

One thing the hurricane didn't take away is the beautiful beach. Miles of white sand and aqua sea await, and this alone is worth the trek.

Sights

Carleton Settlement Ruins

RUINS | Tucked away toward the northwestern end of the Treasure Cay development are the ruins of the very first settlement in Abaco, founded by the Loyalists who left the Carolinas during the American Revolutionary War. The sight is not well marked, but a local can point you in the right direction. ✉ *Treasure Cay.*

Treasure Cay Blue Hole

NATURE SIGHT | You'll need a car or at least a bicycle to visit this natural wonder, but it's worth the trek. Scientists believe the Treasure Cay Blue Hole is 200 feet deep, but feel free to dip your toes into the crystal-clear blue waters or make a splash swinging from one of the rope swings tied to surrounding pine trees. The water is both salt and fresh, and there is no known marine life in the blue hole. ✉ *Off S.C. Bootle Hwy., Treasure Cay* ✥ *Turn left off S.C. Bootle Hwy. just before entrance to Green Turtle Cay Ferry Dock. Take wide dirt road about 2½ miles and follow narrow dirt road at left 500 feet to blue hole.*

Beaches

★ Treasure Cay Beach

BEACH | FAMILY | This beach is world famous for its expanse of truly powder-like sand and breathtaking turquoise water. A hotel and upscale homes line the miles-long beach, but most of it is clear from development since the land is privately owned—and almost clear of footprints. **Amenities:** parking (no fee); **Best for:** sunrise; sunset; swimming; walking. ✉ *Treasure Cay.*

Restaurants

★ Café La Florence

$ | BAKERY | Stop off at this bakery–café in the Treasure Cay shopping strip for just-made muffins and some of the best cinnamon rolls you'll ever try. You'll know you've found it by the smell of those fresh-baked treats and the line of people waiting to indulge. **Known for:** friendly family that owns the place; ice-cream parlor; best spot to grab an early morning coffee. [$] *Average main: $10* ✉ *Treasure Cay* ☎ *242/365–8534* 🕒 *Closed Sun.*

The Pavilion

$$$ | BAHAMIAN | One of the only restaurants that's made a comeback in the Treasure Cay area offers a menu with the standard delicious Bahamian dishes you'd expect for both lunch and dinner. The poolside spot at Bahama Beach Club is known, however, for its varied theme nights. **Known for:** tasty lobster tacos; best sit-down dining in town; romantic candlelit dinners on the beach. [$] *Average main: $40* ✉ *Bahama Beach Club, Treasure Cay* ☎ *242/284–0382, 800/284–0382* 🌐 *www.bahamabeachclub.com.*

Treasure Cay Beach is one of the most beautiful beaches on Great Abaco Island.

Hotels

★ Bahama Beach Club

$$$$ | HOTEL | FAMILY | Ideal for families and small groups, these two- to five-bedroom condos are right on the famous Treasure Cay beach. **Pros:** luxury accommodations on one of the most sublime beaches in the world; large pool area with Jacuzzi; only hotel in Treasure Cay. **Cons:** check-in can be slow; housekeeping is a separate cost; closed September and October. *[$] Rooms from: $525 ✉ Treasure Cay ☎ 800/284–0382 🌐 www.bahamabeach-club.com ⏲ Closed Sept. and Oct. 🛏 87 condos 🍴 No Meals.*

Activities

FISHING

Justin Sands Bonefishing

FISHING | Reservations are a must to go bonefishing with Justin Sands, Abaco's award-winning angler and guide. He's located in Marsh Harbour but accommodates guests all over The Abacos. *✉ Marsh Harbour ☎ 242/359–6890 🌐 www.justfishjs.com 🎟 half day $500; full day $600.*

SCUBA DIVING AND SNORKELING

No Name Cay, Whale Cay, and **Fowl Cays National Park** are popular marine-life sites. The 1865 wreck of the steamship freighter *San Jacinto* also affords scenic diving.

South of Marsh Harbour

Thirty minutes south of Marsh Harbour, the small, eclectic artists' colony of **Little Harbour** was settled by the Johnston family more than 70 years ago. Randolph Johnston moved his family here to escape the consumerist, hectic lifestyle he experienced in the United States and to pursue a simple life where he and his wife could focus on their art. The family is well known for their bronze sculptures, some commissioned nationally.

Just to the south of Little Harbour is the seaside settlement of **Cherokee Sound,** home to fewer than 100 families as well as the longest dock and the smallest museum in The Bahamas. Most of the residents make their living catching crawfish or working in the growing tourism industry; many lead offshore fishing and bonefishing expeditions. The deserted Atlantic beaches and serene salt marshes in this area are breathtaking, and though development at Winding Bay and Little Harbour are progressing, the slow-paced, tranquil feel of daily life here hasn't changed. **Schooner Bay** is a by-design village just a bit farther south. Initially intended as a living, breathing community, it has turned into more of a second-home and vacation destination, but it maintains a quaint island village feel. **Sandy Point,** a fishing village with miles of beckoning beaches and a couple of bonefishing lodges, is slightly more than 50 miles southwest of Marsh Harbour, about a 40-minute drive from Cherokee.

Sights

★ Abaco National Park

NATIONAL PARK | Abaco National Park was established in 1994 as a sanctuary for the endangered Bahama parrot. The mission has been a success as the population at the time was just 1,500, and today there are nearly 9,000 documented. Many other birds call the park home, including the pine warbler and the Bahama yellowthroat.

A 15-mile dirt track passes through the 20,500 protected acres, ending at the Hole in the Wall Lighthouse, a starkly beautiful and desolate location overlooking the ocean. The drive from the paved highway all the way to the lighthouse takes about 1½ hours and can only be done in a 4x4 vehicle. The lighthouse is technically not open to visitors, but people still do climb the rickety stairs to the top, where views of the island and the sea are mesmerizing. ⊠ *South end of Great Abaco* ✛ *The turnoff for park is just before you make final turn on main road leading to Sandy Point*

☎ *242/367–6310 Bahamas National Trust Abaco Office* ⊕ *bnt.bs/explore/abaco/abaco-national-park/.*

Gifts from the Sea Museum

OTHER MUSEUM | One of the tiniest museums in the world is located under the communications tower in Cherokee Sound in a small building that used to house the community telegraph office. Most locals know it as the "Shell Museum" because inside you'll find a collection of more than 200 shells identified by both their Latin and common names. Many of these shells are ones you may find yourself (if you're lucky) as you walk the island's beaches. ⊠ *Cherokee Sound* ☎ *242/366–2053, 242/475–7868* 💲 *Free* ☞ *Call ahead to request entry.*

Hole in the Wall Lighthouse

NATURE SIGHT | Off Great Abaco Highway at the turn in the road that takes you to Sandy Point, a rugged, single-lane dirt track leads you to this navigational lighthouse that stands on Great Abaco's southern tip. The lighthouse was constructed in 1838 against local opposition from islanders who depended on salvaging shipwrecks for their livelihood. Over the years the lighthouse has survived sabotage and hurricanes and was automated in 1995 to continue serving maritime interests. The Bahamas Marine Mammal Research Organisation has leased the site to monitor whale movements and conduct other ocean studies. ⊠ *South of Sandy Point.*

★ The Johnston Art Foundry and Gallery

ART GALLERY | Sculptor Pete Johnston and his sons (direct descendants of Randolph and Margot Johnston, who founded Little Harbour) and acolytes cast magnificent lifelike bronze figures using the age-old lost-wax method at the only bronze foundry in The Bahamas. You can purchase the art in the gallery. ⊠ *Little Harbour, Little Harbour* ☎ *242/577–5487* ⊕ *www.johnstonartfoundry.com.*

★ The Long Dock

BRIDGE | You can walk hundreds of feet along this dock above the shallow aquamarine sea, and it is well worth a visit to the quaint village of Cherokee Sound, especially when you hear the story behind it. The Cherokee Sound community had always boasted about having the longest dock in the country. When Hurricane Dorian washed all 770 feet of it away, leaving little but a few pilings, the community got busy raising money and rebuilding using logs cut from local pine forests. The new bridge is even longer than the original by more than 30 feet and has a series of platforms with benches that make it an even nicer spot to take in the views. ✉ *Cherokee Sound.*

Sawmill Sink Blue Hole

NATURE SIGHT | A half-hour drive south of Marsh Harbour is a crudely marked electric pole directing you to turn right onto an old logging trail. A short drive down this road takes you to an incredible blue hole. It was featured by *National Geographic* in 2010 for the fossils found deep within it. Though you cannot dive this hole, you can swim in it. ✉ *Great Abaco Hwy.*

Beaches

Pelican Cay Beach

BEACH | In a protected park, this is a great spot for snorkeling and diving on nearby Sandy Cay reef. The cay is small and between two ocean cuts, so the water drops off quickly, but its location is also what nurtures the pure white sand. If you get restless, ruins of an old house are hidden in overgrowth at the top of the cay, and they offer fantastic views of the park. **Amenities:** none. **Best for:** snorkeling. ✉ *8 miles north of Cherokee Sound, Cherokee Sound.*

Sandy Point Beach

BEACH | If shelling and solitude are your thing, venture 50 miles southwest of Marsh Harbour to the sleepy fishing village of Sandy Point. Large shells wash up on the sandy beaches, making it great for a stroll and shelling. The best spot for picking up one of nature's souvenirs is between the picnic site and Rocky Point. Well offshore is the private island Castaway Cay, where Disney Cruise Line guests spend a day. **Amenities:** none. **Best for:** solitude; walking. ✉ *Sandy Point.*

Restaurants

★ Pete's Pub

$$ | **BAHAMIAN** | Next door to Pete's Gallery is an outdoor tiki hut restaurant and bar where you can wiggle your toes in the sand while you chow down on fresh seafood, burgers, and cold tropical drinks. Try the mango-glazed grouper, lemon-pepper mahimahi, or coconut-cracked conch while you kick back and enjoy the view of the harbor. **Known for:** refreshing cocktails; occasional wild pig roasts; fun and funky spot to take a dip and grab a bite. [$] *Average main: $22* ✉ *Little Harbour* ☎ *242/357-6648, 242/577–5487* 🌐 *www.petespub.com.*

Hotels

★ The Delphi Club

$$$$ | **B&B/INN** | Although The Delphi Club is billed as a bonefishing lodge, it's a great middle-of-nowhere bed-and-breakfast perfect for anyone looking to get away from it all but not willing to give up style or comfort. **Pros:** private and secluded; lots of on-site activities; situated on a beautiful private beach. **Cons:** very remote; lots of stairs; dinner is always family style at a set time. [$] *Rooms from: $1300* ✣ *Leaving Marsh Harbour, head south 24 miles along Great Abaco Hwy.; turn left when you see large white rock on right-hand side, and follow signs to Delphi Club along unpaved road* ☎ *242/577–1698* 🌐 *www.delphi-bahamas.com* 🛏 *8 rooms* 🍴 *All-Inclusive* ☞ *3-night minimum; fishing or birding packages additional.*

★ Sandpiper Inn & Cottages

$$$ | B&B/INN | With harbor views, luxuriously decorated rooms and suites, and the only restaurant and swimming pool in Schooner Bay right downstairs, this quaint bed-and-breakfast inn is the perfect spot for visitors who want to be taken care of. **Pros:** personalized service; fun on-site bar frequented by boaters docked in the harbor; small and intimate. **Cons:** no organized activities; limited dining options; long way from anything else in Abaco. $ *Rooms from: $305* ☎ *242/577–4656, 242/699–2056* ⊕ *sandpiperabaco. com* ⤏ *7 rooms* ⦶ *No Meals.*

Schooner Bay

$$$$ | HOUSE | FAMILY | Many of the homes and cottages in this designer community are available for rent. **Pros:** homes are completely turnkey; friendly staff; sense of community. **Cons:** no organized activities; just one full restaurant in the village; long way from other communities. $ *Rooms from: $500* ✉ *Schooner Bay Village* ☎ *242/577–1040* ⊕ *schoonerbaybahamas.com* ⤏ *5 homes* ⦶ *No Meals.*

👜 Shopping

ART GALLERIES

★ The Johnston Art Foundry and Gallery

ART GALLERIES | The gallery displays and sells original bronzes by the Johnstons—direct descendants of Randolph and Margot Johnston, who founded Little Harbour—as well as unique gold jewelry, prints, and gifts. ✉ *Little Harbour* ☎ *242/577–5487* ⊕ *www.johnstonartfoundry.com.*

Elbow Cay

Five-mile-long Elbow Cay's main attraction is the charming village of **Hope Town.** The saltbox cottages painted in bright colors—with their white picket fences, flowering gardens, and porches and sills decorated with conch shells—will remind you of a New England seaside community, Bahamian style. The settlement took a direct hit from Hurricane Dorian in 2019, but a strong sense of community—most of the residents' families have lived here for several generations—has helped bring much of it back to life. For an interesting walking or bicycling tour of Hope Town, follow the two narrow lanes that circle the village and harbor. (Most of the village is closed to motor vehicles.)

Although modern conveniences like Wi-Fi and cell service are found throughout the island, most residents remember the day the island first got telephone service—back in 1988. Before that, everyone called each other the way many still do here and in the other Family Islands: by VHF, the party line for boaters. If you are boating and want to communicate with the locals, or would like to make a dinner reservation on one of the cays, you should carry a VHF radio and have it tuned to channel 16.

GETTING HERE AND AROUND
FERRY

Elbow Cay is four miles southeast of Marsh Harbour. Every day except Sunday and holidays, **The Ferry at The Crossing** (☎ *242/367–0290)* leaves Marsh Harbour for the 20-minute ride to Hope Town at 6:15, 7:15, 9, 11, 12:30, 2:30, 3, 3:30, 4:30, and 5:30; ferries make the return trip at 6:45, 8, 9:30, 11:30, 1, 3, 3:30, 4, 5, and 6:15. Sunday and holidays, there is less frequent transport, ending at 4:30/5 pm. A same-day round-trip costs $20. One-way tickets cost $15. Tickets are $5 less for children ages 6–12 and free for children 5 and under.

GOLF CART

Once in Hope Town you can walk everywhere. In fact, only local work vehicles are permitted through town. To visit other parts of the small island, you can rent a bicycle or a golf cart.

CONTACTS The Bike Shop. ✉ *300 feet north of the main Post Office Dock,* *opposite Harbour's Edge, Hope Town* ⊕ *wsailbags.com/thebikeshop.* **Hope Town Cart Rentals.** ☎ *242/458–0442* ⊕ *www. hopetowncartrental.com.* **Island Cart Rent- als.** ☎ *242/366–0448, 561168/208–8160 US number* ⊕ *islandcartrentals.com.*

Sights

★ Elbow Reef Lightstation

LIGHTHOUSE | Upon arrival in Hope Town Harbour, you'll first see a much-pho- tographed Bahamas landmark, an 89-foot-tall, candy-striped lighthouse first manned in 1863. The lighthouse's construction was delayed for several years by acts of vandalism; then-resi- dents feared it would end their profitable wrecking practice. Today the lighthouse is the last hand-turned, kerosene-fueled beacon in operation anywhere in the world. Monday through Saturday, from 9 to 5, you can climb up the spiral staircase to the top for a superb view of the sea and the nearby cays. There are 101 steps in all, and there is no graceful way for an adult to crawl through the small door onto the viewing platform that goes all the way around the top. The lighthouse keepers and their families live in the small cottages at its base, so keep noise to a minimum as one of them is resting up for his night shift. There's no road between the lighthouse and the town proper. You can use your own boat to cross the harbor or take a ferry to the dock and explore the lighthouse; the ferry does not run very frequently, so expect to spend at least an hour here before the next one comes along, to either head back to Marsh Harbour or continue on to Hope Town. ⊠ *Elbow Cay* ⊕ *www. elbowreeflighthousesociety.com* ✉ *Free* ☾ *Closed Sun.*

Beaches

Hope Town Beach

BEACH | A beautiful reef just 30 feet offshore makes this a perfect spot to go snorkeling. Just be careful as the seas can get rough that side of the island. The wide, sandy beach is also a great spot to go for an early morning or late afternoon stroll. Be sure to look out for sea glass. Public access is behind St. John's Meth- odist Church or through the graveyard behind Taylor Park. **Amenities:** none. **Best for:** snorkeling, swimming, walking. ⊠ *Hope Town.*

★ Tahiti Beach

BEACH | FAMILY | This small beach at the southern tip of Elbow Cay is a popular boater's stop. The soft white sand is well protected from the close ocean cut by thick vegetation, a few barrier cays, and shallow water. This shallow area is popular for shelling, and, of course, simply relaxing and watching the tide rise. At low tide, the true beauty of this beach is revealed when a long sand spit emerges, perfect for picnics. It's great for young children, as the water on one side of the spit is ankle deep, stays calm, and remains warm. During peak season the beach can become a bit crowded. **Amen- ities:** floating bar and restaurant on calm afternoons. **Best for:** surfing; swimming. ⊠ *Elbow Cay.*

Restaurants

★ Abaco Inn Restaurant

$$$$ | BAHAMIAN | Set in the country-club- style main lodge splashed with lively Bahamian colors and boasting floor-to- ceiling windows that provide an incredible view of the ocean, the restaurant serves breakfast, lunch, and dinner to guests and visitors in classic island style. Fresh-baked bread, fruit, and lobster or Mexican-style Benedict are breakfast highlights. **Known for:** views of the Sea of Abaco and the Atlantic Ocean; enclosed patio overlooking the ocean; largest wine selection on the island. 💲 *Average main: $50* ✉ *2 miles south of Hope Town, Hope Town* ☎ *242/699-1368* ⊕ *www.abacoinn.com.*

Bridget's Rum Bar

$$$$ | **CARIBBEAN** | Catch the Hope Town Inn & Marina's free boat shuttle from any of the docks across the harbor in Hope Town and pull up a chair under the open octagonal restaurant or hop in and place your order at the swim-up bar. The Caribbean-inspired menu features lots of seafood for lunch and dinner. **Known for:** fun atmosphere; Friday night dancing under the stars; locally inspired sushi. 💲 *Average main: $40* ✉ *Across the harbor, Hope Town* ☎ *242/366–0003* ⊕ *hopetownmarina.com.*

Cap'n Jack's Restaurant and Bar

$$ | **BAHAMIAN** | This casual eatery's seating is out on the pink-and-white-striped dock–patio. Locals, boat people, and land-based tourists gather here for value-priced eats and drinks. **Known for:** Monday night bingo; live music Wednesday and Friday nights; grilled or blackened catch-of-the-day Reuben. 💲 *Average main: $20* ✉ *Hope Town* ☎ *242/366–0247* ⊕ *capnjackshopetown.com* ⊙ *Closed weekends and mid-Aug.–Sept.*

Firefly Bar & Grill

$$$ | **AMERICAN** | Whether you pull in by golf cart or tie up by boat, it's worth the trip to this popular restaurant and bar. Seafood is their specialty, and the extensive menu makes choosing just one dish a challenge. **Known for:** regular live music; offering plant-based options and accommodating food allergies; Sunday Bahamian brunch. 💲 *Average main: $40* ✉ *Hope Town* ☎ *242/366-0145* ⊕ *firefly-sunsetresort.com* ⊙ *closed Mon. and for breakfast except Sun.*

Mackey's Takeout

$$ | **BAHAMIAN** | Breakfast, lunch, and dinner are simple Bahamian and American fare similar to what's on offer at other spots on the island. And while the

delicious Bahamian food menu is worth a stop, it's the ice cream that draws the crowd to this whimsical little takeout restaurant in the middle of the island. **Known for:** delicious cinnamon rolls, banana bread, and other baked goods; excellent breakfast sandwiches and burritos; warm, friendly owner. 💲 *Average main: $20* ✉ *Elbow Cay* ☎ *366-0396* ⊙ *Sun. mornings.*

Munchies

$ | **BAHAMIAN** | For simple Bahamian food that will fill your belly, check out this small dine-in and takeout spot. Try the conch or chicken thigh snack served with fries or the dinner portion, which gives you the choice of two sides. **Known for:** popular spot for ice cream; great breakfast sandwiches; fresh fish dishes. 💲 *Average main: $16* ✉ *1 Russell's La., Hope Town* ☎ *242/804–7484.*

On Da Beach Bar & Grill

$ | **BAHAMIAN** | Burgers, tacos, sandwiches, conch, fish, and icy rum drinks are served up with a terrific Atlantic view at this open-air bar and grill perched high on the beach dunes across the road from the small Turtle Hill resort. Go in your bathing suit and enjoy the beach and snorkeling right out front. **Known for:** regular trivia and DJ nights; one of the few spots for beachside dining; daily fish specials. 💲 *Average main: $15* ✉ *Queens Hwy. between Hope Town and White Sound, Hope Town* ⊕ *www.turtlehill.com/on-da-beach.*

Sea Spray Resort & Marina

$$ | **BAHAMIAN** | A small hut bar overlooking the ocean and a brightly colored food truck serve simple but delicious small bites—conch fritters, fresh-catch ceviche, and fish tacos hit the spot. In true Bahamian style, the bar is open more frequently than the food truck, so be sure to check the schedule before driving all the way out for a bite. **Known for:** live music Thursday and Sunday; fresh seafood prepared perfectly; weekly happy-hour drink specials. 💲 *Average main: $20* ✉ *Elbow*

Cay ☎ *577–4696* 🌐 *seasprayresort.com* 🕒 *food truck closed Sun. through Weds.*

Willie's Kitchen & Bar
$ | **BAHAMIAN** | There are a few plastic tables and chairs outside this basic kitchen spot, but for the most part it's a takeout joint. The menu is limited, but the food is delicious. **Known for:** good, simple food; homemade cinnamon rolls; the fried fish burger. [$] *Average main: $14* ✉ *Elbow Cay* ☎ *242/458-9255* 💳 *No credit cards* 🕒 *Closed Sun. mornings.*

Coffee and Quick Bites

★ Thirsty Cuda
$ | **BAHAMIAN** | **FAMILY** | Be prepared to get wet to order your meal or drink from this floating food truck—it's anchored in waist-deep water off Tahiti Beach at the end of Elbow Cay. The sesame conch bites, burgers, and potent libations are worth wading out for. **Known for:** tasty nibbles; potent tropical drinks; a fun and funky spot to eat, drink, and swim. [$] *Average main: $15* ✉ *Elbow Cay* 🌐 *facebook.com/thirstycuda* 💳 *No credit cards* 🕒 *closed if weather is bad.*

Hotels

PRIVATE VILLA RENTALS

Elbow Cay Properties
HOTEL | Besides being the most cost-efficient way for a family to stay a week or longer on Elbow Cay, a private house or villa is also likely to be the most comfortable. This long-standing rental agency handles nearly 100 properties, from cozy two-bedroom, one-bath cottages, to a seven-bedroom, seven and a half–bath villa better described as a mansion that sleeps 21 people. Many of the rental homes are on the water, with a dock or a sandy beach right out front. The owners are set on finding you a place to match your wishes and budget and can arrange any extra services—from boat rental to a personal chef or yoga classes. There are no Sunday check-ins as the agency is closed, and a three-night minimum is required most weeks; a full week is required during peak holiday seasons. ✉ *Western Harborfront, Elbow Cay* ☎ *561/270–0606* 🌐 *www.elbowcayproperties.com.*

Surfing Elbow Cay

Though it's not well known, there is good surfing off Elbow Cay. If you want to wake up to the waves, stay at the Abaco Inn or rent a house at the end of the island near Tahiti Beach.

HOTELS AND RESORTS

★ Abaco Inn
$$$ | **HOTEL** | The motto here is "Tan your toes in The Abacos," making this beachfront resort the ideal place for a getaway. **Pros:** self-contained resort with one of the best restaurants on the island; easy access to beaches, surfing, and fishing; hypnotic ocean views. **Cons:** 10-minute golf-cart or boat ride to Hope Town; nothing else around; accommodations are basic. [$] *Rooms from: $325* ✉ *2 miles south of Hope Town, Hope Town* ☎ *242/699–1368* 🌐 *www.abacoinn.com* 🛏 *12 rooms* 🍴 *No Meals.*

★ Firefly Sunset Resort
$$$$ | **HOTEL** | Each of these fully equipped, beautifully appointed two- and three-bedroom cottages boasts a stunning view of the Sea of Abaco, and all are situated on the vast property in a way that creates privacy and a sense of true exclusivity. **Pros:** warm and friendly staff; large, beautifully decorated accommodations; one cottage has a small private swimming pool. **Cons:** golf cart or boat is a must for getting around; small man-made beach; minimum three-night stay. [$] *Rooms from: $580* ✉ *Hope Town*

Tahiti Beach on Elbow Cay is a family favorite.

☎ *242/366–0145* 🌐 *fireflysunsetresort.com* 🛏 *5 cottages* 🍴 *No Meals.*

★ Hope Town Inn & Marina
$$ | RESORT | Watch the hustle and bustle (relatively speaking, of course) of Hope Town from this spot across the harbor. **Pros:** great spot for families; swim-up bar serving excellent cocktails; short walk to the lighthouse. **Cons:** across the harbor from everything else; few on-site activities; some cottages are remotely located from the rest of the property. [$] *Rooms from: $275* ✉ *Hope Town* ☎ *242/366–0003, 850/588–4855* 🌐 *www.hopetownmarina.com* 🛏 *24 rooms* 🍴 *No Meals.*

Shopping

SPECIALTY STORES

★ Hope Town Canvas
OTHER SPECIALTY STORE | Bags of all sizes are made by hand out of recycled sails in the upstairs workshop. Sailors consider an old sail from their boat a fair trade for one of the stylish duffel bags, purses, or totes. ✉ *Studio 1 Bldg., Lower Rd., Hope Town* ☎ *806–1094* 🌐 *www.wsailbags.com/hopetown* 🕒 *Closed Sun.*

SOUVENIRS

Da Crazy Crab
SOUVENIRS | Here you'll find a wide selection of souvenirs, beach wraps, T-shirts, arts and crafts, and Cuban cigars. ✉ *Front Street, Hope Town* ☎ *242/819–8630, 242/366-9537* 🌐 *www.facebook.com/p/Da-Crazy-Crab-100057531275526/* 🕒 *Closed Sat. and Sun.*

Ebb Tide Gift Shoppe
SOUVENIRS | This shop is on the upper-path road in a renovated Loyalist home. Come here for such Bahamian gifts as batik clothes, original driftwood carvings and prints, and nautical jewelry. They even sell the brightly colored Androsia fabric by the yard. Browse through the extensive Bahamian book collection. ✉ *Hope Town* ☎ *242/366–0088* 🌐 *www.facebook.com/ebbtidegiftshoppe* 🕒 *closed Sun.*

Activities

BOATING

Hope Town Inn & Marina

BOATING | If you want to get away from the hustle and bustle of Hope Town proper, consider docking your boat at this 50-slip marina that can accommodate up to 125-foot vessels. You'll have access to the standard amenities plus two pools and a restaurant and bar, with a free boat shuttle across the harbor to Hope Town as well as pump-out service. ⊠ *Hope Town Inn, Elbow Cay* ☎ *850/588–4855, 242/366–0003* ⊕ *www.hopetownmarina. com.*

Lighthouse Marina

BOATING | This marina situated at the base of the Elbow Reef Lightstation is relatively small, with just six transient slips that accommodate vessels up to 60 feet, but it has all the expected amenities and more. There's laundry, fuel, bait and tackle, a gift shop, and a liquor store. ⊠ *Hope Town* ☎ *242/577–0283, 242/366–0154* ⊕ *www.htlighthousemarina.com.*

BOAT RENTALS

Island Marine

BOATING | Island Marine rents 17- to 23-foot boats ideal for exploring the Abaco cays. ⊠ *Elbow Cay* ☎ *242/808–4615* ⊕ *www.islandmarine.com* ⊠ *Rentals from $150 per day* ☺ *closed Sun. and mid-Aug. through mid-Oct.*

FISHING

Local Boy Charters

FISHING | Deep-sea charters are available with local boy Justin Russell—an eighth-generation Bahamian who has been fishing these waters for more than 30 years. ⊠ *Hope Town* ☎ *242/458–1685* ⊕ *www.hopetownfishing.com* ⊠ *Charters from $700.*

Seagull Charters

FISHING | This charter company sets up guided deep-sea excursions with Captain Robert Lowe, who has more than 50 years experience in local waters. ⊠ *Hope*
Town ☎ *242/475–3143* ⊕ *abacofishing. com/seagull-cottages-fishing-charters. html* ⊠ *Charters from $550.*

Man-O-War Cay

Fewer than 300 people live on skinny, 2½-mile-long Man-O-War Cay, many of them descendants of early Loyalist settlers who started the tradition of handcrafting boats more than two centuries ago. These residents remain proud of their heritage and continue to build their world-famous fiberglass boats today. The island is secluded, and the old-fashioned, family-oriented roots show in the local policy toward liquor: it isn't sold anywhere on the island. (But most folks won't mind if you bring your own.) A few churches, a one-room schoolhouse, and a couple of small grocery stores that sell sandwiches and the occasional hot meal to make up for the lack of restaurants post–Hurricane Dorian round out the tiny island's offerings.

A mile north of the island, you can dive to the wreck of the USS *Adirondack,* which sank after hitting a reef in 1862. It lies among a host of cannons in 20 feet of water.

GETTING HERE AND AROUND

FERRY

Man-O-War Cay is an easy 20-minute ride from Marsh Harbour by water taxi or aboard a small rented outboard runabout. No cars are allowed on the island, but you'll have no problem walking it, or you can rent a golf cart. The two main roads, Queen's Highway and Sea Road, run parallel.

GOLF CART

CONTACTS Sojer Carts. ⊠ *Man-O-War Cay* ☎ *242/821-9998.*

⊙ Sights

Hero's Wall

HISTORIC SIGHT | This memorial wall is adorned with plaques honoring residents who have helped to develop the community over the years. Notice that most of them share the same last name, as is often the case in small island communities. In this case, Albury and Sweeting are the most common names. ⊠ *Ballfield Rd. and Queen's Hwy., Man-O-War Cay.*

Man-O-War Heritage Museum

HISTORY MUSEUM | Historic artifacts from the boatbuilding industry and local experience over the ages on this tiny island are on display in this small museum, offering a true look back into life as it was way back. The museum is housed in the century-old Sweeting homem and parts of the original island clinic havo aloo been salvaged and are on-site. A portion of the ground floor houses the island's only coffee shop—a great spot for a cup and a delicious pastry and a chance to fund the museum. It's also a great spot to check in with the world as they offer free Wi-Fi. ⊠ *Queen's Hwy. and Pappy Ben Hill, Man-O-War Cay* ⊕ *mowmuseum. wordpress.com* 🎫 *Free* 🕐 *Closed Sun. and Mon. and after 11 am daily.*

☕ Coffee and Quick Bites

★ Man-O-War Heritage Museum Coffee Shop

$ | BAKERY | Pop in for a frappé, iced coffee, or smoothie and a homemade pastry or slice of quiche or casserole at the island's only breakfast spot. The friendly team is also the island's ad hoc visitors center and can point you in the direction of anything you need during your stay. **Known for:** helpful tips; delicious homemade pastries; best (and only) coffee spot on the island. 🅢 *Average main: $9* ⊠ *Queen's Hwy., Man-O-War Cay* ⊕ *mowmuseum.wordpress.com* 🕐 *Closed Sun. and Mon. and after 11 am daily.*

🛍 Shopping

SPECIALTY STORES

★ Albury's Sail Shop

OTHER SPECIALTY STORE | This shop is popular with boaters, who stock up on duffel bags, briefcases, hats, and purses, all made from duck, a colorful, sturdy canvas fabric traditionally used for sails. ⊠ *Lover's La. at Sea Rd., Man-O-War Cay* ⊕ *www.facebook.com/alburyssail-shop* 🕐 *closed Sun.* ☞ *facebook.com/alburyssailshop.*

SOUVENIRS

Joe's Studio

SOUVENIRS | This store sells paintings by local artists, books, clothing, and other nautically oriented gifts, but the most interesting souvenirs are the half-models of sailing dinghies. These mahogany models, which are cut in half and mounted on boards, are meant to be displayed as wall hangings. Artist Joe Albury, one of the store's owners, also crafts full, 3-D boat models. ⊠ *Sea Rd., Man-O-War Cay.*

Great Guana Cay

The essence of Great Guana Cay can be summed up by its unofficial motto, painted on a hand-lettered sign: "It's better in The Bahamas, but it's gooder in Guana." This sliver of an islet just off Great Abaco, accessible by ferry from Marsh Harbour or by private boat, has both beautiful deserted beaches and grassy dunes. Fewer than 100 full-time residents live on 7-mile-long Great Guana Cay, where you're more likely to run into a rooster than a car during your stroll around the tranquil village. Still, there are just enough luxuries here to make your stay comfortable. The island also has easy access to bonefishing flats you can explore on your own.

Nippers Beach Bar & Grill is the best restaurant on Great Guana Cay.

GETTING HERE AND AROUND
Take G & L Ferry to Great Guana Cay from the mainland. They leave from The Crossing in Marsh Harbour. The ride is about 30 minutes. Golf carts are available for rent in Great Guana Cay, though most places are within walking distance.

Beaches

Guana Cay Beach
BEACH | The beaches on Guana Cay stretch along much of the island's ocean side and are often only separated by rocky outcroppings. The sand here is slightly coarse and more of a cream color, with speckles of pink from wave-ground corals. Surfing is popular here, especially on the northern beaches. The North Side Beach, as it is known by locals, offers long, quiet walks. **Amenities:** none. **Best for:** surfing; walking; swimming. ⊠ *Great Guana Cay.*

Restaurants

★ Grabbers Bed, Bar, Dock & Grille
$$ | BAHAMIAN | Enjoy some of the best sunsets you've ever seen from this casual outdoor beachside restaurant. The menu includes all the standard Bahamian and American offerings. **Known for:** huge pizzas loaded with toppings; delicious and strong rum-punch slushies; great, fun atmosphere. $ *Average main: $29* ⊠ *Guana Cay* ☎ 242/809–5133 ⊕ *grabbersatsunset.com.*

Kidd's Cove Seafood Bar & Grill
$$ | BAHAMIAN | Perch on a bar stool on the new deck and enjoy the comings and goings of Guana Cay's harbor and main road. While they boast the "conchiest" conch fritters around, their grilled conch is worth a trip there. **Known for:** great spot for people-watching; potent cocktails; friendly hosts. $ *Average main: $20* ⊠ *Front St., Great Guana Cay* ⊕ *facebook. com/KidsCoveSeafoodBarGrill* ▬ *No credit cards.*

★ **Nippers Beach Bar & Grill**
$$ | **BAHAMIAN** | With awesome ocean views and a snorkeling reef just 10 yards off its perfect beach, this cool bar and restaurant is a must-visit hangout. Linger over a lunch of burgers and sandwiches or a dinner of steak and lobster, then chill out in the pool. **Known for:** tasty grouper sandwiches; best pool and beach party spot in The Abacos; place to rub shoulders with locals. [$] *Average main: $30* ✉ *Great Guana Cay* ☎ *242/365–5111* 🌐 *nippersbar.com* 🕒 *closed Tues.*

Coffee and Quick Bites

Mama's Restaurant & Bar
$ | **BAHAMIAN** | Open for lunch and dinner, Mama's is a delightful little family-owned takeout restaurant with outdoor seating in a tropical garden. Most of the lunch options come grilled. **Known for:** selection of grilled fish; friendly family service; special macaroni and cheese. [$] *Average main: $15* ✉ *Guana Cay* ✥ *From the public dock, head right and take the left up the hill just before you get to Kidd's Cove. They are situated on the corner up the hill.* ☎ *242/813-8981.*

Nightlife

BARS AND PUBS

Grabbers Bed, Bar, Dock & Grill
BARS | This is a popular local spot on weekend nights and not just because it offers the best sunset viewing anywhere around. There's music, cornhole in the sand, and the Guana Grabber, a potent frozen drink designed to lighten any mood. If you're not staying here and want to keep the party going after the last ferry leaves, ask the staff about catching a ride back to Marsh Harbour with them. During the high season, they put on a range of concerts and special theme nights. ✉ *Great Guana Cay* ☎ *242/809–5133* 🌐 *grabbersatsunset.com.*

Shopping

SOUVENIRS

Dive Guana
SOUVENIRS | The Dive Guana shop has everything you need for your beaching and boating vacation—sunscreen, hats, shirts, and snorkel gear, as well as a variety of souvenirs, including locally made straw bags and ceramics. ✉ *Front Street, Great Guana Cay* ☎ *242/557–0661* 🌐 *diveguana.com.*

WINE AND SPIRITS

Fig Tree Wine & Spirits
WINE/SPIRITS | This tiny shop has a large selection of beer, wine, and liquor, as well as soft drinks and snacks. It's also a good spot to load up on ice. ✉ *Located on the dock next to the public ferry dock, Guana Cay.*

Activities

BOATING

Orchid Bay Yacht Club & Marina
BOATING | Orchid Bay Yacht Club & Marina has 16 deep-water slips and full services for boaters at the entrance to the main settlement bay, across from the public docks. Water and fuel are available, laundry service is offered, and there is a small pool that visiting boat passengers and crew can enjoy. ✉ *Great Guana Cay* ☎ *242/365-5175* 🌐 *orchid-bay-marina.com.*

SCUBA DIVING

Dive Guana
DIVING & SNORKELING | This dive shop organizes scuba and snorkeling trips and island-hopping boat charters for up to 10 people. The shop also rents boats, which is the best way to get around and enjoy other nearby cays. ✉ *Great Guana Cay* ☎ *242/577–0661* 🌐 *diveguana.com* 🎟 *Charters start at $1200.*

Green Turtle Cay

This tiny, 3-mile-by-½-mile island is steeped in Loyalist history; some residents can trace their heritage back more than 200 years. Dotted with ancestral New England–style cottage homes, the cay is surrounded by several deep bays, sounds, bonefish flats, and irresistible beaches. **New Plymouth,** first settled in 1783, is Green Turtle's main community. Many of its approximately 500 residents earn a living by diving for conch or selling lobster and fish.

GETTING HERE AND AROUND

FERRY

Many hotels provide an occasional shuttle from the main ferry dock in Green Turtle Cay to their property, and there are a couple of taxis on the island. Most people travel via golf cart or boat. Don't worry, you won't miss having a car; even in the slowest golf cart you can get from one end of the island to the other in 20 minutes or less.

The **Green Turtle Cay Ferry** (☎ *242/475–3841*) leaves the Treasure Cay airport dock at 8:30, 10:30, 11:45, 1:30, 2:30, 3:30, and 5, returning from Green Turtle Cay at 6:30 (from New Plymouth dock only, M–F), 7:30 (from New Plymouth dock onlym M–Sat.), 8, 9, 11, 12:15, 1:30, 3, and 4:30. The trip takes 10 minutes, and one-way fares are $15; same-day round-trip fare is $22. The ferry makes several stops in Green Turtle, including New Plymouth, the Green Turtle Club, and the Bluff House resort.

GOLF CART

CONTACTS D & P Golf Cart Rentals. ✉ *Green Turtle Cay* ☎ *242/365–4655, 954/727–5536 US reservations line* 🌐 *dpcartrentals.com.* **KoolKart Rentals.** ✉ *Green Turtle Cay* ☎ *242/477–5920, 242/577–0211* 🌐 *koolkartrentals.com.* **Seaside Cart Rentals.** ✉ *Green Turtle Cay* ☎ *242/577–5497* 🌐 *seasidecartrentals.com.*

👁 Sights

Loyalist Memorial Sculpture Garden

GARDEN | The past is present in this garden across the street from The New Plymouth Inn (note that it's laid out in the pattern of the British flag). Immortalized in busts perched on pedestals are local residents who have made important contributions to The Bahamas. Plaques detail the accomplishments of British Loyalists, their descendants, and the descendants of those brought as enslaved people, such as Jeanne I. Thompson, a contemporary playwright and the country's second woman to practice law. This is an open garden, free to the public. ✉ *Parliament St., Green Turtle Cay.*

🍴 Restaurants

★ The Club Restaurant at Green Turtle Club Resort

$$ | **EUROPEAN** | Breakfast and lunch are served harborside on a covered, screened-in patio, while dinner takes place in the elegant dining room. At lunch, treat yourself to lobster or fish tacos, conch chowder, or a wrap. **Known for:** best steaks around; burgers piled high with specialty toppings; to-die-for guava crème brûlée. [$] *Average main: $30* ✉ *Green Turtle Club, north end of White Sound, Green Turtle Cay* ☎ *242/816–0625, 443/912–5839* 🌐 *greenturtleclub.com/dining/the-club-restaurant/* ⏲ *Closed mid-Sept.–Oct.*

McIntosh Restaurant & Bakery

$$ | **BAHAMIAN** | This simple diner-style restaurant serves up excellent renditions of local favorites, such as fried grouper and cracked conch, and sandwiches made with thick slices of a slightly sweet Bahamian bun for lunch. At dinner, large portions of pork chops, lobster, fish, and shrimp are served with rib-sticking sides like baked macaroni and cheese, peas and rice, and coleslaw. **Known for:** moist coconut bread; thick and yummy breakfast sandwiches; generous portion sizes. $ *Average main: $25* ✉ *Parliament St., Green Turtle Cay* ☎ *242/699–0381* ⊕ *www.facebook.com/profile. php?id=100041047915245.*

★ Pineapples Bar & Grill
$$ | BAHAMIAN | Hang out, dip in the saltwater pool, and enjoy Bahamian fare with a flair. In Black Sound, at the entrance to The Other Shore Club and Marina, you'll find this simple open-air restaurant with a canopy-shaded bar and picnic tables next to the pool. **Known for:** sensational jerk-spiced grouper; warm and friendly staff; world-famous piña coladas and specialty cocktails. $ *Average main: $20* ✉ *Black Sound, Green Turtle Cay* ☎ *242/821–8892* ⊕ *facebook.com/pineapplessunset.*

★ The Wrecking Tree
$ | BAHAMIAN | The wooden deck at this casual restaurant was built around the wrecking tree, a place where 19th-century wrecking vessels brought their salvage. Today it's a cool place to linger over a cold Kalik and a hearty lunch of some of the best cracked conch you'll find anywhere, fish-and-chips, or zesty conch salad. **Known for:** delicious pastries; baked mac and cheese; lovely spot to watch the comings and goings of New Plymouth. $ *Average main: $18* ✉ *Bay St., Green Turtle Cay* ☎ *242/699-2492* ⊕ *www.facebook.com/pages/The-Wrecking-Tree-on-GTC/338240039639100* ▭ *No credit cards* ⊘ *closed Sun.*

☕ Coffee and Quick Bites

Turtle Crawl Cafe
$ | ICE CREAM | FAMILY | This tiny ice-cream parlor and coffee shop boasts 30 flavors. Located inside a painstakingly renovated island home, there's limited space and seating inside, but across the narrow road are a few picnic benches under the shade of huge trees. **Known for:** local homemade ice cream in interesting flavors like honey avocado; grab-and-go lunches; warm and friendly owners.

$ *Average main: $8* ✉ *Near Sundowners, Queen St., Green Turtle Cay* ☎ *242/727-4129* ⊕ *facebook.com/turtlecrawlcafe* ⊘ *Closed during the day and Mon. and Tues. evenings.*

Hotels

PRIVATE VILLA RENTALS
Abaco Island Rentals
HOTEL | Choose from an eight-bedroom oceanfront mansion with wraparound veranda, three kitchens, and nine bathrooms to a two-bedroom cottage in the heart of New Plymouth. This agency has more than 50 cottages and houses for rent to meet different budgets and needs. It can also help arrange excursions and boat and golf-cart rentals. Most homes have water views, and some have docks for your rental boat. The offices in New Plymouth are in a blue two-story building just down from the ferry dock. ✉ *Various Green Turtle Cay locations, Green Turtle Cay* ☎ *561/202–8333 US number, 242/357–6566* ⊕ *abacoisland-rentals.com.*

HOTELS AND RESORTS
★ Bluff House Beach Resort & Marina
$$ | HOTEL | With its enchanting old-world charm, this historic hotel boasts eight exquisitely furnished suites that offer breathtaking views of the Sea of Abaco. **Pros:** secluded and private beach; safe harbor for boat owners; beautiful decor. **Cons:** golf cart or boat required to get into New Plymouth; lots of steps up to all suites; crowds at on-site bar/restaurant make private beach less secluded. $ *Rooms from: $275* ✉ *Green Turtle Cay* ☎ *954/284–7341, 242/365–4200* ⊕ *www. bluffhouse.com* ⊘ *Closed early Sept.–late Oct.* ⇌ *8 rooms* ⭘ *No Meals.*

Cocobay Cottages
$$$ | B&B/INN | Sandwiched between one beach on the Atlantic and another calmer, sandy stretch on the bay are four spacious cottages—including three three-bedroom cottages and a

Upper suites at Bluff House Beach Resort & Marina have expansive ocean views

two-bedroom cottage—and two villas, all with views of the water. **Pros:** complimentary docking for boats up to 40 ft; great beaches for shell or sea-glass collecting and bonefishing; feels like a home away from home. **Cons:** renting a boat and/or golf cart is essential; five-night minimum stay; not well lit at night. [$] *Rooms from: $375* ✉ *Coco Bay, north of Green Turtle Club, Green Turtle Cay* ☎ *949/734–7367* 🌐 *www.cocobaycottages.com* 🛏 *8 cottages* 🍴 *No Meals.*

★ Green Turtle Club Resort & Marina
$$ | **RESORT** | The long-standing colonial tradition and tone of casual refinement continues at this well-known resort. **Pros:** excellent on-site restaurants for casual or fine dining; easy access to great beaches; personalized service. **Cons:** if you're looking for Bahamian casual, this isn't it; a golf cart or boat is essential to explore the island; some rooms are a long walk from the hotel amenities. [$] *Rooms from: $259* ✉ *North end of White Sound, Green Turtle Cay* ☎ *242/816–0625, 443/912–5839* 🌐 *greenturtleclub.com* 🕓 *Closed mid-Aug.–late Oct.* 🛏 *34 rooms* 🍴 *No Meals.*

Linton's Beach and Harbour Cottages
$$ | **B&B/INN** | These three classic Bahamian-style cottages are ideally placed on 22 private acres between Long Bay and Black Sound. **Pros:** free docking for hotel guests, accommodating yachts up to 70 ft; great value for families and groups; private access to beautiful Long Bay beach. **Cons:** gathering groceries and supplies can be an adventure; no phones or TV in beach cottages; no swimming pool on property. [$] *Rooms from: $300* ✉ *S. Loyalist Rd., Black Sound, Green Turtle Cay* ☎ *772/538–4680* 🌐 *lintoncottages.com* 🛏 *3 cottages* 🍴 *No Meals.*

Nightlife

BARS AND PUBS

★ Miss Emily's Blue Bee Bar
BARS | Head here to find a singing, carousing crowd knocking back the world-famous Goombay Smash. (Or not—many Goombay novices

underestimate the drink's potency, and end up making it an early night.) Mrs. Emily Cooper, creator of the popular Goombay Smash drink, passed away in 1997, but her daughter Violet continues to serve up the famous rum, pineapple juice, and apricot brandy concoction. The actual recipe is top-secret, and in spite of many imitators throughout the islands, you'll never taste a Goombay this good anywhere else. It's worth a special trip to try one. Lunch and dinner are also served here—standard Bahamian fare plus a special Chinese menu on Friday night. ⊠ *Parliament St., Green Turtle Cay* ☎ *242/458–4032* ⊕ *www.facebook.com/profile.php?id=100063627198894* ⊗ *closed Sun.*

Pineapples Bar & Grill

BARS | On the water in front of The Other Shore Club and Marina, this bar has a hopping happy hour from 4 to 6 daily and live music every Friday at 7. Bring your bikini and hang out in the pool or on the shallow beach. ⊠ *Brooklyn Rd., Green Turtle Cay* ☎ *242/821–8892* ⊕ *www.facebook.com/pineapplessunset.*

Sundowners

BARS | Locals hang out at Sundowners, a waterside sports bar and grill with lots of drink specials and a kitchen that is open until midnight for late-night snacks. Grab a mic at Monday karaoke nights. There are also ladies' nights and men's nights as well as full-moon parties. ⊠ *Crown St., Green Turtle Cay* ☎ *242/820–2095* ⊕ *facebook.com/SundownersGTC.*

 Shopping

FOOD AND DRINK

Plymouth Rock Liquors & Cafe

OTHER FOOD & DRINK | This shop sells Cuban cigars and more than 60 kinds of rum. For something completely different, get there early, order one of their famous breakfast sandwiches and brag to your friends that you had breakfast in a liquor store. You can even get the T-shirt to show you've been there, done that. ⊠ *Parliament St., Green Turtle Cay* ☎ *242/699–1330* ⊕ *facebook.com/plymouthrockliquorsGTC* ⊗ *Closed Sun.*

Sid's Food Store

FOOD | Sid's has the most complete line of groceries on the island, plus a gift section that includes books on local Bahamian subjects. You can also buy conch-fritter batter here. ⊠ *Upper Rd., Green Turtle Cay.*

SOUVENIRS

Shavon's Home & Garden

JEWELRY & WATCHES | You'll find an array of T-shirts, hats, and souvenir items here, as well as beautiful silver and gold island-inspired jewelry made by Gary, the patriarch of this family-owned and -operated store. ⊠ *Parliament Street, Green Turtle Cay.*

 Activities

BOATING

It's highly recommended that you reserve your boat rental at the same time you book your hotel or cottage. If you're unable to rent a boat on Green Turtle Cay, try Marsh Harbour.

MARINAS

Bluff House Beach Resort & Marina

BOATING | Here you can find a marina with 46 slips and a full range of services—everything from fuel to laundry facilities and a swimming pool. Five slips are designed to accommodate catamarans. ⊠ *Green Turtle Cay* ☎ *242/365–4200* ⊕ *www.bluffhouse.com.*

Green Turtle Club Resort & Marina

BOATING | Green Turtle Club has 40 slips and offers cable TV and Wi-Fi, as well as a fully stocked commissary. ⊠ *Green Turtle Club, Green Turtle Cay* ☎ *242/816–0625* ⊕ *greenturtleclub.com.*

BOAT RENTALS

Donny's Boat Rentals and Marina

BOATING | The best way to spend your Abaco vacation is exploring the cays by boat. Rent a 17- or 19-foot Whaler, a 20-foot Wellcraft, or a 23-foot Angler for the day or week and find your own deserted beach or island. Bonefishing and deep-sea fishing excursions are also offered. ✉ *Green Turtle Cay* ☎ *242/823–8733, 407/610–7000 toll free from U.S.* 🌐 *donnysboatrentalsgtc.com* 🎟 *Boat rentals from $120 per day, 3 day minimum rental.*

FISHING

Abaco Flyfish Connection and Charters

FISHING | The top recommendation on Green Turtle Cay, Captain Rick Sawyer is one of the best guides in The Abacos. Rick's company offers bonefishing on 17-foot Maverick flats skiffs and reef and offshore fishing aboard his 33-foot Tiara sportfisher. Book as far in advance as you can. ✉ *Green Turtle Cay* ☎ *242/699–0361* 🌐 *abacoflyfish.com.*

Ronnie Sawyer

FISHING | Considered one of the best in the business, Ronnie Sawyer has been fishing the Abaco flats professionally for more than 30 years, so he knows all the best spots. ✉ *Green Turtle Cay* ☎ *242/357–6667* 📧 *ronniesawyergtc@gmail.com* 🎟 *$475 for half day; $600 for full day.*

SCUBA DIVING AND SNORKELING

★ **Brendal's Dive Center**

SCUBA DIVING | **FAMILY** | This dive center leads snorkeling and scuba trips, plus wild-dolphin encounters, fun- and rum-filled day excursions, and more. Personable owner Brendal Stevens has been featured on the Discovery Channel and CNN, and he knows the surrounding reefs so well that he's named some of the groupers, stingrays, and moray eels that you'll have a chance to hand-feed. Trips can include a seafood lunch, grilled on the beach, and complimentary rum punch. A visit to the swimming pigs on nearby No Name Cay has become one of their most popular adventures. ✉ *Green Turtle Cay* ☎ *242/365-4411, 242/458-7868* 🌐 *brendal.com* 🎟 *2-tank dives $175; half-day adventure tours from $55; full-day adventure tours from $165.*

Spanish Cay

Only three miles long, this privately owned island was once the exclusive retreat of millionaires, and many visitors still arrive by yacht or private plane. A well-equipped marina, great fishing, and some fine beaches are among the attractions here.

GETTING HERE AND AROUND

There is no ferry service from Great Abaco, so you'll need a boat to get to the cay. There is also a small, private airstrip. The only facility here is the resort and marina, so no transportation on the island is needed.

Hotels

Spanish Cay Resort and Marina

$$ | **RESORT** | Take your pick here—a beachfront room or a one- or two-room hotel suite tucked away on a hill overlooking the marina and the Sea of Abaco. **Pros:** totally off-the-beaten path location; lots of privacy on remote beaches; full-service marina. **Cons:** for entertainment, you need to rely on yourself; accommodations are dated; you'll need a boat to really explore the islands. [$] *Rooms from: $275* ✉ *Spanish Cay, Cooper's Town* ☎ *242/807–0317* 🌐 *spanishcay.com* 🛏 *12 rooms* 🍴 *No Meals.*

Chapter 6

ANDROS, BIMINI, AND THE BERRY ISLANDS

6

Updated by
Alicia Wallace

👁 Sights	🍴 Restaurants	🛏 Hotels	🛍 Shopping	🍸 Nightlife
★★★★★	★★★☆☆	★★★★☆	★★☆☆☆	★☆☆☆☆

WELCOME TO ANDROS, BIMINI, AND THE BERRY ISLANDS

TOP REASONS TO GO

★ **Bonefish:** Andros, Bimini, and the Berry Islands have world-class reputations for bone-fishing. Hire a guide to show you how to fly-fish, then hunt the bights of Andros or the shallow flats of Bimini and the Berries in pursuit of the elusive "gray ghost."

★ **Day trips:** These islands are closest to both Nassau and South Florida, making them ideal for day trips by ferry or air for gaming, beach-going, dining, and fun shore excursions.

★ **Dive Andros or Bimini:** Go with the diving experts at Small Hope Bay or Kamalame Cay to drop "over the Andros wall" or at Neal Watson's Bimini Scuba Center to explore magnificent wrecks and reefs.

★ **Fish for big game:** Charter a boat and experience the thrill of catching deep-sea prizes such as marlin, mahimahi, tuna, and wahoo.

1 Andros. Vast fishing flats, blue holes, vibrant reefs, and the Tongue of the Ocean make fishing, diving, and snorkeling the main reasons adventurers travel to Andros. The island is mostly flat, lush with pine forests and mangroves, rimmed with white-sand beaches, and laced with lakes.

2 Bimini. Year-round, boaters and tourists from Florida cross the Gulf Stream seeking fish and fun. Many visit North Bimini via the Bimini Fast Ferry to enjoy Resorts World Bimini with its new Hilton hotel, casino, dining, and fun excursions. Fishing and yachting fans frequent Alice Town's quaint hotels, bars, and Bahamian food shacks. South Bimini appeals more to the nature-minded and adventurous visitor.

3 The Berry Islands. For the ultimate remote island getaway, fly in and stay on the small capital of Great Harbour Cay in the north or on semiprivate Chub Cay in the south. In between lies a necklace of island gems accessible only by boat. Both hubs have clubs, villas, and full-service marinas, and both are celebrated for bone-, deep-sea, and bottom-fishing.

Great Stirrup Cay
Great Harbour Cay
Hoffman's Cay
Comfort Cay
Berry Islands **3**
Bond's Cay
Chub Cay
Whale Cay
Joulters Cays
Lowe Sound
Morgan's Bluff
Red Bays
Nicholl's Town
Mastic Point
San Andros
NASSAU
New Providence Island
Barrier Reef
Kamalame Cay
Staniard Creek
Small Hope Bay
Fresh Creek
Andros Town
Tongue of the Ocean
Williams Island
Gold Cay
Andros **1**
Cargill Creek
Behring Point
Barrier Reef
Big Wood Cay
Moxey Town
Lisbon Creek
G R A N D
Wood Cay
Mangrove Cay
Driggs Hill
Yellow Cay
Congo Town
The Bluff
B A H A M A
Kemps Bay
Barrier Reef
Poptop Cay
Deep Creek
B A N K
Mars Bay
Water Cays
Curley Cut Cays

Legends loom large (and small) on these northwestern Bahamas islands. On Bimini, you'll hear about the lost underwater city of Atlantis, Ernest Hemingway's visits, and the Fountain of Youth. Tiny birdlike creatures known as chickcharnies are said to inhabit the pine forests of Andros Island. On both islands, along with the Berry Islands, bonefishing has made legends of mere humans.

Andros, Bimini, and the Berries remain a secret mostly known to avid divers, boaters, and fishermen—fishing and commercial diving sustain the economies here, though Andros also thrives on farming fruit and vegetables. Local produce from a demonstration and training farm is available for sale at The Bahamas Agriculture and Marine Science Institute (BAMSI) located in Central Andros. These islands stash their reputation for superlative blue holes and other natural phenomena away from the glamour of Nassau, just minutes away by plane but a world apart, yet you'll still find some of The Bahamas' most admired resorts here. North Bimini has been transformed into a busier island by Resorts World; its casino and new Hilton hotel feed the island with hundreds of golf-carting tourists who buy packages on the fast ferry from Fort Lauderdale. Although Andros is the largest island in The Bahamas and a favorite of nature-lovers, most of its land is far from any settlement and hardly habitable. All resorts, inns, and lodges lie on a narrow east-coast strip, adjoining beautiful beaches and the barrier reef.

The 30-some cays of the Berry Islands are lesser known still.

The northwestern islands of Andros, Bimini, and Berry lie just off the east coast of Florida. Bimini is 50 miles from Miami; the Berry Islands are a 30-cay chain 100 miles east of Bimini. Andros comprises The Bahamas' largest landmass (about half of all The Bahamas' land in total) and is split into three islands: North and Central Andros, Mangrove Cay, and South Andros. Two tidal estuaries called Northern and Middle Bight separate North and Central Andros from Mangrove Cay, and the Southern Bight splits Mangrove Cay and South Andros. Remote beaches and small settlements stretch along the eastern shores, while a vast wilderness of mangrove estuaries and swamps characterize the western leeward coasts.

Planning

When to Go

Traveling to all islands by plane is possible; by boat is easiest in summer when seas are calmer. Fishing and diving are good year-round, although cold fronts from December to February can cause rough seas. November, March, and April are often the most pleasant months. Temperatures are more comfortable in winter and spring, and during these drier months, mosquitoes and sand flies are fewer. Temperatures usually remain steady enough to enjoy the beaches year-round, but they occasionally drop into the 60s with cold fronts. Hurricane season runs from June through November. August and September, the most likely months for hurricanes, can be hot and steamy, and many resorts and restaurants are closed. Among Andros, Bimini, and the Berries, it seems each hotel or lodge has its own high, low, and shoulder seasons and respective rates. Some hotels, such as the Hilton at Resorts World Bimini, peak in summer, while others, such as bonefish lodges, peak in winter. Highest rates are invariably in the holiday seasons between late December and early January, around Easter in March and April, and for U.S. Labor Day in early September. Bargains can be found in late January, February, October, and early December. Many resorts are quiet during the summer months and may offer better rates based on occupancy.

FESTIVALS

Winter: Junkanoo Celebrations occur all over the islands on Boxing Day (December 26) and New Year's Day, with festivities that include traditional People's Rush mini-Junkanoo parades, music, dancing, and food. They take place in Fresh Creek, Central Andros; Nicholls Town, North Andros; Moxey Town, Mangrove Cay;

Driggs Hill, South Andros; Alice Town, North Bimini; and Bullock's Harbour in Great Harbour Cay, Berry Islands.

Spring: Though the name of the game in Andros is bonefishing, in May, the North Andros town of Red Bays hosts a **Snapper Tournament.** Mangrove Cay comes alive in mid-May with its own local **Mother's Day Homecoming and Regatta,** with islander sloop sailing races, food, drinks, and entertainment.

Summer: Over the second weekend in June, three days of crab races, cook-offs, live Rake 'n' Scrape music, and performances by national musical artists comprise the **All Andros Crab Fest** in Fresh Creek, held at Queen's Park. Expect wild street parties across The Bahamas on July 10, **Independence Day.** The Regattas are often The Family Islands' most attended festivals, featuring passionate rivalry and multiple races of one or more of the A, B, and C class Bahamian sailing sloops. Around The Bahamas' Labour Day in early June, South Andros holds its regatta at The Bluff. The largest sailing festival in the region is the **All Andros & Berry Islands Regatta,** held on Morgan's Bluff Beach the second weekend in July. In Nicholls Town, at the end of July you can also catch the **Junkanoo Summer Festival.** Every Saturday evening in July, Fresh Creek's Queen's Park hosts **Andros Nights,** when locals and visitors gather until midnight to dance and enjoy Bahamian food prepared by women in the community. In Andros, on the third weekend in July, the **Goombay Summer Festival** is held on Friday (noon to midnight) at Morgan's Bluff in North Andros and on Saturday (6 pm to midnight) at Cargill Creek, south Central Andros. Both feature live local bands, Junkanoo, food, drinks, and fun contests such as onion-peeling, watermelon-eating, and sack races. Every Saturday in July, the Berry Islands' Great Harbour Cay Marina hosts the **Junkanoo Summer Fest** with a Junkanoo miniparade, and on the second August weekend, it hosts the **Lobster & Lionfish Derby,** a fishing tournament with prizes and entertainment, including Junkanoo, limbo, fire-dancing, and a lobster cook-off contest. In June and July, Bimini hosts the **Bahamas Boating Flings,** guided flotillas of motor yachts wishing to cross the Gulf Stream, with piloting help organized by The Bahamas Ministry of Tourism's Boating Department. Participating boats gather at a marina in Fort Lauderdale.

Fall: In mid-October, South Andros hosts the three-day **Andros Conch Fest** at Mars Bay Blue Hole Beach and Mars Bay Community Park, when locals and a few lucky visitors are entertained with myriad ways to cook and eat conch amid fun contests, including dancing and conch-cracking. In November, the famous deep-sea fishing resort Bimini Big Game Club hosts its annual **Wahoo Smackdown** fishing tournament. Conviviality abounds when the boats arrive back at the dock and at the evening parties. All are welcome to enter.

Getting Here and Around

AIR
Scheduled nonstop and direct flights from the United States to The Bahamas' northwestern islands are growing in frequency with small, reliable operators from Miami International Airport (MIA), Miami's Watson Island Seaplane Base (XX4), and Fort Lauderdale–Hollywood International (FLL) and Fort Lauderdale Executive (FXE) Airports. Western Air operates direct flights from Nassau (NAS) to San Andros Airport (SAQ) and Nassau to Bimini (BIM). Flamingo Air flies direct from Nassau to Mangrove Cay (MAY), Andros and from Freeport to Bimini (BIM).

FROM NASSAU Flamingo Air. ☎ 242/377–0354 ⊕ flamingoairbah.com. **Glen Air.** ☎ 242/368–2116, 242/471–1860. **LeAir.** ☎ 242/377–2356 ⊕ www.flyleair.com. **Randolph Holdings.** ☎ 242/368–2922,

242/477–1335 ⊕ www.flycharterbahamas.com.

FROM FORT LAUDERDALE AND MIAMI
Air Flight Charters. ☎ 954/359–0320 ⊕ www.airflightcharters.com. **Silver Airways.** ☎ 801/401–9100 ⊕ www.silverairways.com. **Tropic Ocean Airways.** ☎ 800/767–0897 ⊕ www.flytropic.com. **Makers Air.** ☎ 954/771–0330 ⊕ makersair.com.

BOAT AND FERRY
Visiting private boaters must clear Bahamas Customs and Immigration at the nearest port-of-entry, found in Bimini on both South and North Bimini, in the Berry Islands on Great Harbour Cay and Chub Cay, and in Andros at Nicholls Town (Morgan's Bluff Harbour) in North Andros and Fresh Creek Harbour and Driggs Hill Harbour in South Andros. Customs officers are stationed at the nearest airport— San Andros, Andros Town, and Congo Town airports, respectively—so call the airports ahead of time to inform them that you are coming in. Once cleared, you can explore other islands, marinas, and anchorages. You can also clear at gorgeous private island and marina Cat Cay Yacht Club, a few miles south of Bimini. Most ports-of-entry have full-service marinas with amenities, lodging, dining, beaches, and fun activities. From Florida, North Bimini is the only island reachable by ferry. From Nassau's Potter Cay Dock, each main island is served weekly or three times a month by ferry or mail boat. Note that mail boats may make several stops, and due to weather, you may be marooned on your chosen island for days until the next mail boat arrives. Between South and North Bimini, a ferry runs the 15-minute harbor ride every half-hour or so and even until 11 pm. Boating between other islands requires a boat rental or charter. ⇨ See Boat and Ferry for each island for more information.

CONTACTS Bahamas Customs. ☎ 242/347–3100 Alice Town, North Bimini, 242/347–3101 South Bimini airport, 242/325–5788

Chub Cay airport, 242/367–8116 Great Harbour Cay airport, 242/329–2140 San Andros airport (for Nicholls Town, Morgan's Bluff), 242/368–2030 Andros Town airport (for Fresh Creek), 242/369–2640 Congo Town airport (for Drigg's Hill and Kemp's Bay), 242/377–7030 Nassau Airport customs, answers call all hrs, 242/326–4401 through 6 Customs HQ Nassau, business hrs only ⊕ *www. bahamas.gov.bs/customs.* **Bahamas Ferries.** ⊠ *From Potter's Cay Dock, Nassau* ☎ *242/323–2166* ⊕ *www.bahamasferries.com.* **Balearia Caribbean Bimini Fast Ferry.** ⊠ *Miami* ☎ *866/699–6988 toll-free* ⊕ *www.baleariacaribbean.com.* **Potter's Cay Dockmaster's Office.** ⊠ *Nassau* ☎ *242/393–1064.*

CAR

Devoid of rental cars, most of Bimini is accessed on foot or by golf cart. Car rentals are available on Andros and on Great Harbour Cay in the Berry Islands. Don't expect major companies; rentals are done through microenterprises and are usually arranged directly by the hotel or lodge. Rates range between $60 and $120 per day, averaging $85 per day. Be prepared to pay in cash.

Call in advance to have a rental car waiting upon arrival. Some hotels and lodges offer free airport transfers, so be sure to communicate with them about your plans.

TAXI

Taxis are readily available at airports to meet incoming flights and for sightseeing. On larger islands, most mail boats and ferries are greeted by one or two taxis. If not, you can often hitch a ride with a friendly islander going your way. Communicate with your hotel or lodge to make appropriate plans as practices often change based on the season.

Hotels

Find everything from luxury properties to boutique hotels, rentals on private cays (pronounced "keys"), and simple fishing lodges. Comfortable lodge and motel-style accommodations are most common and usually have a restaurant and bar. Some lodges don't have in-room telephones, TVs, or Internet. Most have a phone for guest use on the property, and some will have a computer with Internet in the lounge or lobby. Almost all take credit cards, though very small lodges and nonhotel restaurants may accept cash only. Although places advertise Internet services, connection can be spotty. Rates typically vary between high and low seasons. In some Family Islands, rates are often expressed per cabin, room, or cottage (usually with double occupancy).

While most properties also charge gratuities, not all are registered to charge VAT. All businesses that charge VAT should be registered and certified to do so. The highest rates and busiest times vary with each resort, usually occurring around the Thanksgiving, Christmas, and Easter holidays and from February to June. High season is usually February to April, but these islands can also be busy through June.

Restaurants

With a few notable exceptions, dining here is a casual experience. Most restaurants, lodges, and inns serve traditional Bahamian fare. Call ahead to make sure a restaurant is open—except for roadside and seaside conch shacks, almost all require you to order dinner ahead of time. Resort restaurants have à la carte sit-down meals. Some lodges have all-inclusive meal plans with stays and offer day or night passes for dining nonguests. Many of the favored Bahamian food outlets are takeout places with picnic tables.

A common practice is to take food back to your room to enjoy air-conditioned and fly- and mosquito-free comfort. Thatched conch stands and colorful roadside bars are a great way to mingle with the locals.

⇨ *Restaurant prices are based on the median main course price at dinner, excluding gratuity, typically 10% to 15%, coupled with the new Bahamas Valued Added Tax (VAT) of 10% (on food but not gratuities)—which are usually automatically added to the bill. Hotel prices are for two people in a standard double room in low season, excluding service and 6%–12% tax and 10% VAT. Restaurant and hotel reviews have been shortened. For full information, visit Fodors.com.*

What It Costs in U.S. Dollars

	$	$$	$$$	$$$$
RESTAURANTS				
	under $20	$20–$30	$31–$40	over $40
HOTELS				
	under $200	$200–$300	$301–$400	over $400

Visitor Information

CONTACTS Andros Tourist Offices. ✉ *Fresh Creek* ☎ *242/368–2286 Central Andros, 242/369–1688 South Andros, 242/368–2286 North Andros* ⊕ *www.bahamas.com/islands/andros.* **Association Of Bahamas Marinas.** ✉ *Fort Lauderdale* ☎ *844/556–5290 toll-free, 954/462–4591 U.S. and Canada* ⊕ *www.bahamasmarinas.com.* **Bahama Out Islands Promotion Board.** ✉ *Nassau* ☎ *954/740–8740 U.S. and Canada, 242/322–1140 Nassau office* ⊕ *www.myoutislands.com.* **Berry Islands Tourism Administrator.** ✉ *Great Harbour Cay Airport, Great Harbour Cay* ☎ *242/367–8291 office, 242/451–0404 cell, 242/225–2563 toll-free within Bahamas* ⊕ *www.bahamas.com/islands/berry.*

Bimini Tourist Office. ☎ *242/347–3528 or 29* ⊕ *www.bahamas.com/islands/bimini.*

Andros

The Bahamas' largest island (100 miles long and 40 miles wide) and one of the least explored, Andros is carved up by myriad channels, creeks, lakes, and mangrove-covered cays. The natural **Northern, Middle,** and **Southern Bights** cut through the width of the island, creating shallow boating access between both the east and west coasts. A high concentration of inland blue holes also polka-dot the land. Nestled inside the island's pine and coppice forests, blue-hole exploration, nature hikes, sea kayaking, and snorkeling are draws to this glorious ecotourism island. Above all, Andros is best known for its vast bonefishing flats and diverse diving, particularly high-quality reef dives, wreck dives, and blue hole dives, as well as spectacular wall dives at the edge of the continental shelf.

The Spaniards who came here in the 16th century called Andros *La Isla del Espíritu Santo*—the Island of the Holy Spirit—and it has retained its eerie mystique. The descendants of Seminoles and runaway enslaved people who left Florida in the mid-19th century settled in the North Andros settlement of **Red Bays** and remained hidden until a few decades ago. They continue to celebrate the tribal heritage, making a living by weaving straw goods, along with fishing and harvesting sea sponge. The Seminoles originated the myth of the island's legendary (and elusive) chickcharnies—red-eyed, bearded, green-feathered creatures with three fingers and three toes that hang upside down by their tails from pine trees. These mythical characters supposedly wait deep in the forests to bestow good luck upon the friendly passersby and vent their mischief on the hostile trespasser. The rest of Andros's roughly 8,000 residents live in a dozen settlements on the eastern shore. Farming and commercial fishing sustain the economy.

Andros's undeveloped **West Side** adjoins the Great Bahama Bank, a vast shallow-water haven for lobster, bonefish, and tarpon. Wild orchids and dense pine and mahogany forests cover the island's lush green interior. The marine life–rich **Andros Barrier Reef**—the world's third largest—is within a mile of the eastern shore and runs for 140 miles. Sheltered waters within the reef average 6 to 15 feet, but on the other side ("over the wall"), they plunge to more than 6,000 feet at the **Tongue of the Ocean.**

GETTING HERE AND AROUND
AIR
Consult your hotel to figure out which airport to fly into. From north to south: serving North Andros is the **San Andros Airport (SAQ),** serving Central Andros and Fresh Creek is **Andros Town Airport (ASD)**; **Mangrove Cay Airport (MAY)** serves the island of the same name, and serving South Andros is **Congo Town Airport (TZN).** All except Mangrove Cay are ports of entry, enabling customs clearance for private flights or charters directly from the United States. San Andros (SAQ) is best for hotels between Nicholls Town and Stafford Creek and is reachable from the United States via Makers Air four times a week and from Nassau via Western Air twice daily. Best for all other hotels in North and Central Andros is Andros Town airport, which sees the most traffic and is reachable from the United States by Makers Air four times a week. LeAir operates a twice-daily service from Nassau's domestic terminal and Randolph Holdings air charters usually flies twice a day from Nassau Airport's General Aviation base, a short taxi ride from the main Nassau airport. Mangrove Cay Airport is reachable from Nassau twice daily via LeAir and Flamingo Air. Congo Town in South Andros is served by Makers

Air from Fort Lauderdale Executive and Western Air from Nassau twice daily.

For groups and families, private charters from Miami, Fort Lauderdale, or Nassau can be an affordable, convenient option. From the United States, there are numerous charter services to all Andros airports, including Makers Air and Air Flight Charters. If you're willing to splash out on luxurious travel, a floatplane via Tropic Ocean Airways or a helicopter from Florida can be a highlight.

CONTACTS Andros Town Airport.
☎ 242/368–2134. **Congo Town Airport.**
☎ 242/369–2270. **Mangrove Cay Airport.**
☎ 242/369–0270. **San Andros Airport.**
☎ 242/329–4401.

CAR RENTAL
All airports have SUVs or cars for rent from $70 to $120 a day, plus gas, depending on size and vehicle condition. Note that some resorts or lodges may also offer cars-plus-stay packages and free transfers to and from the airport. Lodges will often offer you a ride to wherever you want to go.

FERRY
Andros is divided by water into three parts: North and Central Andros, Mangrove Cay, and South Andros. Each is serviced by either a ferry or mail boat from Potter's Cay Dock in Nassau. Mail boats are good options for budgeting backpackers, adventurous students, or groups carrying lots of luggage, such as film crews. Passage costs vary between mail boats, from $40 to $70 one way, and may include a meal. The journey is often overnight, and each vessel sails three or four times a month. Nicholls Town and The Bluff in North Andros is served by M/V *Lady Rosalind*; Fresh Creek by Bahamas Ferries and the M/V *KCT*; Mangrove Cay and South Andros by the M/V *Capt. Moxey* and M/V *Lady Katherine*. Note that mail boats may make several stops, and due to their infrequency, you may be marooned on your chosen island for days,

if not weeks, until the next mail boat arrives. For the most up-to-date information on mail boat schedules, passengers should always consult the dockmaster in Potter's Cay in Nassau, weekdays 9 to 5. Once on North and Central Andros, you have to fly or charter a boat to reach its southerly sister islands, but you can take the *Capt. Moxey* mail boat or the free twice-daily government ferry between Mangrove Cay and South Andros. The ferry is run by Frederick Major in a 30-foot outboard from Driggs Hill on South Andros to Lisbon Creek on Mangrove Cay, at 8 am and 4 pm. The journey takes around 15 minutes.

CONTACTS Frederick Major's Ferry Service.
✉ *Driggs Hill* ☎ *242/376–8533* ⊕ *www. bahamas.com/vendor/south-andros-tourist-office.* **Potter's Cay Dockmaster's Office.** ✉ *Nassau* ☎ *242/393–1064.* **South Andros Tourist Office.** ✉ *Congo Town* ☎ *242/369–1688* ⊕ *www.bahamas.com/andros.*

TAXI

Confirm with the hotel to see if your taxi will meet airplanes and ferries. Rates run around $1.50 per mile, though most fares are set and generally known. In North or South Andros fares can be quite a surprise; always ask your hotel for assistance and always agree on a fare before you set foot in a taxi. Taxis are also available for touring around the islands, and because of their friendliness, local knowledge, and insight, they often become vacation highlights. Tours will take you to shops, farms, restaurants, beaches, historic ruins, and blue holes—giving you a sense of the scene and recommendations on where to dine and more. Tour rates vary: for five passengers and up, they start from $50 per person for a half day and $100 per person for a full day.

North Andros

The northern part of Andros spreads from the settlements of **Morgan's Bluff, Nicholls Town, Lowe Sound,** and **Red Bays** to **Stafford Creek.** North Andros consists of long stretches of pine forests, limestone bluffs, and fields and gardens of ground crops. Seminoles, formerly enslaved people, and Mennonites settled this land along with the West Indian population. White-sand beaches, mostly deserted, line the island's eastern face, interrupted by creeks, inlets, and rock outcroppings. Logging supported North Andros in the 1940s and 1950s and laid the foundation for its roads. Tourism, farming, and commercial fishing, especially in the west and the northernmost Joulter Cays, drives the economy today.

San Andros is home to North Andros's airport, but **Nicholls Town** is the port and largest settlement here and in all of Andros. Once home to a vogue resort in the 1960s (Andros Beach Hotel), today it is mostly residential, inhabited in part by snowbirds, who own the adorable Bahamian-style, brightly painted cottages that were once part of the storied resort. Although recent repaving has improved the main highway, you'll often encounter potholes. Near the airport, road conditions are good; don't worry about traffic—you'll be lucky if you see more than 20 vehicles on the highway in a single day.

GETTING HERE AND AROUND

The San Andros airport (SAQ) has flights from Nassau through SkyBahamas and Western Air. Taxis meet incoming flights. You can get around on foot in Nicholls Town; car rentals are available for exploring the island's 65 miles of Queen's Highway and feeder roads in the north. They run about $85 to $130 a day. Main roads in Central Andros are in good shape, but watch out for potholes in North Andros. If you're renting a car, call in advance to make sure your car is available at the airport.

CAR RENTAL CONTACTS

CJ's Car Rental. ✉ *Nicholl's Town* ☎ *242/471–3386.* **Executive Car Rentals.** ✉ *Nicholl's Town* ☎ *242/471–5259, 242/329–4081.* **Gaitor's Car Rental.** ✉ *Nicholl's Town* ☎ *242/471–1550, 242/464–3151.*

Sights

Morgan's Bluff & Beach

BEACH | Three miles north of Nicholls Town is a crescent beach, a headland known as Morgan's Bluff, and a set of caves named after the 17th-century pirate Captain Henry Morgan, who allegedly dropped off some of his stolen loot in the area. The beach and park serve as the site for Regatta Village, a colorful collection of stands and stalls that set up in July when the big event, the All Andros & Berry Islands Regatta, takes place. Adjacent is the Government Dock and a safe harbor, with a small, popular island bar and restaurant. ✉ *Nicholl's Town.*

Nicholls Town

TOWN | Nicholls Town, on Andros's northeastern corner, is a spread-out settlement with its eastern shore lying on a beautiful beach and its northern shore on Morgan's Bluff beach. It's the island's largest settlement, with a population of about 600. This friendly community, with its agriculture- and fishing-based economy, has grocery and supplies stores, a few motels, a public medical clinic, government offices, and more. Adorable cottages, a throwback from the town's big resort era of the 1960s, house the island's wintering population from the United States, Canada, and Europe. ✉ *Nicholl's Town.*

Red Bays

TOWN | Fourteen miles west of Nicholls Town, Red Bays is the sole west-coast settlement in all of Andros. The town was settled by Seminoles and runaway enslaved Africans escaping Florida pre–Civil War and was cut off from the rest of Andros until a highway connected it to Nicholls Town in the 1980s. Residents are known for their craftsmanship, particularly straw basketry and wood carving. Tightly plaited baskets, some woven with scraps of colorful Androsia batik, have become a signature craft of Andros. Artisans have their wares on display in front of their homes (with fixed prices). Despite opening their homes to buyers, Red Bays locals don't seem very used to visitors. Expect a lot of curious stares and occasional smiles. ✉ *Red Bay Settlement.*

Uncle Charlie's Blue Hole

NATURE SIGHT | Mystical and mesmerizing, blue holes pock Andros's marine landscape in greater concentration than anywhere else on Earth—an estimated 160-plus—and provide entry into the islands' network of coral-rock caves. Offshore, some holes drop off to 200 feet or more. Inland blue holes reach depths of 120 feet, layered with fresh, brackish, and salt water. Uncle Charlie's Blue Hole, with a 40-feet diameter, is one of Andros's most popular and is lined with picnic benches and a ladder. ✉ *North Andros, north of San Andros airport, 300 yards off main highway after turnoff for Owen Town.*

Beaches

If solitude is what you're searching for, you'll definitely find it on the beaches of North Andros. Long and secluded, you might find each beach has just one small resort or bar close by—and a few reefs for snorkeling.

Conch Sound & Ocean Hole

BEACH | South of Nicholls Town's eastern shore, Conch Sound is a wide bay with strands of white sand and tranquil waters where you can also find Conch Sound Ocean Hole, a sea-filled blue hole where you can snorkel around and see the rich

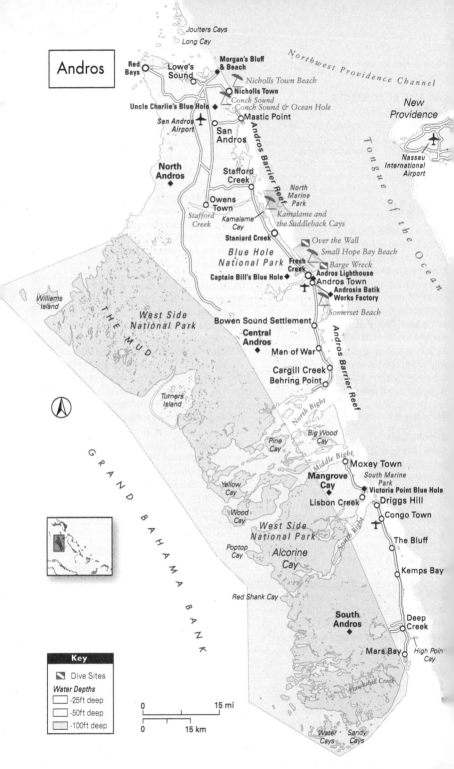

Andros

Joulters Cays
Long Cay

Northwest Providence Channel

Red Bays
Lowe's Sound
Morgan's Bluff & Beach
Nicholls Town Beach
Nicholls Town
Conch Sound
Conch Sound & Ocean Hole
Uncle Charlie's Blue Hole
Mastic Point
San Andros Airport
San Andros

New Providence

Nassau International Airport

North Andros

Stafford Creek
Owens Town
Stafford Creek
Kamalame Cay
North Marine Park
Kamalame and the Saddleback Cays

Staniard Creek

Blue Hole National Park
Fresh Creek
Over the Wall
Small Hope Bay Beach
Barge Wreck
Captain Bill's Blue Hole
Andros Lighthouse
Andros Town
Androsia Batik Works Factory
Somerset Beach

Williams Island

THE MUD

West Side National Park

Bowen Sound Settlement
Central Andros
Man of War

Turners Island

Cargill Creek
Behring Point

North Bight

Big Wood Cay

Andros Barrier Reef

Tongue of the Ocean

Pine Cay

Middle Bight
Moxey Town
South Marine Park
Mangrove Cay
Victoria Point Blue Hole
Driggs Hill
Lisbon Creek

Yellow Cay

Wood Cay

West Side National Park

Alcorine Cay

Congo Town
South Bight
The Bluff

G R A N D   B A H A M A   B A N K

Poptop Cay

Kemps Bay

Red Shank Cay

South Andros

Deep Creek

Mars Bay
High Point Cay

Hawksbill Creek

Water Cays
Sandy Cays

Key

◣ Dive Sites

Water Depths

-25ft deep

-50ft deep

-100ft deep

0 — 15 mi

0 — 15 km

marine life. The flats are a convenient wading spot for bonefishers, who can wade for hours. Commercial fishermen bring their catches to a little beach park nearby. You can buy fresh catch and dine at a couple of shacks. **Amenities:** only at nearby restaurants. **Best for:** solitude; fishing; snorkeling. ⊠ *Nicholl's Town.*

Nicholls Town Beach

BEACH | Two-and-a-half miles east of Nicholls Town's commercial center, the settlement reaches the east-facing coast along beautiful and long Nicholls Town Beach, which catches the easterly breezes and is by far the preferred beach in this area. It adjoins Conch Sound to the south. You might be on your own except for guests at the renovated Andros Island Beach Resort, with its tiki bar and restaurant, where you can rent kayaks or snorkeling gear. **Amenities:** resort nearby. **Best for:** solitude; swimming; walking. ⊠ *Nicholl's Town.*

Restaurants

F&H Takeaway

$ | **BAHAMIAN** | This tiny shack on the water in Lowe's Sound is the quintessential Bahamian conch shack experience, where the owner will wade out in the water, select, and hammer out the conch before your eyes. Ask him to eat the extraneous pistile or bibby for a laugh. **Known for:** authentic Bahamian experience; extremely fresh catches; delicious seafood. ⓢ *Average main: $10* ⊠ *Nicholl's Town* ✚ *Lowes Sound, 2 miles north of Nicholls Town* ☎ *242/329–7143* ▭ *No credit cards.*

Lil' Anchor Restaurant

$ | **BAHAMIAN** | On the water at Conch Sound, this cute shack of a restaurant is a great place for island-fresh fish, conch, and lobster in season. Watch the fishermen come in with their catches. **Known for:** local patronage; waterfront location; fresh fish and conch. ⓢ *Average main:*

$12 ⊠ *Nicholl's Town* ☎ *242/464–3049, 242/429–4387* ▭ *No credit cards.*

Hotels

Andros Island Beach Resort

$ | **RESORT** | **FAMILY** | Facing east on long, pristine Nicholls Town Beach, this palm tree–festooned property offers three secluded beachfront cottages, four villas, and a beachside tiki bar and restaurant with beautiful views. **Pros:** gorgeous beach and water activities; on-site restaurant and bar; spacious villas with kitchens. **Cons:** breakfast usually self-catered; bug spray essential in summer and fall; rental car necessary. ⓢ *Rooms from: $185* ⊠ *Nicholl's Town* ☎ *242/329–1009* ⊕ *www.androsislandbeachresorts.com* ➲ *4 villas, 3 suites.*

Love at First Sight

$ | **B&B/INN** | At the mouth of Stafford Creek, self-sufficient anglers and do-it-yourself vacationers can sit on the sundeck or at the bar, sip a cold local beer or a cocktail, and contemplate the superb fishing and diving in Central Andros. **Pros:** nature excursions can be arranged; restaurant and bar overlooking creek; quiet and clean. **Cons:** rental car necessary; basic rooms with amenities; not on beach. ⓢ *Rooms from: $150* ⊠ *On main highway at mouth of Stafford Creek* ☎ *242/368–6082* ⊕ *www.loveatfirst-sights.com* ➲ *10 rooms* ⦿ *No Meals.*

Pineville Motel

$ | **B&B/INN** | This truly one-of-a-kind, eye-popping plot of land fits in 17 rooms, a petting zoo, a small disco, a movie theater, a bar, and a DIY gift shop—made mostly of recycled materials such as tires, reclaimed wood, and seashells. **Pros:** unique experience; cheap rates; enthusiastic owner. **Cons:** not near beach; basic accommodations; overcrowded petting zoo. ⓢ *Rooms from: $55* ⊠ *Nicholl's Town* ☎ *242/329–2788, 242/557–4354* ➲ *17 rooms* ⦿ *No Meals.*

Did You Know?

Andros is the largest yet one of the most sparsely developed islands in the Bahamas. Putting the first footprints of the day on an empty beach might become your favorite activity.

The Red Bay Sunset Lodge
$$$$ | B&B/INN | Owner and flats guide Benry Smith built this humble three-room lodge, with a dining room for visitors eager to go bonefishing in North Andros. **Pros:** owner is a flatfishing guide; right on the water; complimentary beer and wine in dining room. **Cons:** very modest accommodations; only if you're a serious angler; three-night minimum. $ *Rooms from: $2450 ⌧ North Andros ☎ 242/471–6319 ⊕ www.redbaysunset.com ⇆ 3 rooms* ⏽◯❙ *All-Inclusive.*

Nightlife

BARS AND PUBS
Da Big Shop
BARS | Overlooking Nicholls Town Beach, Da Big Shop is as local as it gets. The 200-year-old building used to be Andros's only trading post for sponge harvesters; unfortunately, the building has not aged well, but the interior bar, open daily from noon until late, is a good time. On the weekends it has DJs, and on some holidays, a live band. For lunch or dinner, try Da Big Shop's island dinners, sandwiches, burgers, and pastas. It tends to attract local anglers and North Andros's younger demographic. You might be the only tourists here. ⌧ *Nicholl's Town* ☎ *242/225–2947, 242/329–2047.*

Activities

FISHING
Bonefishing
FISHING | North Andros's north coast and the string of Joulter Cays lying 5 to 10 miles offshore are among the country's richest fly-fishing grounds for bonefish and permit. Conch Sound and Lowe's Sound are reachable by car and good for DIY fishing by wading, but to have the full scope of the best fishing spots and to learn about this tricky craft of catching spooky bonefish, hire a skiff and Bahamian guide. Some of the country's leading guides operate in North Andros,

and visiting enthusiasts flock to the local lodges to fish with them. They can also arrange diving and snorkeling tours. ⌧ *North Andros* ☎ *242/471–5299 Elias Griffin, 242/471–1535 Keith Russell, 242/357–2781 Phillip Rolle, 242/329–2661 North Andros Flyfishing ⊕ www.northandrosflyfishing.com.*

Deep Sea and Bottom Fishing
FISHING | From Morgan's Bluff Harbour, Craig Curry takes out fishing charters to the reefs and shelves for grouper and snapper bottom-fishing and to the deep-ocean Tongue of the Ocean for bill- and game fish. His 35-foot Open Fisherman comfortably accommodates six; the larger 55-foot yacht can fit 10. Craig can also arrange snorkeling and scuba-diving tours. Call for rates. ⌧ *North Andros* ☎ *242/558–3799, 242/471–3339.*

WILDLIFE-WATCHING
Wild Boar Hunting
WILDLIFE-WATCHING | Perhaps oddly for such a passionate animal-lover, Eugene Campbell of Pineville Motel offers sometimes-thrilling guided wild-boar hunting in the scrub forests of mid-west North Andros. With a vast national park to escape to and live in, the boars have a similarly vast non-park habitat. They are not endangered and often hard to track down. Eugene closely guides up to three hunters, and because hunting the tusk-bearing boars is dangerous, he gives a mandatory safety lecture. Prices include hunting gear, transportation, and lunch. ⌧ *North Andros* ☎ *242/329–2788, 242/557–4354 ⌑ $350 for half day and $600 for full day, with gear, transportation, and lunch included.*

Central Andros

Those arriving in **Central Andros** by Bahamas Ferries from Nassau will arrive in the village of **Fresh Creek**; those arriving by plane will arrive in neighboring **Andros Town** (the petite transportation and governmental hub). Both Fresh Creek and

Andros Town, joined by a small bridge over the creek, are found midisland, on the east coast of North and Central Andros.

Heading north from Andros Town and Fresh Creek, Central Andros extends as far north as Stafford Creek, near Kamalame Cay, where the land officially becomes North Andros (though it's debated exactly where Central ends). As you head south from Andros Town airport, scrub pine forests and brush give way to mangroves and hardwood coppice. Long beaches scallop the eastern shoreline, and the sole road, Queen's Highway, will bring you to the bonefishing villages of **Cargill Creek** and **Behring Point.** Here, along the bonefish sweet spot of **Northern Bight,** you'll find nice homes with flowering gardens, palm trees, and sea grapes that overlook the ocean or the wide estuary.

Central Andros accounts for 60% of Andros's entire hotel inventory. Those expecting the glitz and glamour of The Bahamas' megaresorts and more touristy islands should look elsewhere. Here the glamour is the romantic, natural type, with open vistas of the beaches, tidal estuaries, pine forests, and distant barrier reef. However rustic it may seem, you'll find pockets of extraordinary excellence and success, notably the award-winning, luxurious private island resort **Kamalame Cay,** as well as the more homey, family-friendly, all-inclusive **Small Hope Bay Lodge,** and private villa **KettleStone.** This part of Andros has many simpler home rentals and bonefishing lodges with lodging, dining, and fishing packages. All lodging types attract many repeat visitors who come year after year (or a couple of times every year) to savor Andros's beautiful beaches, reefs, and world-class diving and fishing.

Central Andros's famed and remote **West Side** is a national park that teems with mangrove estuaries rich with marine life, including conch, lobster, bonefish barracuda, and small sharks. Flocks of West Indian pink flamingos, more commonly associated with the Southern Islands, also find habitat in the Andros West Side National Park. This uninhabited region is accessible only by private boat. Central Andros has several national parks, including two marine parks offshore, Blue Holes National Park north of Fresh Creek and the Crab Replenishment Reserve south of it.

GETTING HERE AND AROUND

Fly into Andros Town airport (ASD) with LeAir from Nassau, with Makers Air from Fort Lauderdale Executive (FXE) or Tropic Ocean Airways from Miami's Seaplane base at Watson Island or Fort Lauderdale International Airport (FLL). Randolph Holdings and Glen Air fly here regularly, even a couple of times a day. Alternatively, take the three-hour Sealink ferry with Bahamas Ferries from Nassau to Fresh Creek. Taxis meet airplanes and ferries. The fare from the airport to Fresh Creek is about $20; to the Cargill Creek area, some 20 miles south of the airport, it costs about $50.

A number of car-rental operators are available (rentals start at $85 a day), but if you're staying in the Cargill Creek area, you'll probably be doing most of your traveling by boat. Many lodges will pick you up at the airport. In Andros Town and Fresh Creek, you can easily get around to the local restaurants, beaches, and blue holes by bike and on foot. Good advice is to take a taxi tour early in your stay to get the lay of the land and meet a well-informed local. They know all the places to go and where to shop and dine.

CAR RENTAL CONTACTS Adderley's Car Rental. ⊠ *Fresh Creek, Central Andros* ☎ *242/357–2149.* **Rooney's Auto Car Rental.** ⊠ *Fresh Creek* ☎ *242/471–0346,.*

Sights

Andros Lighthouse

LIGHTHOUSE | As you enter Fresh Creek Harbour, you'll see this historical lighthouse built circa 1892 to navigate boats into the southern entrance of Fresh Creek Channel. No longer in use, the lighthouse, with a brace of rusty cannon near a delightful small beach, is an island landmark and offers a picturesque view, including a large, rusty old shipwreck. ⊠ *Andros Town* ☞ *Free.*

Androsia Batik Works Factory

FACTORY | The Androsia Batik Works Factory in Andros Town is home to the famous Androsia batik that has been adopted as the official fabric of The Bahamas. Small Hope Bay Lodge's Birch family established it in 1973 to boost employment in Andros. The brightly colored hand-dyed cotton batik has designs inspired by Andros's flora, fauna, and culture. You can prearrange a batik lesson ($30) and make your own design on a choice of fabric, garment, or bag. Self-tours are free. The unique brand is seen and sold throughout The Bahamas, the Caribbean, and online. The outlet store (with different opening times) offers bargains on shirts, skirts, wraps, fabric, jewelry, books, crafts, and souvenirs. ⊠ *Andros Town* ☎ *242/376–9339* ⊕ *www.androsia.com.*

Captain Bill's Blue Hole

NATURE SIGHT | One famous sight that nature lovers should catch is Captain Bill's Blue Hole in Blue Hole National Park. Blue holes are the top of extensive water-filled underground cave systems formed in the ice age, and there are hundreds on Andros. Located northwest of Small Hope Bay, the National Trust has made Captain Bill's popular and comfortable with a boardwalk and a shady gazebo. Steps allow you to jump 30 feet down to cool off, and there's a nature trail around the hole's 400-foot diameter. Accessible by car or bike, Captain Bill's is included on most guided tours. ⊠ *Fresh Creek*

✥ *Go 2 miles north from Small Hope Bay, turn left (west) in Love Hill, and take white road 2.7 miles west* ⊕ *www.bnt.bs/parks/andros* ☞ *Free.*

Fresh Creek

TOWN | Fresh Creek is an estuary, a hamlet, and a harbor, forming the north side of Andros Town and the south side of the Fresh Creek settlement, both joined by a small bridge. The north Fresh Creek side is more built up, with a few docks, stores, churches, motels, and restaurants, including Hank's Place, a local hot spot. On the south Andros Town side, the ferry and mail boats off-load at the dock next to the closed Andros Lighthouse Beach Club & Marina. You can still walk around the resort's point to get close to the lighthouse, with its small beach and shipwreck. The Andros Tourist Office and some shops are a short walk away. The creek itself cuts over 16 miles into the island, creating tranquil bonefishing flats and welcoming mangrove-lined bays that boaters and sea kayakers can explore. Upstream, there's even a remote Sunset Point houseboat, where you can stay surrounded by the flowing water and scintillating views. ⊠ *Fresh Creek* ⊕ *www.bahamas.com/islands/andros* ☞ *Free.*

Staniard Creek

TOWN | Sand banks that turn gold at low tide lie off the northern tip of Staniard Creek, a small island settlement 9 miles north of Fresh Creek, accessed by a bridge off the main highway. Coconut palms and casuarinas shade the oceanside beaches, and offshore breezes are pleasantly cooling. Kamalame Cove, part of nearby luxurious resort and private Kamalame Cay, is at the northern end of the settlement. Three creeks snake into the mainland, forming extensive mangrove-lined back bays and flats, good for wading and bonefishing. ⊠ *Staniard Creek.*

Beaches

Because they're famous for their off-the-chart fishing and diving, the islands of Andros often get shorted when talk turns to beaches. This is a great injustice, especially in the cases of the long, deserted beaches defining Central Andros's east coast and the abandoned white-sand beaches of Central Andros's outlying cays.

Kamalame and the Saddleback Cays
BEACH | East of Staniard Creek lies a series of serene cays, idyllic for beach drops or consummating the ultimate Robinson Crusoe fantasies. The first is Kamalame Cay, home to the luxurious resort of the same name. Just past Kamalame, uninhabited Big and Little Saddleback Cays boast sparkling, white-sand beaches and crystal-clear waters. You'll need a small, private boat to reach either (note that these cays are a regular drop-point for guests of Kamalame Cay). Little Saddleback is tiny with no shade, so bring plenty of sunblock. Big Saddleback has a wider crescent beach, with plenty of shade from the pine trees. Also nearby is Rat Cay, which offers excellent snorkeling, especially around the adjacent blue hole. **Amenities:** none. **Best for:** solitude; snorkeling; swimming; walking. ✉ *Staniard Creek.*

Small Hope Bay Beach
BEACH | Small Hope Bay Lodge is planted squarely on this long, coved beach where the near-shore snorkeling is excellent and the sand is white. Sign up for a resort course, a dive excursion, or simply enjoy a $55 beachside lunch buffet (with advance notice). A full day of beach fun with breakfast, lunch, and dinner, and all drinks and water sports included, is $199. Nonguests can also enjoy the dinner buffet with its open bar and music. **Amenities:** food and drink; showers; toilets; water sports. **Best for:** snorkeling; swimming; walking. ✉ *Small Hope Bay Lodge, Central Andros* ☎ *855/841–6966 toll-free U.S. and Canada, 242/368–2014 office* 🌐 *www.smallhope.com.*

Somerset Beach
BEACH | Two miles south of the Andros Town airport, off a long, beaten-up bare road through an arch of Australian pines, is Somerset Beach, a stunning, long, and wide beach with offshore sandbars that let you walk offshore for half a mile. The pines offer shade, and there's a picnic table built by the workers from AUTEC, the nearby U.S. Navy submarine-testing base. Bring a camera as this is one of the most beautiful beach sights in The Bahamas. **Amenities:** none. **Best for:** photography; shelling; swimming; walking.

Restaurants

Hank's Place Restaurant and Bar
$ | **BAHAMIAN** | On the north side of Fresh Creek, near the bridge, this restaurant and bar juts out into the harbor and is graced with sweeping views. Locals, visitors, and workers from the nearby naval base enjoy Hank's for decent Bahamian dinners (chicken, fish, lobster, and pork) and for the popular dance party on Saturday night. **Known for:** Hanky Panky frozen cocktail; harbor views; dance parties. [$] *Average main: $18* ✉ *Fresh Creek* ☎ *242/368–2447* 🌐 *www.hankplace.com* 🕓 *Closed Sun. and Mon.*

★ **Kamalame Cay**
$$ | **CARIBBEAN** | If you're not a guest at Kamalame Cay's private island resort, you might have to travel miles to enjoy this casual but luxurious dining experience, which is every bit worthwhile. Set on one of The Bahamas' most beautiful beaches, Kamalame draws guests to cocktails at the poolside Tiki Bar, then to The Great House to enjoy Andros's top cuisine. **Known for:** romantic setting; fixed menu; innovative dishes. [$] *Average main: $30* ✉ *Kamalame Cay Resort, Staniard Creek* 🌐 *www.kamalame.com.*

Small Hope Bay Lodge

$$$$ | **BAHAMIAN** | Unless you're a lucky all-inclusive guest at this resort famous for its diving and fishing, the best way to enjoy it is to buy an all-inclusive $199 day pass allowing you breakfast, lunch, dinner, and bar drinks (starting at lunchtime). From 7 am to 10 pm, you can enjoy all the facilities and equipment on Small Hope's gorgeous beach: kayaks, windsurfers, sailboats, snorkeling, paddleboards, and a fresh whirlpool. Just dinner and wine is $90 per person, which does not include bar drinks. **Known for:** communal dining experience; beach activities; Bahamian fare. $ *Average main: $99* ⊠ *Small Hope Bay* ☎ *242/368-2014* ⊕ *www.smallhope.com.*

Hotels

Andros Island Bonefish Club (AIBC)

$$ | **B&B/INN** | If you're a dedicated bonefisher, AIBC is the place for you, with access to 100 square miles of lightly fished flats, including wadable (at low tide) flats right out front. **Pros:** outdoor deck and bar idyllic for fishing stories; prime location on Cargill Creek; waterslide. **Cons:** not much for nonanglers; basic accommodations. $ *Rooms from: $200* ⊠ *Cargill Creek* ☎ *242/368-5167* ⊕ *www. androsbonefishing.com* ➥ *12 rooms* ⦿ *All-Inclusive.*

Big Charlie & Fatiha's Fishing Lodge

$$$$ | **B&B/INN** | On the banks of Cargill Creek, this small and charming bonefishing lodge is run by Charlie Neymour, a bonefishing legend, and his wife, Fatiha, who serves deliciously aromatic Moroccan and Mediterranean cuisine in the dining room—with tasty fresh seafood Bahamian-style as well. **Pros:** pristine facilities; fridges, satellite TV, and Wi-Fi in rooms; unusually good cuisine for a lodge. **Cons:** beach is some distance; only for fishing fans. $ *Rooms from: $500* ⊠ *Cargill Creek* ☎ *242/368-4297* ⊕ *www.bigcharlieandros.com* ➥ *4 rooms* ⦿ *All-Inclusive.*

Hank's Place

$ | **B&B/INN** | Hank's Place, with its restaurant and bar next door, offers four spacious, comfy rooms on the water for $100 double occupancy, including Wi-Fi. **Pros:** central convenience; on the water; on-site restaurant. **Cons:** basic but clean; loud music Saturday night; three-night minimum. $ *Rooms from: $100* ⊠ *Fresh Creek* ☎ *242/357-2214 cell, 242/368-2447* ⊕ *www.hankplace.com* ➥ *4 rooms* ⦿ *All-Inclusive.*

★ Kamalame Cay

$$$$ | **RESORT** | An all-inclusive resort with individual villas spaced along a 3-mile beach, the breathtaking and private 96-acre Kamalame Cay occupies a Bahamian pinnacle in luxury island retreats—and is surprisingly affordable. **Pros:** discreet pampering; delicious, innovative food; on-site over-water spa. **Cons:** Wi-Fi only in reception area; eye mask needed for sleeping past sunrise; round-trip airport transfers are costly. $ *Rooms from: $575* ⊠ *Staniard Creek* ⊕ *At north end of Staniard Creek* ☎ *242/368-6281, 800/790-7971 from U.S.* ⊕ *www. kamalame.com* ⊗ *Closed Aug.–Oct.* ➥ *20 bungalows* ⦿ *All-Inclusive.*

★ KettleStone Luxury Villa

$$$$ | **HOUSE** | **FAMILY** | Perched on a small bluff overlooking the Andros Barrier Reef, this dreamy luxury villa provides a consummate private getaway. **Pros:** oceanfront luxury; very private; near town; freshwater pool and free snorkeling. **Cons:** must drive to beach; self-catered or hired chef; not a resort. $ *Rooms from: $857* ⊠ *Fresh Creek* ☎ *242/357-2746 cell, 800/827-7048 toll-free in U.S. and Canada* ⊕ *www.kettlestoneluxuryvilla. com* ➥ *3 bedrooms sleeping 6 standard guests (Maximum 2 additional guests at $50 per person)* ⦿ *No Meals.*

★ Small Hope Bay Lodge

$$$ | **HOTEL** | **FAMILY** | This casual, lusciously palm-shaded beach and oceanfront property has been going strong for more than 50 years and offers 17 private cottages,

with a main dining clubhouse, lounge, and waterfront terrace and bar. **Pros:** best dive operation on Andros; air-conditioning; free Wi-Fi in public areas. **Cons:** in summer you'll need insect repellent; hot tub instead of pool. [$] *Rooms from: $325* ✉ *Small Hope Bay* ☎ *242/368–2014 resort, 800/223-6961 toll-free* 🌐 *www.smallhope.com* 🛏 *17 cottages* 🍴 *All-Inclusive.*

Sunset Point Houseboat

$$ | **B&B/INN** | If you're into nature and relaxation, this B&B on Fresh Creek lets you snorkel under your lodge and view birds, fish, rays, and maybe even dolphins passing mere feet away. **Pros:** private, serene, and eco-immersed; self-catered or cook for hire; expert Andros tourism guide. **Cons:** too quiet for some; children must be eight years or older and able to swim; car rental often needed. [$] *Rooms from: $300* ✉ *Fresh Creek* ✣ *1¼ miles west of Fresh Creek Bridge, on southern side of estuary* ☎ *242/357–2061 cell* 🌐 *facebook.com/SunsetPointHouseboat* 🛏 *3 beds, 3 baths, available for 2 to 6 persons* 🍴 *No Meals.*

Nightlife

BARS AND PUBS

Hank's Place

BARS | The overwater bar at Hank's Place Restaurant and Bar is *the* place to be on Saturday and some Fridays. Sunset is more of a relaxed scene, but come late-night, the music gets louder, people get "happier," and the dancing begins! It's also enjoyed by mostly young workers from the nearby AUTEC U.S. naval base. It's open from 2 pm to 10 pm Tuesday to Friday, and until 3 am on Saturday. ✉ *Fresh Creek* ☎ *242/368–2447, 242/357–2214 cell* 🌐 *www.hankplace.com.*

Did You Know?

In The Bahamas, mail is still delivered by mail boats, as it has been for decades. Mail boats leave Nassau's Potter's Cay carrying mail, cars, produce, consumer goods, and passengers on trips to more than 30 Bahamian islands, including Andros, a four-hour cruise.

Shopping

SOUVENIRS

★ **Androsia Store**

SOUVENIRS | Adjacent to the Androsia Batik Works Factory is the Androsia Store, where you can buy original fabrics, clothing, bags, souvenirs, and stuffed toys. Designed with island-inspired natural and cultural motifs, Androsia is popular nationwide and has been adopted by many as the official fabric of The Bahamas. ✉ *Andros Town* ☎ *242/376–9339* 🌐 *www.androsia.com* 🕒 *Closed Sun.*

Mangrove Cay

Home to 800 resilient, friendly locals, remote Mangrove Cay is sandwiched between two sea-green bights, separating it from Central and South Andros and creating an island of shorelines strewn with washed-up black coral, gleaming deserted beaches, and dense pine forests. **Moxey Town,** known locally as Little Harbour, is historically based on commercial fishing and conch and sponge harvesting and rests on the northeast corner in a coconut grove. Pink piles of conch shells and mounds of porous sponges dot the small harbor. Anglers come on a mission, in search of giant bonefish on flats called "the promised land" and "land of the giants." A five-minute boat ride takes fly-fishers to Gibson Cay to wade hard sand flats sprinkled with starfish.

GETTING HERE AND AROUND

Flamingo Air and LeAir fly a scheduled service from Nassau to Mangrove Cay Airport (MAY), located in Moxey Town. You can charter from Nassau or from Fort Lauderdale with many services, including Tropic Ocean Airways' floatplanes or Makers Air. Taxis meet airplanes and mail boats from Nassau, and taxi tours are a great way to get to know the island with all its shops, restaurants, and attractions.

Rent a car from Gaitor's or PB's car rentals at the airport for $80 to $100 a day. The cay's main road runs south from Moxey Town, past the airport, and then along coconut-tree-shaded beaches to the settlement of Lisbon Creek.

Frederick Major runs the free government ferry linking Mangrove Cay with South Andros. In his 30-foot outboard, it takes a few minutes to run from Lisson Creek to Driggs Hill—or a few more minutes to reach Tiamo Resort and a lodge along the Southern Bight's north shore. The ferry leaves Driggs Hill twice a day, at 8 am and 4 pm. The proposed ferry link from Mangrove Cay to Central Andros Island (Behring Point) has been put on hold.

TRANSPORT CONTACTS Frederick Major Ferry Services. ⊠ *Mangrove Cay* ☎ *242/376–8533, 242/323–6111 Nassau office, 242/554–1880 cell.* **Gaitor's Car Rental.** ⊠ *Mangrove Cay* ☎ *242/471– 1550, 242/464–3151.* **Henson "Harry" Saunders Taxi & Tours.** ⊠ *Mangrove Cay* ☎ *242/357–2365.* **Patrick King Taxi & Tours.** ⊠ *Mangrove Cay* ☎ *242/471–1126.*

◉ Sights

With beautiful wildlife along its coastline, tidal flats, and limestone caves, Mangrove Cay offers days of adventuresome exploring and sightseeing. Ask your local lodge about guided tours. Patrick King

or Harry Saunders will take you around the cay's 8 miles to see Little Harbour and the fisherman's dock with its fresh catches of lobster, conch, grouper, and snapper. You can also explore caves, myriad churches, and small souvenir stalls replete with Mangrove Cay sponges. Ask to visit Ralph Moxey, another kind of Andros legend, in his case, in the crafts of boatbuilding and carving. Ralph has built many island sloops, won many races, and, today, carves miniatures out of local woods like Andros mahogany and sapodilla along with shell crafts. He can also teach you about bush medicine and the healing qualities of local plants such as noni, naked wood, strongback, and more. Visit Diane Cash's souvenir and craft store to browse her raffia-and-shell-decorated straw dolls, hats, bags, billfolds, and fish- and star-shape bags. Dine at and sample tropical homemade breads from Rosa Bullard's Four Kids' Bakery & Restaurant.

Victoria Point Blue Hole

NATURE SIGHT | On an island known for magical blue holes, the Victoria Point Blue Hole is Mangrove Cay's superb ocean hole for snorkeling and diving. Just ask the folks at Swain's Cay Lodge or Seascape Inn—or any local—where to find it. ⊠ *Mangrove Cay.*

🍴 Restaurants

If you stay at one of Mangrove Cay's lodges, you're sure to be served fresh, delicious island fare, usually as part of your lodging and fishing package. You can, however, also explore other lodges. It's a great way to get to know them, so long as you book a day ahead. Swain's Cay Lodge has a restaurant on the beach, 3 miles south of the airport on the main road. Call ahead, especially during the low season, to confirm that you can enjoy fresh catches, conch, lobster, and more island dishes either alfresco on the beachfront porch or in the cool inside. The island's famous conch stand is

Shine's One-Stop Conch Shack north and then west of the airport road, sitting on the edge of Middle Bight. Here, enclosed in air-conditioning and away from flies, enjoy conch and fresh fish myriad ways. Some snowbirds and second-home owners treat themselves to Tiamo Resort's finer dining by taking the Tiamo's free ferry from Lisbon Creek (south Mangrove Cay) to the resort on South Andros. Explore other eateries as you bike, drive, or walk around other settlements on the 7-mile-long cay.

Seascape Inn's Barefoot Bar and Grill
$ | **BAHAMIAN** | Every table has a nice ocean view at this warm and friendly beachfront restaurant and bar at the Seascape Inn. Owners Mickey and Joan McGowan do the baking and cooking themselves. **Known for:** homemade ice cream; chocolate ganache; fresh catch of the day. [$] *Average main: $18* ✉ *Seascape Inn, Mangrove Cay* ☎ *242/369–0342* 🌐 *www.seascapeinn.com.*

Shine's One-Stop Conch Shack
$ | **BAHAMIAN** | Also known as Greene's after its owner Ornald "Shine" Greene, this waterfront spot on Little Harbour is as close to nightlife as you'll get on Mangrove Cay—live music is rare (save for during homecoming and regatta festivals) but if the island's busy or a big group requests it, they'll arrange a live band. Dominoes and backgammon with reggae and calypso tunes add to the upbeat ambience as you view the harbor, sip a beer or Goombay Smash, and tuck into the daily catch of fish, conch, and lobster. **Known for:** lively ambience; outstanding hospitality; excellent fresh ceviche. [$] *Average main: $12* ✉ *Mangrove Cay* ☎ *242/369–0078* 💳 *No credit cards.*

Swain's Cay Reefside Restaurant
$$ | **BAHAMIAN** | Swain's Cay Lodge's beachside Reefside Restaurant & Bar is a local dining and cocktail-sipping hot spot serving delicious authentic Bahamian cuisine for breakfast, lunch, and dinner, supported by a well-stocked bar. (Nonguests are welcome, but book in advance.) The decor is modern contemporary, and big windows and glass doors give it a bright ambience. Dine inside in air-conditioned comfort or on the beachside deck. **Known for:** extensive drinks menu; warm hospitality; modern, contemporary decor. [$] *Average main: $22* ✉ *Swain's Cay Lodge, Mangrove Cay* ☎ *242/422–5018 cell* 🌐 *www.swainscaylodge.com.*

🛏 Hotels

Mangrove Cay Club
$$$$ | **B&B/INN** | Located on the rocky south shore of the Middle Bight, 1½ miles northwest of Mangrove Cay Airport, is this purely-for-bonefishing club that only offers fishing-dining-lodging packages normally sold through fishing and hunting agencies. **Pros:** close to prized bonefish areas; great fishing gear and skiffs; superbly trained guides. **Cons:** hard-to-swim-in currents; no beach; somewhat remote. [$] *Rooms from: $3700* ✉ *Mangrove Cay* ☎ *242/369–0731 lodge, 402/222–0624 U.S. office* 🌐 *mangrovecayclub.com* 🛏 *8 waterfront suites sleeping 16* 🍴 *All-Inclusive.*

Seascape Inn
$ | **B&B/INN** | One of Andros's few lodging options catering to more than fishermen, Seascape Inn is a small, rustic beachfront gem; five individual, well-maintained cottages with private decks overlook the glass-clear ocean. **Pros:** quiet beachfront location; outstanding food; great snorkeling, kayaking, and bird-watching on-site. **Cons:** no air-conditioning; no TV; insect repellent a must. [$] *Rooms from: $198* ✉ *Mangrove Cay* ☎ *242/369–0342* 🌐 *www.seascapeinn.com* 🛏 *5 cottages* 🍴 *Free Breakfast.*

Swain's Cay Lodge
$$ | **B&B/INN** | This petite, beachfront resort is a gem for bonefishing fans and escape artists who want to enjoy Andros's natural beauty in peace and quiet. **Pros:** beachfront; excellent island

Undersea Adventures in Andros

Andros probably has the largest number of dive sites in the country. With the third-longest barrier reef in the world (behind those of Australia and Belize), the island offers about 100 miles of drop-off diving into the Tongue of the Ocean.

Uncounted numbers of **blue holes** are forming in the area. In some places these constitute vast submarine networks that can extend more than 200 feet down into the coral (Fresh Creek, 40–100 feet; North Andros, 40–200-plus feet; South Bight, 40–200 feet). Blue holes are named for their inky-blue aura when viewed from above and for the light-blue filtered sunlight that is visible from many feet below. Some of the holes have vast interior chambers with stalactites and stalagmites, offshoot tunnels, and seemingly endless corridors. Others have distinct thermoclines (temperature changes) between layers of water and are subject to tidal flow.

The dramatic Fresh Creek site provides insight into the complex Andros cave system. There isn't much coral growth, but there are plenty of midnight parrotfish, big southern stingrays, and some blacktip sharks. Similar blue holes are all along the barrier reef, including several at Mastic Point in the north and the ones explored and filmed off South Bight.

Undersea adventurers can also investigate wrecks such as the *Potomac*, a steel-hulled freighter that sank in 1952 and lies in 40 feet of water off Nicholls Town. And off the waters of Fresh Creek, at 70 feet, lies the deteriorated 56-foot-long World War II LCM (landing craft mechanized) known only as the **Barge Wreck**, which was

sunk in 1963 to create an artificial reef. Newer and more intact, the *Marian* wreck lies at 70 feet. Both are encrusted with coral and are home to a school of groupers and a blizzard of tiny silverfish. You'll find fish-cleaning stations where miniature cleaning shrimp and yellow gobies clean grouper and rockfish by swimming into their mouths and out of their gills, picking up food particles. It's an excellent subject matter for close-up photography.

The multilevel **Over the Wall** dive at Fresh Creek takes novices to depths of 65–80 feet and experienced divers to 120–185 feet. The wall is covered with black coral and all kinds of tube sponges. **Small Hope Bay Lodge** is the most long-respected dive resort on Andros. It's a friendly, informal place where the only thing taken seriously is diving and fishing. There's a fully equipped dive center with a wide variety of specialty dives, including customized family-dive trips with a private dive boat and dive master. If you're not certified, check out the lodge's morning resort course and be ready to explore the depths by afternoon. If you are certified, don't forget to bring your C card.

If you are leery of diving but want to view the spectacular undersea world, try snorkeling. Shallow reefs, beginning in 6 feet of water and extending down to 60 feet or more, are ideal locations for spotting myriad brightly colored fish, sea urchins, and starfish. Don't forget your underwater camera.

Winter water temperatures average about 74°F. In summer, water temperatures average about 84°F.

Tiamo Resort is the most luxurious resort in South Andros.

food; free transfers to airport and tours. **Cons:** sleeps only 22; beach is shallow for swimming. $ *Rooms from: $250* ✉ *Mangrove Cay* ☎ *242/422–5018* ⊕ *www. swainscaylodge.com* ⇨ *7 units* ❍❙ *Free Breakfast.*

South Andros

South Andros's road stretches 25 miles from **Driggs Hill**—a small settlement of pastel houses, a tiny church, a grocery store, the government dock, and the Emerald Palms Resort—to Mars Bay. Eight miles farther south, the Bluff settlement sprawls atop a hill overlooking miles of golden beaches, lush cays, and the Tongue of the Ocean. Here skeletons of Arawak peoples were found huddled together. A local resident attests that another skeleton was found—this one of a 4-foot-tall, one-eyed owl, which may have given rise to the legend of the mythical, elf-like chickcharnie. South Andros is laced with an almost continuous set of beaches on the northwest and east coasts, and more than 15 boutique resorts, bonefishing lodges, inns, and rentals are scattered among the island's many small settlements. It's a magnet for serious anglers and divers alike.

GETTING HERE AND AROUND

The Congo Town Airport (TZN) is 4 miles south of Driggs Hill and receives flights four times a week from Fort Lauderdale Executive Airport (FXE) via Makers Air and daily flights from Nassau (NAS) via Western Air. Nassau-based Golden Wings Charters is a respected charter company that can be used to reach South Andros. For the ultimate thrill and the convenience of flying direct to your resort's beach or dock, charter a seaplane either with Miami Seaplane Tours & Charters or Safari Seaplanes from Nassau. Taxis and many lodges and hotels meet incoming flights and ferries.

A free government ferry operated by Frederick Major's Ferry Service makes the quick trip between Mangrove Cay and South Andros twice daily. It departs from South Andros at 8 am and 5 pm and from Mangrove Cay soon after. Schedules (and weather) are subject to change.

TRANSPORT CONTACTS Frederick Major Ferry Services. ✉ *Mangrove Cay* ☎ *242/376–8533, 242/323–6111 Nassau office, 242/554–1880 cell.* **Lee Meadows Taxi Service.** ☎ *242/369–5029.* **Lenglo Car Rental.** ✉ *South Andros, Congo Town* ☎ *242/369–1702.* **Rahming's Rental Car.** ✉ *Congo Town* ☎ *242/369–1608.* **Shirley Forbes Taxi Service.** ✉ *Congo Town* ☎ *242/369–2930.*

Hotels

Andros Beach Club
$$$$ | **ALL-INCLUSIVE** | In Kemp's Bay, 10 miles south of Congo Town Airport, Andros Beach Club lies on a beach of powder-soft sand that stretches uninterrupted for almost 4 miles north. **Pros:** on fabulous beach, excellent diving and instructing; safe and secluded. **Cons:** remote and petite; fairly basic. [$] *Rooms from: $550* ✉ *Deep Creek* ✣ *10 miles south of Congo Town Airport* ☎ *954/681–4818, 242/369–1454 resort* 🌐 *www.androsbeachclub.com* 🛏 *7 rooms* 🍴 *All-Inclusive.*

★ **Caerula Mar Club**
$$$$ | **RESORT** | This chic oceanfront property on South Andros wows with its understated luxury, suites and villas with outdoor living spaces, and light, airy decor complementing its natural surroundings. **Pros:** complimentary use of water-sports equipment; good on-site restaurant and poolside beach bar; luxurious accommodations away from it all. **Cons:** three-night minimum; no kids under 12 allowed; no other restaurants within walking distance. [$] *Rooms from: $785* ✉ *South Andros, Driggs Hill* ☎ *800/790–6845* 🌐 *www.caerulamar.com* 🛏 *24 units* 🍴 *No Meals.*

The Pointe Resort & Marina
$ | **HOTEL** | Making great use of the views on a breathtaking point south of Kemp's Bay, this modern, smart, two-story resort has six suites and a restaurant, bar, and small marina. **Pros:** clean and modern ambience; gorgeous views; popular on-site restaurant good for groups. **Cons:** long taxi ride from airport; call in advance for dining; not on beach. [$] *Rooms from: $140* ✉ *Deep Creek* ☎ *242/471–9366* 🌐 *https://thepointesouthandros.com/* 🛏 *4 rooms with kitchettes* 🍴 *No Meals.*

★ **Tiamo Resort & Spa**
$$$$ | **RESORT** | At this luxurious hideaway for jet-setters in the know, you might feel like you're in French Polynesia, yet it is one of the Atlantic's last great secrets. **Pros:** 1½-to-1 staff-to-guest ratio; spectacular private beachfront location; great cuisine and water sports. **Cons:** alcohol not included in rates; insect repellent a must; only accessible by resort's ferry. [$] *Rooms from: $1155* ✉ *South Bight, Driggs Hill* ✣ *3 mile boat ride from Driggs Hill or Lisbon Creek (Mangrove Cay)* ☎ *242/225–6871 within Bahamas, 786/374–2442 in U.S. and Canada* 🌐 *www.tiamoresorts.com* 🕒 *Closed Sept. and Oct.* 🛏 *2 rooms, 11 villas* 🍴 *All-Inclusive.*

Activities

FISHING

Reel Tight Charters
FISHING | Usually operated by Jesse from Abaco Beach Club, an experienced diving instructor, this renowned charter company is often hired by other resorts and lodges on South Andros. With their 25-foot 300HP catamaran and 14-foot skiff, they offer a variety of excursions, mostly in South Andros but also farther afield, such as Green Cay on the other side of the Tongue of the Ocean. Tours are available, including deep-sea, reef-, and spearfishing, plus diving, snorkeling, private island picnics, and blue hole–exploring. They also rent water-sports gear and kayaks. ✉ *Driggs Hill Marina, Driggs Hill* ☎ *242/369–1454 Bahamas, 954/681–4818 in U.S. and Canada.*

Bimini

Bimini has long been known as The Bahamas' game-fishing capital. Bimini's strong tourist season falls from spring through summer, when calmer seas mean the arrival of fishing and pleasure boats from south Florida. The nearest of the Bahamian islands to the U.S. mainland, Bimini consists of two main islands and a few cays just 50 miles east of Miami, across the Gulf Stream that sweeps the area's western shores. Most visitors spend their time on bustling North Bimini; South Bimini is quieter and more eco-oriented. Except for the vast new Resorts World Bimini development that occupies the island's northern third, most of the hotels, restaurants, churches, and stores in Bimini are in the capital, **Alice Town,** and neighboring **Bailey Town** and **Porgy Bay,** along North Bimini's King's and Queen's Highways. Along the east coast of North Bimini are long beaches; on the west, the protected harbor, docks, and marinas. Most of the islands' 3,000 inhabitants reside in South Bimini, although they travel to North Bimini daily for work and school. Although the local communities in North Bimini are walkable, the preferred (and fun) way to scoot around is by golf cart. Resorts World Bimini has increased North Bimini's bustle and economy. Three times a week, the Balearia Fast Ferry takes up to 650 passengers to Bimini in two hours from Fort Lauderdale, who spread around the island enjoying its beaches, eateries, bars, nightclubs, and casino.

Sparsely populated **South Bimini** is where Juan Ponce de León allegedly looked for the Fountain of Youth in 1513, and a site with a well and natural trail memorializes it. More engaging, however, is the island's biological field station, known as the Sharklab for its study of lemon-, hammerhead-, and nurse-shark behavior and tracking, among other things. The main resort on this island is the modern, marina-based Bimini Sands Resort & Marina that sits atop a gorgeous mile-long beach. South Bimini is much more low-key than North Bimini, a slower pace loved by hundreds of visiting residents (and some visiting boating partiers), who have built nearly 80 homes in Port Royal on the island's southern tip.

Salvagers, gunrunners, rum-runners, and the legendary Ernest Hemingway have peopled the history of Bimini. Hemingway wrote much of *To Have and Have Not* and *Islands in the Stream* here between fishing forays and street brawls. Finding solace and inspiration in the natural environment, civil rights icon Dr. Martin Luther King Jr. penned one of his last speeches in Bimini.

GETTING HERE AND AROUND
AIR
South Bimini's small airport (BIM) was enlarged and improved in 2015 thanks to help from Resorts World Bimini, to cope with the extra traffic it brings. Silver Airways, with its feeder network of many Florida cities, flies in from Fort Lauderdale (FLL) twice a day. Tropic Ocean Airways with its floatplanes flies from Miami's Watson Island Seaplane base (MPB) and Fort Lauderdale International (FLL) straight to North Bimini Harbour (NSB), docking at Resort World. From Nassau, Western Air and Flamingo Air fly to South Bimini daily, and Flamingo also has a daily schedule from Grand Bahama Airport (FPO). Numerous operators from Florida and Nassau fly into South Bimini. More than six charter airlines fly from Fort Lauderdale: Apollo Jets from FLL, Island Air Charters and Makers Air and Bahamas Express from FXE. To reach North Bimini (Alice Town) from South Bimini Airport, you take a short taxi ride ($3) from the airport and a five-minute ferry ($2). The ferry runs until 10 pm or so for staff and guests who live on South Bimini.

CONTACTS Bimini Airport.
☎ *242/347–4111.*

Sunsets in Bimini can be otherworldly.

BOAT AND FERRY

Three times a week (Wednesday, Friday, and Sunday) Balearia Bimini's fast ferry whisks visitors and day-trippers to North Bimini, docking at Resorts World's new ocean-side pier. Accommodating more than 600 passengers in relatively spacious comfort, the high-speed catamaran *Jaume II* departs Terminal 21 in Port Everglades, Florida, and covers the 49 nautical miles in only two hours. Business Class includes everything in Economy Class but adds a light lunch and snack and discounts at the duty-free store. You can choose day trips from $75 plus taxes, giving you seven hours on Bimini. (Oddly, if you book a ferry ticket for longer, such as three days, the price rises to $198 per person.) You can book a ferry-and-stay at the Hilton, which, for the lodging, works out to be around $235 per night, double occupancy. RWB's website, however, usually offers great ferry-and-stay specials as well as exciting party weekends with live bands and more. Of course, with a ferry-only ticket, you don't have to stay at the Hilton; you can choose any of Bimini's hotels or inns.

Although rarely chosen, you can also sail to Bimini by old-fashioned mail boat. Contact the dockmaster in Potter's Cay in Nassau or the Bimini mail boat office at ☎ *242/347–3203* for an up-to-date schedule. M/V *Sherice M* usually leaves Potter's Cay, Nassau, on Thursday afternoon for Chub Cay, North Bimini, and Cat Cay, returning on Monday morning. The one-way trip takes about 12 hours and costs $50. Going between North and South Bimini requires a five-minute ferry crossing, managed by the local government ($2 each way; with the airport taxi's $3, a total of $5). It runs from early morning to fairly late at night.

Bimini's eight marinas accommodate private yachts and fishing boats in droves, with most crossing the Gulf Stream from Florida, a distance of around 48 nautical miles. As you enter port, fly the yellow quarantine flag. Coming into North Bimini, you have to clear Customs and Immigration in Alice Town at the

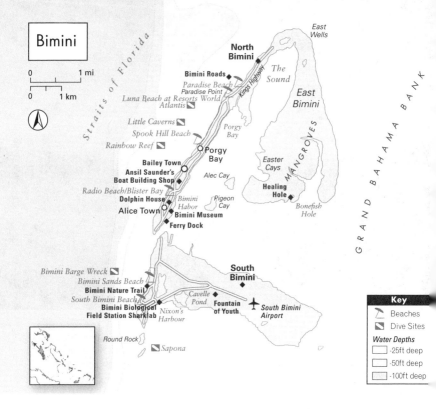

Bimini Big Game Club or at the government buildings in Bailey Town. Coming into South Bimini, dock at Bimini Sands Resort & Marina and take a taxi to clear at Customs and Immigration at the airport, 2 miles away.

Once docked, only the captain can leave the boat in order to clear with local Customs and Immigration. All crew are required to remain on board until the captain returns having been cleared. The clearance fee is $150 for boats up to 30 feet in length and $300 for boats over 30 feet, which covers the cruising permit, fishing permit, Customs and Immigration charges, and a $25-per-person departure tax for up to three persons. Additional persons over the age of six are charged an additional $25 departure tax.

CONTACTS Balaeria Bimini Fast Ferry. ✉ North Bimini ☎ 866/699–6988 ⊕ www.

baleariacaribbean.com. **Bimini Customs Office.** ☎ 242/347–3100. **Nassau Dockmaster's Office.** ✉ Nassau ☎ 242/393–1064.

VISITOR INFORMATION
CONTACTS Bimini Tourist Office. ☎ 242/347–3528, 242/347–3529 ⊕ www. bahamas.com/bimini.

North Bimini

Bimini's capital, **Alice Town,** is at North Bimini's southern end. It's colorful, painted in happy Caribbean pastels, and by night and day is buzzing with golf-carting visitors from Resorts World and the marinas along the main road of King's Highway. In a prominent location stand the ruins of the Compleat Angler Hotel, Ernest Hemingway's famous haunt, which burned down in 2006. A short walk away on the west coast is Radio

Beach (aka Alice Town Beach), and in the center of town are the Bimini Native Straw and Craft Market, the tourist office, the government dock, the marinas, and many restaurants and bars.

In quick succession, Alice Town turns into **Bailey Town,** then **Porgy Bay.** Going north you'll see conch stands, restaurants, and the pink-color government center and clinic. The beaches here are less frequented. Beyond Porgy Town, the north third of the island is the expansive Resorts World Bimini development.

GETTING HERE AND AROUND

If arriving by plane, catch a taxi ($3) at the South Bimini Airport and a ferry ($2) to the new government dock in Alice Town. The entire process costs $5. You can walk, take a taxi, or hire a golf cart to reach your accommodations. From Resorts World, you can hire a golf cart or taxi into Alice Town, or take the free hourly tram.

Most people get around North Bimini on gas-powered golf carts, available for rent from various vendors for $70 to $100 per day. At smaller rental companies, try bargaining. Note that the speed limit is 25 mph and that the roads follow the British system—driving on the left.

GOLF CART RENTAL CONTACTS ABC

Rentals. ⊠ *King's Hwy., Alice Town* 📞 *242/473–0286 cell.* **Elite Golf Carts At Resorts World.** ⊠ *North Bimini* 📞 *242/464–5025.* **Sue & Joys Rentals.** 📞 *242/347–6081.*

Sights

Ansil Saunder's Boatbuilding Shop

HISTORIC SIGHT | In Bailey Town, near the government park, is Ansil Saunder's boatbuilding shop, where you can see his beautiful flats fishing boat called the *Bimini Bonefisher.* Ansil is firstly a bone-fisherman of some repute, having scared up a 16-pound, 3-ounce bonefish for Jerry Lavenstein in 1971—the still-standing

bonefish world record. Ansil is equally famous for taking Dr. Martin Luther King Jr. on a guided boat tour to the East Bimini wilderness. Dr. King wanted inspiration for an upcoming speech to be given for striking sanitation workers in Memphis. He found it in the mangroves, so rich in life and full of God's creation, says Ansil, who recited his creation psalm to King. Three days after the Memphis speech, Dr. King was killed. At the time, with some foreboding, Ansil says that Dr. King mentioned to him that he didn't think he would live very long. To those who inquire, Ansil proudly shows memorabilia from Dr. King's wife and various VIPs. Saunders became an active member of The Bahamas independence movement. Saunders is regarded as one of The Bahamas' living legends—and a consummate ambassador. You probably can't find, in all the country, a more historically rich guide to take you fishing or to the Healing Hole in one of the boats he crafted. ⊠ *Bailey Town, on harbor front, Alice Town* 📞 *242/347–2178 shop* 💬 *Donations accepted.*

Bailey Town

TOWN | Most of the island's residents live in Bailey Town in small, pastel-color concrete houses just off King's Highway, north of the Bimini Big Game Club and before Porgy Bay. Bailey Town has two of Bimini's biggest grocery stores, where goods and produce come in by mail boat, usually on Thursday; Friday is the best day to shop. It's also a good place to find a home-cooked meal or conch salad from shacks along the waterfront. Don't miss a bite at Joe's Conch Stand; it's a local institution. ⊠ *North Bimini.*

Bimini Museum

HISTORY MUSEUM | The Bimini Museum, sheltered in the restored (1921) two-story original post office and jail—a two-minute walk from the ferry dock, across from the island straw market—showcases varied artifacts, including Adam Clayton Powell's domino set and photos, a fishing log, and rare fishing films of Ernest Hemingway with artifacts from the old Rod & Gun Club. You can also view photos from Bimini's Prohibition rum-running era, rum kegs, old cannonballs, and Martin Luther King Jr.'s immigration card from 1964. The exhibit includes films shot on the island as early as 1922. The museum is privately managed. ⊠ *King's Hwy., Alice Town* 🕾 *242/347–3038, 242/473–1252 cell* 🖃 *$2 donation requested.*

Bimini Roads

NATURE SIGHT | Avid divers shouldn't miss a trip to underwater Bimini Roads, aka The Road to Atlantis. This curious rock formation under about 20 feet of water, 500 yards offshore at Bimini Bay, is shaped like a backward letter J, some 600 feet long at the longest end. It's the shorter 300-foot extension that piques the interest of scientists and visitors. The precision patchwork of large, curved-edge stones forms a perfect rectangle measuring about 30 feet across. A few of the stones are 16 feet square. It's purported to be the "lost city" whose discovery was predicted by Edgar Cayce (1877–1945), a psychic with an interest in prehistoric civilizations. Archaeologists estimate the formation to be between 5,000 and 10,000 years old. Carvings in the rock appear to some scientists to resemble a network of highways. ⊠ *North Bimini.*

Dolphin House

HISTORY MUSEUM | Bimini historian and poet laureate Ashley Saunders has spent decades constructing this eclectic home and guesthouse from materials salvaged from local construction sites and the sea, while writing a two-volume set on Bimini's history. He offers walking tours, which begin with a tour of his structure—named for the 27 mosaic, sculpted, and painted dolphins throughout—then continue through Alice Town to tell the island's history. His books on the history of Bimini make for a fascinating read and souvenir. You'll see intricate conch shell

and coconut crafts for sale. ⊠ *Alice Town between King's and Queen's Hwys., Alice Town* 🕾 *242/347–3201* 🖃 *Tours $20/hr.*

Healing Hole

NATURE SIGHT | Hidden in the west coast mangroves of East Bimini is the Healing Hole—a cold spring of freshwater amid the hot sea saltwater with, some say, real, and others, mythical, healing powers. Hard to get to and find, it's best to hire a guide in a shallow boat, or, if you want exercise, in a kayak. You can only get there in mid-to-high tide, and make sure to take insect repellent. You'll see much life above and below water. For ecolovers and adventure-seekers only. ⊠ *North Bimini.*

 # Beaches

Luna Beach at Resorts World

BEACH | On Resorts World's long Paradise Beach, Luna Beach brings chic luxury to fun-in-the-sun and beach parties at night. Upscale food, exquisite cocktails, mod music, and beach toys are all part of the mix, centered on the open-air clubhouse. The solar-powered private cabanas even have phone-charging ports. For more action, jump on a Jet Ski, paddleboard, or kayak, or simply sun bake on a float. You can even book stingray and snorkeling tours here. During Sunset Sessions Happy Hour, DJ Arlette reverbs the beach with danceable tunes. On special full-moon weekends, Luna Beach imports live bands for its moonlight beach parties, also featuring Bahamian bands and mini-Junkanoo breakouts. Cocktails are half price from 8 to 9 pm. Open Sunday to Wednesday noon–7 pm; Friday and Saturday, noon–11 pm. **Amenities:** food and drink; lifeguards. **Best for:** partiers; snorkeling; swimming ⊠ *Resort World, North Bimini* ⊕ *www.rwbimini.com.*

Radio Beach/ Blister Bay

BEACH | Alice Town's Radio Beach and Bailey Town's Blister Bay form a continuous

You can kayak in North Bimini's mangrove flats.

stretch of beach off Queen's Highway, easily accessible in many places. Also called Alice Town Beach, its southern part is often busier and where spring breakers and the young like to party together. CJ's bar and grill, among other stands, is the default HQ, serving affordable beers, drinks, burgers, and island dinners. Eat inside (away from the flies), on the deck, or on the beach. **Amenities:** food and drink. **Best for:** partiers; swimming. ⊠ *Alice Town.*

South Bimini Beach

BEACH | Many would say Bimini's finest beach is on South Bimini, stretching about a mile from Bimini Sands Resort & Marina to South Bimini Beach Club (now closed) at Port Royal where the sand loops round the point and collects in a wide crescent—a favorite of spring breakers and Florida boaters. At South Bimini Beach Club is a protected anchorage and docks, but if you have a boat, it's best to slide into the marina at the north end of the beach. There you have amenities and an infinity pool with a bar serving food and drinks. From North Bimini, take an $8 ferry plus a taxi to reach the resort—it's well worth the trip to get away from it all. **Amenities:** food and drink. **Best for:** partiers; swimming. ⊠ *South Bimini* ☎ *242/347–3500* ⊕ *www. thebiminisands.com.*

Spook Hill Beach

BEACH | North of Radio Beach and named for its proximity to the local cemetery and Bimini's memorial park, Spook Hill Beach is quieter than Radio and Blister Bay Beaches and caters mostly to families looking for quiet sands and calm waters. Shallow shores are ideal for wading, and the crystal-clear waters make for great snorkeling. There is a permanent snack bar here, and usually, a few pop-up beach bars add to the fun. The beach is heavily lined with pine trees and is narrow at high tide. **Amenities:** food and drink. **Best for:** solitude; snorkeling; swimming. ⊠ *North Bimini.*

🍴 Restaurants

Bimini Big Game Bar & Grill
$$ | BAHAMIAN | A favorite place for boaters and anglers, this popular restaurant has a large, cool (and insect-free) interior and a patio deck with excellent second-story views of the marina, boats passing in the harbor, and shimmering flats beyond. Enjoy beers, cocktails, and island and American fare at reasonable prices. **Known for:** great place to watch sports; lovely views; camaraderie and atmosphere. $ *Average main: $26* ⋈ *Alice Town* ☎ *242/347–3391* ⊕ *biggameclubbimini.com* ☾ *No dinner Mon.–Wed.*

Joe's Conch Shack
$ | BAHAMIAN | This small island-style open-air conch stand lies on a tiny beach between Bailey Town and Resorts World. Both locals and visitors swear the salad has more conch and is more tender here than anywhere, and his fritters and lobster salad are favorites. Joe personally extracts conch (with his eyes on you) while serving with a big smile. **Known for:** genuine Bahamian experience; fresh conch; harbor views. $ *Average main: $12* ⋈ *North Bailey Town, North Bimini* ☎ *242/554–5183* ▭ *No credit cards.*

Hotels

Bimini Big Game Club Resort & Marina (*BBGC*)
$$ | HOTEL | This king of Alice Town's marina-based resorts has an illustrious fishing history since 1936, and today it has a renewed spark and charm, with and a focus on quality service. **Pros:** spacious rooms; excellent marina for fishing boats; great base with good restaurant. **Cons:** only fishing- and diving-oriented; most rooms ground level; not on the beach. $ *Rooms from: $249* ⋈ *King's Hwy., Alice Town* ☎ *242/347–3391 resort, 800/867–4764 reservations* ⊕ *www.biggameclubbimini.com* ⇶ *51 rooms* ⦿ *No Meals* ↝ *On-site is Bimini Scuba Center, a top Bahamas dive operator. Also on-site*

are Bahamas Customs & Immigration for quick clearing for yachts.

★ Resorts World Bimini Hilton & Marina
$$ | RESORT | FAMILY | This pastel-splashed luxury resort boasts a boutique casino and a stunning Hilton hotel with a rooftop infinity pool, a luxury spa, and a fitness center. **Pros:** top-quality marinas with all services; children's activity center; shuttle service around the property. **Cons:** restaurant opening times irregular; north-end units are a long walk from town; beach can get crowded. $ *Rooms from: $239* ⋈ *King's Hwy., North of Bailey Town, North Bimini* ☎ *888/930–8688 reservations, 242/347–8000 Hilton, 242/347–2900 front desk, 305/374–6664 marina* ⊕ *rwbimini.com* ⇶ *374 units* ⦿ *No Meals.*

Sea Crest Hotel & Marina
$ | HOTEL | Near Radio Beach, this small marina has two buildings: one with three stories, down a little lane leading to the beach, and one with two stories, on the marina. **Pros:** free Wi-Fi; central location; welcoming service. **Cons:** rooms are motel style; rooms lack decor; no restaurant. $ *Rooms from: $149* ⋈ *King's Hwy., Alice Town* ☎ *242/347–3071 hotel, 242/473–8083 reservations* ⊕ *www.seacrestbimini.com* ⇶ *27 rooms* ⦿ *No Meals.*

Nightlife

BARS AND PUBS
Big John's Bar & Grill
BARS | This waterside sports bar, restaurant, and tiny marina, patronized by the younger set, is one of the most popular places on-island to party, dance, and grab a cold beer, burger, or island snack. It's open from noon until late. It now sports a snazzy humidor with authentic Cuban cigars. Come nightfall Thursday to Saturday, a fabulous local Bimini band plays live music combining pop, Bahamian hits, reggae, and soca. At midnight, a local DJ takes over and spins until 3 am. If

you want to book a room in the boutique hotel upstairs, be mindful of the noise. ⊠ *King's Hwy., Alice Town* ☎ *239/347–3117* ⊗ *Closed Mon.*

 ## Shopping

SHOPPING CENTERS
Bimini Craft Centre & Straw Market
CRAFTS | Near the Government Public Dock in Alice Town, this craft center features the original straw, wood-carving, and craft works of myriad islanders. Products are showcased over 17 stalls. A great place for tie-dye resort wear and T-shirts, there's also some amazing food to be had. Make sure to stop at Nathalie Thompson's Bread stand to try a loaf of decadent Bimini bread. Think hot challah with sugar glaze. ⊠ *Next to a big pink government building and government dock, Alice Town* ☎ *242/347–3520.*

Fisherman's Village Marina
NEIGHBORHOODS | This 136-slip full-service marina, one of two marinas at Resorts World Resort & Marina, doubles as North Bimini's main touristic shopping village. Adjacent to the reception area, the "village" houses Bimini Undersea dive shop, a liquor and grocery store, an ice-cream shop, a gourmet pizzeria, a café and deli, a clothing boutique, and the surprisingly affordable and good-value Healing Hole Rum Bar & Grill (only open 11 am–4 pm, Monday, Wednesday, and Friday). ⊠ *North Bimini* ☎ *242/347–2900, 786/280–6861 Bimini Undersea Tours* ⊕ *rwbimini.com/things-to-do/fishermans-village.*

Trev Inn Marketplace
MARKET | Trev Inn has probably the largest selection of groceries and produce on North Bimini. It's located four buildings south of the pink-color Bimini Clinic in Porgy Bay, a short distance from Resorts World. (Also, Brown's is nearby, and farther south is Roberts' Grocery Store, near the big power station in Bailey Town, and Jontra's, near the Bimini Big Game

Club.) The mail boat comes in Thursday, so it's best to shop for fresh produce Thursday evening, Friday, and Saturday. Exploring local grocery stores is quaint and amusing except when you get to the cash register: with costly freight, import duties, and 7.5% VAT, expect to pay about double. To save money, bring coolers packed with fresh and frozen food. ⊠ *King's Hwy., Porgy Town, Alice Town* ☎ *242/347–2452.*

 ## Activities

BOATING AND FISHING
Bimini is not only one of the big-game fishing capitals of the world, it also holds six bonefishing world records. Hire one of the island's famous guides—and great characters—to hunt for the spooky "gray ghost." Full-day fishing excursions cost upward of $600. Reef and deep-sea fishing excursions are also available, from $400 for a half day. The best bonefishing guides must be booked well in advance.

Bimini Big Game Club Resort & Marina
DIVING & SNORKELING | Bimini Big Game Club Resort & Marina is a great base for fishing, diving, and snorkeling charters. They book the island's top bonefish guides and bottom and deep-sea fishing captains. You can also rent a small boat here, as well as kayaks, paddleboards, and snorkeling gear, and you can buy bait. There's a convenience store on property for mid-dive and mid-tour snacks (and liquor)—along with a Bahama Customs and Immigration office for port-of-entry clearance for boats. It's also the new home of the famous Neal Watson's PADI Bimini Scuba Center. ⊠ *Alice Town* ☎ *800/867–4764 toll-free, 242/473–8816 dive center* ⊕ *biggameclubbimini.com.*

Bonefish Ebbie David
FISHING | With his personality-plus, you'll get more laughs out of Ebbie David than fish—or will you? He's one of Bimini's most famous and highly recommended bonefishing guides and the recipient of

This large bonefish was caught on Bimini's shallow flats.

a coveted Ministry of Tourism Cacique Award for his excellence in the sport and in hospitality. Ebbie now runs his own bonefishing lodge. ⊠ *Alice Town* ☎ *242/347–2053.*

Golden Dream Charters

FISHING | Ex–commercial fisherman and island-born Captain Stephen Knowles has a special insight for when and where the fish are biting. His Ocean Yachts 46-foot Convertible *Golden Dream* is purpose-made for comfortable, fun fishing. Stephen heads to the Gulf Stream, trolling for big game: blue marlin, sailfish, mahimahi, wahoo, and tuna. Bimini abounds with bottom-fishing spots, where he'll set you on groupers, snappers, porgies, and yellowtails. In his 46-foot luxury sportfishing cabin cruiser, it's $800 for a half day, and $1,600 for a full day. ⊠ *Alice Town* ☎ *242/727–8144 cell, 242/347–3391 Bimini Big Game Club marina.*

SCUBA DIVING AND SNORKELING

The **Bimini Barge Wreck** (a World War II landing craft) rests in 100 feet of water. **Little Caverns** is a medium-depth dive with scattered coral heads, small tunnels, and swim-throughs. **Rainbow Reef** is a shallow dive popular for fish gazing. **Moray Alley** teems with captivating moray eels, and **Bull Run** is famous for its profusion of sharks. And, of course, there's **Bimini Roads (aka, Road to Atlantis),** thought to be the famous "lost city." Dive packages are available through most Bimini hotels. You can also check out the best diving options through the **Bahamas Diving Association** (☎ *954/236–9292* or *800/866–3483*).

Bimini Undersea

SCUBA DIVING | Headquartered in Fisherman's Village at Resorts World, the highly rated Bimini Undersea tour operator offers myriad excursions and experiences, including scuba diving, shark dives and stingray adventures, nature boat tours, fishing, and snorkeling with wild spotted dolphins. They run Sunset

Celebration Cruises, and near the marina and on Paradise Beach at the new Luna Beach Club, they offer Jet Skis, kayaks, and paddleboards. You can also rent or buy snorkel and diving gear. They offer two, two-tank dives a day and introductory scuba lessons. Dive packages with accommodations at Resorts World are available, and day-trippers are also welcome to join. ⊠ *Resorts World Bimini & Marina, North Bimini* ☎ *242/347–2941, 786/280–6861 in U.S. and Canada* ⊕ *www.biminiundersea.net.*

Neal Watson's PADI Bimini Scuba Center
DIVING & SNORKELING | The PADI-certified Bimini Scuba Center, located at Bimini Big Game Club Resort & Marina, offers two-tank dives in the morning and one-tank dives in the afternoon. Besides exciting great hammerhead shark dives (from October to March), bull shark dives near Cat Cay, and Caribbean reef and lemon shark dives, BSC also offers wild spotted dolphin snorkeling excursions. (You may need patience and understanding; after all, these are free and wild creatures.) The operator visits all of Bimini's popular dive spots: the Sapona Wreck, the Bimini Barge, Atlantis Road, Tuna Alley, Victory Reef, the Nodules, the Strip, Rainbow Reef, and much more. They offer a full range of rentals and tank fills, as well as kayaks and paddleboards for exploring the harbor and flats beyond. You can also arrange for small boat rentals and all types of fishing charters. Novices can safely train in the resort's pool, then grab a quick bite and drink. With everything so convenient, Bimini Scuba Center is an excellent choice for a diving or fishing vacation. ⊠ *Alice Town* ☎ *242/347–3391 resort, 800/867–4764 toll-free in U.S. and Canada, 242/473–8816 cell* ⊕ *www.biminiscubacenter. com.*

South Bimini

Bigger, with nicer beaches and a higher elevation than low-lying North Bimini, South Bimini is nonetheless the quieter of the two islands. Home to the island's only airport, it has a smattering of shops near the ferry landing, where boats make regular crossings between the two islands, a short five-minute ride. Bimini Sands Resort is the biggest property on the island, with its safe-harbor marina, condos, and nature trail. The resort helps preserve the island's ecofocus by staying low-key and keeping much of its land undeveloped. It helps maintain the little Fountain of Youth Park, the Sharklab, and beautiful beaches. South of the main resort in Port Royal are 80-plus vacation homes, some docks, and a scalloped beach that's a favorite of visiting boaters.

GETTING AROUND
Visitors do not need a car on Bimini, and there are no car-rental agencies. A taxi from the airport to Bimini Sands Resort is $3. Hitching a ride is common.

◉ Sights

Bimini Biological Field Station Sharklab
WILDLIFE REFUGE | Often featured on Discovery Channel and other TV shows, the Bimini Biological Field Station Foundation's Sharklab was founded decades ago by Dr. Samuel Gruber, a shark biologist at the University of Miami. Important research on the lemon, hammerhead, nurse, bull, and other shark species has furthered awareness and understanding of the misunderstood creatures. Visitors can tour the lab at low tide. The highlight is wading into the bay, where the lab keeps several lemon sharks, rotating them on a regular basis. The tour leader gets in the pen with the sharks, captures one in a net, and speaks about its behaviors and common misconceptions people have of the lemon. The hands-on presentation, done by the research

assistants or researchers themselves, is entertaining and educational. Tours are offered daily, but visitors must call in advance; the times aim for low tide. This is a special vacation highlight for families with children. ✉ *South Bimini, 15 Elizabeth Dr., South Bimini* ✛ *End of long road to south of island, turn left* ☎ *242/347–4538* ⊕ *www.biminisharklab. com* ✉ *$10 donation desirable.*

Bimini Nature Trail

TRAIL | FAMILY | Developed by Bimini Sands Resort on undeveloped property, this mile-loop trail is one of the best of its kind in The Bahamas. Its slight rise in elevation means a lovely shaded walk under hardwood trees such as gumbo-limbos, poisonwood (marked with "Don't Touch" signs), and buttonwood. Check out the ruins of the historic Conch House, a great place for sunset-gazing. There is also a pirate's well exhibit devoted to the island's swashbuckling history. Excellent signage guides you through the island's fauna and flora if you prefer doing a self-guided tour. However, for the best interpretation and learning experience, book a guided tour through the front desk at Bimini Sands. Kids always love petting the indigenous Bimini boa on the guided tour. The trail was recently improved by Bahamian bird-watchers such as Erika Gates of Freeport's famous Garden of the Groves reserve. ✉ *South Bimini, South Bimini* ☎ *242/347–3500 resort* ✉ *Free. Guided tours $12.*

Fountain of Youth

HISTORIC SIGHT | Famous explorer Juan Ponce de León heard about a Fountain of Youth possibly located in Bimini, so in 1513, on his way to discovering Florida and the Gulf Stream, he landed on Bimini but never found the fountain. The historical result? Somehow Biminites adopted a freshwater natural well that was carved out of limestone by groundwater thousands of years ago and used it to commemorate Ponce de León's search. Now there's a plaque to celebrate the myth.

So, nonetheless, go there and make a wish (without casting a penny—this is an eco-island). You'll find the Fountain of Youth on the road to the airport. ✉ *South Bimini* ☎ *242/347–3500 Bimini Sands Resort & Marina* ✉ *Free.*

Beaches

South Bimini claims Bimini's prettiest beaches, with a pristine, mile-long stretch on the western side, and near Port Royal, a sandy cove and point on the southern side, with some of the best from-shore snorkeling around. In the far south, the point's gorgeous beach is there to enjoy for all and sundry. It's a favorite beach for boaters, with a couple of docks and safe anchorages from northerly or easterly winds. The partiers tend to congregate here, leaving the northern beaches relatively secluded. At the north end of the long beach is Bimini Sands Resort & Marina. Dock there and you can use their infinity pool and other amenities (and a fuel dock, too). The Pool Bar, with its refreshments and food, is welcome to all beach walkers.

Bimini Sands Beach

BEACH | Patrons of Bimini Sands Resort & Marina are not the only ones who love the mile-long Bimini Sands beach. This gorgeous stretch of white-sand powder, with its offshore snorkeling, is so enticing that vacationers from North Bimini and even Floridians often take the quick ferry over or boat across the Gulf Stream for the day. The southern cove and point once had facilities that are, at this writing, closed, but the beach and beautiful waters are still a magnet for boaters. To clear Bahamas Customs, who are stationed at the airport, it's best to slide into the Bimini Sands marina, where you have access to amenities, including the Pool Bar and a freshwater pool. The southern beach gets particularly busy during spring break, but the northern stretch stays relatively secluded. **Amenities:** food and drink. **Best for:** partiers; snorkeling; swimming

✉ *South Bimini* ☎ *242/347–3500 Bimini Sands Resort & Marina* 🌐 *Free. Ferry plus taxi from North Bimini $5.*

🍴 Restaurants

The Petite Conch

$ | **BAHAMIAN** | This second-story, cozy little diner/café overlooks Bimini Sands Marina, and although they don't serve fancy cuisine, it does have excellent and comforting Bahamian dishes at a reasonable cost. Very convenient for the resort's and marina's guests, The Petite Conch serves breakfast, lunch, and dinner with American and local favorites. **Known for:** cozy ambience; convenient for resort and marina guests; fast and friendly service. $ *Average main: $10* ✉ *South Bimini* ☎ *242/347–3500.*

🛏 Hotels

Bimini Sands Resort & Marina

$$ | **RESORT** | **FAMILY** | Overlooking the Straits of Florida on a stunning beach, this well-designed property rents one-to three-bedroom condominiums with direct marina access. **Pros:** full-service marina with customs nearby; small restaurant with pool bar and café; good tour operations. **Cons:** limited nightlife on South Bimini (party is daytime here); sometimes a shortage of lounge chairs; somewhat remote. $ *Rooms from: $250* ✉ *South Bimini, South Bimini* ☎ *242/347–3500 resort, 888/588–2464 in U.S. and Canada* ⤵ *206 condominiums.*

🏃 Activities

BOATING, FISHING, AND DIVING

Bimini Sands Resort & Marina

BOATING | Bimini Sands Resort & Marina arranges and has access to all the tours and excursions offered by the excursion and dive operators in North Bimini including the shark, stingray, wreck, reef, and wild spotted dolphin tours offered by Neal Watson's Bimini Scuba Center. You

Plan Ahead

Even though you're going to the laid-back islands, you need to reserve your guides, boats, cars, and golf carts in advance. And if you ask, these friendly islanders might include an airport greeting and transfer to your hotel.

can join those tours either by taking the $5 ferry-plus-a-taxi option to Alice Town or by asking the tour boat to pick you up at the Bimini Sands Marina. The resort itself offers kayaks, snorkeling gear, and boat rentals so you can go and discover Bimini's many reefs and wrecks on your own. ✉ *Bimini Sands Resort & Marina, South Bimini* ☎ *242/347–3500.*

SCUBA DIVING AND SNORKELING

Bimini has excellent diving opportunities, particularly for watching marine life. Off the shore of South Bimini, the concrete wreck of the SS *Sapona* attracts snorkelers as well as partiers.

The Berry Islands

The Berry Islands consist of more than two dozen small islands and almost a hundred tiny cays stretching in a thin crescent to the north of Andros and Nassau. Although a few of the islands are privately owned, most of them are uninhabited—except by rare birds who use the territory as their nesting grounds, or by visiting yachters dropping anchor in secluded havens. The Berry Islands start in the north at **Great Stirrup Cay** and **Coco-Cay,** where thousands of cruise passengers enjoy Bahama-island experiences and the Stingray City Bahamas attraction on neighboring Goat Cay. The Berries end in the south at **Chub Cay,** only 35 miles north of Nassau.

Most of the islands' 700 residents live on the tranquil, 10-mile-long **Great Harbour Cay,** the largest of the Berry Islands. Its main settlement, **Bullock's Harbour,** aka "the Village," has a couple of good restaurants, grocery and liquor stores, and some small shops. A mile west, the Great Harbour Cay's beach area was developed in the early 1970s. More homes, condos, and villas have been built or remodeled since. The 65-slip protected marina has also been renovated and is once again popular with yachties. There are no big resorts on Great Harbour; instead, there's a delightful, world-class boutique hotel called Carriearl, a former house of a famous Hollywood star matchmaker, who invited his guests here to party within their tight circle. There's a small hotel at the marina and homes and villas for rent on the marina and beaches. The GHC Property Owners Association is active and provides many fun activities and events, including the partial upkeep of 9 holes of the original golf course. Many private pilots have homes and fly in here. The Berries are reputed to have one of the world's highest concentrations of millionaires per square mile, but, surprisingly, there are no banks or ATMs, so make sure you bring some cash with your credit cards.

In recent years, family, wedding, honeymoon, and beach-seeking vacations and bonefishing have become more popular. In the south, Chub Cay is close to a deep-sea pocket where the Tongue of the Ocean meets the North West Providence Channel—a junction that traps big game fish. Remote flats south of Great Harbour, from Anderson Cay to Money Cay, are excellent bonefish habitats, as are the flats around Chub Cay. Deeper-water flats hold permit and tarpon.

Chub Cay, a popular halfway point for boaters crossing to and from Florida, is also experiencing a comeback with millions having been recently invested in the Chub Cay Resort & Marina, which is soon to become private, catering more to investors who own or build homes on the island. On Chub, you'll certainly connect with your friends and young ones, but make sure you have a boat to give you freedom to explore, dive, and fish. Bring food, drinks, and snacks for your stay. The new, luxury-looking clubhouse has a well-stocked convenience store. Most rental units come with kitchens.

GETTING HERE AND AROUND

AIR

In the Berry Islands, Great Harbour Cay (GHC) Airport receives regular flights from Fort Lauderdale airport (FLL) through Tropic Ocean Airways, with their land-capable floatplanes, on Friday and Sunday. Four times weekly Makers Air flies to Chub Cay (CCZ) and GHC from Fort Lauderdale Executive Airport (FXE). From Nassau (NAS), two flights a day come in via LeAir. Many other charter operators with props, jets, and helicopters fly in from Florida. For a full list of schedule and charter flights see ⊕ *www. bahamas.com/islands/berry-islands/ getting-here.*

Chub Cay is served from Nassau every Monday, Wednesday, and Friday by Captain Bill Munroe's Bill Air (☏ *242/434–0374*), who can vary the aircraft's size according to passenger numbers. It's $100 one-way.

On Great Harbour Cay, one of the few taxis will take you to your resort or villa. After that, renting an SUV, golf cart, or at least a bike is sensible, although walking around the Bullock's Harbour village itself is a nice 40-minute stroll. On 6-mile-long Chub Cay, it's only a mile from the marina resort to the airport.

BOAT

Great Harbour Cay and Chub Cay are popular yachting destinations and stop-offs for boats going farther afield. Both are ports of entry with friendly service by Customs and Immigration for entry clearance and gaining the mandatory cruising permits. Both have excellent marinas with fuel and full services. From Nassau, the mail boat M/V *Capt. Gurth Dean* sets sail twice or three time a month from Potter's Cay Dock on Wednesday night, arriving Thursday morning to supply the GHC with groceries, supplies, and general cargo.

Take a boat or hire a guide and island hop to explore the cays' splendid turquoise serenity and wildlife on land and undersea. The Berries are favored among bone- and deep-sea fishermen in-the-know and who want to get away from crowds. World-class fishing tournaments used to be held here and at the start of the crawfish season on August 1; many boats from Nassau chose to spearfish here for its westerly lee-side shelters, its proximity, and the lucrative bounty. On Little Harbour Cay, 16 miles southeast of Great Harbour, is the famous outpost Flo's Conch Bar, now run by Flo's family. Visit the Stingray City Bahamas's tour to snorkel with stingrays off Goat Cay by catching the company's staff boat from Great Harbour Cay.

CONTACTS Chub Cay Resort & Marina. ☎ 242/325–1490 *resort and marina,* *786/209–0025 in U.S. and Canada.* **Great Harbour Cay Marina.** ⊠ *Great Harbour Cay* ☎ 242/367–8005 *marina* ⊕ *www. greatharbourcay.com.*

ISLAND TRANSPORTATION

On Great Harbour Cay, you can get to most places on foot, which is convenient as there are not a lot of ground transportation options. There is one car-rental provider with vehicles ranging from $75 up to $90. On Chub Cay you can rent golf carts at the marina and elsewhere. On both islands, transport may be included in your villa rental. Hopefully you'll get on to the water and sightsee some Berry magic by renting a small boat or doing some fishing. Make sure you have a reliable VHF radio and plot your course on a good chart that you can buy at the marinas: these islands have many hazardous reefs and sandbars. Gas is around $5 a gallon.

CONTACTS Happy People Rentals. ⊠ *Great Harbour Cay Marina, Great Harbour Cay* ☎ 242/367–8117 *shop,* 242/359–9052 *cell.* **Krum's Rentals.** ⊠ *Great Harbour Cay* ☎ 242/367–8370.

Beaches

Off these always secluded, immaculate beaches, the clarity of Bahamian waters is especially evident when you reach the Berry Islands. Starfish abound, and you can often catch a glimpse of a gliding stingray, eagle ray, barracuda, or needle fish. You'll find ocean beaches with gentle lapping waves, sultry beaches with sandbar flats where you can walk half a mile, and private coves enclosed by cliffs.

Chub Cay Beach

BEACH | As well as the 400-yard beach right at the marina, Chub Cay has a splendid 1¼-mile strand with great swimming and nearby snorkeling. The Club House with its pool is a mere 400 yards away for refreshments. **Amenities:** none. **Best for:** swimming; snorkeling. ⊠ *Chub Cay's southern coast* ☎ 242/325–1490 *clubhouse and marina office.*

Great Harbour Cay Beach

BEACH | Two crescents scoop Great Harbour Cay's east coast with 5 miles of almost unbroken powder. Travel north to discover Sugar Beach with its bluff-surrounding romantic private coves. Progressing south, the beach becomes Lover's Beach, thinning out until Hotel Point Beach, where the strand widens and you can see waves clash from two directions. Farther south still is famous Great Harbour Beach itself, where you'll encounter the fabulous boutique hotel Carriearl and its fine pool, restaurant, and bar. On the south end of Great Harbour Beach near the airport, you'll find The Beach Club, a popular daytime bar and grill with a gift shop. Play beach volleyball, or take a yoga class. (They may ask for a small donation.) At the extreme south are the shallow, simmering sandbars of Shelling Beach that let you wade out for yards. At low tide, you can cross the tidal Shark Beach Creek to the pristine Haines Cay, which, hidden from the north by a hill, offers an even more splendid, long beach. Along Great Harbour Cay's powdery 5-mile stretch, nearby reefs beckon snorkelers, and gin-clear waters invite kayakers and paddleboarders. **Amenities:** food and drink. **Best for:** shelling; swimming; walking; snorkeling. ✉ *Great Harbour Cay* ✥ *5 miles long with varying names* ☎ *242/367–8005 marina and resort* 🌐 *www.greatharbourcay.com.*

Haines Cay Beach

BEACH | At low tide, walk across from Shelling Beach estuary, round the point, and walk south a half mile, and you'll discover one of The Bahamas's most unspoiled, beautiful beaches. It's 2 miles long, with excellent snorkeling on its north end and swimming all along. Wear some sturdy footwear for the land walk. It's also reachable by kayak. There are no trees for shade, so an umbrella, lots of fluids, and sunscreen are advisable. **Amenities:** none. **Best for:** swimming; walking; snorkeling; solitude. ✉ *Great Harbour Cay* ✥ *½ mile west of Shelling Beach.*

Sugar Beach

BEACH | Sugar Beach is the northernmost of the island's beaches, where rock bluffs divide the sand into romantic "private" coves of various lengths. Explore the caves or snorkel in calm waters. On top of one of the hills are the ghostly remains of the Sugar Beach Hotel, a 1950s lair built by the Hollywood Rat Pack—Sammy Davis Jr., Dean Martin, Frank Sinatra, Peter Lawford, and Joey Bishop. Female stars invited there included Marilyn Monroe, Shirley MacLaine, Lauren Bacall, Angie Dickinson, and Judy Garland. This was their scenic escape from paparazzi. The hilltop ruins are decrepit and surrounded by bush and cliffs, so explore with caution. **Amenities:** none. **Best for:** swimming; walking; snorkeling; solitude. ✉ *Great Harbour Cay.*

Early-Bird Dinners 🍴

Dinner is commonly served in most restaurants starting at 6 pm and can be over by 8:30. It's always best to call ahead for reservations and to let the restaurant know you are coming as hours can be irregular; they may decide to close if they think they aren't going to be busy. Some like to have your order ahead of time.

🍴 Restaurants

★ The Carriearl Roost

$$$ | **BAHAMIAN** | Guests who discover The Carriearl Roost are pleasantly stunned that a restaurant of such charm and caliber just happens to be on their tiny island. The staff provide excellent service, and they are responsive and amiable. **Known for:** tropical chic atmosphere; reservation only; signature fried chicken. [$] *Average main: $35* ✉ *Soul Fly Lodge, Great Harbour Cay Beach, Great Harbour Cay* ☎ *242/367–8785* 🌐 *www.soulfly-lodge.com/the-carriearl-roost* 🕒 *No lunch except Sun. brunch, closed Mon.–Wed.*

Coolie Mae's Sunset Restaurant

$$ | **BAHAMIAN** | In the island food category, expats, locals, and visitors rate Mae's food as true-true excellent. Her bright sign makes the casual 60-seat restaurant, on Bullock's Harbour's central seafront, easy to find. **Known for:** conch salad; Bahamian specialties like peas-and-rice; reservations recommended. [$] *Average main: $22* ✉ *In middle of Bullock's Harbour's west peninsula, Great Harbour Cay* ☎ *242/367–8730* 💳 *No credit cards* 🕒 *Closed Sun.*

Kayaks line the beach at Little Stirrup Cay in the Berry Islands.

Hotels

★ Chub Cay Resort & Marina

$$$$ | **HOTEL** | Chub Cay Resort & Marina has been speedily and most beautifully restored to what is a luxury oasis on an otherwise rustic cay. **Pros:** excellent location for flats and offshore fishing; quality bar and restaurant serves three meals; luxury-style clubhouse and well-appointed rooms with balconies. **Cons:** construction may occur, but away from hotel; not much to do on land, but plenty on the sea. [$] *Rooms from: $425* ✉ *Chub Cay* ☎ *242/325–1490 hotel, 786/209–0025 in U.S. and Canada* 🌐 *www.chubcay.com* 💳 *No credit cards* 🛏 *31 units* 🍴 *No Meals.*

Great Harbour Inn

$ | **B&B/INN** | Perched above the marina in Great Harbour Cay, this five-suite inn is basic but conveniently located near the marina and less than a mile from the beach. **Pros:** a basic, no-frills economical getaway; near marina; now has cable TV and Internet, but call first to ensure they're operational. **Cons:** needs an upgrade; can be hot and buggy when the wind is down. [$] *Rooms from: $130* ✉ *Above Great Harbour Cay marina, Great Harbour Cay* ☎ *242/367–8370, 242/451–0579 cell* 💳 *No credit cards* 🛏 *5 suites.*

★ Soul Fly Lodge

$$$$ | **B&B/INN** | An unassuming front entrance hides what many say is one of The Bahamas' top small vacation retreats, and guests love having 7 miles of powdery beach to themselves. **Pros:** right on 7 miles of silky sand beach; superb restaurant and bar; excellent, attentive, and friendly service. **Cons:**; only four rooms; one of the more expensive options. [$] *Rooms from: $475* ✉ *Great Harbour Cay* ☎ *242/367–8785 hotel* 🌐 *www.soulflylodge.com* 🛏 *4 rooms* 🍴 *No Meals.*

Activities

BOATING

The water's depth is seldom more than 20 feet here. Grass patches and an occasional coral head or flat coral patch dot the light-sand bottom. You might spot the odd turtle, and if you care to jump over the boat's side with a mask, you might also pick up a conch or two in the grass. Good snorkeling and bonefishing and peaceful anchorages can be found on the lee shores of the Hoffmans and Little Harbour Cays. Flo's Conch Bar, at the southern end of Little Harbour Cay, serves fresh conch prepared every way.

Great Harbour Cay Marina

BOATING | In the upper Berry Islands, the full-service Great Harbour Cay Marina has 65 slips for yachts up to 150 feet. This is the island's touristic nerve center, where you can book fishing and snorkeling charters and arrange boat rentals. Accessed through an 80-foot-wide channel from the west, the marina has almost no motion even in rough weather: it's a top hurricane hole. This sleepy and crime-free island on a gorgeous beach still has plenty to do: join a game of pétanque in the street with free rum punch on Wednesday evening, or the Chill 'N' Grill ($10–$15) get-together on Friday night, or weekly yoga, fitness classes, and beach volleyball at The Beach Club. You can even play nine holes of golf on the rather weedy course. The marina is a great base for boating, snorkeling, and fishing. HeuBoo's Deli on the dock is a good place for ice cream and pastries. Fuel is at a separate dock west of the marina. The marina's management company also rents out town houses. ⊠ *Great Harbour Cay* ☎ *242/367–8005 dock, 242/457–4216 cell* ⊕ *www.greatharbourcay.com.*

Happy People Boat Rental

BOATING | At Great Harbour Cay Marina, Elon Rolle, who can be found in a small convenience store on the dock, hires for the day, half day, or hour, an unsinkable 20-foot Boston Outrage with 200HP ($250 a day plus gas; using about $150 for 30 gallons for a day). Snorkeling, spear, and fishing gear are extra. It also comes with VHF radio. ⊠ *Great Harbour Cay Marina, Great Harbour Cay* ☎ *242/367–8117 marina, 242/367–8761 home, 242/359–9052 cell.*

FISHING

Percy Darville's Bonefishing

BOATING | Percy Darville and his family and crew know the flats of the Berries better than anyone. The fleet comprises four skiffs. Percy has a speedy 26-foot Mako with 400HP, ideal for bottom-fishing and taking tours to highlights such as Hoffman's Cay Blue Hole. Contact this top crew well in advance as they are much in demand. In 2007, Captain Percy was awarded the Cacique Award for Sports and Leisure, The Bahamas' prestigious award for hospitality and for his contribution to tourism. ⊠ *Great Harbour Cay* ☎ *242/464–4149 cell, 242/367–8119 home.*

SNORKELING

Stingray City

DIVING & SNORKELING | **FAMILY** | A snorkel trip by boat to this spot on Goat Island is a favorite experience of both cruise passengers and anyone staying in Great Harbour Cay. Visitors interact in the pristine, sparkling, and shallow water with southern rays and swimming pigs. ⊠ *Great Harbour Cay* ☎ *242/364–1032 Nassau office* ⊕ *www.stingraybahamas.com.*

Chapter 7

ELEUTHERA AND HARBOUR ISLAND

7

Updated by
Sheri-kae McLeod

● Sights	♛ Restaurants	🏨 Hotels	🛍 Shopping	🍸 Nightlife
★★★★★	★★★☆☆	★★★★☆	★★☆☆☆	★☆☆☆☆

WELCOME TO ELEUTHERA AND HARBOUR ISLAND

TOP REASONS TO GO

★ **Play in pink sand:**
Glorious, soft, pink sand, the ethereal shade of the first blush of dawn, draws beach connoisseurs to Harbour Island. Plenty of pretty pink beaches also dot Eleuthera's east and north coasts.

★ **Ogle island architecture:** Historic homes with storybook gables and gingerbread verandas are the norm on Harbour Island and in Spanish Wells. Picturesque Victorian houses overlook Governor's Harbour in Eleuthera.

★ **Savor soulful sounds:** Nights here rock with the Bahamian group Afro Band, the hip-hop of TaDa, the traditional sound of Jaynell Ingraham, and the calypso of Doctor Seabreeze.

★ **Indulge in alfresco dining:** Harbour Island's intimate restaurants have reinvented regional cuisine. On Eleuthera, Governor's Harbour has a number of laid-back restaurants with memorable menus and magnificent views.

Eleuthera's undeveloped, serene north holds some of the island's most celebrated natural wonders: the Glass Window Bridge, a heart-racing span between 80-foot cliffs often buffeted by a raging Atlantic; the 17th-century Preacher's Cave; and the thrilling waves of Surfer's Beach.

1 Hatchet Bay. "The country's safest harbour" is Hatchet Bay's claim to fame. The naturally protected harbor is a popular place to anchor sailboats and fishing vessels.

2 Governor's Harbour. The administrative capital of Governor's Harbour is a pretty, Victorian town, with a lively harbor that's a frequent stop for mail boats, ferries, and yachts. The town offers upscale restaurants and down-home conch cafés, boutique inns, and inexpensive apartments.

3 Rock Sound and South Eleuthera. Rock Sound, the original capital of Eleuthera, is a quaint seaside settlement with 19th-century homes. Thirty miles away, yachties stop at Cape Eleuthera peninsula for a few nights of luxury in elegant townhouses. Environmentalists also come here from around the world to learn about the self-sustaining Island School.

4 Harbour Island. Dunmore Town, the first capital of The Bahamas, has historic Loyalist houses, fronted by white picket fences, some with cutouts of pineapples and boats, festooned with red bougainvillea and tumbling purple morning glories. Luxurious inns, renowned restaurants, and the magnificent pink beach attract celebrities.

5 Spanish Wells. A quaint town of tidy clapboard white houses is on windswept St. George's Cay, a destination for those who don't want to bump elbows with other tourists. Idyllic white- and pink-sand beaches are the main attractions.

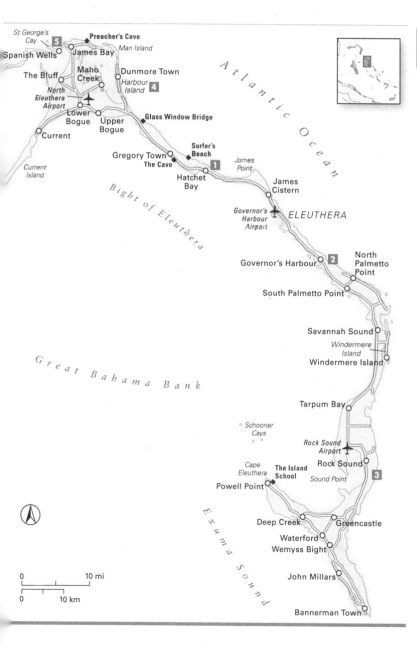

St George's Cay
Preacher's Cave
5
Spanish Wells
James Bay
Man Island
The Bluff
Maho Creek
Dunmore Town
North Eleuthera Airport
Harbour Island
4
Lower Bogue
Upper Bogue
Glass Window Bridge
Current
Gregory Town
The Cave
Surfer's Beach
1
James Point
Hatchet Bay
James Cistern
Current Island
Governor's Harbour Airport
ELEUTHERA
Bight of Eleuthera
Governor's Harbour
2
North Palmetto Point
South Palmetto Point
Savannah Sound
Windermere Island
Windermere Island
Great Bahama Bank
Tarpum Bay
Schooner Cays
Rock Sound Airport
Rock Sound
Cape Eleuthera
The Island School
Sound Point
3
Powell Point
Deep Creek
Greencastle
Waterford
Wemyss Bight
John Millars
Atlantic Ocean
Exuma Sound
Bannerman Town

0   10 mi
0   10 km

You haven't experienced a real escape until you've vacationed in Eleuthera. Simple luxury resorts are the norm, deserted expanses of white- or pink-sand beaches are your playground, and islanders are genuinely friendly. Seclusion, sun, and starry skies are abundant here.

Eleuthera was founded in 1648 by a British group fleeing religious persecution; the name is taken from the Greek word for freedom. These settlers, who called themselves the Eleutheran Adventurers, gave The Bahamas its first written constitution. "Adventurers" has taken on new meaning as a clarion call to sailors, tourists, and, more recently, retirees looking for adventures of their own.

Largely undeveloped rolling green hills and untrammeled sandy coves, along with sleepy 19th-century towns, offer an authentic Bahamas experience that is quickly disappearing. Try not to notice the ubiquitous HG Christie and Sotheby's "For Sale" signs unless, of course, you're so smitten you want to stay. Rent a car—or even better, an SUV—for washboard back roads, and explore the island's secluded beaches and sandy coves fringing turquoise and aqua water that rivals anything in the Caribbean. The island is among the prettiest in The Bahamas, with gentle hills, unspoiled "bush" (backwoods), and gardens of tumbling purple lantana and sky-blue plumbago. Hotels and inns are painted in the shades of Bahamian bays and sunset, which is best watched from the comfort of verandas and seaside decks.

If you're looking for all of this and a bit more action, ferry over to Harbour Island, Eleuthera's chic neighbor. With its uninterrupted three-mile pink-sand beach, top-notch dining, and sumptuous inns, the island has long been a favorite hideaway for jet-setters and celebrities. For splendid beaches with few, if any, tourists head to Spanish Wells, a quiet, secluded settlement located on St. George's Cay, approximately 500 meters off the northern tip of Eleuthera. Eleuthera and Harbour Island beaches are some of the best in the world, thanks to their pristine beauty and dazzling variety.

Eleuthera, at the center of The Bahamas chain, is a narrow, 110-mile island. The fierce, deep-blue Atlantic is to the east, and the usually placid azure and teal shallows of the Bight of Eleuthera and the Great Bahama Bank are to the west. Eleuthera's mainland holds the majority of the island's residents, about 8,000. The rest of the 3,000 residents are split between three-mile Harbour Island, one mile off Eleuthera's northeast coast, and two-mile Spanish Wells, one mile off Eleuthera's northern coast. The island is 200 miles east of Florida and 50 miles east of Nassau.

Planning

When to Go

High tourist season in Eleuthera runs from December through April. Low temperatures might dip into the 60s, and the water can be chilly. Bring a sweater and a jacket, especially if you plan on boating. Expect to pay higher rates for rooms, boat rentals, and airfare during this time. For the cheapest hotel rates and some of the best deals on water-sports packages, visit in summer or fall, when the ocean is generally calm and warm. Be aware, however, that hurricane season runs June through November, with the highest risk of storms from August to October. During this time weather can be steamy and rainy.

The liveliest times to visit Eleuthera are when island-wide festivals and celebrations are held, like the annual Junkanoo celebration during Christmas, the Pineapple Festival and Deep Creek Conch Fest in June, and the Rock Sound Homecoming during Easter. Reserve hotel rooms early.

FESTIVALS

Deep Creek Conch Fest
FESTIVALS | This festival celebrating Deep Creek's cultural heritage, featuring live Rake 'n' Scrape performances, takes place in June in Rock Sound. ⊠ *Rock Sound.*

Junkanoo
FESTIVALS | This annual celebration happens in Rock Sound and on Harbour Island on December 26. Celebrations start around 7 pm. ⊠ *Rock Sound.*

North Eleuthera/Harbour Island Sailing Regatta
FESTIVALS | Each October this regatta provides five days of exciting competition of Bahamian Class A, B, and C boats. Onshore activities based on Harbour Island include live bands, Bahamian

music, cultural shows, food, and drink. ⊠ *Dunmore Town.*

Pineapple Fest
FESTIVALS | Pineapple Fest was started in 1988 as a way to celebrate the many pineapple farmers on the island. The event is held every Labor Day in The Bahamas (the first Friday in June) and features activities like pineapple-eating contests, pineapple-cooking contests, and even sporting events involving pineapple. ⊠ *Gregory Town.*

Getting Here and Around

AIR

Eleuthera has three airports: **North Eleuthera (ELH),** mid-island **Governor's Harbour (GHB),** and **Rock Sound International (RSD)** in the south. Taxis usually wait for scheduled flights at the airports. Taxi service for two people from North Eleuthera Airport to Gregory Town is around $60 ($80 from Governor's Harbour Airport); from Governor's Harbour Airport to Pineapple Fields, $50; and from Rock Sound Airport to Cape Eleuthera, $75. Visitors going to Harbour Island and Spanish Wells should fly into North Eleuthera Airport.

CONTACTS Governor's Harbour Airport.
⊠ *Governor's Harbour* ☎ *242/332–3270.*
North Eleuthera Airport. ☎ *242/335–1242.*
Rock Sound Airport. ⊠ *Rock Sound*
☎ *242/334–2125.*

BOAT AND FERRY

Mail boats leave from Nassau's Potter's Cay for the five-hour trip to Eleuthera. One-way tickets cost $30. M/V *Current Pride* sails to Current Island, Hatchet Bay, the Bluff, and Long Bay Cay on Thursday, returning Tuesday to Nassau. M/V *Bahamas Daybreak III* leaves Nassau on Monday and Wednesday for Harbour Island, Rock Sound, and Davis Harbour, returning to Nassau Tuesday and Sunday. The *Eleuthera Express* sails for Governor's Harbour, Rock Sound, Spanish

Wells, and Harbour Island on Monday and Thursday, returning to Nassau on Tuesday and Sunday. Contact the **Dockmaster's Office. Bahamas Ferries'** high-speed catamarans connect Nassau to Harbour Island, Governor's Harbour, and Spanish Wells. The trip takes three hours and costs $250 round-trip.

CONTACTS Bahamas Ferries. ☎ 242/323–2166 ⊕ bahamasferries.com. **Dockmaster's Office.** ☎ 242/393–1064.

CAR

Rent a car if you plan to travel around Eleuthera. You can drive north to south in about three hours. Daily rentals run about $70. Request a four-wheel drive if you plan to visit Preacher's Cave or Surfer's Beach.

CONTACTS Big E's Eleuthera Car Rentals. ✉ Governor's Harbour ☎ 242/818–1522 ⊕ bigescarrental.com. **Central Auto Rentals.** ☎ 242/470–8513 ⊕ careleuthera. com. **Eleuthera Car Rental.** ☎ 242/470–0844 ⊕ eleutheracars.com. **Major's Car Rental & Taxi Service.** ☎ 242/359–7163. **Turnquest Car Rentals.** ✉ Governor's Harbour ☎ 242/359–7575, 242/470–4350 ⊕ turnquestcarrentals.com. **Taylor and Taylor Car Rentals.** ✉ North Palmetto Point, Governor's Harbour ☎ 242/332–1665 ⊕ eleutheracar.com.

GOLF CART

You'll want a golf cart if you spend more than a couple of days on Harbour Island or in Spanish Wells. Four-seater carts start at about $60 a day. Carts can be rented at most hotels and at the docks.

CONTACTS Dunmore Rentals. ✉ Bay St., Dunmore Town ☎ 242/557–7897 ⊕ dunmorerentals.com. **Harbourside Rentals.** ✉ 5th St., Spanish Wells ☎ 242/333–5022 ⊕ harboursidebahamas.com. **Major's Golf Cart Rentals.** ✉ Princess St., Dunmore Town ☎ 242/470–5064, 242/465–7329 ⊕ majorsrentals.com. **Ross Golf Cart Rentals.** ✉ Colebrook St., Dunmore Town ☎ 242/333–2122 ⊕ rossgolfcartrentals. com. **Kiplin Golf Cart Rentals.** ✉ Colebrook

St., Dunmore Town ☎ 242/470–2400 ⊕ kiplinrentals.com.

TAXI

Taxis are almost always waiting at airports and at the North Eleuthera and Harbour Island water-taxi docks. Your hotel can call a taxi for you; let them know a half hour before you need it.

CONTACTS Arthur Nixon Taxi and Rentals. ✉ Governor's Harbour ☎ 242/359–7879. **Fine Thread Taxi Service.** ☎ 242/359–7780, 242/436–5989. **J.Q. Taxi Service.** ☎ 242/553–6781. **Royal Williams Taxi Service.** ✉ Spanish Wells ☎ 242/335–1175.

Hotels

Harbour Island, more than any other Family Island, is where the cognoscenti come to bask in luxurious inns and atmospheric small resorts. Follow the celebrities to $600-a-night cottages with views of the beach or to elegant rooms in Dunmore Town. Eleuthera offers elegant, intimate, beach-adjacent resorts pleasantly empty of crowds. You'll also find plenty of friendly, tidy, and affordable inns, a few on the beach, for around $200 a night. For urbanites who want all-out American luxury, there are modern town houses with stainless-steel appliances and granite in the kitchens and bedrooms for the entire family. Whether you spend a lot or a little the staff on this friendly island will know your name after a day. Many hotels are closed in September and October.

Restaurants

Don't let the outdoor dining on rustic wood tables fool you—Harbour Island and Eleuthera offer sophisticated cuisine that rivals that of any restaurant in Nassau. Although the place is usually casual and you never have to wear a tie, the food is taken seriously. Island specialties such as cracked conch, barbecued pork or chicken, and the succulent Bahamian lobster (known locally as crawfish) still abound, but you'll also find cappuccinos, steak, and lobster ravioli. For delicious conch, stop by one of the seafood restaurants on Bay Street, north of the Government Dock, where you can eat fresh conch salad on decks next to the water.

Most eateries are closed Sunday in addition to seasonal closure during the hurricane season. During the months of September and October, call before visiting restaurants on the island. Many restaurants have entertainment on regular nights, so plan your dining schedule accordingly.

⇨ *Restaurant prices are based on the median main course price at dinner, excluding gratuity, typically 15%, which is often automatically added to the bill. Hotel prices are for two people in a standard double room in high season, excluding service and 10% tax. Restaurant and hotel reviews have been shortened. For full information, visit Fodors.com.*

What It Costs in U.S. Dollars

$	$$	$$$	$$$$
RESTAURANTS			
under $20	$20–$30	$31–$40	over $40
HOTELS			
under $200	$200–$300	$301–$400	over $400

Visitor Information

CONTACTS Eleuthera Tourist Office. ✉ *Governor's Harbour* ☎ *242/332–2142, 242/302–2000* ⊕ *bahamas.com.* **Harbour Island Tourist Office.** ✉ *Dunmore St.* ☎ *242/333–2621, 819/489–1293* ⊕ *officialharbourisland.com.* **Bahama Out Islands Promotion Board.** ✉ *Nassau* ⊕ *myoutislands.com.*

Gregory Town and North Eleuthera

Gregory Town is a sleepy community, except on Friday night when people are looking for music, whether that's speakers blasting reggae or a local musician playing Rake 'n' Scrape at a roadside barbecue. There's action, too, at Surfer's Beach, where summer and winter waves bring surfers from around the world. The famous Glass Window Bridge is north of town, and Preacher's Cave, the landing of the earliest settlers, is on the northern tip of the island. Gregory Town is home to a little more than 600 people, residing in small houses on a hillside that slides down to the sea. The town's annual Pineapple Festival is held on Bahamian Labor Day weekend, at the beginning of June, with live music continuing into the wee hours.

GETTING HERE AND AROUND

The North Eleuthera Airport is closer to Gregory Town hotels than the airport in Governor's Harbour. The taxi fare from the North Eleuthera Airport to Gregory Town is around $60 for two people. Rent a car at the airport unless you plan to stay at a resort for most of your visit.

⊙ Sights

★ Glass Window Bridge

NATURE SIGHT | At a narrow point of the island a few miles north of Gregory Town, a slender concrete bridge links two sea-battered bluffs that separate the island's Central and North Districts. Sailors going south in the waters between New Providence and Eleuthera supposedly named this area the Glass Window because they could see through the natural limestone arch to the Atlantic on the other side. Stop to watch the northeasterly deep-azure Atlantic swirl together under the bridge with the southwesterly turquoise Bight of Eleuthera, producing

Great Itineraries

If You Have 3 Days

Fly into North Eleuthera and take the ferry to **Harbour Island**. Base yourself at a hotel near the famous three-mile pink-sand beach or in historic Dunmore Town. Relax on the beach and have lunch at an ocean-side restaurant. Stroll through **Dunmore Town** in the afternoon, stopping at crafts stands and fashionable shops, admiring colonial houses along Bay Street, and visiting historic churches. At night, dine at one of the island's fine restaurants, such as Rock House, Blue Bar at Pink Sands, or Acquapazza. On Day 2, go scuba diving or snorkeling, or hire a guide and try to snag a canny bonefish. Visit the conch shacks on Bay Street for a low-key beachside dinner. On Day 3, get some last-minute color on the beach or some in-room spa pampering; stop by Daddy D's or Gusty's for late-night music.

If You Have 5 Days

Head back to **Eleuthera** for the next two days. Rent a car at the North Eleuthera Airport (reserve in advance) and drive south past the **Glass Window Bridge**, where you can stand in one spot and see the brilliantly blue and often fierce Atlantic Ocean to the east and the placid Bight of Eleuthera to the west. Continue to **Governor's Harbour**, the island's largest town, and grab lunch at Tippy's or the Buccaneer Club, two of the most popular restaurants in town. Stay at one of the beach resorts and enjoy the incredible water views. Head into town if you're looking for some nightlife or dining options.

If You Have 7 Days

On your last two days, drive back to **North Eleuthera**, base yourself at the Daddy Joe's inn, where you can enjoy great food and live music at the restaurant. Gaulding's Cay Beach is also just across the street. On your final day take the ferry to **Spanish Wells**, where you can rent a golf cart and spend a half day exploring the tiny town and relaxing on a white-sand beach with no tourists. Or stay put and explore Surfer's Beach nearby.

a brilliant aquamarine froth. Artist Winslow Homer found the site stunning and painted *Glass Window* in 1885. The original stone arch, created by Mother Nature, was destroyed by a combination of storms in the 1940s. Subsequent concrete bridges were destroyed by hurricanes in 1992 and 1999. Drive carefully because there is frequent maintenance work going on. ⊠ *Queen's Hwy., North of Gregory Town, Gregory Town.*

Preacher's Cave

NATURE SIGHT | At the island's northern tip, this cave is where the Eleutheran Adventurers (the island's founders) took refuge and held services when their ship wrecked in 1648. Note the original stone altar inside the cave, built by Captain William Sayle in the 1600s. Across from the cave is a long succession of deserted pink-sand beaches. ⊠ *North Eleuthera* ✛ *Follow Queen's Hwy. to T-intersection at north end of island. Turn right and follow signs to cave.*

The Queen's Baths

NATURE SIGHT | Much like natural hot tubs or "moon pools" (as the locals call them), the Queen's Baths are a warm collection of tidal pools that were formed from the erosion of nearby rocks. The clear, dark-blue waters of the Atlantic Ocean, which fill the pools, are warmed by the Bahamian sun, providing a warm and calming alternative to a crowded and sometimes chilly beach. The best time to visit the pools is during low and medium tides, so be sure to check before going to take a dip. Wear hard-bottom shoes to avoid slipping on rocks. ⊠ *Queen's Hwy., Gregory Town* ✛ *Located between the Glass Window Bridge and Daddy Joe's restaurant. A 'Queen's Bath' sign marks the entrance.*

★ **Sapphire Blue Hole**
NATURE SIGHT | This natural sinkhole located at the northern tip of Eleuthera is a popular spot for divers in the know. The water is an unbelievably bright turquoise but clear enough that you can see straight to the bottom. Though the hole doesn't look deep, it's about 30 feet. Note that because this is a natural attraction, Sapphire Blue Hole is surrounded by rocks, so be sure to wear comfortable shoes. There's no ladder to climb out of the water (only a rope), so this isn't recommended for young children or those who aren't physically fit. ⊠ *North Eleuthera* ✛ *2 min west of Preacher's Cave.*

 Beaches

★ **Ben Bay Beach**
BEACH | The horseshoe-shape Ben Bay Beach is mostly accessed via boats, but it is one of the top beaches for swimming in Eleuthera. The turquoise waters are clear and almost always calm, with rosy pink sand along its shores. The beach is somewhat hard to find, so don't expect to ever encounter crowds of people here. Take advantage of the seclusion and nap under the palm trees, or go snorkeling along the rocky areas of the cove. **Amenities:** none. **Best for:** solitude; snorkeling; swimming. ⊠ *North Eleuthera* ↪ *If driving, take an SUV or similar vehicle due to road conditions.*

Gaulding Cay Beach
BEACH | Snorkelers and divers will want to spend time at this beach, three miles north of Gregory Town. You'll most likely have the long stretch of white sand and shallow aqua water all to yourself, and it's great for shelling. At low tide, you can walk or swim to Gaulding's Cay, a tiny rock island with a few casuarina trees. There's great snorkeling around the island; you'll see a concentration of sea anemones so spectacular it dazzled even Jacques Cousteau's biologists. **Amenities:** none. **Best for:** snorkeling; sunset. ⊠ *Queen's Hwy., across from Daddy Joe's restaurant, Gregory Town.*

Surfer's Beach
BEACH | This is Gregory Town's claim to fame and one of the few beaches in The Bahamas known for surfing. Serious surfers have gathered here since the 1960s for decent waves from December to April. If you don't have a jeep, you can walk the ¾ mile to this Atlantic-side beach—take a right onto the paved road past the Hatchet Bay silos, just south of Gregory Town. Look for a young crowd sitting around bonfires at night. **Amenities:** water sports. **Best for:** surfing. ⊠ *Queen's Hwy., Gregory Town.*

Tay Bay Beach
BEACH | Steps from historical Preacher's Cave, this beach offers a long expanse of powdery white sand. The area is remote, so you're likely to have the beach to yourself. There are plenty of palmetto trees to relax underneath for a quiet afternoon. Just offshore is Devil's Backbone, where the Eleutheran Adventurers shipwrecked and sought shelter in the cave. **Amenities:** none. **Best for:** solitude; walking. ⊠ *North Eleuthera* ✛ *Follow Queen's Hwy. to T-intersection at north end of island. Turn right and follow signs to Preacher's Cave.*

 Restaurants

Daddy Joe's
$$ | **BAHAMIAN** | Located just south of the Glass Window Bridge, this restaurant serves up what it describes as "Bahamian Soul Food" along with hosting local bands every Sunday. Order conch bites

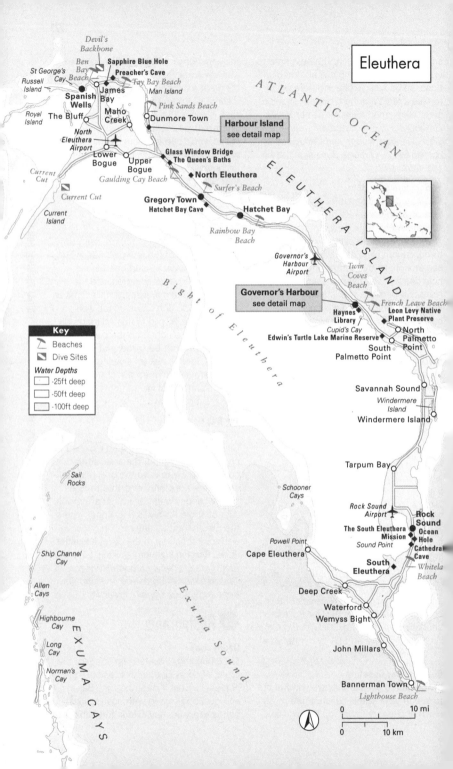

Eleuthera

ATLANTIC OCEAN

ELEUTHERA ISLAND

Devil's Backbone

Ben Bay Beach
Sapphire Blue Hole
Preacher's Cave

St George's Cay
Russell Island

Royal Island

Spanish Wells
James Bay
Maho Creek
The Bluff

Tay Bay Beach
Man Island

Pink Sands Beach
Dunmore Town

Harbour Island
see detail map

North Eleuthera Airport

Lower Bogue
Upper Bogue
Gaulding Cay Beach

Glass Window Bridge
The Queen's Baths
◆ North Eleuthera

Current Cut

Current Island

Gregory Town
Hatchet Bay Cave
Surfer's Beach

Hatchet Bay

Rainbow Bay Beach

Bight of Eleuthera

Governor's Harbour Airport

Twin Coves Beach

Governor's Harbour
see detail map

French Leave Beach

Leon Levy Native Plant Preserve

Haynes Library
Cupid's Cay
Edwin's Turtle Lake Marine Reserve ◆

○ North Palmetto Point

South Palmetto Point

Savannah Sound

Windermere Island
Windermere Island

Key

⌐ Beaches
◣ Dive Sites

Water Depths
⬚ -25ft deep
⬚ -50ft deep
⬚ -100ft deep

Sail Rocks

Schooner Cays

Tarpum Bay

Rock Sound Airport

Rock Sound
The South Eleuthera Mission
Sound Point

Ocean Hole
Cathedral Cave

Whitela Beach

South Eleuthera ◆

Ship Channel Cay

Powell Point
Cape Eleuthera

Allen Cays

Deep Creek
Waterford
Wemyss Bight

Highbourne Cay

Exuma Sound

Long Cay

John Millars

Norman's Cay

E X U M A   C A Y S

Bannerman Town
Lighthouse Beach

0 ___ 10 mi

0 ___ 10 km

as a starter to complement the long list of tropical concoctions, including the aptly named "Da Glass Window." In addition to wings and burgers, Daddy Joe's also offers grilled options like fresh seafood and chicken. **Known for:** taco Tuesday with drink special; famous loaded Daddy Joe's burger; warm and friendly staff. $ *Average main: $28* ✉ *Queen's Hwy., Gregory Town* ☎ *242/335–5688* ⊕ *facebook.com/mydaddyjoes* ⊙ *Closed Wed. and Sept.*

★ Freedom Restaurant & Sushi Bar

$$$ | EUROPEAN | This recently renovated, window-lined restaurant serves three meals a day, combining classic Asian dishes with fresh Bahamian fare. An extensive cocktail list from the Freedom Bar— which features a stunning view of the hilltop pool— includes the Glass Window Bridge, with the exquisite landmark of the same name just a short drive away. **Known for:** famous Cove sushi roll; flavorful seafood dishes like stone crab and scallops; variety of vegetarian dishes on the menu. $ *Average main: $38* ✉ *The Cove Eleuthera, Queen's Hwy., Gregory Town* ☎ *242/335–5142 reservations, 866/644-4452* ⊕ *thecoveeleuthera.com* ⊙ *Closed mid-Aug.-Nov.*

Glass Window Bar & Grill

$$ | BAHAMIAN | Just a stone's throw away from one of Eleuthera's most popular natural treasures is this casual, open-air restaurant offering classic Bahamian dishes and stunning views of the sea. Stop here for a cold beer or enjoy one of the special featured dishes, like grilled pineapple or the El Karaka Salad—a signature dish named in honor of the owner's father. **Known for:** delicious wraps filled with lobster, conch, or chicken; secluded beach nearby; fun and friendly vibe. $ *Average main: $30* ✉ *Queen's Hwy., Gregory Town* ✛ *About ½ mile north of Glass Window Bridge, on the left* ☎ *242/422–5277* ⊕ *www.facebook.com/p/Glass-Window-Bar-Grill-100088739455026/* ▭ *No credit cards* ⊙ *Closed mid-Sept.–mid-Nov.*

Pineapple Express

Pineapples remain Eleuthera's most famous product, even though the industry has been greatly reduced since the late 1800s when the island dominated the world's pineapple market. These intensely sweet fruits are still grown on family farms, primarily in northern Eleuthera. Don't miss Gregory Town's Pineapple Festival in June.

Unca Gene's Seafood Restaurant & Bar

$$ | BAHAMIAN | You'll find the most delicious Bahamian meals at Unca Gene's casual, seaside restaurant, as well as delicious burgers and pasta dishes. The restaurant has a homey feel, painted in light blue, with an outside dining patio where guests can enjoy the cool sea breeze while they eat. **Known for:** super-friendly staff; fettuccine Alfredo (shrimp, lobster, conch); generously poured cocktails. $ *Average main: $20* ✉ *Queen's Hwy., Gregory Town* ✛ *Beside Island Made Gift Shop* ☎ *242/335–5060* ⊕ *www.facebook.com/profile.php?id=100064730795030* ⊙ *Closed Sun.*

Hotels

★ The Cove Eleuthera

$$$$ | RESORT | Forty secluded acres studded with scenic beach cottages set the tone for this relaxing island escape; a rocky promontory separates two coves, each with a sandy beach and calm water, perfect for snorkeling. **Pros:** decadent holistic body and beauty treatments at the resort's spa; top-rated amenities; one of the most luxurious places to stay on the island. **Cons:** need a car if you want to do anything outside the property; limited dining options; some lower-budget rooms

lack the privacy of the bungalows and villas. [$] *Rooms from: $650* ✉ *Queen's Hwy., Gregory Town* ✣ *1½ miles north of Gregory Town* ☎ *242/335–5142, 866/644–4452* 🌐 *thecoveeleuthera.com* 🕑 *Closed mid-Aug.–Nov.* 🛏 *29 rooms* 🍴 *No Meals.*

Daddy Joe's

$ | **B&B/INN** | Daddy Joe's is already quite popular among locals of Eleuthera for its delicious food, but traditional Bahamian hospitality and a friendly staff draw visitors to the inn. **Pros:** quiet location; games and activities provided for kids; live entertainment at restaurant on some nights. **Cons:** not many amenities; limited dining options; might be too remote. [$] *Rooms from: $150* ✉ *Queen's Hwy., Gregory Town* ☎ *242/335–5688* 🌐 *facebook.com/mydaddyjoes* 🛏 *15 rooms* 🍴 *No Meals.*

★ Ocean Tally

$$$$ | **B&B/INN** | Set atop a rocky cliff on Whale Point, Ocean Tally is a luxurious bed-and-breakfast surrounded by Eleuthera's natural beauty. **Pros:** well-maintained property; stunning and very private accommodation; friendly and accommodating owners. **Cons:** limited amenities; you'll need to rent a car to go into the town; might be too remote. [$] *Rooms from: $425* ✉ *Whale Point Dr., North Eleuthera, Gregory Town* ☎ *242/359–7676* 🌐 *oceantally.com* 🛏 *3 cottages* 🍴 *Free Breakfast.*

Nightlife

BARS AND PUBS

Champion's Sports Bar and Grill

BARS | For afternoon or nighttime fun in Gregory Town, head to Champion's Bar on Queen's Highway. The bar hosts live bands and parties on weekends, along with karaoke and pool tables. There's a restaurant serving local Bahamian food and a bar stocked with assorted beers and cocktails. The outdoor tiki bar opens in the afternoon, serving drinks and bar snacks. ✉ *Queen's Hwy., Gregory Town* ☎ *242/335–5026.*

Shopping

CRAFTS

★ Island Made Gift Shop

CRAFTS | This shop, run by Pam and Greg Thompson, is a good place to shop for Bahamian arts and crafts, including Androsia batik (made on Andros Island), driftwood paintings, Abaco ceramics, neem products, and prints. Look for the old foam buoys that have been carved and painted into fun faces. ✉ *Queen's Hwy., Gregory Town* ☎ *242/335–5369* 🌐 *www.facebook.com/IslandMadeGiftShop* 🕑 *Closed Sun.*

Activities

ISLAND TOURS

Arthur Nixon Tours

GUIDED TOURS | Arthur Nixon is one of the most popular tour operators in Eleuthera, offering taxi services, car rentals, and tours of the island. ✉ *Gregory Town* ☎ *242/359–7879* 🎫 *Tours range from $160 to $300 (for two people).*

Freedom Vacation Tours

DRIVING TOURS | Freedom Vacation Tours offers a range of tours throughout Eleuthera, Harbour Island, and Spanish Wells. They also provide accommodations and dining. ✉ *Gregory Town* ☎ *242/335–1700, 242/324–6884* 🌐 *freedomvacationtours.com* 🎫 *Tours range from $300 to $800 for up to five persons.*

SCUBA DIVING AND SNORKELING

Foster Neilly

SCUBA DIVING | Foster Neilly offers snorkeling and diving tours to Current Cut, which isn't recommended without a guide due to its fast (and sometimes dangerous) current. Foster also offers boat trips for those who want to explore further. Call a few days in advance. ✉ *End of Current road, Current* ☎ *242/448–1609* *cell, 242/332–1745* 🎫 *Tours start at $150; boat trips start at $200.*

SURFING

Rebecca's Beach Shop

SURFING | In Gregory Town, stop by Rebecca's Beach Shop, a general store, crafts shop, and, most important, surf shop, where local surf guru "Ponytail Pete" rents surfboards, fishing and snorkel gear, and more. A chalkboard lists surf conditions and tidal reports. He also gives surf lessons. ✉ *Queen's Hwy., Gregory Town* ☎ *242/335–5436.*

Hatchet Bay

"The country's safest harbour," Hatchet Bay (also known as "Alice Town"), which has one of mid-Eleuthera's few marinas, is a good place to find a fishing guide and friendly locals or to anchor sailboats and fishing vessels when storms are coming. Take note of the town's side roads, which have such colorful names as Lazy Road, Happy Hill Road, and Smile Lane. Just south of town, The Rainbow Inn and restaurant is the hub of activity for this stretch of the island. Don't miss James Cistern, a seaside settlement to the south.

GETTING HERE AND AROUND

Hatchet Bay is equidistant between the Governor's Harbour and North Eleuthera airports. The taxi fare from either airport is about $60 for two people. It's best to rent a car at the airport unless you plan to stay at a resort for most of your visit.

Sights

Hatchet Bay Cave

NATURE SIGHT | North of Hatchet Bay lies a subterranean, bat-populated tunnel complete with stalagmites and stalactites. Pirates supposedly once used it to hide their loot. An underground path leads for more than a mile to the sea, ending in a lofty, cathedral-like cavern. Within its depths, fish swim in total darkness. The adventurous may wish to explore this area with a flashlight (follow the length of guide string along the cavern's floor), but it's best to inquire first at one of the local stores or The Rainbow Inn for a guide. ✉ *Queen's Hwy., Hatchet Bay* ✥ *2 miles north of Hatchet Bay, turn left at sign for "Hatchet Bay Caves".*

Beaches

★ **Rainbow Bay Beach**

BEACH | Located at Rainbow Cay to the south of Hatchet Bay, this small, pristine beach with miles of powdery, baby-pink sand is one of the most visited in the area. The water is calm and clear, with an abundance of marine life that make the beach a great snorkeling or fishing spot. Relax under the deck or one of the many thatch umbrellas with picnic tables along the beach, or take advantage of the kayaks that are available for use. **Amenities:** water sports; parking. **Best for:** snorkeling; swimming. ✉ *Wandering Shore Dr, off Queen's Hwy., Hatchet Bay.*

Restaurants

The Front Porch

$$$$ | **SEAFOOD** | This little roadside restaurant features a beautiful view of the bay, particularly at sunset when the orange horizon is freckled with the silhouettes of moored sailboats. The menu is island-inspired European cuisine and always includes fresh seafood. **Known for:** delicious local crawfish tail; stunning sunset views from deck; varied seafood platter with large portions. [$] *Average main: $42* ✉ *Queen's Hwy., Hatchet Bay* ☎ *242/335–0727.*

★ **The Rainbow Room**

$$$ | **EUROPEAN** | With a classy but no-fuss aura and exhibition windows that face gorgeous sunsets, this restaurant is well known for its steaks, which are flown in daily, and fresh seafood. Guests have 180-degree views of the ocean from the screened patio or dining room. **Known for:** great local desserts like guava or pineapple cheesecake; popular Eluetheran pizza with conch topping; lively atmosphere. [$] *Average main: $37* ✉ *Queen's Hwy., Hatchet Bay* ✣ *2½ miles south of Hatchet Bay* ☎ *242/551–3220* 🌐 *sunsetcoveeleuthera.com.*

Twin Brothers
$$ | **BAHAMIAN** | This brightly painted restaurant is famous for its frozen daiquiris and range of local cuisine. Icy mixes of strawberry and piña colada are swirled into a striking (and delicious) dessert cocktail. **Known for:** popular Miami Vice frozen daiquiri; must-try guava duff dessert; Bahamian specialties like cracked conch and conch salad. [$] *Average main: $25* ✉ *West off Queen's Hwy., Hatchet Bay* ☎ *242/335–0730* 🕒 *Closed Mon.*

Hotels

★ **Sunset Cove**
$$ | **B&B/INN** | Immaculate and generously sized cottages, some octagonal—all with large private porches—have sweeping views of the ocean. **Pros:** snorkeling gear available for borrowing; all rooms and cottages have either kitchenette or full kitchen; gracious and accommodating hosts. **Cons:** not on the beach; not close to a town or shops; not many amenities. [$] *Rooms from: $250* ✉ *Queen's Hwy., Hatchet Bay* ✣ *2½ miles south of Hatchet Bay* ☎ *242/551–3219* 🌐 *sunsetcoveeleuthera.com* 🛏 *11 rooms* 🍴 *No Meals.*

Nightlife

LIVE MUSIC

Doctor Sea Breeze
LIVE MUSIC | The debonair, one-man band Cedric Bethel, better known as Doctor Seabreeze, strums his acoustic guitar while singing island songs at Sunset Cove in Hatchet Bay and Ronnie's Hi-D-Way in Governor's Harbour. Call to find out which day he'll be there. ✉ *Hatchet Bay* 🌐 *www.facebook.com/DrSeabreezeBook/.*

Governor's Harbour

Governor's Harbour, the capital of Eleuthera and home to government offices, is the largest town on the island and one of the prettiest. Victorian-era houses were built on Buccaneer Hill, which overlooks the harbor, bordered on the south by a narrow peninsula and Cupid's Cay at the tip. To fully understand its appeal, you have to settle in for a few days and explore on foot—if you don't mind the steep climb up the narrow lanes. The town is a step into a gentler, more genteel time. Everyone says hello, and entertainment means wading into the harbor to cast a line or taking an art class at the pink 19th-century library. You can see a current movie at the balconied Globe Princess, the only theater on the island, which also serves the best hamburgers in town. Or, swim at the gorgeous beaches on either side of town, which stretch from the pink sands bordering the ocean to the white sands of the Bight of Eleuthera. Home to some of the island's wealthiest residents, who prefer the quiet of Eleuthera to the fashionable party scene of Harbour Island, there are few banks or grocery stores.

GETTING HERE AND AROUND

Fly into Governor's Harbour Airport north of town or arrive by mail boat from Nassau. You will want to rent a car at the airport, even if you plan to stay in Governor's Harbour, to best explore the beaches and restaurants.

Sights

Edwin's Turtle Lake Marine Reserve
NATURE PRESERVE | This 43-acre, deep-blue saltwater lake is the perfect place to see much of The Bahamas' beautiful marine life up close. The marine reserve was established in 1954 by the Burrows

Family to protect the endangered green sea turtles and the other various kinds of fish, lobster, and other marine life that call the lake home. One-hour guided kayak tours are available. You can also rent kayaks and canoes for off-property use. Call to book reservations before visiting. ⊠ *Queen's Hwy., Governor's Harbour* ☎ *242/426–1323, 242/818–7447* ⊕ *edwinsmarinepreserve.com* ⊘ *Closed Sun.*

Haynes Library

LIBRARY | The heart of the community, this 19th-century building has a local book club and offers art classes and Tuesday-morning coffee hours for visitors and residents. The library has a wide selection of books and computers, with gorgeous views of the harbor. ⊠ *Haynes Ave., Governor's Harbour* ☎ *242/332–2877* ⊕ *hayneslibrary.com* ⊘ *Closed weekends.*

Leon Levy Native Plant Preserve

GARDEN | Walk miles of scenic trails in this 25-acre nature preserve located on Banks Road. Funded by the Leon Levy Foundation and operated by the Bahamas National Trust, the preserve serves as an environmental education center with a focus on traditional bush medicine. Follow the boardwalk over a small waterfall and take the path to the Observation Tower to see hundreds of indigenous trees, plants, and wildlife, such as mangroves, five-finger plants, and bullfinches. Group tours are available, or if you'd prefer to tour the preserve on your own, the welcome center will provide you with a map and a plant identification guide. ⊠ *Banks Rd., Governor's Harbour* ☎ *242/332–3831* ⊕ *levypreserve.org* ☞ *$11* ⛁ *levypreserve.org.*

 Beaches

French Leave Beach

BEACH | This stretch of pink sand is home to French Leave Resort. The gorgeous Atlantic-side beach is anchored by

Why Is the Sand Pink?

Contrary to popular belief, pink sand comes primarily from the crushed pink and red shells of microscopic insects called foraminifera, not coral. Foraminifera live on the underside of reefs and the sea floor. After the insects die, the waves smash the shells, which wash ashore along with sand and bits of pink coral. The intensity of the rosy hues depends on the slant of the sun.

fantastic bistros like The Buccaneer Club and Tippy's. The wide expanse, ringed by casuarina trees, is often deserted and makes a great outpost for romantics. **Amenities:** food and drink. **Best for:** solitude; swimming; walking. ⊠ *Banks Rd., Governor's Harbour.*

Twin Coves Beach

BEACH | This unique beach got its name because of its interesting geography: being split into two coves by a narrow sand bridge. Frequent sightings of nurse sharks, lobster, various kinds of fish, rays, and other marine life are what you'll find on either side of the beach. Not many people visit here during the week, so it's the perfect place to relax and go swimming or snorkeling. **Amenities:** parking (free). **Best for:** swimming; snorkeling; solitude. ⊠ *Bank's Rd., Twin Cove, Governor's Harbour.*

🍴 Restaurants

The Buccaneer Club

$$$ | **BAHAMIAN** | On the top of Buccaneer Hill overlooking the town and harbor, this mid-19th-century farmhouse is now a must-try restaurant that serves three meals a day. The outdoor dining area is located under a huge tree, with candlelit

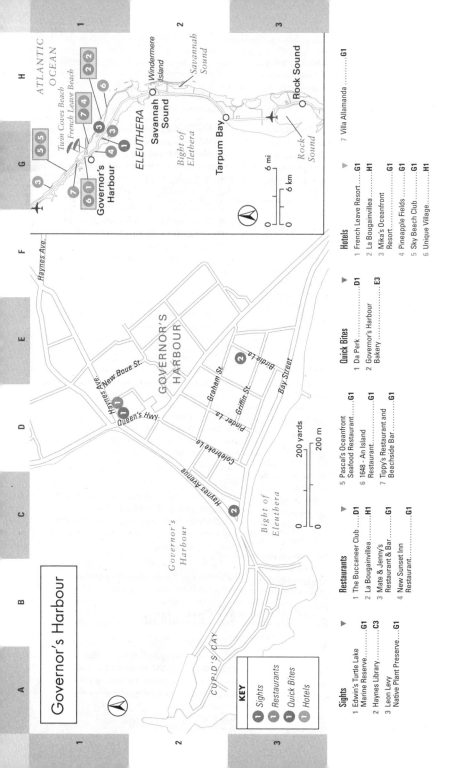

Governor's Harbour

KEY
- ① Sights
- ① Restaurants
- ① Quick Bites
- ① Hotels

Sights ▶
1. Edwin's Turtle Lake Marine Reserve......**G1**
2. Haynes Library......**C3**
3. Leon Levy Native Plant Preserve....**G1**

Restaurants ▶
1. The Buccaneer Club ...**D1**
2. La Bougainvillea **H1**
3. Mate & Jenny's Restaurant & Bar.........**G1**
4. New Sunset Inn Restaurant........**G1**
5. Pascal's Oceanfront Seafood Restaurant......**G1**
6. 1648 - An Island Restaurant.........**G1**
7. Tippy's Restaurant and Beachside Bar.........**G1**

Quick Bites ▶
1. Da Perk **D1**
2. Governor's Harbour Bakery **E3**

Hotels ▶
1. French Leave Resort.....**G1**
2. La Bougainvillea **H1**
3. Mika's Oceanfront Resort.................**G1**
4. Pineapple Fields **G1**
5. Sky Beach Club..........**G1**
6. Unique Village...........**H1**
7. Villa Allamanda **G1**

tables and soft jazz music playing in the background. **Known for:** local specialties such as grouper, conch, and crawfish; scenic dining; live music on Tuesday. [$] *Average main: $35* ✉ *Haynes Ave., Governor's Harbour* ☎ *242/332–2000* ⏲ *Closed Wed. and Sept.–Nov.*

La Bougainvillea

$$ | **ITALIAN** | Enjoy an electric fusion of classic Italian dishes and Bahamian cuisine served at the stunning oceanfront La Bougainvillea property. The resort has a luxurious ambience, but the restaurant is calm and inviting while simultaneously maintaining a fine-dining experience. **Known for:** views of the ocean; live music on Thursday; wood-fired homemade pizza. [$] *Average main: $30* ✉ *North Palmetto Point, Banks Rd., Governor's Harbour* ☎ *242/813–7436* 🌐 *www.labougainvillea.com/the restaurant.html.*

Mate & Jenny's Restaurant & Bar

$$ | **PIZZA** | A few miles south of Governor's Harbour, this casual neighborhood restaurant specializes in pizza but also serves sandwiches, cocktails, and Bahamian favorites. The walls are painted with tropical sunset scenes and decorated with photos and random memorabilia, which add to the restaurant's local flair. **Known for:** conch-topped pizza; lively atmosphere; charming owners. [$] *Average main: $27* ✉ *South Palmetto Point, Governor's Harbour* ☎ *242/332–1504* 💳 *No credit cards* ⏲ *Closed Tues., No lunch Sun.* ☞ *takeout only.*

New Sunset Inn Restaurant

$$ | **BAHAMIAN** | This easily overlooked restaurant is a favorite among Eleuthera natives. While it may not look like it from the outside, New Sunset Inn serves some of the most delicious Bahamian dishes on the island. **Known for:** affordable prices; delicious rum punch; fresh seafood dishes like grouper, conch, and shrimp. [$] *Average main: $25* ✉ *Queen's Hwy., Governor's Harbour* ☎ *242/332–2487.*

★ **Pascal's Oceanfront Seafood Restaurant**

$$$ | **ECLECTIC** | In addition to ocean-view seating from its dining room, Pascal's also features a swim-up bar, perfect for a leisurely lunch. Relax in the infinity-edge pool while you savor a mango daiquiri and cheeseburger and take in the magnificent view of the Atlantic. **Known for:** variety of cocktails; delicious curry grouper dish; Sunday barbecue pool party. [$] *Average main: $37* ✉ *Sky Beach Club, Queen's Hwy., Governor's Harbour* ☎ *242/332–3422* 🌐 *skybeachclub.com/pascals/* ⏲ *Closed Mon.*

★ **1648—An Island Restaurant**

$$$ | **ECLECTIC** | Take in the sunset view as you enjoy a glass of wine and an island-inspired pizza or seafood meal. Located at French Leave Resort, 1648 boasts a sweeping view of the Bight of Eleuthera and its stunning turquoise water. **Known for:** conch rangoons starter; tropical cocktails; poolside dining. [$] *Average main: $38* ✉ *French Leave Resort, Queen's Hwy., Governor's Harbour* ☎ *242/332–3777* 🌐 *frenchleaveresort.com.*

★ **Tippy's Restaurant and Beachside Bar**

$$ | **ECLECTIC** | Despite its barefoot-casual environment (old window shutters used as tabletops, sand in the floor's crevices), the menu at this open-air beach bistro is a sophisticated mix of Bahamian and European cuisine, with items that change daily based on the availability of fresh local products. Expect things like lobster tails, specialty pizza, and fresh fish prepared with some sort of delectable twist. **Known for:** unique menu items like coconut conch tacos and conch chowder; deck overlooking the beach; live music on weekends. [$] *Average main: $29* ✉ *Banks Rd., Governor's Harbour* ☎ *242/332–3331* 🌐 *tippysbeachbar.com* ⏲ *Closed Mon. and Sept. and Oct.*

 Coffee and Quick Bites

★ Da Perk

$ | **CAFÉ** | This tidy restaurant offers free Wi-Fi and is an excellent place to catch up on e-mails over dessert and coffee. The café is located in the middle of town, making it a convenient spot for a quick bite at breakfast or lunch. **Known for:** breakfast bagels; delicious deli sandwiches; gluten-free menu options. $ *Average main: $18* ✉ *Queen's Hwy., Governor's Harbour* ☎ *242/332–2620* ▭ *No credit cards.*

Governor's Harbour Bakery

$ | **BAKERY** | A Governor's Harbour staple since 1989, this bakery serves delicious pastries and breads, baked fresh daily. Stop in to pick up some of the popular Danish coffee cake or sample johnny cakes and hot patties—Bahamian favorites. **Known for:** fresh coconut and cinnamon bread; homemade jam and scones; conch and beef patties. $ *Average main: $10* ✉ *Tucker La., Governor's Harbour* ⊹ *South past Burrow's Grocery Store* ☎ *242/332–2071* ▭ *No credit cards* ⊗ *Closed Sun.*

Hotels

★ French Leave Resort

$$$$ | **RESORT** | This Governor's Harbour resort offers gorgeous waterfront villas, a harbor-view bar and grill, and dozens of other luxurious amenities. **Pros:** high-end appliances, like iPads and flat-screen TVs, in rooms; most villas fully equipped with kitchen and washer/dryer; heated pool with loungers on-site. **Cons:** you'll need a car if you want to explore the island; limited food options; beach is on the other side of the island. $ *Rooms from: $600* ✉ *Queen's Hwy., Governor's Harbour* ☎ *242/332–3778* ⊕ *frenchleaveresort. com* ⊐ *22 villas* ⦿ *No Meals.*

La Bougainvillea

$$ | **RESORT** | This stunning oceanfront boutique hotel provides a tranquil island experience on one of Eleuthera's breathtaking pink-sand beaches, and many of the resort's luxurious suites feature views of the ocean. **Pros:** snorkeling gear and paddleboards available for use; massage therapist on staff; stocked full-service bar on-site. **Cons:** no phone or TV in suites; on-site restaurant can get expensive; not many facilities. $ *Rooms from: $300* ✉ *North Palmetto Point, Banks Rd., Governor's Harbour* ☎ *242/813–7436, 242/813–5355* ⊕ *labougainvillea.com* ⊐ *12 suites* ⦿ *No Meals.*

Mika's Oceanfront Resort

$$ | **RESORT** | Founded by Louisiana native Mika Ann Webb in 2019, Mika's Resort is a small, modern beachfront resort with Caribbean flair and luxury amenities. **Pros:** snorkeling gear and kayaks available for use; spa services offered on-site; all rooms are oceanfront. **Cons:** no swimming pool; no on-site restaurant; limited facilities. $ *Rooms from: $220* ✉ *3 Knowles Dr, Governor's Harbour* ☎ *833/634–0007* ⊕ *mikasresort.com* ⊐ *5 rooms* ⦿ *No Meals.*

Pineapple Fields

$$ | **RESORT** | **FAMILY** | Across the street from a pink-sand Atlantic beach and Tippy's oceanfront bistro, Pineapple Fields is the perfect base for a disappearing act; hole up in one of 32 condo units, each with front and back verandas, a full kitchen, and a living room with pull-out queen sofa. **Pros:** large pool with loungers and umbrellas; location close to airport; stunning secluded beach nearby. **Cons:** not many activities on-site; necessary to drive to town; not oceanfront. $ *Rooms from: $280* ✉ *Banks Rd., Governor's Harbour* ☎ *242/332–2221* ⊕ *pineapplefields. com* ⊗ *Closed mid-Sept.–Oct.* ⊐ *32 rooms* ⦿ *No Meals.*

★ Sky Beach Club

$$$ | **RESORT** | Perched on 22 acres of oceanfront property, this modern resort features three poolside one-bedroom bungalows and four large four-bedroom houses. **Pros:** secluded pink-sand beach;

infinity-edge pool on-site; private chef and masseuse available. **Cons:** need a car to get to town; restaurant and pool often get crowded and noisy; some facilities not well-maintained. $ *Rooms from: $325* ✉ *Queen's Hwy., Governor's Harbour* ☎ *242/422–9597* ⊕ *skybeachclub. com* ⇨ *7 suites* ⦿ *No Meals.*

Unique Village

$ | **HOTEL** | Just south of Governor's Harbour near North Palmetto Point on marvelous pink Poponi Beach, this resort has large, tropical-style rooms with French doors opening to private balconies. **Pros:** on a gorgeous pink beach; great on-site restaurant that serves three meals a day; large pool with gazebo and lounge chairs. **Cons:** not close to any stores or shops; a 10-minute drive to Governor's Harbour; some rooms and amenities are dated. $ *Rooms from: $120* ✉ *North Palmetto Point, Resort Dr., Governor's Harbour* ☎ *877/610–3874* ⊕ *uniquevillageresort. com* ⇨ *14 rooms* ⦿ *No Meals.*

Villa Allamanda

$ | **B&B/INN** | Located on one of Governor's Harbour's most picturesque hilltops in Cigatoo Estates, surrounded by lush forest, is this laid-back and colorful guesthouse. **Pros:** quiet property; close to the beach; stunning views from every room. **Cons:** limited dining options; not many facilities; car needed to access restaurants and sights. $ *Rooms from: $194* ✉ *Cigatoo Estates, Jacaranda Dr., Governor's Harbour* ☎ *242/332–3934* ⊕ *villaallamanda.com* ⇨ *8 rooms* ⦿ *No Meals.*

 Nightlife

BARS AND PUBS

Ronnie's Hi-D-Way

BARS | With a pool table, outdoor basketball court, and large dance floor, Ronnie's is the most popular local hangout in Governor's Harbour. The scene really takes off on Friday and Saturday nights, when the bar hosts a DJ. If you drop in for a drink on the weekend, expect to stay a while for dancing to popular reggae and hip-hop tunes. ✉ *Cupid's Cay, Governor's Harbour* ☎ *242/332– 2307* ⊕ *www.facebook.com/ Ronnies-Hi-D-Way-100054897484302/.*

Secrets VIP Sporting Lounge

BARS | Some of the best DJs on the island start and keep the party going at Secrets VIP until late at night on weekends. The bar has a variety of cocktails and popular Bahamian drinks. You can also get quick bites like wings and conch fritters from the kitchen. ✉ *Queen's Hwy., South Palmetto Point, Governor's Harbour* ☎ *242/332–1155* ⊕ *www.facebook.com/ profile.php?id=100068801642597.*

FISH FRY

Anchor Bay Fish Fry

GATHERING PLACES | After a long week, locals and tourists alike flock to Anchor Bay Fish Fry on Friday night to let loose and de-stress. The menu is simple, with fried fish, barbecue chicken and pork, and local sides. It's the liquor and lively atmosphere that draw the crowd. Fish Fry's signature drink, Rum Bubbas, is a must-try—and is the perfect liquid courage to get you participating in limbo and outdoor dances. ✉ *Bay St., Dunmore Town* ⦿ *Closed Sun.-Thurs.*

 Performing Arts

FILM

Globe Princess Theatre

FILM | The Globe Princess hosts a showing of one current film each night at 8:15 pm. Movies change weekly. The concession serves some of the best hamburgers in town and is open for lunch 11–3 weekdays. ✉ *Queen's Hwy., Governor's Harbour* ☎ *242/332–2735* ⦿ *Closed Thurs.*

236

Shopping

SOUVENIRS

The Blue Seahorse Gift Shop

SOUVENIRS | This unique shop is one of the best places to get cool Bahamian souvenirs. They sell handcrafted items, made from shells, sea glass, and pink sand, all from the beaches on the island. ⊠ *Queen's Hwy., Governor's Harbour* ⊹ *½ mile north of French Leave Resort. Take the first left turn north of the Resort on Queen's Hwy.* ☎ *242/332–2167, 242/470–2358* ⊕ *www.facebook.com/ blueseahorsegiftshop/* ⊗ *Closed Sun.*

Norma's Gift Shop

SOUVENIRS | A range of unique souvenirs, including handcrafted items, fine china, crystal, and leather goods are sold at this tiny, colorful gift shop. You'll also find clothing (mostly T-shirts and beach sandals), jewelry, and fragrances. ⊠ *Haynes Ave., Governor's Harbour* ⊹ *At the corner of Haynes Ave., between Da Perk and First Caribbean Bank* ☎ *242/332–2002* ⊕ *www.facebook.com/normasgiftshop/* ⊗ *Closed Sun.*

Activities

FISHING

Paul Petty

FISHING | Paul is one of the best in the business for guiding anglers through the flats in Governor's Harbour. With his help, you're sure to hook a bonefish. He is also a knowledgeable reef-fishing and deep-sea-fishing guide. ⊠ *Governor's Harbour* ☎ *242/557-7269, 242/332–2963* ⊡ *Bone fishing: half day $500, full day $1000; reef fishing: half day $750, full day $1400.*

Rock Sound and South Eleuthera

One of Eleuthera's largest settlements, the village of **Rock Sound** has a small airport serving the island's southern part. Front Street, the main thoroughfare, runs along the seashore, where fishing boats are tied up. If you walk down the street, you'll eventually come to the whitewashed St. Luke's Anglican Church, a contrast to the deep-blue and green houses nearby with their colorful gardens full of poinsettia, hibiscus, and marigolds. If you pass the church on a Sunday, you'll surely hear fervent hymn singing through the open windows. Rock Sound has the island's largest supermarket shopping center, where locals stock up on groceries and supplies.

The tiny settlement of **Bannerman Town** (population of about 100) is 25 miles from Rock Sound at the island's southern tip, which is punctuated by an old clifftop lighthouse. Rent an SUV if you plan to drive out to it; the rutted sand road is often barely passable. The pink-sand beach here is gorgeous, and on a clear day, you can see The Bahamas' highest point, Mt. Alvernia (elevation 206 feet), on distant Cat Island. The town lies about 30 miles from the residential Cotton Bay Club, past the quiet little fishing villages of Wemyss Bight (named after Lord Gordon Wemyss, a 17th-century Scottish slave owner) and John Millars (population 15), barely touched over the years.

GETTING HERE AND AROUND

Fly into Rock Sound Airport and rent a car. The airport is just north of town, and The Island School is a 22-mile drive south. If you fly into Governor's Harbour, plan to rent a car at the airport—Rock Sound is about 34 miles south. Taxis are available at both airports but can be expensive.

👁 Sights

Cathedral Cave

CAVE | This short but impressive cave is one of South Eleuthera's most unique hidden gems, located behind the ocean hole just south of Rock Sound. A wooden staircase leads down to the relatively small cave formed by karst. Despite the nickname, "spider cave," you won't find many spiders here (even though there are plenty of spider webs). The cave also has high, open ceilings, so there isn't a need for a flashlight. ⊠ *Shermans Hwy.* ⊹ *1 mile south of Ocean Hole. Entrance is across from the Allen Chapel AME Church (white building).*

★ Ocean Hole

NATURE SIGHT | A small inland saltwater lake a mile southeast of Rock Sound is connected by tunnels to the sea. Steps have been cut into the coral on the shore so visitors can climb down to the lake's edge. Bring a piece of bread or some fries and watch the fish emerge for their hors d'oeuvres, swimming their way in from the sea. A local diver estimates the hole is about 75 feet deep. He reports that there are a couple of cars at the bottom, too. Local children learn to swim here. ⊠ *Queen's Hwy., Rock Sound* ⊹ *A Bahamas Heritage sign, across street from church, marks path to Ocean Hole.*

The South Eleuthera Mission

HISTORIC SIGHT | A superb example of a historic Bahamian colonial building, The South Eleuthera Mission, also called Mission House, sits on the Rock Sound waterfront and is open to visitors during regular business hours. Originally built in the 1850s, the reconstruction of a Methodist manse was overseen by volunteer Patricia Rose Maclean, a British designer highly experienced in period restoration. The facility now houses a library and Internet café and offers free tours to visitors who want to view the historical house. They also offer after-school programs for kids, a summer youth

Learning in Paradise 👁

The Island School is a pioneering program for high-school students that's a model of sustainability—students and teachers work together to run a campus where rainwater is captured for use, solar and wind energy are harnessed, food comes from its own small farm, wastewater is filtered and reused to irrigate landscaping, and biofuel is made from cruise ships' restaurant grease to power vehicles and generators. For more information, call ☎ *242/334–8551* or visit ⊕ *islandschool.org.*

program, and other community-based programs. ⊠ *Meridian Hwy., Rock Sound* ☎ *242/225–9870, 242/334–2948* ⊕ *facebook.com/TheSouthEleutheraMission* ⊘ *Closed weekends.*

🏖 Beaches

Whiteland Beach

BEACH | The long, bumpy road is worth driving on just to get to this beautiful secluded beach located on the Atlantic side of the island. Whiteland Beach features an incredible stretch of clear, white sands with beautiful blue waters. The beach is never crowded, so it's a great place to relax privately. There are also reef and rock formations close to the shore, which make it a great place for snorkeling. **Amenities:** none. **Best for:** solitude; snorkeling; walking. ⊠ *Shermans Hwy., Rock Sound* ⊹ *Opposite Charles Bay.*

🍴 Restaurants

★ Frigate's Bar & Grill
$$$ | **BAHAMIAN** | This charming restaurant embodies everything that people love about Eleuthera. The menu offers a range of local favorites, the property is right on the beach (with chairs for lounging after a meal), and the restaurant has an amazing outside deck with a stunning view of Rock Sound's harbor. **Known for:** several platter options to choose from; top-rated cracked conch and conch salad; hearty fisherman's platter with a variety of seafood. [$] *Average main: $36* ✉ *Meridian Hwy., Rock Sound* ☎ *242/334–2778, 242/829-0257* 🌐 *frigatesbarandgrill.com.*

Harbour Pointe Restaurant
$$ | **CARIBBEAN** | Located at Cape Eleuthera Resort and Marina, with a breathtaking sunset view, Harbour Pointe offers Caribbean cuisine in a casual setting. The restaurant features indoor and outdoor seating with panoramic views of the pool, marina, and ocean. **Known for:** must-try grilled fish tacos; vegetarian options on menu; delicious rum punch and other cocktails. [$] *Average main: $30* ✉ *Cape Eleuthera Resort and Marina, Rock Sound* ☎ *242/334–8500* 🌐 *capeeleuthera.com.*

Sammy's Place
$ | **BAHAMIAN** | Owned by Sammy Culmer and managed by his friendly daughter Margarita, Sammy's is a casual restaurant where you can enjoy great service and authentic Eleutheran food. Sammy's serves conch and fish burgers, a baked chicken dinner, and a variety of club sandwiches and salads. **Known for:** delicious conch stew; specialty pizzas on Friday; friendly service. [$] *Average main: $20* ✉ *Albury La., Rock Sound* ☎ *242/334–2121* 🌐 *www.facebook.com/profile.php?id=100063493361480* 💳 *No credit cards.*

Softball: The Sport of the Island

Fast-pitch softball is a ubiquitous sport on Eleuthera. On most any weekend afternoon from March to November, you can find locals playing at Rock Sound or Palmetto baseball parks on the island, known as the Softball Capital of The Bahamas. Eleuthera pitchers and brothers Edney and Edmond Bethel are both players for The Bahamas national team, which has been consistently in the top 10 in the world.

★ Wild Orchids Waterfront Restaurant
$$$ | **BAHAMIAN** | With a menu of delicious Bahamian and American dishes along with stunning views of the ocean, Wild Orchids Waterfront Restaurant provides one of the best dining experiences in Rock Sound. The restaurant is a restored beach house that's more than a century old, and its interior has a traditional Bahamian design that's comforting and familiar. **Known for:** dining deck that's steps away from the beach; wild orchids quesadilla; tasty crab cakes. [$] *Average main: $34* ✉ *William St., Rock Sound* ☎ *242/334–2000* 🌐 *facebook.com/wildorchidseleuthera* 🕒 *Closed Sun.*

🛏 Hotels

★ Cape Eleuthera Resort and Marina
$$ | **RESORT** | **FAMILY** | Nestled between the aquamarine and emerald waters of Rock and Exuma Sounds, gigantic villas have two bright bedrooms, a full bath, and a stainless-steel kitchen, while the beach cottages feature a luxury bathroom and wet bar. **Pros:** beach bonfires with live music on Sunday; professional and friendly staff; gear rental on-site for water and

land excursions (some with fee). **Cons:** isolated from rest of island; need a car to leave resort; on-property restaurant is the only dining option nearby. $ Rooms from: $265 ⊠ Cape Eleuthera Dr., Rock Sound ☎ 242/334–8500, 844/884–1014 ⊕ capeeleuthera.com ⇆ 38 suites ⊚ No Meals.

Northside Inn Cottages

$ | B&B/INN | These quaint cottages are nestled into a hillside with an extraordinary view of the Atlantic. **Pros:** stunning secluded beaches nearby; owner makes delicious homecooked meals for guests; friendly staff. **Cons:** steep walk down to the beach; the area is remote; extra fee for air-conditioning. $ Rooms from: $140 ⊠ Beach Rd., Rock Sound ↔ Turn off Queen's Hwy. in Rock Sound onto Fish St. Turn left at T-intersection onto Northshore Dr, then right at end of pavement ☎ 242/334–2573 ⊕ northsideinneleuthera.com ⊟ No credit cards ⇆ 3 cottages ⊚ No Meals.

Activities

TOURS
Eleuthera Tours

ADVENTURE TOURS | On a guided tour with Eleuthera Tours, you can spend the day at Schooners Cay or go swimming with sea turtles at Turtle Creek. They offer a range of ocean and outdoor adventure tours and provide lunch for an additional cost. ⊠ Meridian Hwy., Rock Sound ☎ 242/557–7381 ⊕ eleutheratours.com ⇆ Tours from $90 per person.

Harbour Island

Harbour Island has often been called the Nantucket of the Caribbean and the most gorgeous of the Family Islands because of its powdery pink-sand beaches (three miles worth!) and its pastel-color clapboard houses with dormer windows, set among white picket fences, narrow lanes, cute shops, and tropical flowers.

The frequent parade of the fashionable and famous, and the chic small inns that accommodate them, have earned the island another name: the St. Bart's of The Bahamas. But residents have long called it Briland, their faster way of pronouncing "Harbour Island." These inhabitants include families who go back generations to the island's early settlement, as well as a growing number of celebrities, supermodels, and tycoons who feel that Briland is the perfect haven to bask in small-town charm against a stunning oceanscape. Some of The Bahamas' most handsome small hotels, each strikingly distinct, are tucked within the island's two square miles. Several are perched on a bluff above the shore, and you can fall asleep with the windows open and listen to the waves lapping the beach. Take a walking tour of the narrow streets of **Dunmore Town,** named after the 18th-century royal governor of The Bahamas, Lord Dunmore, who built a summer home here and laid out the town, which served as the first capital of The Bahamas. It's the only town on Harbour Island, and you can take in all its attractions during a 20-minute stroll.

GETTING HERE AND AROUND
Access Harbour Island via a 10-minute ferry ride from the North Eleuthera dock. Fares are $5 per person in a boat of two or more ($10 if just one person), plus an extra dollar to be dropped off at the private Romora Bay Resort docks and for nighttime rides.

The best way to get around the island is to rent a golf cart or bike or to hire a taxi since climbing the island's hills can be strenuous in the midday heat. Staying in Dunmore Town puts you within walking distance of everything you'll need.

Sights

Haunted House of Harbour Island
HISTORIC HOME | According to local tales, this huge mansion was built by

Harbour Island is a tranquil place to spend some time.

newlyweds in 1945. After an argument one night, both the wife and husband left the house and were never seen again. The table was set for dinner; the food on the stove and all of their clothing and wedding gifts were left behind. The property has been damaged over the years but is still open for visitors. It's a great place to let your imagination run wild. ⊠ *Dunmore Town* ✛ *Located next to the Aquapazza Restaurant. Follow the pink board signs* ☎ *242/333–2621 Harbour Island Tourist Board.*

Lone Tree

NATURE SIGHT | If you stroll to the end of Bay Street and follow the curve to the western edge of the island, you'll find the Lone Tree, one of the most photographed sights on Harbour Island. This enormous piece of driftwood is said to have washed up on shore after a bad storm and anchored itself on the shallow sandbar in a picturesque upright position, providing the perfect photo op for countless tourists. ⊠ *Bay St., Dunmore Town.*

Beaches

★ Pink Sands Beach

BEACH | This is the fairest pink beach of them all: three miles of pale pink sand behind some of the most expensive and posh inns in The Bahamas. Its sand is of such a fine consistency that it's almost as soft as talcum powder, and the gentle slope of the shore makes small waves break hundreds of yards offshore; you have to walk out quite a distance to get past your waist. This is the place to see the rich and famous in designer resort wear or to ride a horse bareback across the sand and into the sea. **Amenities:** food and drink; toilets; showers. **Best for:** partiers; sunrise; swimming; walking. ⊠ *Court Rd., Dunmore Town.*

🍴 Restaurants

Many Harbour Island hotels and restaurants are closed from September through mid-to-late October.

★ Acquapazza

$$$ | ITALIAN | Briland's only Italian restaurant offers a change of pace from the island's standard fare–and a change of scenery, too. It's located at the top of the hill at Romora Bay Resort, with a dockside terrace where you can take in the sunset while sipping one of its exclusively imported Italian wines. **Known for:** excellent grilled octopus; fantastic daiquiris; generous meal portions and fair prices. $ *Average main: $38* ⊠ *Romora Bay Resort & Marina, Colebrooke St., Dunmore Town* ☎ *242/333–3240, 242/359–7133* ⊕ *acquapazzabahamas. net.*

★ Beach Bar at Coral Sands

$$ | ECLECTIC | For lunch with a view, try the oceanfront bar and restaurant at Coral Sands, where executive chef Ken Gomes creates delicious lunch options that go perfectly with a tropical cocktail or a glass of white wine. In addition to seafood options like conch fritters, lobster salad sandwiches, and grilled mahimahi, the restaurant also serves gourmet pizzas and popular local cocktails. **Known for:** shrimp po'boy; special menu for kids; extensive wine list. $ *Average main: $30* ⊠ *Coral Sands Hotel, Chapel St., Dunmore Town* ☎ *242/333–2350* ⊕ *coralsands.com* ⊗ *Closed mid-Aug.–mid-Oct. No dinner.*

★ Blue Bar & Kitchen at Pink Sands

$$$ | ECLECTIC | Blue Bar & Kitchen at Pink Sands is a famed, open-air restaurant and bar featuring blue and white decor that complements the pristine pink sand and clear, blue ocean that the restaurant overlooks. You'll have an unbeatable view while sipping one of their signature cocktails and enjoying conch tacos, a tuna poke bowl, or any of the other island-inspired menu options. **Known**

for: popular "pinky cocktail"; a variety of breakfast options; must-try open-face lamb burger. $ *Average main: $34* ⊠ *Pink Sands Resort, Chapel St., Dunmore Town* ☎ *242/333–2030* ⊕ *pinksandsresort.com* ⊗ *No dinner.*

The Dunmore

$$$$ | CARIBBEAN | Start with a signature cocktail at the handsome mahogany bar before enjoying dinner under the stars on the ocean-view porch. The executive chef creates island-inspired dishes that change seasonally—lobster and grouper meals are always on the menu. **Known for:** homemade ice cream and sorbet; delicious tuna poke bowl; expansive wine selection. $ *Average main: $52* ⊠ *The Dunmore, Gaol La., Dunmore Town* ☎ *242/333–2200* ⊕ *dunmorebeach.com* ⊗ *Closed mid-Aug.–mid-Nov., No dinner Tues.*

★ The Landing

$$$$ | ECLECTIC | You never know which actor or rock star you'll rub elbows with—Richard Gere and Dave Matthews like to dine here—at the Hemingway-esque bar, but none of it matters once you've moved on to the dining room and are under the spell of chef Madelene Pedican, whose dishes soar with a Southeast Asian flair. Standouts include the goat cheese ravioli with shrimp and spicy crab capellini. **Known for:** exceptional ambience and service; spectacular lobster with lemongrass risotto; the most delcious banana upside-down cake, with ice cream. $ *Average main: $50* ⊠ *The Landing, Bay St., Dunmore Town* ☎ *242/333–2707* ⊕ *harbourislandlanding. com* ⊗ *Closed Wed. and mid-Aug.–Nov. No lunch.*

Ma Ruby's Restaurant

$$ | BAHAMIAN | Although you can sample local Bahamian fare at this famous eatery, the star of the menu is the cheeseburger, purportedly the inspiration for Jimmy Buffett's "Cheeseburger in Paradise" song. Maybe it's the rustic charm of the breezy patio or the secret

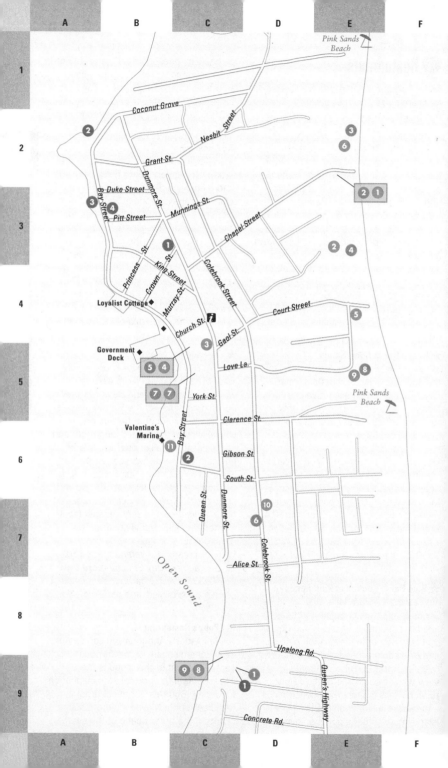

Pink Sands
Beach

Coconut Grove

Nesbit Street

Grant St.

Duke Street

Dunmore St.

Bay Street

Pitt Street

Munnings St.

Chapel Street

King Street

Princess St.

Crown St.

Murray St.

Colebrook Street

Loyalist Cottage ◆

Church St.

Court Street

Gaol St.

Government
Dock

Love La.

York St.

Pink Sands
Beach

Bay Street

Clarence St.

Valentine's
Marina

Gibson St.

South St.

Queen St.

Dunmore St.

Open Sound

Colebrook St.

Alice St.

Upalong Rd.

Queen's Highway

Concrete Rd.

Harbour Island

KEY

- **1** Sights
- **1** Restaurants
- **1** Quick Bites
- **1** Hotels

ATLANTIC OCEAN

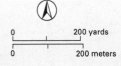

0   200 yards

0   200 meters

Did You Know?

The horses that visitors can ride on Pink Sands Beach are wild Bahamian horses from South Eleuthera, trained by Harbour Island resident Martin Saunders. They roam free on the beach and roll in the surf when they're not carrying riders. One of the horses is infamous for going to the nearby cemetery and turning on the faucet for water.

seasonings on the melt-in-your-mouth patty, but this burger served between thick slices of homemade Bahamian bread is definitely otherworldly. **Known for:** specialties include cracked conch and shrimp; delicious cocktails, including the Bahama Mama; island charm and friendly staff. $ *Average main: $27* ⊠ *Tingum Village Hotel, Colebrooke St., Dunmore Town* ☎ *242/333–2161* ⊕ *tingumvillage.com/ma-rubys-restaurant/.*

★ Rock House Restaurant

$$$$ | MODERN AMERICAN | Splendid harbor views and a transporting Mediterranean-loggia vibe create the perfect backdrop for the continental menu, infused with tropical accents, at the restaurant at the Rock House hotel. Rock House also takes its drinks seriously, with an extensive list showcasing California boutique wines. **Known for:** delicious rum cake dessert, with homemade ice cream; inventive dishes such as lobster and corn agnolotti; extensive wine list. $ *Average main: $48* ⊠ *The Rock House Hotel, Bay St., Dunmore Town* ☎ *242/333–2053* ⊕ *rockhousebahamas.com* ⊗ *Closed mid-Aug.–Nov. and Mon.* ☞ *Lunch for Rock House guests only.*

Runaway Hill Inn Restaurant

$$$$ | CARIBBEAN | Enjoy a moonlit dinner on Runaway Hill's beachfront veranda, with views of the pink-sand beach and turquoise waters along with sounds of the ocean waves. Chef Krishna Higgs specializes in Bahamian cuisine, combining local ingredients with global flavors. **Known for:** stunning ocean views; seafood crepes; signature coconut curry grouper. $ *Average main: $45* ⊠ *Colebrooke St., Dunmore Town* ☎ *242/333–2150* ⊕ *runawayhill.com* ⊗ *Closed mid-July–early Nov.*

Sunsets Restaurant & Bar

$$ | BAHAMIAN | FAMILY | This waterfront pavilion at Romora Bay Resort perfectly frames sunsets over Harbour Island, so be sure to get here in time to snag a good seat for the show. Popular with locals, the restaurant serves mid-priced Bahamian specialties, such as conch fritters, for a casual lunch or dinner. **Known for:** Sunset's burger; pasta pomodoro; top Bahamian musicians play local island music during dinner hours. $ *Average main: $28* ⊠ *Romora Bay Resort and Marina, Dunmore St., Dunmore Town* ☎ *242/333–2325* ⊕ *romorabay.com* ⊗ *Closed Sept.*

☕ Coffee and Quick Bites

Arthur's Bakery

$ | CAFÉ | The friendly café has a quiet garden nook where you can savor your morning brew with an apple turnover, banana pancakes, or any of the daily breakfast offerings. The most popular item to take back is the jalapeño-and-cheese bread. **Known for:** free Wi-Fi for customers; amazing mini-doughnuts; delicious fruit smoothies. $ *Average main: $20* ⊠ *Crown St. and Dunmore St., Dunmore Town* ☎ *242/333–2285* ⊕ *www.facebook.com/p/Arthurs-Bakery-100063728615705/* ▭ *No credit cards* ⊗ *Closed Sun.*

★ Cocoa Coffee House

$ | CAFÉ | Located on the western end of the island with a view of the harbor, this charming coffee shop has lots of space to sit and relax while you enjoy a latte and a sandwich. They also serve nondairy drinks like smoothies and organic juices, plus a variety of breakfast sandwiches, salads, pastries, and acai bowls. **Known for:** tasty croissant sandwiches; affordable prices; fast, free Wi-Fi for guests. $ *Average main: $16* ⊠ *Bay St., Dunmore Town* ☎ *242/333–1323* ⊕ *www.cocoacoffeehouse.com.*

★ Queen Conch

$$ | BAHAMIAN | Four blocks from the ferry dock on Bay Street, with a deck overlooking the water, this small, colorful shack—presided over by Lavaughn Percentie—is renowned for its freshly caught conch salad. They also serve local dishes like conch fritters, conch sandwiches, and stone crab. **Known for:** homemade sauces and dressings; delicious Bahamian cocktails; laid-back atmosphere. $ *Average main: $20* ⌾ *Bay St., Dunmore Town* ☎ *242/333-3811* ⊟ *No credit cards* ⊘ *Closed Sun.*

★ **Sweet Spot Café**

$ | **CAFÉ** | Sweet Spot is the only 100% vegan and vegetarian café on Harbour Island. Their menu includes a variety of healthy favorites like acai bowls, whole-wheat pancakes, and various wraps and salads. **Known for:** delicious vegan lox bagel; great Turkish coffee; a variety of sorbet with unique flavors like Campari grapefruit and strawberry basil. $ *Average main: $16* ⌾ *Bay St., Dunmore Town* ☎ *242/809-0768* ⊕ *www.sweetspotcafe.net.*

 Hotels

Coral Sands Hotel

$$$$ | **RESORT** | **FAMILY** | An elegant yet energetic flair accents this eight-acre oceanfront resort, right on the beach. **Pros:** stunning infinity pool, surrounded by palm trees; tennis courts, gym, and yoga studio on-property; great restaurants on-site. **Cons:** limited food options; expensive on-site dining; some rooms have dated fixtures. $ *Rooms from: $430* ⌾ *Chapel St.* ☎ *242/333-2350, 561/228-1432 within the U.S.* ⊕ *coralsands.com* ⊘ *Closed mid-Aug.–mid-Oct.* ⇨ *40 suites* ‖◎‖ *Free Breakfast.*

The Dunmore

$$$$ | **RESORT** | This charming, retro-glam hotel with private cottages evokes a 1940s club in the tropics—with its mahogany bar, casual yet elegant dining room, and faded paperbacks in the clubhouse library, it's a favorite with the New England yachting set. **Pros:** on the beach with ocean-side bar service; variety of outdoor activities and water sports offered; private terraces and lawn chairs for every cottage. **Cons:** cottages

Heavenly Music

The best live music on Harbour Island is at the Lighthouse Church of God on Chapel Street in Dunmore Town on Sunday morning. Mick Jagger and Lenny Kravitz have dropped by to hear the incredible choir.

too close for real privacy; limited facilities; not all cottages have a view of the ocean. $ *Rooms from: $750* ⌾ *Gaol La., Dunmore Town* ☎ *242/333-2200, 877/891-3100* ⊕ *dunmorebeach.com* ⊘ *Closed Aug. 15–Nov. 15* ⇨ *18 cottages* ‖◎‖ *No Meals.*

Eleven Bahama House

$$$$ | **B&B/INN** | Originally deeded in 1796 and built by Thomas W. Johnson, Briland's first doctor and justice of the peace, this handsome B&B, in a garden filled with bougainvillea, royal poincianas, and hibiscus, thrives thanks to the loving preservation work of genial innkeeper John Hersh. **Pros:** central location in the middle of Dunmore Town; access to a stunning private beach nearby; five-star service. **Cons:** not beachfront; limited hotel services; no on-site restaurant. $ *Rooms from: $700* ⌾ *Dunmore St., Dunmore Town* ☎ *970/315-7625* ⊕ *elevenexperience.com/bahama-house-harbour-island* ⊘ *Closed Aug.–Nov.* ⇨ *11 rooms* ‖◎‖ *Free Breakfast.*

The Landing

$$$ | **B&B/INN** | Sparse white walls and crisp white linens evoke a timeless, understated chic at The Landing, which is acclaimed as much for its singular style as for its superb cuisine. **Pros:** top-notch drinks at the bar; fun games like scrabble and backgammon sets available for use; acclaimed dining. **Cons:** basic amenities; limited hotel services; not on the beach.

[$] *Rooms from: $315* ✉ *Bay St., Dunmore Town* ☎ *242/333–2707* 🌐 *harbourislandlanding.com* 🕒 *Closed mid-Aug.–Nov.* 🛏 *13 rooms* 🍴 *No Meals.*

★ Ocean View Club

$$$ | **RESORT** | The spectacular view of Harbour Island's Pink Sands Beach is the major selling point for this luxury boutique hotel. **Pros:** outstanding restaurant; most rooms are oceanfront; honor system self-service bar. **Cons:** not many facilities; some amenities are outdated; limited dining options. [$] *Rooms from: $395* ✉ *Gaol La., Dunmore Town* ☎ *242/333–2276* 🌐 *ilovetheoceanview.com* 🕒 *Closed mid-Aug–early Nov.* 🛏 *14 rooms* 🍴 *Free Breakfast.*

★ Pink Sands

$$$$ | **RESORT** | Harbour Island's famed beachfront resort has long been praised by celebrities—Martha Stewart, Nicole Kidman, and Brooke Shields, to name a few—and honeymooners alike for its 25 secluded acres of beautiful rambling gardens and private cottages and villas. **Pros:** truly private accommodations; snorkeling equipment, kayaks, and paddleboards available; discreet and well-trained staff. **Cons:** some accommodations are a long walk from the restaurant and beach; cottages don't have kitchens; pool and fitness center are small. [$] *Rooms from: $750* ✉ *Chapel St., Dunmore Town* ☎ *242/333–2030* 🌐 *pinksandsresort.com* 🛏 *29 cottages* 🍴 *No Meals.*

★ Rock House

$$$$ | **HOTEL** | Originally a complex of historic harbor-side buildings, Rock House was designed by the late Wallace Tutt (the builder of Gianni Versace's mansion in Miami) and owner Don Purdy, who attentively orchestrates a pampering, intimate haven for his discriminating international clientele. **Pros:** Harbour Island's most luxurious boutique hotel; many rooms have an enclosed terrace or a private cabana; amazing food (especially dinner) at on-site restaurant. **Cons:** not on the beach; lack of views from some rooms; not ideal for families with young children. [$] *Rooms from: $450* ✉ *Bay St., Dunmore Town* ☎ *305/433–2024, 242/333–2053* 🌐 *rockhousebahamas.com* 🕒 *Closed Aug.–mid-Nov.* 🛏 *10 rooms* 🍴 *Free Breakfast.*

Romora Bay Resort and Marina

$$$ | **RESORT** | **FAMILY** | Pink Adirondack chairs on the dock welcome you to this colorful and casual resort situated on the bay side of the island. **Pros:** new 40-slip marina on-site; water views from every room; private bayside beach. **Cons:** sloping steps from dock to cottages are a hassle for luggage; some room amenities are dated; no breakfast at either restaurant. [$] *Rooms from: $400* ✉ *South end of Dunmore St., Dunmore Town* ☎ *242/333–2325* 🌐 *romorabay.com* 🛏 *15 rooms* 🍴 *No Meals.*

Runaway Hill Inn

$$$$ | **B&B/INN** | This quiet seaside inn on gorgeous, rolling grounds feels far removed from the rest of the island, which is precisely the point. **Pros:** kayaks, paddleboards, and other water sports equipment available; stunning private beach; sand toys and activities available for kids. **Cons:** limited service; not as chic a vibe as nearby resorts; some amenities are dated. [$] *Rooms from: $450* ✉ *Colebrooke St., Dunmore Town* ☎ *242/333–2150, 843/278–1724* 🌐 *runawayhill.com* 🕒 *Closed mid-July.–early Nov.* 🛏 *12 rooms* 🍴 *No Meals.*

Tingum Village Hotel

$$ | **B&B/INN** | **FAMILY** | Each of the rustic cottages on this property, owned by the Percentie family, is named after a different island of The Bahamas. **Pros:** family-friendly larger cottages with kitchenettes; local flavor; Ma Ruby's restaurant on-site. **Cons:** no-frills interior and furnishings; not on beach or harbor; rustic grounds. [$] *Rooms from: $201* ✉ *Colebrooke St., Dunmore Town* ☎ *242/333–2161* 🌐 *tingumvillage.com* 🛏 *30 rooms* 🍴 *Free Breakfast.*

Valentines Resort & Marina
$$$ | **RESORT** | **FAMILY** | With the largest marina on Harbour Island, equipped with 51 slips capable of accommodating yachts up to 160 feet, this resort is ideal if you're a self-sufficient traveler or family that doesn't require many amenities but enjoys spacious condo-style rooms and water-focused activities. **Pros:** modern rooms; luxurious bathrooms come with soaking tubs, glass shower stalls, and premium toiletries; large swimming pool. **Cons:** not oceanfront; impersonal condo-style quality; many rooms lack harbor views. $ *Rooms from: $385* ⊠ *Bay St., Dunmore Town* ☎ *242/333–2142* ⊕ *valentinesresort.com* ⤳ *41 rooms* ⦿ *No Meals.*

 ## Nightlife

BARS AND PUBS
Beyond the Reef
BARS | The party starts at this waterfront bar at sunset and extends well into the evening. Drink specials are available all day, and you can find great Bahamian food at any one of its neighboring vendors. Sunday is karaoke night, and there's live music on weekends. ⊠ *Bay St., Dunmore Town* ☎ *242/699–5141* ⊕ *www.facebook.com/beyondthereef300.*

Gusty's
BARS | Enjoy a brew on the wraparound patio of Gusty's, on Harbour Island's northern point. This lively, rustic hot spot has a few tables, great drinks, and a pool table. On weekends, holidays, and in high season, it's an extremely crowded and happening dance spot, especially after 10 pm. ⊠ *Bay St., Dunmore Town* ☎ *242/333–2165* ⊕ *facebook.com/sunsetsatGustys.*

DANCE CLUBS
★ **Daddy D's**
DANCE CLUBS | This is the place to be on the weekends and holidays in Harbour Island. The dance floor takes off around midnight and is a popular spot for young locals and tourists alike. DJ and owner Devon "Daddy D" Sawyer spins pop music, hip-hop, and reggae tunes late into the night. There are also live bands on select days. Karaoke night is every Tuesday, and they host themed events on some holidays. ⊠ *Dunmore St., Dunmore Town* ☎ *242/359–7006* ⊕ *daddyd.com.*

 ## Shopping

ART GALLERIES
Princess Street Gallery
ART GALLERIES | Princess Street Gallery displays original art by local and internationally renowned artists, as well as a diverse selection of illustrated books, home accessories, and locally made crafts. ⊠ *Princess St., Dunmore Town* ☎ *242/333–2788* ⊕ *harbourislandgallery.com* ☉ *Closed Sun.*

CLOTHING
Blue Rooster
WOMEN'S CLOTHING | This is the place to go for festive party dresses, sexy swimwear, fun accessories, and gifts. ⊠ *King St., Dunmore Town* ☎ *242/333–2240* ☉ *Closed Sun.*

Calico Trading Co.
DEPARTMENT STORE | This high-end boutique offers a variety of designer clothing for men, women, and children. They also sell unique gift items, sandals, and jewelry. ⊠ *Dunmore St., Dunmore Town* ⚓ *beside Arthur's Bakery* ☎ *242/333–3826* ⊕ *www.facebook.com/CalicoTradingCo* ☉ *Closed Sun.*

Dake's Shoppe
DEPARTMENT STORE | Dake's Shoppe sells an exquisite collection of clothing, jewelry, and other accessories, and candles made by local and international designers. ⊠ *Duncane La., Dunmore Town* ⚓ *Intersection of Dunmore St. and King St.* ☎ *242/333–3045* ⊕ *www.dakesshoppe.com* ☉ *Closed Sun. and Sept.–Oct.*

Harbour Island Canvas

CRAFTS | Harbour Island Canvas sells a variety of handmade tote bags, backpacks, duffle bags, wallets, and more. They also have a sister store in Hope Town, Abaco. ⊠ *Murry St., Dunmore Town* ✛ *Corner of Dunmore St. and King St.* ⊕ *www.wsailbags.com/harbourisland* ☾ *Closed Sun.*

The Sugar Mill

WOMEN'S CLOTHING | Owned by former fashion model India Hicks, the cousin of King Charles, this upscale boutique is where you'll find a glamorous selection of resort wear, accessories, and gifts from designers around the world. ⊠ *Bay St., Dunmore Town* ☎ *242/333–3558, 242/470–5694* ⊕ *indiahicks.com/the-sugar-mill* ☾ *Closed Sun.*

GIFTS AND SOUVENIRS

A and A Hidden Treasures

CRAFTS | This family-owned souvenir shop sells authentic handmade Bahamian crafts. You'll find wonderful straw bags, baskets, and hats, as well as conch shell necklaces and bracelets. ⊠ *Colebrook St., Dunmore Town* ☎ *242/470–7141* ⊕ *www.facebook.com/AandAHiddenTreasures/.*

Dilly Dally

SOUVENIRS | Here you can find Bahamian-made jewelry, maps, T-shirts, CDs, and decorations, and other fun island souvenirs. ⊠ *Dunmore St., Dunmore Town* ☎ *242/333–3109* ☾ *Closed Sun.*

Pink Sands Gift Shop

SOUVENIRS | The gift shop at the Pink Sands resort offers a trendy selection of swimwear, accessories, casual clothing, and trinkets. ⊠ *Pink Sands Resort, Chapel St., Dunmore Town* ☎ *242/333–2030* ⊕ *www.pinksandsresort.com.*

 Activities

BIKING

Michael's Cycles

BIKING | Bicycles are a popular way to explore Harbour Island; rent one—or a golf cart, motorboat, or kayak—at Michael's Cycles. ⊠ *Colebrooke St., Dunmore Town* ☎ *242/333–2384, 242/464–0994* ⊕ *michaelscyclesbriland. com* ⚏ *Bike rental $15 per day.*

BOATING AND FISHING

Harbour Island's marine ecosystem provides great opportunities for deep-sea fishing, bonefishing, spearfishing, and spin fishing. The Harbour Island Tourist Office can help organize bone- and bottom-fishing excursions, as can all of the major hotels.

Stuart Cleare

FISHING | Bonefish Stuart is one of Harbour Island's best bonefishing guides. You'll want to call well in advance to arrange a trip with him. ⊠ *Dunmore Town* ☎ *242/333–2072, 242/464–0148* ✉ *bonefishstuart@live.com* ⚏ *$400 for half-day, $800 for full-day trips.*

SCUBA DIVING AND SNORKELING

Valentines Dive Center

SCUBA DIVING | This dive center rents and sells equipment and provides all levels of instruction and certification. They also offer daily snorkeling and dive trips. ⊠ *Valentine's Resort & Marina, Bay St., Dunmore Town* ☎ *242/333–2080* ⊕ *valentinesdive.com* ⚏ *Dives from $140.*

SPAS

The Island Spa

SPAS | For romantic couples' massages in the privacy of your own room, book Jamie at The Island Spa. She makes in-room visits and offers evening beach massages, body scrubs, and aromatherapy. In addition to massages, The Island Spa can also do bridal hair and makeup, manicures, and pedicures—ideal for a destination wedding. ⊠ *Colebrook St., Dunmore Town* ☎ *242/333–3326*

🌐 *theharbourislandspa.com* 💆 *Massages from $125.*

Spanish Wells

Off Eleuthera's northern tip lies St. George's Cay, the site of **Spanish Wells.** The Spaniards used this as a safe harbor during the 17th century while they transferred their riches from the New World to the Old. Residents—the few surnames go back generations—live on the island's eastern end in clapboard houses that look as if they've been transported from a New England fishing village. Descendants of the Eleutheran Adventurers continue to sail these waters and bring back to shore fish and lobster (most of The Bahamas' langoustes are caught here), which are prepared and boxed for export in a factory at the dock. So lucrative is the trade in crawfish, the local term for Bahamian lobsters, that the 1,500 inhabitants may be the most prosperous Family Islanders.

GETTING HERE AND AROUND

You can reach Spanish Wells by taking a five-minute ferry ride ($7) from the Gene's Bay dock in North Eleuthera. You can easily explore the area on foot, or rent a golf cart.

🍴 Restaurants

Budda's Snack Shack

$$ | **BAHAMIAN** | Housed in an old school bus, Budda's Snack Shack is one of the most unique restaurants in all of Eleuthera. The quirky restaurant is a favorite among locals and tourists for its delicious food and laid-back atmosphere. **Known for:** burgers with homemade buns; the popular fried chicken; variety of excellent appetizers. [$] *Average main: $25* ✉ *12th St., Spanish Wells* ☎ *242/333–4111* 🌐 *buddabahamas.com* 🕒 *Closed Sun.*

★ **The Shipyard**

$$$ | **ECLECTIC** | Located on the eastern tip of Spanish Wells, just where the ocean separates the town from North Eleuthera, the waterfront views from here are stunning. The dinner menu includes classic Bahamian meals as well as international dishes like English pub fish-and-chips and cubano pork. **Known for:** fresh catch of the day; famed lobster macaroni and cheese; discounted cocktails during Friday happy hour. [$] *Average main: $36* ✉ *Main St., Spanish Wells* ☎ *242/333–5010* 🌐 *www.facebook.com/shipyardsw.*

★ **Wreckers Restaurant & Bar**

$$$$ | **MEDITERRANEAN** | The scenic views over the harbor, great service, and variety of flavorful Bahamian meals make Wreckers a culinary delight. Choose from the menu of local Bahamian dishes or the specialty flatbread pizzas. **Known for:** amazing truffle mushroom pizza; delicious lobster pasta; freshly caught fish and shrimp. [$] *Average main: $41* ✉ *Spanish Wells Yacht Haven & Resort, South St., Spanish Wells* ☎ *242/333–5222* 🌐 *swyachthaven.com/dining/.*

☕ Coffee and Quick Bites

Papa's Scoops

$ | **CAFÉ** | This small and unassuming shack is where you'll find the best dessert in Spanish Wells. Soft-serve homemade ice cream in a variety of flavors like white chocolate, coconut, and cheesecake keeps visitors coming back every night to Papa's Scoops' front yard. **Known for:** unique ice-cream flavors; delicious daiquiris; variety of ice-cream sandwiches and cookies. [$] *Average main: $8* ✉ *Main St., Spanish Wells* ☎ *242/333–4364* 🌐 *www.facebook.com/papascoops* 💳 *No credit cards.*

Hotels

Howard Beach House

$$$$ | **HOUSE** | **FAMILY** | The private Howard Beach House is the perfect luxury vacation home, especially for large groups. **Pros:** completely private property; accommodating hosts; kayaks, paddleboards, and bicycles available for use. **Cons:** located in a secluded area; limited amenities; expensive housekeeping fee. [$] *Rooms from: $525* ✉ *North Beach, 13th St. N, Spanish Wells* ☎ *519/823–6600* 🌐 *howardbeachhouse.com* 🛏 *4 rooms* 🍴 *No Meals.*

Spanish Wells Yacht Haven & Resort

$$ | **B&B/INN** | In peaceful Spanish Wells is this gorgeous boutique hotel with six guest rooms, each complete with an en suite bathroom and a wet bar, and one villa with a full-service kitchen and dining and lounge areas. **Pros:** all rooms have a terrace with pool and marina views; great on-site restaurant; well-maintained amenities. **Cons:** no beach access; rooms don't have full-service kitchens; not many facilities. [$] *Rooms from: $265* ✉ *South St., Spanish Wells* ☎ *242/333–4255* 🌐 *swyachthaven.com* 🛏 *7 rooms* 🍴 *No Meals.*

Shopping

SOUVENIRS

The Islander Shop

SOUVENIRS | In addition to being the number one place to get fabric and sewing equipment, The Islander Shop also has a variety of arts and crafts, local souvenirs, home decor items, and even clothing and accessories. ✉ *Main St., Spanish Wells* ☎ *242/322–3103* 🌐 *homefabricsltd.com* 🕒 *Closed Sun.*

SPORTING GOODS

Island Custom Rod and Tackle

SPORTING GOODS | This quaint shop has all you need for fishing in Spanish Wells. They sell rods and reels, fishing gaffs, spears, and much more. They also do rod repairs. ✉ *28th St. N, Spanish Wells* ☎ *242/333–4515, 242/470-5322* 🌐 *www.facebook.com/IslandCustomRodAndTackle/.*

Ronald's Service Center

GENERAL STORE | Ron, the friendly and helpful owner, sells boating parts and equipment and also does repairs. You can also get calamari, a variety of fish, and other seafood here. ✉ *3rd St., Spanish Wells* ☎ *242/333-4022* 🕒 *Closed Sun.*

Activities

FISHING

Bahamas Ocean Safaris

FISHING | Jamie, the owner, acts as guide and captain, offering reef-bottom fishing at Dutch Bar, just five miles off the coast of Spanish Wells. He also does scuba-diving tours, reef explorations, and other ocean adventures. ✉ *12th St., Spanish Wells* ☎ *242/470-1930* 🌐 *bahamasoceansafaris.com* 🎟 *half day $1200, full day $2000.*

Spanish Wells Fishing

FISHING | For decades, Spanish Wells Fishing has been offering guided fishing tours, excursions, and other beach adventures in Spanish Wells. ✉ *South St., Spanish Wells* ☎ *242/359–7894* 🌐 *www.spanishwellsfishing.com* 🎟 *Fishing: half day $950, full day $1650.*

ADVENTURE TOURS

Uncle Rob's Great Adventures

BOAT TOURS | Spanish Wells native Rob Pinder provides snorkeling, starfish hunting, and a variety of other boating tours throughout Spanish Wells and Eleuthera Island. ✉ *2nd St., Spanish Wells* ☎ *242/557–7655* 🌐 *www.unclerobsgreatadventures.com* 🎟 *Tours start at $750.*

Chapter 8

THE EXUMAS

8

Updated by
Sheri-kae McLeod

⊙ Sights	🍴 Restaurants	🛏 Hotels	🛍 Shopping	🍸 Nightlife
★★★★☆	★★★★★	★★★★☆	★★☆☆☆	★★★☆☆

WELCOME TO THE EXUMAS

TOP REASONS TO GO

★ **Party like a local:** Hot spots include Santanna's Bar & Grill, Shirley's at The Fish Fry shacks for cracked conch and fresh seafood, and Chat 'N' Chill on Stocking Island for Sunday pig roasts.

★ **Island-hop:** Spend a couple of days boating through the 365 cays (one for every day of the year, as the locals say), and spot iguanas, swimming pigs, and giant starfish.

★ **Enjoy empty beaches:** Empty stretches of bleach-white sand are yours to explore.

★ **Explore the Land and Sea Park:** Snorkel in the 176-square-mile Exuma Cays Land and Sea Park and see queen conchs, starfish, and thriving coral reefs, as well as the endangered hawksbill and threatened green and loggerhead turtles.

Thirty-five miles southeast of Nassau, Allan's Cay sits at the top of The Exumas chain of 365 islands (most uninhabited) that skip like stones for 120 miles south across the Tropic of Cancer. Flanked by the Great Bahama Bank and Exuma Sound, the islands are at the center of The Bahamas. George Town, The Exumas' capital and hub of activity, is on Great Exuma, the mainland and largest island, near the bottom of the chain. Little Exuma is to the south and connected to the mainland by a bridge. Together, these two islands span fifty miles.

1 **Great Exuma.** George Town hosts the 10-day George Town Cruising Regatta and the Bahamian Music and Heritage Festival. Dazzling white beaches and fish fries offering cold Kaliks crop up along the coasts of the entire island. Visitors come to fish, dive, and snorkel. Luxurious resorts and inns offer solitude or hopping beach parties.

2 **Little Exuma.** The Tropic of Cancer runs through the chain's second-largest island, which is duly noted on the steps leading to Tropic of Cancer Beach, one of the most spectacular on the island.

3 **The Exuma Cays.** If you're looking for a true escape, boat over to the cays where celebrities like Johnny Depp own spectacular islands. The renowned Exuma Cays Land and Sea Park toward the chain's north end has gorgeous crystal-clear water and white sand.

Sail Rocks

Ship Channel Cay

Allan's Cays
Leaf Cay
Highbourne Cay
Highbourne

Long Cay

Norman's Cay

Shroud Cay

Hawksbill Cay

Exuma Cays Land and Sea Park

3

Waderick Wells Cay

Halls Pond Cay

O'Brian's Cay

Bells Cay
Fowl Cay

Compass Cay
Joe Cay
Thomas Cay

Sampson Cay
Thunderball
Big Major's Cay
Grotto
Staniel Cay

Harvey's Cays

Black Point

Great Guana Cay

E X U M A   C A Y S

EXUMA SOUND

Little Farmer's Cay
Big Farmer's Cay

Musha Cay
Cave Cay
Rudder Cut Cay

Darby Island
Young Island

Block Cay
Normans Pond Cay

Lee Stocking Island

G R A N D   B A H A M A   B A N K

Brigantine Cays
Barraterre

Rolleville
Steventon
Queen's Hwy.

Great Exuma Island

1

Exuma Int'l Airport

Mt. Thompson

Moss Town

Stocking Island

Jolly Hall
Fish Fry

George Town

Channel Cays

Rolle Town
Tropic of Cancer Beach

2

Forbes Hill

Williams Town

Little Exuma Island

15 mi

15 km

EXUMA CAYS LAND AND SEA PARK

Established by The Bahamas in 1958, and now overseen by the Bahamas National Trust, the 176-square-mile Exuma Cays Land and Sea Park was the first of its kind in the world—an enormous open aquarium with pristine reefs, an abundance of marine life, and sandy cays.

The park appeals to divers, who appreciate the vast underworld of limestone, reefs, drop-offs, blue holes, and caves, as well as the multitude of exotic marine life, including one of The Bahamas' most impressive stands of rare pillar coral. Since the park's waters have essentially never been fished, you can see what the ocean looked like before humans intervened. For landlubbers, there are hiking trails and birding sites; stop in the main office for maps. More than 200 bird species have been spotted here. At Shroud Cay, jump into the strong current that creates a natural whirlpool whipping you around a rocky outcropping to a powdery beach.

BEST TIME TO GO

In summer, the water is as warm as bathwater and usually just as calm. The park has vastly fewer boats than in the busy winter season when the channel becomes a blue highway for a parade of sailing and motor vessels. Bring insect repellent in summer and fall.

BEST WAYS TO EXPLORE

By boat. Boaters can explore the sandy cays and many islets that are little more than sandbars. The water is so clear it's hard to determine depths without a depth finder, so go slow and use your charts. Some routes are only passable at high tide. Get detailed directions before you go into the park, and be sure to stop by the park headquarters on Warderick Wells Cay for more information. Make sure you have a VHF marine radio on the boat or carry a handheld VHF radio so you can call for help or directions.

On foot. The park headquarters has a map of hiking trails—most are on Warderick Wells Cay—that range from two-mile walks to two-hour treks. Wear sturdy shoes because trails are rocky. You'll see red, black, and white mangroves, limestone cliffs, and lots of birds—white-tail tropic birds, green herons, blue herons, black-bellied plovers, royal terns, and ospreys. Take sunscreen and water, and be aware that there's very little shade.

By kayak. Visitors do sometimes take kayak trips from neighboring cays into the park and camp on the beach. The park has kayaks that can be used by boaters moored in the park. As you paddle, look for sea turtles, which might pop up beside you.

Underwater. You have to go underwater to see the best part of the park—spiny lobsters walking on stilt legs on the sandy floor, seagrass waving in the currents, curious hawksbill turtles (critically endangered), solemn-faced groupers,

Wildlife abounds in Exuma Cays Land & Sea Park.

and the coral reefs that support an astonishing range of sea life. Bring your own equipment.

FUN FACT
The park has one native land mammal—the hutia, a critically endangered nocturnal rodent that looks similar to a gray squirrel.

MAKING A DIFFERENCE
How successful has the Exuma Cays Land and Sea Park been? About 74% of the grouper in the northern Exumas' cays come from the park. Crawfish tagged in the park have been found repopulating areas around Cat Island 70 miles away. The concentration of conch inside the park is 31 times higher than the concentration outside. This conservatively provides several million conchs outside the park for fishermen to harvest each year.

A sign marks where to find blow holes at the park.

The Exumas are known for their gorgeous 365 cays. Get the wind and sea salt in your hair as you cruise through the pristine 120-mile chain. Combine the epic scenery with fresh seafood and friendly locals, and you have one of the best vacation destinations in The Bahamas.

There is not a casino or cruise ship in sight on The Exumas, and those who love the remote beauty of the windswept cays keep coming back.

In 1783, Englishman Denys Rolle sent 150 enslaved people to Great Exuma to build a cotton plantation. His son, Lord John Rolle, later gave all of his 5,000 acres to his freed former slaves, and they took the Rolle name.

On Great Exuma and Little Exuma, you'll still find wild cotton and testaments from plantations first established by Loyalists after the American Revolutionary War. Today, The Exumas are known as The Bahamas' onion capital, and many of the 7,000 residents earn a living by fishing and farming, as well as tourism.

The Exumas attract fishermen after bonefish, the feisty breed that prefers the shallow sandy flats that surround these islands. The healthiest coral reefs and fish populations in the country make for excellent diving and snorkeling.

Some cays are no bigger than a sandbar, but you won't stay on the sand long as Perrier-clear waters beckon. Beaches won't be hard to find on the tiny cays; on Great Exuma, look for "Beach Access" signs on Queen's Highway.

Planning

When to Go

High season is December through April when the weather is in the 70s (lows can dip into the 60s). Hotels sell out for events such as the George Town Cruising Regatta and the Bahamian Music and Heritage Festival in February and March, and the National Family Island Regatta in April.

Room rates are cheaper in summer, but fall (late August through November, the height of hurricane season) offers the best deals. The weather during this time can be rainy and hot. Some inns close for September and October.

FESTIVALS

George Town Cruising Regatta
FESTIVALS | The George Town Cruising Regatta in February is 10 days of festivities, including sailing, a conch-blowing contest, dance, food and entertainment, and sports competitions. ✉ *George Town* ☎ *242/554–5351*.

Junkanoo Parade
CULTURAL FESTIVALS | The Exumas' Junkanoo Parade on New Year's Day starts at

7 pm in George Town and normally ends around 10 pm at Regatta Park. Dancing, barbecues, and music happen before and after the parade. ⊠ *George Town.*

Junkanoo Summer Festival
CULTURAL FESTIVALS | The Junkanoo Summer Festival in June and July is held beachside at The Fish Fry in George Town and features local and visiting bands, kids' sunfish sailing, arts and crafts, and boat-building displays. It typically takes place on a Saturday afternoon. ⊠ *George Town.*

National Island Family Regatta
FESTIVALS | One of the oldest and most important traditions in The Bahamas, the National Island Family Regatta brings together sailors and families during the last weekend in April. ⊠ *Elizabeth Harbour, George Town* ⊕ *nationalfamilyislandregatta.com.*

Getting Here and Around

AIR
The airport is 15 miles north of George Town. Taxis wait at the airport for incoming flights; a trip to George Town costs $30 for two people; to William's Town, $80; to February Point, $30; to Emerald Bay, $30; and to Grand Isle, $30. Each additional person is $3. Staniel Cay Airport accepts charter flights and private planes.

CONTACTS Exuma International Airport (GGT). ☎ *242/345–0607, 242/524–9118 Airport Manager* ⊕ *exumaairport.com.*

BOAT AND FERRY
The mail boat M/V *Grand Master* travels from Nassau to George Town on Tuesday and returns to Nassau on Thursday. The trip takes 14 hours and costs $45 each way. M/V *Captain C* leaves Nassau on Tuesday for Staniel Cay, Big Farmer's Cay, and Ragged Island, returning to Nassau on Friday. The trip is 14 hours and costs between $45 and $60. Contact the Dockmaster's Office for more information.

Elvis Ferguson operates a boat taxi from Government Dock to Chat 'N' Chill on the hour throughout the day. If you plan on leaving the island after 6 pm, tell the captain in advance.

CONTACTS Dockmaster's Office. ⊠ *Potter's Cay, Nassau* ☎ *242/393–1064.* **Captain Elvis Ferguson.** ⊠ *Government Dock, George Town* ☎ *242/464–1558* ⊕ *elviswatertaxi.com.*

CAR
If you want to explore Great Exuma and Little Exuma, you'll need to rent a car. Most hotels can arrange car rentals. Car rental costs typically start at around $60 per day.

CONTACTS Airport Car Rentals. ⊠ *George Town Airport, George Town* ☎ *242/345–0090, 242/225–4267* ⊕ *exumacarrental.com.* **Berlies Car Rental.** ⊠ *Exuma International Airport, George Town* ☎ *242/336–3290* ⊕ *berliescarrentals.com.* **Thompson's Rentals.** ⊠ *George Town* ☎ *242/336–2442, 242/345–0058* ⊕ *exumacars.com.*

TAXI
Taxis are plentiful on Great Exuma, and most offer island tours. A half-day tour of George Town and Little Exuma is about $150 for two people.

CONTACTS Exuma Travel and Transportation Limited. ⊠ *George Town* ☎ *242/345–0232.* **Luther Rolle Taxi Service.** ⊠ *George Town* ☎ *242/357–0662, 242/345-5003.*

Hotels

Stay in simple stilt cottages, fabulous rooms with butler service, atmospheric old inns, modern condo rentals, all-inclusives, ecolodges, or bed-and-breakfasts—temporary homes-away-from-home for every taste and price point.

The mainland of Great Exuma has had an energetic growth spurt that includes some of the country's most luxurious hotels, including Sandals Emerald Bay,

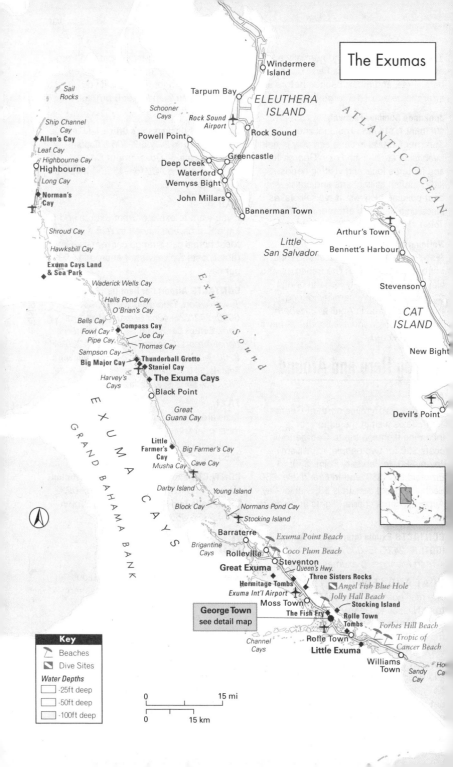

Grand Isle Resort and Residences, and Hideaways at Palm Bay.

Restaurants

Exuma restaurants are known for terrific Bahamian home cooking—cracked conch, fried chicken served with peas-and-rice, and macaroni baked with egg and loads of cheese. Try conch salad at the cluster of wooden shacks called The Fish Fry, just north of George Town. Pea soup with dumplings is a specialty here, and many local restaurants serve it as a weekly lunch special. Lots of restaurants on the island close during the hurricane season, especially from August to November. Be sure to check or call before visiting.

Restaurants at larger resorts have upscale dining, including Continental twists on local cuisine as well as imported steaks and gourmet pizzas.

⇨ *Restaurant prices are based on the median main course price at dinner, excluding gratuity, typically 15%, which is often automatically added to the bill. Hotel prices are for two people in a standard double room in high season, excluding service and 10% tax. Restaurant and hotel reviews have been shortened. For full information, visit Fodors.com.*

What It Costs in U.S. Dollars

	$	$$	$$$	$$$$
RESTAURANTS	under $20	$20–$30	$31–$40	over $40
HOTELS	under $200	$200–$300	$301–$400	over $400

Activities

SCUBA DIVING AND SNORKELING

Exuma Cays Land and Sea Park and **Thunderball Grotto** are excellent snorkeling and dive sites.

Dive Exuma

DIVING & SNORKELING | Located in the heart of George Town on the Government Dock, this company offers daily dives, PADI courses, snorkel tours, and private charters. ✉ George Town ☎ 242/357–0313, 242/336–2893 ⊕ dive-exuma.com ⌨ One tank dives from $80.

Minns Water Sports

BOATING | Minns Water Sports offers boat rentals for those who want to explore Great Exuma. They require renters to stay within the Elizabeth Harbour area. ☎ 242/336–3483, 242/336–2604 ⊕ mwsboats.com ⌨ One day rentals from $237.

Staniel Cay Adventures

SCUBA DIVING | Explore the beautiful waters of Staniel Cay with Staniel Cay Adventures. The company provides a boutique scuba-diving experience, catering to small groups of up to eight people. ✉ Staniel Cay ☎ 242/524–8062 ⊕ stanielcayadventures.com ⌨ Group dives from $330 per person.

Tours

BOAT TOURS

Charter World

BOAT TOURS | This company offers a variety of yacht charters throughout The Bahamas. ☎ 954/603–7830 ⊕ charterworld.com.

Four C's Adventures

BOAT TOURS | Various private and group charters are available through Four C's Adventures, including snorkeling at Thunderball Grotto, fishing, and sightseeing tours. ☎ 242/357–0328, 954/793–4329 ⊕ exumawatertours.com ⌨ Tours start at $550 for three people.

Sun Fun Tours

BOAT TOURS | Operated by Captain Tyrone in Little Farmer's Cay, Sun Fun Tours offers a range of private tour packages through the cays of Exuma. All tours include complimentary drinks, water, and snacks. ✉ *Little Farmer's Cay* ☎ *242/434–6225, 242/225–9818* ⊕ *sunfunexuma. com* 🖾 *Half-day tours $1800; full day $2950.*

ISLAND TOURS

Exuma Travel and Transportation Limited
BUS TOURS | This company provides bus tours of Great Exuma and Little Exuma and can accommodate large parties. ✉ *George Town* ☎ *242/345-0232.*

Island Routes
ADVENTURE TOURS | From reading road trips at local schools to historical tours and ocean adventures, Island Routes offers the opportunity to experience the best of Exuma. ☎ *800/744–1150, 305/663–4364* ⊕ *islandroutes.com* 🖾 *Tours from $162.*

Visitor Information

CONTACTS Exuma Tourist Office.
✉ *Queen's Hwy., George Town* ☎ *242/336–2430* ⊕ *bahamas.com.* **Out Islands Promotion Board.** ⊕ *myoutislands. com.*

Great Exuma

George Town is the capital and largest town on the mainland, a lovely seaside community with darling pink government buildings overlooking Elizabeth Harbour. The white-pillared, colonial-style Government Administration Building was modeled on Nassau's Government House and houses the commissioner's office, police headquarters, courts, and a jail. Atop a hill across from it is the whitewashed St. Andrew's Anglican Church, originally built around 1802. Behind the church is the small, saltwater Lake Victoria. It was

once used for soaking sisal used for making baskets and ropes. The straw market, a half dozen outdoor shops shaded by a huge African fig tree, is a short walk from town. You can bargain with fishermen for some of the day's catch at the Government Dock, where the mail boat comes in.

Small settlements make up the rest of the island. **Rolle Town,** a typical Exuma village devoid of tourist trappings, sits atop a hill overlooking the ocean five miles south of George Town. Some of the buildings are over a century old. **Rolleville** overlooks a harbor twenty miles north of George Town. Its old slave quarters have been transformed into livable cottages.

GETTING AROUND

Dining and sightseeing beyond your resort may require you to rent a car, as taxis can get expensive if you're going long distances.

 Sights

The Fish Fry
RESTAURANT | The Fish Fry is the name given to a jumble of beachside restaurants about two miles north of George Town. They're favored by locals for made-to-order fish and barbecue. Some shacks are open on weekends only, but most are open nightly until at least 11 pm. Music blares on a nightly basis, but on Sunday night, locals crowd the shacks for karaoke. Eat at picnic tables by the water and watch the fishing boats come into the harbor. This is a popular after-work meeting place on Friday night, and a sports bar attracts locals and expats for American basketball and football games. ✉ *Queen's Hwy., George Town.*

Rolle Town Tombs
CEMETERY | Seek out the three Rolle Town Tombs, which date back to the time of the Loyalists. The largest tomb bears this poignant inscription: "Within this tomb interred the body of Ann McKay, the wife of Alexander McKay who departed this

life the 8th November 1792. Aged twenty-six years and their infant child." The tombs are off the main road; look for a sign. The settlement has brightly painted buildings, several more than a century old. ✉ *Rolletown*.

★ Stocking Island

ISLAND | Slightly more than a mile off George Town's shore lies Stocking Island. The four-mile-long island has very few inhabitants, the upscale Kahari Resort, Saint Francis Resort, lots of walking trails, two gorgeous white beaches rich in seashells and popular with surfers, and plenty of good snorkeling sites. Jacques Cousteau's team is said to have traveled some 1,700 feet into Mystery Cave, a blue-hole grotto 70 feet beneath the island. Stocking Island is the headquarters for the wildly popular George Town Cruising Regatta.

Three Sisters Rocks

VIEWPOINT | From the top of Mt. Thompson, rising from Three Sisters Beach, there is a pleasing view of the Three Sisters Rocks jutting above the water just offshore. Legend has it that the rocks were formed when three sisters, all unwittingly in love with the same English sailor, waded out into deep water upon his departure, drowned, and turned into stone. If you look carefully next to each "sister," you'll see smaller boulders. These represent the "children" who the fickle sailor left with the three sisters. This site is also a great snorkeling and diving spot. ✉ *Queen's Hwy., Mount Thompson* ✢ *Mt. Thompson is about 12 miles north of George Town, past Moss Town.*

Beaches

★ Coco Plum Beach

BEACH | This stunning white-sand beach in Great Exuma is known for its great shelling and sand dollars during low tide. The beach is dotted with palm trees that provide shaded areas perfect for picnics

Capturing Waves

Here are a few tips for capturing the water's incredible shades of blue: shoot early—before 9 am—on a sunny day, or late in the afternoon. Make sure the sun is behind you. Use a tripod, or hold the camera still. Find a contrasting color—a bright red umbrella or a yellow fishing boat.

and relaxing on the sand. During low tide, the sandbars formed allow for a peaceful beach stroll. Watching the kitesurfers who sometimes frequent the beach is another way to pass the time. **Amenities:** parking (free). **Best for:** swimming; solitude. ✉ *Queens Hwy.* ✢ *Near Blow Hole Cay, in between Steventon and Rolleville.*

Exuma Point Beach

BEACH | Starfish, baby reef sharks, and stingrays are among the species at Exuma Point Beach. Located at the edge of the peninsula in Rolleville, this beach is uncrowded and serene, perfect for those who crave a relaxing beach day. It also has extremely low tide, with sandbars stretching for miles out into the ocean. The abundance of marine life also makes it a great place for bonefishing. **Amenities:** none. **Best for:** solitude; walking. ✉ *Queen's Hwy, Rolleville.*

Jolly Hall Beach

BEACH | A curve of sparkling white sand shaded by casuarina trees, this long beach is located just north of Hideaways at Palm Bay. It's quiet, and the shallow azure water makes it a great spot for families or romantics. When it's time for lunch, walk over to Hideways or Augusta Bay, two nearby boutique hotels. Watch your bags when high tide comes in; much of the beach is swallowed by the sea. That's the signal for a cold Kalik and

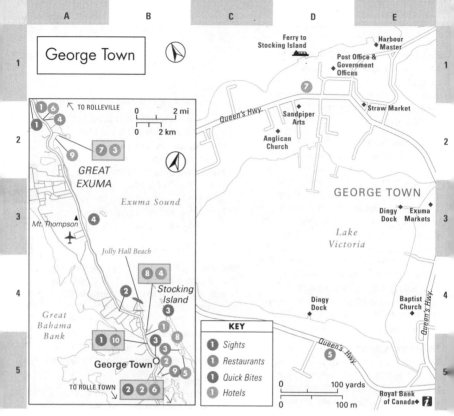

George Town

TO ROLLEVILLE

0 — 2 mi

0 — 2 km

GREAT EXUMA

Exuma Sound

Mt. Thompson

Jolly Hall Beach

Stocking Island

Great Bahama Bank

George Town

TO ROLLE TOWN

Ferry to Stocking Island

Harbour Master

Post Office & Goverment Offices

Queen's Hwy.

Sandpiper Arts

Straw Market

Anglican Church

GEORGE TOWN

Dingy Dock

Exuma Markets

Lake Victoria

Dingy Dock

Baptist Church

Queen's Hwy.

Queen's Hwy.

Royal Bank of Canada

KEY

1 Sights

1 Restaurants

1 Quick Bites

1 Hotels

0 — 100 yards

0 — 100 m

Sights ▼

1	The Fish Fry	B5
2	Rolle Town Tombs	B5
3	Stocking Island	B4
4	Three Sisters Rocks	A3

Restaurants ▼

1	Big D's Conch Spot	A2
2	Blu on the Water Restaurant & Bar	B5
3	Chat 'N' Chill	B5
4	Cocoplum Bistro	A2
5	Eddie's Edgewater	D5
6	Haulover Bay Bar & Grill Resturant	B5
7	Palapa at Grand Isle Resort	A2
8	The Rusty Anchor	B4
9	Shirley's at The Fish Fry	B5
10	Splash Beach Bar	B5

Quick Bites ▼

1	Lighthouse Cafe & Ice Cream Parlor	A2
2	Prime Island Meats and Deli	B4
3	Sandpiper Cafe	B5

Hotels ▼

1	Augusta Bay	B5
2	February Point Resort Estates	B5
3	Grand Isle Resort & Residences	A2
4	Hideaways at Palm Bay	B4
5	Kahari Resort	B5
6	Paradise Bay Bahamas	A2
7	Peace & Plenty Resort and Beach Club	D1
8	St. Francis Resort & Marina	B5
9	Sandals Emerald Bay	A2

a grouper sandwich. **Amenities:** none. **Best for:** solitude; sunrise; swimming; snorkeling. ⊠ *Queen's Hwy., George Town.*

🍴 Restaurants

★ Big D's Conch Spot
$$$ | BAHAMIAN | For the freshest—and according to locals, best—conch salad and the coldest beer, look for the splatter-painted seaside shack a stone's throw from Grand Isle Resort. Big D catches the conch right outside the restaurant, and the salads are often prepared in front of customers. **Known for:** very friendly staff; great local cocktails; must-try conch salad and burger. $ *Average main: $32* ⊠ *Queen's Hwy., Steventon* ☏ *242/358–0059* ⊕ *bigdsconchspot.com* ⊗ *Closed Mon and Tues. Closed Aug. 1 to early Oct.* ☞ *The card machines tend to go out sometimes so carry cash.*

★ Blu on the Water Restaurant & Bar
$$$ | FUSION | Blu on the Water is a must-have dining experience when visiting Great Exuma. Chef Ty Wong has crafted a delicious fusion of Asian and Bahamian dishes that will sweep you into culinary heaven. **Known for:** must-try Bang Bang conch appetizer; fantastic seafood risotto and other pastas; delicious desserts. $ *Average main: $40* ⊠ *Queens Hwy., Rolletown, George Town* ☏ *242/345–5258* ⊕ *bahamasblu.com* ⊗ *Closed Wed.*

★ Chat 'N' Chill
$$ | BAHAMIAN | Yacht folks, locals, and visitors alike rub shoulders at Kenneth Bowe's funky open-air beach bar on the point at Stocking Island. All the food is grilled over an open fire; awesome conch burgers with secret spices, freshly made conch salad, burgers, and a variety of drinks attract diners from all over Great Exuma. **Known for:** famed barbecue ribs; fun beach activities like volleyball and feeding stingrays; gift shop with local souvenirs. $ *Average main: $20* ⊠ *1*

Stocking Island ☏ *305/504–5100* ⊕ *chatnchill.com.*

★ Cocoplum Bistro
$$ | BAHAMIAN | Whether you want a quick breakfast before heading to the beach or dinner under the stars, this open-air beachside bistro at Paradise Bay is a top place to dine. This bistro serves three meals a day, combining Bahamian and French cuisines. **Known for:** great desserts like éclairs and lemon custard pies; variety of poke bowls; delicious cocktails. $ *Average main: $30* ⊠ *Queen's Hwy., Rokers Point Settlement* ☏ *242/524-8116* ⊕ *cocoplumbistroexuma.com.*

Eddie's Edgewater
$$ | BAHAMIAN | In the heart of George Town, this authentic Bahamian restaurant is open for lunch and dinner. The dining terrace offers a stunning view of Lake Victoria, while the indoor dining room and large bar at the front is a popular hangout spot on Monday, when there's live music, lots of drinking, and dancing. **Known for:** Monday night Rake 'n' Scrape; cracked chicken; large portions. $ *Average main: $20* ⊠ *Queens Hwy., George Town* ☏ *242/336–2050* ⊗ *Closed Sun.*

Haulover Bay Bar & Grill Restaurant
$$ | BAHAMIAN | Tucked away in quaint Rolle Town by the bay, Haulover Bay Restaurant is a popular lunch spot serving delicious Bahamian meals and drinks. After your meal, you can walk out to the sandbar and hang out by the water, where you're guaranteed to see starfish, sea turtles, and possibly, a lemon shark. **Known for:** must-try cracked chicken meal; delicious local cocktails; relaxed atmosphere. $ *Average main: $30* ⊠ *Queens Hwy., Rolletown* ☏ *242/447–3772* ⊕ *haulover-bay-bar-grill-resturant.business.site* ▭ *No credit cards* ⊗ *Closed Sat.*

Palapa at Grand Isle Resort
$$$ | EUROPEAN | The fusion of Caribbean and Bahamian spices, fresh seafood, and the tropical outdoor setting is not

to be missed at Palapa. This poolside restaurant serves three meals a day and offers a stunning view of the ocean. **Known for:** unique location; special house drinks and wines; variety of pizzas and sandwiches are menu staples. $ *Average main: $37 ⊠ Grand Isle Resort, Queen's Hwy., Rokers Point Settlement ☎ 242/358–5000 ⊕ grandisleresort.com/dining/palapa.*

★ **The Rusty Anchor**

$$$ | INTERNATIONAL | Sip on a cucumber cooler drink while taking in the stunning ocean views at this idyllic, open-air restaurant located at February Point. The menu is varied with a range of Bahamian favorites, along with steak, pasta, and seafood dishes — complemented by a well-stocked bar. **Known for:** great cocktails; top-rated chicken parmesan; delicious grilled lobster tail. $ *Average main: $40 ⊠ February Point, George Town ☎ 242/336-2400 ⊕ facebook.com/therustyanchoratfebruarypoint ۞ Closed Mon. and Tues.*

★ **Shirley's at The Fish Fry**

$$ | BAHAMIAN | At buzzing The Fish Fry hot spot in Great Exuma, Shirley's is the most popular restaurant of them all, with its chill atmosphere and delicious food. The colorful, quaint little shack is just a stone's throw away from the beach, so there's a great view from the outdoor dining deck. **Known for:** coconut grouper is the best on the island; large portions; variety of delicious pies for dessert. $ *Average main: $30 ⊠ Queens Hwy., George Town ☎ 242/336–3737 ۞ Closed Tues. and Wed. Closed Sept. and Oct.*

★ **Splash Beach Bar**

$$ | BAHAMIAN | Splash, located at Hideaways at Palm Bay, is a fun eatery with a stunning view of the harbor and Stocking Island, which you can see from the wraparound windows. There's also an outdoor dining area if you prefer feeling the ocean breeze and warm weather while you eat. **Known for:** stuffed burgers; bar with swings; beach access. $ *Average*

The Golden Ticket

Sandals restaurants are only open to guests at the hotel—unless you buy a $200 day pass (from 10 am to 6 pm) or evening pass, at the same cost, (from 6 pm to 2 am) that gives you access to all the restaurants and bars. An all-day pass, valid for 24 hours, costs $350.

main: $25 ⊠ Queen's Hwy., George Town ☎ 242/336–2787 ⊕ hideawayspalmbay.com ۞ Closed mid-Aug.–Nov. 1.

☕ Coffee and Quick Bites

Lighthouse Cafe & Ice Cream Parlor

$ | ICE CREAM | The number one place to stop for ice cream in Great Exuma is this quaint, colorful restaurant that sits on the beach. Visitors usually plan to make it a quick stop, but end up staying for the stunning ocean views from the back deck. **Known for:** affordable prices; unique ice-cream flavors like butter pecan and cherry vanilla peach; delicious barbecue chicken with homemade sauces. $ *Average main: $12 ⊠ Queen's Hwy., Steventon ☎ 242/358-0400 ▭ No credit cards ۞ Closed Tues.*

Prime Island Meats and Deli

$ | SANDWICHES | Stop by this deli to stock up on deli meats, cheeses, and gourmet meats like steak, filet mignon, pork chops, and more for your stay. Owners Ron and Susan Kemp also sell delicious chicken salad, crab salad, potato salad, and more. **Known for:** fantastic rotisserie chicken and quality beef; delicious homemade cookies; widest selection of meats in Great Exuma. $ *Average main: $15 ⊠ Queen's Hwy., Hoopers Bay, George Town ☎ 242/336–3627 ⊕ facebook.com/PrimeIslandMeatsAndDeli ۞ Closed Sun.*

Sandals Emerald Bay on Great Exuma has one of the island's best beaches.

Sandpiper Cafe

$ | SANDWICHES | Located in central George Town, just across from Peace & Plenty, this Sandpiper Cafe (formerly Driftwood Cafe) is a pleasant spot for a cup of coffee and a hot breakfast sandwich in the morning. Sandpiper also offers lunch, with specialties such as pizza, subs, and salads, served with fresh lemonade or iced tea. **Known for:** homemade bread; signature eggs Benedict; delicious milkshakes and smoothies. $ *Average main: $18* ✉ *Queen's Hwy., George Town* ☎ *242/801–6531* ⊕ *www. instagram.com/sandpipercafeexuma/* ⊘ *Closed Sun.*

 ## Hotels

Augusta Bay

$$$ | RESORT | The perfect balance of luxury and casual chic, without the megaresort feel, this eighteen-room resort on 300 feet of narrow beach is a mile north of George Town. **Pros:** quiet property; resort provides snorkeling and sea kayaking; on-site ocean-view bar has top-rated rum punch and cocktails. **Cons:** some fixtures and furnishings show wear; need a car to drive to town and shops; many services come at an extra cost. $ *Rooms from: $310* ✉ *Queen's Hwy., George Town* ☎ *242/336–2251* ⊕ *augustabaybahamas.com* ⮒ *18 rooms* ⦿ *Free Breakfast.*

February Point Resort Estates

$$$$ | RESORT | FAMILY | This gated residential community and resort is a world all on its own—with oceanfront residences, penthouses, custom homes, and vacation villas that are available as guest accommodations. **Pros:** beach club with an infinity pool and sundeck; great restaurant on-property; villas are completely private. **Cons:** more like a gated community than a resort; a small number of guests per villa; no entertainment within the community. $ *Rooms from: $550* ✉ *Queen's Hwy., George Town* ☎ *242/336–2660* ⊕ *februarypoint.com* ⮒ *8 villas* ⦿ *No Meals.*

★ Grand Isle Resort & Residences
$$$$ | **RESORT** | **FAMILY** | This luxurious 78-villa complex boasts one of the island's few spas, an infinity pool overlooking the ocean, and a poolside patio restaurant. **Pros:** the ultimate in luxury accommodations; villas have fully loaded kitchens, private patios, and washers and dryers; each villa has its own golf cart. **Cons:** 20-minute drive from George Town and not much to do near the resort; lacks local flavor; golf-cart parking is extra. [$] *Rooms from: $544* ✉ *Off Queens Hwy., Rokers Point Settlement* ☎ *242/358–5000* 🌐 *grandisleresort.com* 🛏 *78 villas* 🍴 *No Meals.*

Hideaways at Palm Bay
$$ | **RESORT** | **FAMILY** | One of George Town's most modern accommodations, Hideaways is all about light and color. **Pros:** roomy accommodations; a short drive to George Town's restaurants; great restaurant and bar on-site. **Cons:** beach all but disappears at high tide; accommodations are close together; free Wi-Fi is unreliable. [$] *Rooms from: $215* ✉ *Queen's Hwy.* ✥ *1 mile from George Town* ☎ *242/336–2787* 🌐 *hideawayspalmbay.com* 🛏 *40 rooms* 🍴 *Free Breakfast.*

★ Kahari Resort
$$$$ | **HOTEL** | Kahari Resort on Stocking Island, just off the coast of Great Exuma, offers privacy, exclusivity, and tranquility. **Pros:** convenient water taxis available to travel between islands; access to two stunning beaches; great on-site spa that offers a range of body and beauty treatments. **Cons:** can only be accessed via boat from airport; location is very isolated; many of the services cost extra. [$] *Rooms from: $750* ✉ *Stocking Island, George Town* ☎ *242/524–8889* 🌐 *www.kahariresort.com* 🛏 *12 rooms* 🍴 *No Meals.*

★ Paradise Bay Bahamas
$$ | **RESORT** | Sitting right on the beach in Great Exuma, Paradise Bay is a charming boutique hotel with a cheerful Franco-Bahamian style. **Pros:** kayaks and other water sports available; convenience stores and restaurants are nearby; ocean view from rooms. **Cons:** limited amenities; need to rent a car to go into the town; cottages are close together, so little privacy. [$] *Rooms from: $250* ✉ *Queen's Hwy.* ☎ *242/358–5229* 🌐 *paradise-bay-bahamas.com* 🕒 *Closed late Aug. to mid-Oct.* 🛏 *11 rooms* 🍴 *Free Breakfast.*

Peace & Plenty Resort and Beach Club
$$$ | **HOTEL** | The first Exumas hotel and granddaddy of the island's omnipresent Peace & Plenty empire, this pink, two-story lodge is in the heart of the action in George Town. **Pros:** resort has a marina, stunning pool, and business center; friendly staff; ocean-view balconies in some rooms. **Cons:** no beach; have to take a water taxi to Stocking Island; some furniture shows signs of wear and tear. [$] *Rooms from: $310* ✉ *Queen's Hwy., George Town* ☎ *242/524–9197* 🌐 *peaceandplenty.com* 🛏 *34 rooms* 🍴 *Free Breakfast.*

Saint Francis Resort & Marina
$$$ | **HOTEL** | The idyllic Saint Francis Resort on Stocking Island is the perfect tropical getaway for those looking for a beautiful and quiet property surrounded by lush forests, blue holes, and gorgeous beaches. **Pros:** great food at restaurant; accommodating and friendly staff; water sports like snorkeling, kayaking, and paddleboarding offered. **Cons:** no TVs in the rooms; few amenities; property is very remote. [$] *Rooms from: $400* ✉ *Stocking Island, George Town* ☎ *242/557–9629, 772/763–8135* 🌐 *stfrancisresort.com* 🛏 *8 rooms* 🍴 *Free Breakfast.*

★ Sandals Emerald Bay
$$$$ | **RESORT** | Sandals Emerald Bay is Great Exuma's most luxurious all-inclusive resort, with cream and aqua buildings facing a mile-long stretch of powdery white sand and a half-acre zero-entry pool in the center of the property. **Pros:** luxe butler suites available; popular spa with 16 treatment rooms;

The Straw Market in George Town features handmade crafts.

has the only 18-hole golf course on the island. **Cons:** the resort is isolated; lacks Bahamian flavor; rooms near entertainment areas can be noisy. [$] *Rooms from: $1200* ✉ *Queen's Hwy., Rokers Point Settlement* ☎ *242/336–6800, 800/726–3157* 🌐 *sandals.com* 🛏 *249 suites* 🍴 *All-Inclusive.*

Nightlife

BARS AND PUBS

Roy's Bar & Lounge

BARS | Locals and tourists alike flock to Roy's Lounge on Saturday for karaoke night. On other nights, it's a relaxed after-work chill spot where Bahamians come to enjoy old-school music, great drinks, and quick bites. ✉ *Old Airport Rd., George Town* ☎ *242/524-1191* 🕓 *Closed Mon. and Tues.*

FISH FRY

The Fish Fry

GATHERING PLACES | There's always something going on at The Fish Fry, a cluster of shacks two miles north of George Town. A DJ is usually there on Friday and Sunday. ✉ *Queen's Hwy., George Town.*

LIVE MUSIC

Eddie's Edgewater

LIVE MUSIC | On Monday, head to Eddie's Edgewater for rousing Rake 'n' Scrape music. The front porch is a popular spot, where locals hang out all week long. ✉ *Queens Hwy., George Town* ☎ *242/336–2050* 🕓 *Closed Sun.*

Shopping

MARKETS

★ Exuma Markets

FOOD | At this grocery store located in the center of George Town, yachties tie up at the skiff docks in the rear, on Lake Victoria. Boaters can also send emergency e-mails and faxes from this location. You can also order groceries online and have them delivered or pick them up. ✉ *Queen's Hwy., George Town* ☎ *242/336–2033* 🌐 *shopexuma.com.*

You'll swim among multicolored tropical fish at Staniel Cay.

SOUVENIRS

★ Marilyn's Gift Shop

SOUVENIRS | This quaint and pristine shop in George Town is fully stocked with souvenirs. Clothing, Bahamian handmade crafts, jewelry, and much more are sold here. A second location is at Exuma International Airport. ⊠ *Queens Hwy., George Town* ✛ *Beside Driftwood Café* ☎ *242/357–0321* ⊕ *www.facebook.com/p/Marilyns-Gift-Shop-100063628916686/* ⊗ *Closed Sun.*

Sandpiper Arts & Crafts

SOUVENIRS | Here you can find upscale souvenirs, from high-quality cards and books to batik clothing and art. ⊠ *Queen's Hwy., George Town* ✛ *Beside Minnis Water Sports* ☎ *242/336–2084* ⊗ *Closed Sun.*

Straw Market

SOUVENIRS | The Straw Market offers a wide range of Bahamian straw bags, hats, and beachwear at scores of open-air shops and stalls. Prices are negotiable. ⊠ *Queen's Hwy., George Town* ⊗ *Closed Sun.*

Activities

ADVENTURE TOURS

★ Island Boy Adventures

BOATING | Floating down the lazy river at Moriah Harbour Park, boating through the Exuma Cays to swim with the pigs, and diving for lobster are just a few of the activities offered by experienced Captains Evvie and Tonio. If you're not sure what to choose, let Island Boy Adventures help you plan your day—you won't be disappointed. ⊠ *Queens Hwy., George Town* ☎ *242/422–2697* ⊕ *islandboyadventures.com* ✉ *Private charters for up to 8 people from $2,800.*

BOATING

Because of its wealth of safe harbors and regatta events, the Exumas are a favorite spot for yachtsmen. Renting a boat allows you to explore the cays near George Town and beyond, and a number of hotels in town allow guests to tie up rental boats at their docks. For those who want to take a water jaunt through Stocking Island's hurricane holes, sailboats are ideal.

FISHING

In the shallow flats off Exuma's windward coast the elusive bonefish, the "ghosts of the sea," roam. Patient fishermen put featherweight, thumbnail-size flies on the lines, calculate the tides and currents, and cast out about 50 feet in hope of catching one. For sure success, avid fishermen pay guides about $300 a day to help them outsmart the skinny gray fish that streak through the crystal water. Most hotels can arrange for expert local guides, and a list is also available from the Exuma Tourist Office. The season is year-round and highly prized among fly-fishers.

Fish Rowe Charters

FISHING | This charter company has a 40-foot Hatteras that holds up to four fishers. ☎ 242/357-0870 ⊕ fishrowecharters.com ▢ Deep-water charters from $1,500 for a half day.

Steve Ferguson

FISHING | Stevie is the go-to guide for all things bonefishing in Great Exuma. He will provide a cooler with ice for refreshments and lunch upon request during his fishing trips. ☎ 242/422-7033, 242/345-0153 ⊕ bonefishstevie.com ▢ half day $450; $700 full day for up to two persons.

GOLF

Sandals Emerald Bay Golf Course

GOLF | Golf legend Greg Norman designed the 18-hole, par-72 championship course, featuring six ocean-side holes, at Sandals Emerald Bay, the island's only golf course. There are preferred tee times for hotel guests. ⊠ Sandals, Queen's Hwy., Rokers Point Settlement ☎ 242/336-6800 ⊕ www.sandals.com/golf/bahamas/ ▢ from $110 ⛳ 18 holes, 7000 yards, par 72.

SCUBA DIVING

The popular **Angelfish Blue Hole,** just minutes from George Town, is filled with angelfish, spotted rays, snapper, and the occasional reef shark. However, while it is full of mesmerizing schools of colorful fish, it is for experienced divers only. There are plenty of other dive sites like **The Washing Machine** and the **Barracuda Shoals** for less experienced divers.

Dive Exuma

SCUBA DIVING | This outfitter provides dive instruction, certification courses, scuba trips, and snorkel tours. ⊠ Government Dock, George Town ☎ 242/357-0313 ⊕ www.dive-exuma.com ▢ One-tank dives; $80; two-tank dives $154; private snorkel charter starts at $550.

SNORKELING

Minns Water Sports

DIVING & SNORKELING | You can rent or purchase snorkeling gear at Minns. They also offer boat rentals by the day. ⊠ Queen's Hwy., George Town ☎ 242/336-3483 ⊕ mwsboats.com.

SPAS

Exuma Massage & Yoga

SPAS | Schedule a private yoga session in the comfort of your home or at your hotel, or relax and indulge with one of the relaxing massages from Lyn, the owner, who is the only person to offer mobile services in Exuma. ⊠ George Town ☎ 242/357-0684 ⊕ exumamassage.com ▢ One hr massage $150 ☞ Services: Swedish massage, after-sun relief, Thai yoga massage, private yoga sessions.

★ **Red Lane Spa**

SPAS | Located on the Sandals Emerald Bay property, this elegant spa has 16 treatment rooms, a steam room, and a fitness center. Couples massages and "sun lover" relief are among the treatments offered. The spa is open to the public, but you'll need to call ahead to make your appointment. ⊠ Sandals Emerald Bay, Queen's Hwy., Rokers Point Settlement ☎ 242/336-6800

⊕ *www.sandals.com/redlane-spa/* *1 hr massage from $174* ☞ *Steam room. Gym with: cardiovascular machines, free weights, weight-training equipment. Services: body wraps, facials, massage, scrubs, nail treatment. Classes and programs: Pilates, yoga.*

SeaStar Spa

SPAS | Seawater therapy, or the art of marine healing, is the philosophy at SeaStar Spa, located at Grand Isle Resort. Relax in one of three treatment rooms, including one designed especially for couples. The spa is open every day and offers a number of massages, scrubs, and wraps utilizing natural ingredients such as ginger, lime, coconut, and island spices. SeaStar also has a special "children's spa" menu, which includes shorter massages and pedicures as well as hair braiding. ⊠ *Grand Isle Resort, Rokers Point Settlement* ☎ *242/358– 5000* ⊕ *grandisleresort.com/amenities/ seastar-spa* *1hr massages starting at $130* ☞ *Services: aromatherapy, massage, nail treatment, scrubs, waxing, facials, children's spa.*

Little Exuma

Scenes from two *Pirates of the Caribbean* movies were filmed on the southern end of Little Exuma—only 12 square miles— and on one of the little cays just offshore. But that's just one of the many reasons people are drawn to this lovely island, which is connected to Great Exuma to the north by a narrow bridge. Rolling green hills, purple morning glories spilling over fences, small settlements with only a dozen houses, and glistening white beaches make this a romantic afternoon escape. Near **William's Town** is an eerie salt lake, still and ghostly, where salt was once scooped up and shipped away. You can hike old footpaths and look for ruins of old plantation buildings built in the 1700s near The Hermitage, but you'll have to look beneath the bushes and vines to

find them. Little Exuma's most popular beach is Tropic of Cancer Beach; it's a thrill to stand on the line that marks the spot. You're officially in the tropics now.

GETTING HERE AND AROUND

Little Exuma is hot, with little shade. It's possible to walk or bike, but a car, golf cart, or scooter is the best way to get around the island.

VISITOR INFORMATION
People-to-People Program

CULTURAL TOURS | This group hosts a tea where visitors can learn about bush medicine and other aspects of local life while getting to know Exuma islanders. ☎ *242/336–2430* ⊕ *bahamas.com/ our-people-people-experience.*

⊙ Sights

Hermitage Tombs

HISTORIC HOME | The Hermitage estate ruins are testaments to the cotton-plantation days. The small settlement was built by the Ferguson family from the Carolinas, who settled here after the American Revolutionary War. Visitors can see the foundations of the main house and tombs that date back to the 1700s. The tombs hold George Butler (1759– 1822), Henderson Ferguson (1772–1825), and Constance McDonald (1755–59). An unnamed grave is believed to be that of an enslaved person. ⊠ *Little Exuma.*

❶ Beaches

Forbes Hill Beach

BEACH | This is one of The Exumas' most stunning beaches, favored among those looking for somewhere quiet to relax and soak up the sun, or a secluded beach to snorkel. The small beach is a cove with plenty of marine life — a variety of fish and conch are among what you'll find near the reef, making it a great place to fish as well. There's a small pavilion where you can eat and a tire swing. **Amenities:** none. **Best for:** solitude; snorkeling; swimming;

Did You Know?

The Tropic of Cancer cuts through Little Exuma. A helpful painted line marking the spot on the steps leading down to Tropic of Cancer Beach makes a great photo op.

walking. ⊠ *Queen's Hwy., Forbes Hill, Little Exuma.*

★ **Tropic of Cancer Beach** (*Pelican Beach*)
BEACH | This is the beach most visitors come to The Exumas for, although don't be surprised if you're the only one here at noon on a Saturday. It's right on the Tropic of Cancer; a helpful line marking the spot on the steps leading down to the sand makes a great photo op. The beach is a white-sand crescent in a protected cove, where the water is usually as calm as a pond. A shady wooden cabana makes a comfortable place to admire the beach and water. *Pirates of the Caribbean* 2 and 3 were filmed on nearby Sandy Cay. **Amenities:** none. **Best for:** solitude; snorkeling; swimming; walking. ⊠ *Moore Hill, Little Exuma.*

Restaurants

★ Santanna's Bar & Grill
$$ | **BAHAMIAN** | Santanna's claim to fame, besides the beautiful ocean view and the delicious food, is that it was a favorite dining and hangout spot for the cast and crew during the filming of *Pirates of the Caribbean.* The menu features a range of Bahamian and American dishes, and Mom's Bakery next door is famous for its fresh bread and mouthwatering rum cakes. **Known for:** shark feeding at the beach; delicious fried lobster; best place to get jerk chicken in Little Exuma. $ *Average main: $25* ⊠ *Queen's Hwy., William's Town, Little Exuma* ☎ *954/371–8045, 242/345–4102* ⊕ *www.santannas-barngrill.com* ⊗ *Closed Sun.*

★ Tropic Breeze Beach Bar & Grill
$$ | **CARIBBEAN** | With an outdoor dining area that wraps around the restaurant so you can enjoy the tropical sea breeze and views of the Caribbean Sea, this is one of the most tranquil restaurants in Little Exuma. Chef Khriston, a Le Cordon Bleu graduate, prepares the best and most popular Caribbean dishes — be sure to try the Jerk Wings with a

cold beer. **Known for:** delicious seafood platter with shrimp, fish, and lobster; excellent rum punch; friendly chef who sometimes serenades his guests. $ *Average main: $28* ⊠ *Queens Hwy., William's Town, Little Exuma* ☎ *242/345–4100* ⊕ *www.facebook.com/profile.php?id= 100063489795877* ⊗ *Closed Sun. and Mon. Closed Aug.–Sept.*

Hotels

★ The Conch House
$$$$ | **B&B/INN** | This elegant and luxurious beachfront property, with its own private beach, could be yours while you enjoy a relaxing stay in Little Exuma. **Pros:** stunning pool on property; luxurious Bahamian-style decor; house has a fully fitted and equipped kitchen. **Cons:** might be too remote; you will need a car to get to restaurants; limited facilities on property. $ *Rooms from: $1250* ⊠ *Marine Dr., Little Exuma* ⊕ *theconchhouselittleexuma.com* ➳ *4 rooms* �‖*No Meals.*

Tropical View Villas
$$ | **B&B/INN** | If you ever want to be surrounded by stunning beaches and lush forests, then you'll find Tropical View Villas to be the perfect island getaway. **Pros:** close to airport; property is quiet; a range of services are provided by staff upon request. **Cons:** far from any restaurants; no amenities; limited activities found nearby. $ *Rooms from: $240* ⊠ *Moore Hill, Queens Hwy., Little Exuma* ☎ *242/345–4195* ⊕ *vrbo.com/622100* ➳ *2 rooms* �‖*No Meals.*

The Exuma Cays

A band of cays—with names like **Rudder Cut, Big Farmer's, Great Guana,** and **Leaf**—stretches northwest from Great Exuma. It will take you a full day to boat through all 365 cays, most uninhabited, some owned by celebrities. Along the way, you'll find giant starfish, wild iguanas, swimming pigs, dolphins, sharks, and

The famous swimming pigs of Big Majors Cay will be happy to meet you at your boat.

picture-perfect sandbars. The Land & Sea Park, toward the northern end of the chain, is world-renowned.

GETTING HERE AND AROUND

Most people visit the cays with their own boats; you'll need one to island-hop, although you can fly into Staniel Cay. The channels are confusing for inexperienced boaters, especially at low tide, and high tide can hide reefs and sandbars just underneath the surface. If this sounds intimidating, look into booking a boat tour. Once on a cay, most are small enough to walk around. Golf carts are popular on Staniel Cay.

Sights

Allen's Cay

ISLAND | Allen's Cay is at The Exumas' northernmost tip and home to the rare northern Bahamian rock iguana. Bring along some grapes and a stick to put them on, and these little guys will quickly become your new best friends. ⊠ Allan's Cay.

Big Major Cay

ISLAND | FAMILY | Just north of Staniel Cay, Big Major Cay is home to the famous swimming pigs (it's also called Pig Beach). These guys aren't shy; as you pull up to the island, they'll dive in and swim out to greet you. Don't forget to bring some scraps; Staniel Cay restaurant gives guests bags before they depart.

Compass Cay

ISLAND | Explore the many paths on the island, which is 1½ miles long and one mile wide, or sit on the dock and watch the sharks swim below—don't worry, they're harmless nurse sharks. Several houses and Airbnbs are on the island for rent. There are also two small convenience stores stocked with snacks and beverages. ⊠ Compass Cay ⊕ compass-caymarina.com.

★ Exuma Cays Land and Sea Park

NATURE PRESERVE | Created by The Bahamas in 1958 and now overseen by the Bahamas National Trust, the 176-square-mile Exuma Cays Land and Sea Park was the first of its kind in the world—an enormous open aquarium with pristine reefs, an abundance of marine life, and sandy cays. For landlubbers there are hiking trails and birding sites. At Shroud Cay, jump into the strong current that creates a natural whirlpool whipping you around a rocky outcropping to a powdery beach. On top of the hill overlooking the beach is Camp Driftwood, made famous by a hermit who dug steps to the top, leaving behind pieces of driftwood. ⊠ *Park Headquarters* ☎ *242/601–7438* ⊕ *bnt.bs/ explore/exuma/exuma-cays-land-sea-park/* ⌁ *VHF Channel 9.*

Little Farmer's Cay

ISLAND | If you're looking for a little civilization, stop off at Little Farmer's Cay, the first inhabited cay in the chain, about 40 minutes (18 miles) from Great Exuma. The island has two restaurants and a small grocery store where locals gather to play dominoes. But don't expect too big of a party; just around 70 people live on the island. A walk up the hill will reward you with fantastic island views.

Norman's Cay

ISLAND | North of the Exuma Cays Land and Sea Park is Norman's Cay, an island with 10 miles of rarely trod white beaches that attracts the occasional yachter. It was once the private domain of Colombian drug smuggler Carlos Lehder. It's now owned by a group of American investors. Stop by Norman's Cay Beach Club at MacDuff's for lunch or an early dinner and its "always five-o'clock-somewhere" beach cocktail. ⊠ *Norman's Cay.*

★ **Staniel Cay**

ISLAND | This is the hub of activity in the cays, and a favorite destination of yachters thanks to the Staniel Cay Yacht Club. Shack up in one of the cotton candy–color cottages and visit the club's restaurant for lunch, dinner, and nightlife. The island has an airstrip, two hotels, and paved roads, and everything is within walking distance. ⊠ *Staniel Cay.*

★ **Thunderball Grotto**

CAVE | Just across the water from the Staniel Cay Yacht Club is one of The Bahamas' most unforgettable attractions: Thunderball Grotto, a lovely marine cave that snorkelers (at low tide) and experienced scuba divers can explore. In the central cavern, shimmering shafts of sunlight pour through holes in the soaring ceiling and illuminate the glass-clear water. You'll see right away why this cave was chosen as an exotic setting for such movies as 007's *Thunderball* and *Never Say Never Again,* and the mermaid tale *Splash.* ⊠ *Staniel Cay.*

🍽 Restaurants

★ **Hill House Restaurant**

$$$$ | BAHAMIAN | Housed in a charming British-style villa at Fowl Cay Resort, this upscale restaurant serves fresh Bahamian-inspired modern cuisine alongside spectacular 360-degree views of the surrounding islands and sea. The cocktail hour is followed by an amazing four-course gourmet dinner featuring a creative blend of Bahamian-inspired modern cuisine that the chef prepares daily with the freshest seafood and local ingredients. **Known for:** new menu daily; delectable hors d'oeuvres and innovative cuisine; lively cocktail hour. $ *Average main: $50* ⊠ *Fowl Cay Resort, Big Major's Cay* ☎ *242/557–3179 reservations* ⊕ *www.fowlcay.com/ dining* 🕐 *Closed Sept.* ⌁ *VHF Channel 16 for dinner reservations.*

★ **Lorraine's Cafe**

$$ | BAHAMIAN | Located at the Black Point Marina on Great Guana Cay, this quaint restaurant is popular for its barbecue buffet and happy hour combo on Wednesday and Saturday evenings. Lorraine's serves three meals per day, but lunch is the most hectic, with flocks of tourists, typically on excursions, stopping by to eat. **Known for:** delicious ribs and mac and cheese; amazing specialty drinks by bartender Killer Ralph; coconut bread freshly baked by

Staniel Cay Yacht Club

Lorraine's mom. $ *Average main: $30* ⊠ *Black Point Marina, Great Guana Cay* ☏ *242/355–3095* ⊕ *www.facebook. com/p/Lorraines-Cafe-100063615760310/.*

MacDuff's Restaurant

$$$$ | **BAHAMIAN** | MacDuff's Restaurant offers a mellow fine-dining experience with delicious food and world-class service. Chef Jason Wallace prepares a blend of contemporary and Bahamian meals, and while at the bar, you'll find bartenders serving specialty cocktails and local favorites. **Known for:** friendly staff; comfortable sofa and cabana to relax; delicious MacDuff cheeseburger. $ *Average main: $45* ⊠ *Norman's Cay* ☏ *242/805–2235 reservations* ⊕ *macduffscottages.com.*

Sea Level at Staniel Cay Yacht Club

$$ | **BAHAMIAN** | This waterfront restaurant serves up Bahamian specialties such as cracked conch, fresh grouper, snapper, and grilled lobster, with homemade bread. A dinner bell rings when dinner is ready and diners move from the bar to the dining room. **Known**

for: serves breakfast, lunch, and dinner; must-try conch po'boy; some ingredients come from the restaurant's own garden. $ *Average main: $38* ⊠ *Staniel Cay Yacht Club, Staniel Cay* ☏ *242/355–2024* ⊕ *www.stanielcay.com/dining/* ☞ *VHF Channel 16 for reservations.*

Hotels

Compass Cay Marina

$$$$ | **B&B/INN** | Five spacious houses on the island, which is 1½ miles long and one mile wide, are separated by lush palm and hardwood hammocks and so far apart that you feel you have the island to yourself. **Pros:** remote tranquility; boat included; all houses are fully equipped with amenities. **Cons:** expensive to get to; too remote; not many activities. $ *Rooms from: $2400* ⊠ *Compass Cay* ☏ *772/532–4793* ⊕ *compasscaymarina. com* ⇌ *5 villas* ⏐◎⏐ *No Meals.*

Embrace Resort

$$ | **HOTEL** | Less than two minutes away from the Staniel Cay Airport is Embrace

Resort, a charming boutique hotel that prides itself on offering top-notch Bahamian hospitality. **Pros:** most villas have a balcony; complimentary airport and marina transfers; staff will book excursions upon request. **Cons:** most services are at an extra cost; on-site pool is small; basic rooms. $ *Rooms from: $250* ✉ *Staniel Cay* ☎ *242/524–7447, 242/524–0951 whatsapp* ⊕ *www.embraceresort.com* ⇆ *7 villas* ⦿ *Free Breakfast* ☞ *Breakfast not offered on Sunday.*

★ Fowl Cay Resort

$$$$ | **RESORT** | The all-inclusive Fowl Cay Resort is a Caribbean paradise; set in the breathtaking turquoise waters of the central Exumas chain of little islands and cays in The Bahamas, it was originally used to keep chickens by the locals (hence the name). **Pros:** spacious and tasteful villas; each villa has its own personal boat and golf cart; three private beaches nearby. **Cons:** villas are costly; villas can't be booked for less than a week; resort pool is small. $ *Rooms from: $2000* ✉ *Fowl Cay* ✛ *7-minute boat ride from Staniel Cay airstrip* ☎ *877/845–5275, 242/557–3179* ⊕ *fowlcay.com* ☾ *Closed Sept.* ⇆ *6 villas* ⦿ *All-Inclusive.*

MacDuff's Cottages

$$$$ | **B&B/INN** | Surrounded by tranquil seas, lush landscapes, and remote island living, this stunning retreat, with six oceanfront cottages and a restaurant, offers the beauty of a tropical paradise and the remoteness of a private escape. **Pros:** staff will arrange excursions to nearby cays; kayaking, snorkeling, and paddleboarding available; all cottages feature a large covered porch with ocean view. **Cons:** expensive to get there; might be too remote; not many activities. $ *Rooms from: $850* ✉ *Norman's Cay* ☎ *242/357–9501* ⊕ *macduffscottages. com* ⇆ *6 cottages* ⦿ *No Meals.*

★ Staniel Cay Yacht Club

$$$$ | **B&B/INN** | The Staniel Cay Yacht Club is nothing short of legendary, once drawing such luminaries as Malcolm Forbes and Robert Mitchum to its property. **Pros:** great restaurant; authentic Bahamian experience; great for families, and children's activities can be arranged. **Cons:** expensive to get to without a private boat or plane; no TVs in many of the rooms; most services cost extra. $ *Rooms from: $700* ✉ *Staniel Cay* ☎ *242/355–2024, 954/467–6658* ⊕ *stanielcay.com* ⇆ *15 cottages* ⦿ *No Meals.*

Nightlife

BARS AND PUBS

Staniel Cay Yacht Club

BARS | Staniel Cay Yacht Club has a relatively busy bar, hopping with yachters from all over the world. There's no dress code, but shirts and cover-ups are required after 5 pm. No reservations are required either, but only adults (18+) are allowed after 10 pm. ✉ *Main Street, Staniel Cay* ☎ *242/355–2024* ⊕ *stanielcay.com.*

Activities

BOATING AND FISHING

L&C Island Rentals

BOATING | Boating enthusiasts can rent between a 17-foot and a 22-foot Yamaha at L&C Island Rentals. Guides can also be hired for inexperienced boaters, and snorkeling gear is available for rent. ✉ *Staniel Cay* ☎ *242/524-8191* ⊕ *stanielrentals.com* ✉ *Starting at $400 per day plus fuel.*

Staniel Cay Adventures

BOATING | Staniel Cay Adventures provides fishing charters, snorkeling trips, private tours, and group excursions throughout the Exuma Cays. ✉ *Main Street, Staniel Cay* ☎ *242/524–8062* ⊕ *www.stanielcayadventures.com* ✉ *tours start at $330.*

BICYCLING

Staniel Cay Golf Cart Rentals also rents bicycles, starting at $20 for a half day.

278

THE SOUTHERN FAMILY ISLANDS

Updated by
Alicia Wallace

⊙ Sights	🍴 Restaurants	🛏 Hotels	🛍 Shopping	🍸 Nightlife
★★★★★	★★★★☆	★★★☆☆	★☆☆☆☆	★★☆☆☆

WELCOME TO
THE SOUTHERN FAMILY ISLANDS

TOP REASONS TO GO

★ **Take time for yourself:** Discover the joy of slowing down on islands off the trampled tourist track. Glistening sand, calm coves, or rolling ocean waves—you'll have your pick.

★ **Tell your own tall fishing tale:** Whether deep-sea fishing off southern Inagua or bonefishing in the crystal-clear shallows on Cat Island's east coast, your fishing adventures will be remembered forever.

★ **Explore historic lighthouses:** Surrounded by treacherous shoals and reefs, the Southern Family Islands have the country's most famous 19th-century lighthouses, most of which you can climb for stunning views.

★ **Discover a world beneath the surface:** Spectacular diving and snorkeling, and even specialty shark dives, are on the menu for nature lovers when visiting these secluded southern isles with their calm, clear waters.

1 Cat Island. Stunning beaches, the highest point in the country (the 206-foot Mt. Alvernia), 200-year-old deserted stone cottages, incredible straw work, and superb diving and fishing attract loyal visitors.

2 San Salvador. Located on one of the largest reefs in the world, the tiny island's crystal clear waters are a scuba diver's dream. A single road loops around the island, showcasing its spectacular beaches.

3 Long Island. Ringed with stunning beaches, this island offers comfortable resorts and inns as well as the world's deepest blue hole.

4 Crooked Island and Acklins. Fishing and more fishing are the reasons to come here, but be sure to take a day off to dive and snorkel. The Wall, a famed dive site about 50 yards off Crooked Island's coast, drops from 45 feet to thousands.

5 Inagua. The biggest attraction here is the island's 80,000 pink flamingos, but there are also caves waiting to be explored. Anglers come to fish tarpon and bonefish, and to explore the Spanish galleons that sank off the coast.

wn

Bight

Alvernia

San Salvador 2

Cockburn Town○

ption y

Stella Marls

Rum Cay

Port Nelson○

Long Island 3

Cay○

Clarence Town○

A T L A N T I C   O C E A N

Crooked Island passage

Samana Cay

Colonel Hill○

Richmond○

Crooked Island 4

Long Cay

Plana Cay

Mayaguana passage

Mayaguana Island

Spring Point○

Acklins Island

0 ————————————— 30 mi
0 ————————————— 30 km

Little Inagua Island

Great Inagua Island 5

Lake Windsor

Matthew Town○

INAGUA NATIONAL PARK

Flamingos catching fish in the water.

Nothing quite prepares you for your first glimpse of the West Indian flamingos that nest in Inagua National Park. They are a brilliant crimson-pink, up to 5 feet tall, and have black-tipped wings. A dozen flamingos will suddenly fly across a pond, intermixed with fantastic pink roseate spoonbills.

It's a moving experience, but because of the island's remote location, as few as 100 people witness it every year. By 1952, Inagua's flamingos had dwindled to about 5,000. The birds were hunted for their meat—especially the tongue—and feathers. The government established the 287-square-mile park in 1963, and today 60,000 flamingos nest here—the world's largest breeding colony of West Indian flamingos. The birds like the many salt ponds in Inagua that supply their favorite meal—brine shrimp.

Contact the **Bahamas National Trust** Nassau office (☎ 242/393–1317 or ⊕ www. bnt.bs) or **Wardens Henry Nixon and**

Randolph "Casper "Burrows (☎ 242/464–7618, 242/395–0856) or the Inagua office (☎ 242/339–2128) to make reservations for your visit. Visits to the park are by special arrangement. ✉ 10 miles west of Matthew Town.

BEST TIME TO GO
Flamingos are on the island year-round, but for the greatest concentration, visit during nesting season from late February through June. Early in March, their courtship displays are an elaborate mass dance, and the chorus fills the air for miles. They parade shoulder-to-shoulder, performing wing salutes, head wagging, and contorted preening with expanded wings.

The courtship displays end in April. The pairs then build small volcano-like nest mounds up to two feet tall. Early morning and late afternoon are the best times to come. If you visit right after their hatching, the flocks of fuzzy, gray baby flamingos are entertaining, and the 50 shades of gray and pink are a photographer's delight.

BEST WAYS TO EXPLORE

With a guide. Senior Park Warden Henry Nixon or Deputy Randolph "Casper" Burrows lead all tours into the park and to Union Creek Reserve. They'll drive you past small flocks of flamingos in the salt ponds and answer questions. Contact them before your trip, or ask around when you get to Inagua and someone will connect you within minutes.

By kayak. You can't kayak in the park's salt ponds because they're too shallow, but you can in Lake Windsor, also called Lake Rosa (locally known as "The Pond")—a huge inland lake with its eastern half in the park. You'll need a good 4x4 SUV or truck to reach the lake.

On foot. The best way to see flamingos up close is by parking the car and walking, or sitting quietly for a while in a thicket of mangroves. Flamingos are skittish and easily spooked. Although

There are plenty of tropical animals to see in this park.

Bahamas national bird, the West Indian flamingo.

the ponds and mangroves look a lot like the Florida Everglades, there are no alligators or poisonous snakes here. Make sure you have insect repellent on before you take off; the mosquitoes are in abundance.

FLAMINGO FACTS

Flamingos are the national bird and protected from hunters by law.

Females lay one egg a year, and both parents take turns sitting on it for 28 days. Both parents also produce milk in the crop at the base of the neck for the chick for three months. The parents' feathers turn white while they feed the chick because they lose carotene.

Flamingos are monogamous and usually mate for life but are extremely social birds that like to live in groups.

Their "knees," which seem to bend backward, are actually ankles. The knees are tucked under their feathers. What looks like the leg is actually the foot extending from the ankle.

Standing on one leg is the most comfortable position for a flamingo.

Brine shrimp, the flamingos' main source of food, give the mature bird its brilliant deep-pink coloring.

RAKE 'N' SCRAPE

Welcoming Rake 'N' Scrape musicians.

Rake 'n' Scrape music's contagious cadence, created by instruments made mostly from recycled objects, brings on a particularly strong urge to get up and shake it.

Most closely linked in sound, rhythm, and composition to zydeco music out of New Orleans, Rake 'n' Scrape is folk music at its best. It's unclear just where Rake 'n' Scrape originated, but most believe it has roots in Africa, made the voyage to The Bahamas with enslaved people, and was adapted over the years. Today's Rake 'n' Scrape was cultivated on remote Cat Island. Lacking money for and access to modern instruments, the resourceful locals made use of whatever supplies were available. Years later, many of these musicians could have their pick of shiny, finely tuned instruments, but sticking with what they know makes beautiful music.

HAVE A LISTEN
International recording artist and Cat Islander **Tony McKay,** who went by the stage name Exuma, incorporated Rake 'n' Scrape into his compositions. He paid homage to the style with the song "Goin' to Cat Island."

George Symonette's "Don't Touch Me Tomato" had a resurgence in a television commercial for Cable Bahamas. Symonette is associated with Goombay, a music style popular in Nassau in the 1950s. Goombay soon died out, giving way to closely related Rake 'n' Scrape.

Comprised of six Harbour Islanders, **The Brilanders** have toured with Jimmy Buffet. Their hit song "Backyard Party" is a soundtrack standard at just about any Bahamian party.

The Lassie Doh Boys put their stamp on Rake 'n' Scrape in 2006 with "Rake 'n' Scrape Mama."

Bahamian schoolchildren still learn their multiplication tables to **Ed Moxey's Rake 'n' Scrape**'s version of the old Bahamian folk song "The Timestable."

INSTRUMENTS
An authentic Rake 'n' Scrape band uses recycled objects to make music. An ordinary saw held in a musician's lap, then bent and scraped, becomes an instrument. A piece of wood, some fishing line, and a tin washtub is a good stand-in for the brass section. Plastic juice bottles are filled with pigeon peas, painted in bright colors, and turned into maracas. Add a goatskin drum, and you have all you need for a Rake 'n' Scrape ensemble, although many bands now add a concertina, guitar, or saxophone.

MAJOR PLAYERS
Authentic Rake 'n' Scrape is a dying art. The handful of groups scattered throughout The Bahamas are comprised of older people. Today **Ophie & Da Websites, The Brilanders, Thomas Cartwright,** and **Bo Hogg** are among the few groups still performing old-style Rake 'n' Scrape. Other modern Bahamian

Recycled objects are used as instruments.

musicians, such as **K.B., Phil Stubbs, D-Mac** and **Rhythm and Youth** work the sound and rhythm into their own signature styles. On Cat Island, you can ask around for **Pompey** and **Cedel.**

The popular four-day **Rake 'n' Scrape Festival** each June on Cat Island hosts dozens of bands from all over The Bahamas and the Caribbean.

In Nassau, July's **Junkanoo Summer Festival** showcases notable Rake 'n' Scrape bands alongside current headliners.

On Harbour Island, **Gusty's** and **Vic-Hum Club** usually work at least one night of Rake 'n' Scrape into the weekly live music schedule. **The Brilanders** often play at **Seagrapes.**

DANCE LIKE A LOCAL
The Rake 'n' Scrape rhythm is so captivating that even the most rhythmically challenged will be hard-pressed to stand still. As the first beats are played, look around and see what the old folk do. It's not unusual to see a man stick his leg out, lift his pants leg a bit, and let his footwork get fancy.

At festivals, schoolchildren usually dance the quadrille or heel-toe polka. If you ask a Bahamian to show you how to "mash da roach" or dance "the conch style," they may jump up and put on a show.

Traditional goatskin drum.

Wild and windswept, the southern Bahamian islands are idyllic Edens for those adventurers who want to battle a tarpon, dive a "wall" that drops thousands of feet, photograph the world's largest group of West Indian flamingos, or just sprawl on a sun-splashed beach with no sign of life—except maybe for a Bahama parrot pelting seeds from a guinep tree.

The quiet, simpler way of life on the Southern Family (or Out) Islands is startlingly different from Nassau's fast pace, and even more secluded than the northern Family Islands. You won't find huge resorts, casinos, or fast-food restaurants here, not to mention stoplights. Instead, you'll be rewarded with a serene vacation that will make your blood pressure drop faster than a fisherman's hook and sinker.

Sportsmen and -women are drawn to the Southern Islands to outsmart the swift bonefish and fish for marlin, black and bluefin tuna, wahoo, and swordfish. Yachties roam these islands on their way to the Caribbean, and vacationers rent Hobie Cats and kayaks. On all these islands, divers and snorkelers come to see healthy reefs, abundant underwater wildlife, and even sharks. Romantics and honeymooners head south for the glorious sunsets viewed from the verandas of beachside cottages and for the lovely pink beaches. Bird-watchers arrive with binoculars in hand to see the green-and-red Bahama parrots, Bahama pintails, tricolor and crested night herons, and, of course, flamingos. They can also try to spot the Bahama woodstar hummingbird, which is very similar to one of the world's newest discovered species, the Inaguan lyretail hummingbird.

Back-to-back hurricanes in the past decade damaged portions of the Southern Islands—yet, in many cases, seemed to prove how resilient these hardy and community-minded folk are. Friends, families, and companies from neighboring islands and the United States and Canada poured in generous donations. While never fully complete, repairs to infrastructure and in the tourism sector were relatively quick.

The neighborliness and hospitality of the residents is well-known, and visitors are often taken aback by their instant inclusion in the community. You can't walk 100 feet without someone offering a welcome ride on a hot day or a taxi driver offering you fresh fruit from his car trunk. Ask an islander where a certain restaurant is and they will walk with you until you see it. On Inagua, express any disappointment such as not seeing a flamingo up close, and the person standing behind you at the store will get on their cell phone. The scenery is gorgeous, but this genuine rapport is what brings regulars back time and again to these tiny communities.

The southernmost Bahama islands are remote, exposed to the open Atlantic, and ruggedly dramatic. Cat Island, 130 miles southeast of Nassau, lies to the west of diminutive San Salvador. Long Island stretches 80 miles across the Tropic of Cancer, due south of Cat Island. Windswept Crooked Island and Acklins, with about 300 and 600 residents, respectively, are southeast of Long Island. And way down at the southernmost point of the country is Inagua, only 55 miles northeast of Cuba and 60 miles north of Haiti.

Planning

When to Go

Few visitors make it to these Southern Islands, but those who do come at different times. Europeans tend to arrive in summer and stay for a month or longer. Sailors come through on their way to the southern Caribbean in fall and return to The Bahamas in spring or summer on trips back to North America. Fishers arrive all year, and divers prefer the calm seas in summer. Those looking for a winter warm-up visit from December to April, when temperatures are in the 70s. These months have the lowest rainfall of the year, but the ocean is chilly and, during cold fronts, is choppy for divers and boaters. Christmas, New Year's, and Easter are usually booked, so reserve rooms months in advance.

Many inns and resorts are closed in September and October for annual repairs, owners' vacations, and hurricane season, which technically runs from June through November. Mosquito repellent is usually needed year-round (except when winds blow), but is imperative in summer and fall, especially after a period of rain when both mosquitoes and no-see-ums come out in full force, especially at sunset. Note that they remain in the sand on your feet and towels even after you leave the beach, so make sure to rinse or leave your towel outside your room.

The Southern Islands are generally a couple of degrees warmer than Nassau, but farther south are more consistent trade winds in summer. You may need a windbreaker in winter, particularly on a boat. If possible, time your visit for Junkanoo on New Year's morning, sailing regattas in June and July, and special events, such as Cat Island's Rake 'n' Scrape Festival in early June.

FESTIVALS

Cat Island Rake 'n' Scrape Festival
MUSIC FESTIVALS | The annual Cat Island Rake 'n' Scrape Festival celebrating indigenous music is held in early June on Bahamian Labour Day weekend. Each day the festivities begin with breakfast and lunch in the park, with games of dominoes and checkers. At 7 pm, the site is cleared for the Battle of the Rake 'n' Scrape Bands. You can also enjoy a gospel concert, cultural dance troupes, a children's corner with games, arts and crafts, and a fishers' and farmers' market. Nearby restaurants expand their menus for the after-parties. Between 1,000 and 2,000 people attend and fill local hotels, inns, and guesthouses, so book early. Two mail boats, Bahamasair, and private charters serve the festival, which takes place in the town square near Arthur's Town Airport. ✉ *Arthur's Town Square, North Cat Island, Arthur's Town* 🚢 *$20.*

Cat Island Regatta
CULTURAL FESTIVALS | Growing in popularity (thanks to its Kalik Beer sponsorship), the annual Cat Island Regatta, held on the beach in New Bight over the Emancipation holiday weekend in early August, has parties, live music, games, dancing,

and lots of island cooking. Some 30–40 island sloops compete in various classes over three days. Expect some Rake 'n' Scrape and party music from national and local live entertainers. Games can include dominoes, water relay races, ugliest man, water balloon toss, hula hoop relays, coconut races, and more. Book flights and lodging well in advance. ⊠ New Bight ⊕ bahamas.com/events ☒ Free.

Discovery Day Festival
CULTURAL FESTIVALS | Though October 12 is now known as National Heroes Day across The Bahamas, it was not too long ago commemorated as "Discovery Day." However, the island of San Salvador continues to recognize the day Christopher Columbus arrived in the new world, since he landed right on one of their beaches. The Discovery Day Homecoming Festival is a week-long event that takes places at various venues across the island, including Graham's Harbour on the far north of the island and Long Bay, where memorials mark the spot where Columbus landed. Festival days depend on when the public holiday falls, but always include food, drink, craft, a mix of live bands, DJs, and fun games such as sack races, coconut barking, pineapple eating, beer drinking, and a staged cultural dancing show. An evening ecumenical service and gospel concert usually kicks things off while a Beach Bash closes out the festivities. ⊠ Graham's Harbour on San Salvador's far north beach, and Long Bay Beach, south of Cockburn Town ⊕ www.bahamas.com/islands/san-salvador ☒ Free except for main concert area.

Inagua Heritage & Salty Festival
CULTURAL FESTIVALS | More oriented to locals and their families, and sponsored by the Morton Salt Company, this homecoming-type heritage festival takes place over the Emancipation holiday weekend in early August. Most activities are in Matthew Town's marketplace, with a Sunday Beach Bash on Farquharson Beach, 8 miles north of the town. Visitors are most welcome and encouraged to join in. Celebrations include an ecumenical church service, gospel choirs, a Junkanoo rushout, fireworks, live bands, games, and cultural activities, including the plaiting of the maypole and climbing the greasy pole. Along with festival staples, such as barbecued meats and fresh seafood, it's a great chance to savor some of the island's more unusual delicacies, such as spiced souses and baked breads and tarts. ⊠ Matthew Town ⊕ www.bahamas.com/islands/inagua ☒ Free.

Junkanoo
CULTURAL FESTIVALS | Inagua puts on spirited Junkanoo parades on Boxing Day, December 26, and New Year's Day. Parades start at 4:30 am; you have to make the decision to stay up all night or get up early. There's food at the fish fry at Kiwanis Park in the center of town where the parades end. ⊠ Matthew Town.

Long Island Sailing Regatta
FESTIVALS | The annual Long Island Sailing Regatta, featuring Bahamian-made boats, is a three-day event the first weekend of June. Held in Salt Pond, the regatta is the island's biggest event and The Bahamas' second-largest regatta, attracting competitors from all over the islands. Booths featuring handmade crafts and Bahamian food and drink dot the site, and local bands provide lively entertainment beginning at sundown. Salt Pond is 10 miles south of Simms. ⊠ Salt Pond ⊕ bahamas.com/events.

Getting Here and Around

AIR
All of the Southern Family Islands have at least one airport, and several have multiple airports. Flights are primarily from the Nassau hub using local airlines and charter companies. San Salvador has scheduled flights from Montreal in Canada, Fort Lauderdale in Florida, and from Paris in France.

⇨ *See individual island sections for more details.*

BOAT AND FERRY

Mail boats link all these islands to Nassau, and, only for a popular festival, Bahamas Ferries may add a special service to supply the extra demand.

⇨ *See individual island sections for more details.*

If you plan to use the mail boat for transportation, check schedules by calling the Dockmaster's Office in Nassau. They change frequently.

CONTACTS Association of Bahamas Marinas. ☎ *844/356 5772 toll-free, 954/462–4591 Florida* ⊕ *www.bahamasmarinas.com.* **Mailboat Port/Dockmaster's Office in Nassau.** ✉ *Potter's Cay, Nassau* ☎ *242/393–1064 Dockmaster's office, 242/394–1237.*

CAR AND TAXI

You can rent a car on all the islands. Taxi service is also available. Regardless, transportation tends to be expensive because of the isolation and cost of fuel.

Hotels

The inns in the Southern Family Islands are small and intimate and usually cater to a specific crowd, such as anglers, divers, or those who just want a quiet beach experience. Club Med Columbus Isle, an upscale resort on San Salvador, is an exception, with 236 rooms and a wide range of activities. Fernandez Bay Village in southern Cat Island is also more of a full-service resort, with seven cottages, five villas, and a long menu of activities and dining.

Most inns are on the beach, and many have one- and two-bedroom cottages with private verandas, offering three meals a day or self-catering along with free kayaks, paddleboards, and bikes. They'll either pick you up at the airport, ask you to get a taxi, or arrange a car

rental. Fishing guides, charters, dive trips, and sightseeing tours are just a call away, but you should book them in advance. If the hotel doesn't close in the off-season, some of the best deals are available in September through early December. U.S. holidays and local holidays or festivals can quickly fill the islands' rooms.

Restaurants

Family Island restaurants are often family-run and focus on home-style dishes. If you want to dine at a restaurant or another inn, it's crucial to call ahead. Dinner choices largely depend on what's planned or what fishermen and mail boats bring in; be prepared for limited choices. If you are renting, bring snacks and be prepared to grocery shop.

Anticipate tasty Bahamian fresh fish, lobster, and conch, fresh-baked bread, and coconut tarts, along with a smattering of American and international dishes. Fish, lobster, and conch—which is served stewed, as a salad, or cracked (battered and deep fried)—is served at almost every restaurant for lunch and dinner. Chicken served many ways is a Bahamian staple, and the skills of Bahamian cooks to prepare tasty chicken are legendary. These islands have breezy roadside conch stands—typically near a settlement or a beach—that deserve a special trip from your hotel. On Friday and Saturday nights many restaurants and bars crank up the music, and visitors and locals will drink and dance 'til late.

⇨ *Restaurant prices are based on the median main course price at dinner, excluding gratuity, typically 15%, which is often automatically added to the bill as well as 10% VAT. Hotel prices are for two people in a standard double room in high season, excluding service and the 10% VAT. Some resorts can charge a 6% resort levy that goes to the Bahamas Out Island Promotion Board. These BOIPB hotels typically offer a higher standard of service. Restaurant and hotel reviews have been shortened. For full information, visit Fodors.com.*

What It Costs in U.S. Dollars			
$	$$	$$$	$$$$
RESTAURANTS			
under $20	$20–$30	$31–$40	over $40
HOTELS			
under $200	$200–$300	$301–$400	over $400

Visitor Information

CONTACTS Association of Bahamas Marinas. ☎ *844/356 5772 toll-free, 954/462-4591 Florida* ⊕ *www.bahamasmarinas.com.* **The Bahamas Ministry of Tourism.** ☎ *242/302–2000 in Nassau* ⊕ *www.bahamas.com.* **Bahamas Out Islands Promotion Board.** ☎ *242/322–1140 in Nassau* ⊕ *www.myoutislands.com.*

Cat Island

Cat Island is made up of exquisite pink-sand beaches and sparkling white-sand-ringed coves as calm and clear as a spa pool. Largely undeveloped, the island has the tallest hill in The Bahamas, a dizzying 206 feet high, with a historic tiny stone abbey on top. The two-lane Queen's Highway runs the 48-mile length of the island from north to south, mostly along the gorgeous sandy western coastline, through quaint seaside settlements and past hundreds of abandoned stone cottages. Some are 200-year-old slave houses, crumbling testaments to cotton and sisal plantation days, while others, too old to have modern utilities, were abandoned. Trees and vines twist through spaces that used to be windows and roofs, and the deep-blue ocean can be seen through missing walls. In 1938 the island had 5,000 residents and today only about 1,500. Many of the inhabitants left the cottages long ago out of necessity, to find work in Nassau and Florida, but the houses remain because they still mark family land.

Cat Island was named after a frequent visitor, the notorious pirate Arthur Catt, a contemporary of Edward "Blackbeard" Teach. Another famous islander is Sir Sidney Poitier, who grew up here before leaving to become a groundbreaking Academy Award–winning movie actor and director.

GETTING HERE AND AROUND
AIR
Cat Island has two airports: Arthur's Town (ATC) in the north and New Bight (TBI) mid-island. Two airlines fly in from Nassau to both airports: Southern Air four days a week, and SkyBahamas daily. (SkyBahamas has a connecting flight from Fort Lauderdale to Nassau in the early morning four days a week, providing convenient connections from Florida.) To reach these Southern Islands from Nassau, Stella Maris Air Service has a great reputation and, from Fort Lauderdale or Miami, you can arrange a charter through Eastern Air Express, Monarch Air Group, or Triton Airways to fly you direct, avoiding Nassau. For the best price, call around for a plane with the right number of seats. If you are going to Fernandez Bay Village or Hawk's Nest Resort, fly into the Bight. If you are going to Pigeon Cay, Orange Creek Inn, Shannas Cove, or Tailwinds, fly to Arthur's Town. For a full list of scheduled and charter airlines see ⊕ *www.bahamas.com/islands/cat-island/getting-here.*

⇨ *For contact information of individual airlines, see also Air Travel in Travel Smart.*

AIRPORT CONTACTS New Bight Airport. ✉ *New Bight* ☎ *242/342–2256.*

Great Itineraries

Note: If you don't have a boat, island-hopping is difficult in these parts because to fly between these islands you either have to transfer back to Nassau or charter your own plane. Most visitors choose one island as a base.

If You Have 5 Days

Fly into **The Bight** on Cat Island, check into **Rollezz Villas Beach Resort** or another inn and catch what's left of the day on the gorgeous Old Bight beach, enjoying the shaded cabanas and paddleboards made available to guests. Dine at the open-air restaurant on the property. On Day 2 jump in your rental car and head north to explore Cat Island and visit **Arthur's Town**. Go on a prearranged afternoon **snorkel or dive excursion** at **Shannas Cove**, staying to enjoy their beach. From the clubhouse's high balcony, enjoy the views at dusk with a Goombay Smash and their excellent cuisine. Stop off at **The Hot Spot** for a Bahama Mama nightcap on your way home. Book Day 3 with a morning fishing charter at **Hawk's Nest Resort & Marina** to catch some game fish off the ocean wall. Drive back, touring **Old Bight** with its ancient plantation ruins and **New Bight** for some souvenir shopping. Then climb The Bahamas's highest "mountain," the 206-foot **Mt. Alvernia**, to see **The Hermitage**, the ruins of a famous little abbey. Enjoy the evening at the Fish Fry on **New Bight Beach** with some island music and fresh conch, fish, or lobster, washed down with sky juice. Day 4 is for relaxing around Rollezz Villas and getting to know the local owners and managers, who live on-site. Walk the white-sand beach, sink in the soft powder, and snorkel or paddle a kayak into the shallows to the south, where you can turtle spot in the mangrove creeks. Day 5, take an early morning flight.

If You Have 10 Days

Day 6. Arrive at **Stella Maris Airport** and check in to the famed resort there. Head down to the **Moonshine Bar & Grill** on the ocean, capture views from the boardwalk, and take a dip in the man-made, wave-washed ocean hole. Enjoy dinner at the resort. On Day 7, book a morning **snorkel or dive** at the resort's dive shop, with fabulous reef, wreck, shark, night, and wall dives. In the afternoon, join the resort's excursion to a beach on the western side for some **snorkeling or kayaking**. Arrange for dinner at **Chez Pierre's** in Miller's Bay, a small inn celebrated for its cuisine. Day 8, pack an ice chest, bring your swimsuits, and rent a car. Make it your goal to see and swim at **Dean's Blue Hole**, a stunning ocean hole surrounded by cliffs and a beach. First, head south to Dean's. Then if you have time, head farther south to see **Galloway's Landing Beach**. Heading back, enjoy lunch at **Flying Fish Marina's Outer Edge Grill**, see **Hamilton's Cave** near Deadman's Cay, and stop at **Max Conch Bar & Grill**. On Day 9, book a **Bonafide Bonefishing** tour for the morning, then take Stella Maris's excursion to **Cape Eleuthera** to enjoy the stunning beach. (If you have a four-wheel drive, you can even negotiate the rocky road to **Columbus Monument** and see some breathtaking hilltop views.) At Cape Eleuthera, enjoy gorgeous sunsets, cocktails, and a delightful dinner. Day 10, shop for souvenirs at a resort's boutique and go for a final swim in the pool.

BOAT

Mail boats that bring supplies to the island each week make for an adventurous way to get around. You'll ride with groceries, large and small appliances, automobiles, and sometimes even livestock. All boats depart from Potter's Cay in Nassau. The M/V *New G* and the M/V *KCT* sails to north and south Cat Island. Contact the Dockmaster's Office for schedules and fares as they change frequently.

CONTACT Mailboat Port/Dockmaster's Office in Nassau. ✉ *Potter's Cay, Nassau* ☎ *242/393–1064 Dockmaster's office, 242/394–1237.*

CAR

The best way to enjoy the overall Cat Island experience is to rent a car. Various settlements are not within walking distance. The two-lane, potholed Queen's Highway runs the 48-mile length of the island from north to south. You can also tour the island with a guide from Cat Island Experience.

The New Bight Service Station and Gilbert's New Bight Market rent cars on the southern end of Cat Island and will pick you up from the New Bight Airport. Robon Enterprises rents cars for the north (for those flying into Arthur's Town). It's important to rent a car from an agency that services the end of the island where you are staying because companies will not deliver cars to renters at the opposite end of the island. However, all inns and resorts can arrange rental cars for you upon arrival, and many people arrange their cars through their lodging. Rates depend on the number of days you're renting but are expensive, averaging $85 per day plus gas (which is also very expensive).

CAR RENTAL CONTACTS Alvernia Food's & Car Rental. ✉ *Smith's Bay* ☎ *242/342–2042* ⊕ *alvernia-food-store.business. site.* **Gilbert's Car Rentals and Market.** ✉ *Across from Gilbert's Inn, New Bight*

☎ *242/342–3011.* **New Bight Car Rentals.** ✉ *New Bight* ☎ *242/342–3014.* **Robon Enterprises Car Rental.** ✉ *In Bennett's Harbour, near Arthur's Town Airport, Arthur's Town* ☎ *242/354–6120, 242/359–9643.*

TAXI

Taxis wait for incoming flights at the New Bight and Arthur's Town airports, but be warned that fares can be expensive, starting at about $20 for the 10-minute trip from New Bight Airport to the community of New Bight. Most inns and resorts will make arrangements for airport transfers, often complimentary.

Arthur's Town and Bennett's Harbour

Arthur's Town's claim to fame is that it was the boyhood home of actor Sidney Poitier, who wrote about growing up here in his autobiography *The Measure of a Man*. His parents and relatives were farmers. The presence of Young Marine Explorers, a local marine conservation nonprofit, has mobilized the local community around many environmental conservation initiatives, including coral reef restoration projects.

When you drive south from Arthur's Town, which is nearly at the island's northernmost tip, you'll wind along a road that passes through small villages and past bays where fishing boats are tied up. Fifteen miles south of Arthur's Town is Bennett's Harbour, one of the island's oldest settlements. Fresh-baked breads and fruit are sometimes sold at makeshift stands at the government dock, and there is good bonefishing in the creek.

🍽 Restaurants

★ **Shannas Cove Restaurant**
$$$$ | EUROPEAN | This resort restaurant boasts a beautiful towering view above the sea and the north point of the island and offers three meals a day on the

breezy veranda or in the cool interior. The German owners take their European cuisine seriously, and they please and surprise hotel guests and those from other resorts who drive far to dine here. **Known for:** homemade breads; extensive menu; reservations necessary. $ *Average main: $48 ⊠ Shanna's Cove, north of Orange Creek, Bennett's Harbour* 🕾 *242/354–4249* ⊕ *www.shannas-cove. com* ▭ *No credit cards* 🛇 *Closed Sept.*

Yardie's Restaurant, Bar & Conch Stand
$ | JAMAICAN | Yardie's owners, Odette and Derrick Rolle, serve up large-size genuine Jamaican and Bahamian dishes such as jerk chicken, steamed pork chops, curried mutton, barbecue ribs, and their famous fresh conch salad. If you really want an island meal, try the breakfast grits with tuna or corned beef. **Known for:** conch salad; open all day; no frills. $ *Average main: $15 ⊠ North Cat Island, Bennett's Harbour* 🕾 *242/354–6076* ▭ *No credit cards.*

 ## Hotels

Pigeon Cay Beach Club
$$ | RESORT | In a wide bay a half mile off the main road just south of Alligator Point, this resort, owned and operated by an American family, has seven deluxe cottages and a "big house" with several rooms, which are all colorfully decorated and perched steps away from a secluded 3-mile stretch of pristine sugary white beach. **Pros:** fully equipped kitchens in rooms; bicycles, kayaks, and snorkel gear available; cars available for a small fee. **Cons:** not wheelchair-accessible; surcharge for airport transfers; meals are served only a few times a week. $ *Rooms from: $215 ⊠ Rokers ✛ 3 miles south of Bennett's Harbour* 🕾 *242/354–5084* ⊕ *www.pigeoncaybahamas.com* 🛏 *11 rooms* ⦿ *No Meals.*

Shannas Cove Resort
$$ | RESORT | This quiet and secluded owner-run beach resort is perched high on the hill on the northern tip of Cat Island, granting sweeping views of the beautiful beach at Shannas Cove and the north of the island. **Pros:** stunning private beach; excellent on-site restaurant; nicely designed, roomy cottages with air-conditioning. **Cons:** no TVs; isolated from the rest of the island; no children. $ *Rooms from: $269 ⊠ North of Orange Creek, Arthur's Town* 🕾 *242/354–4249* ⊕ *www. shannas-cove.com* 🛇 *Closed Sept.* 🛏 *5 villas* ⦿ *No Meals.*

 ## Nightlife

BARS AND PUBS
The Hot Spot Restaurant & Karaoke Bar
BARS | Owners Ted and Melony (the latter is also the fabulous cook here) entertain locals and visitors with great Bahamian food and karaoke. It is known for the Bahamian touches, like sky juice, the 46-ounce Como Hill cocktail, and other drinks served in pea cans. Some claim Melony's food, served on palms and sea grape leaves, is the best they've had. Spurred on by tuneful locals and visitors pumping out a great selection of music, this place can rock until 3 am. If the music's too loud, you can dine and drink on the deck. This is the north's best nightlife spot. ⊠ *North Cat Island, Arthur's Town* 🕾 *242/464–6505.*

 ## Activities

SCUBA DIVING
Coral reefs teeming with fish and mysterious shipwrecks make for great diving off the north end of the island, where visibility ranges from 165 to 200 feet thanks to a natural filtering system of limestone and rich fauna.

Diving with Shannas Cove Resort
SCUBA DIVING | This is not a certified dive shop, but Frank, one of the owners of Shannas Cove, is a master diver and takes only up to four divers at a time—making it very safe for beginners and pros alike. Shannas offers north Cat

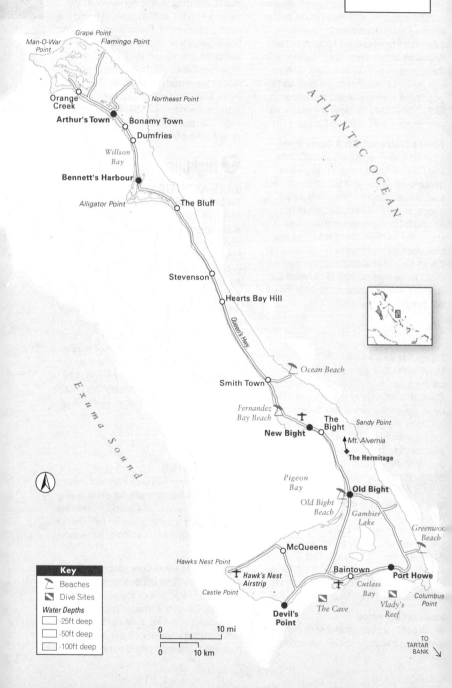

Cat Island

Man-O-War Point
Grape Point
Flamingo Point

Northeast Point

Orange Creek
Arthur's Town
Bonamy Town
Dumfries

Willson Bay

Bennett's Harbour

Alligator Point

The Bluff

Stevenson

Hearts Bay Hill

Queen's Hwy.

ATLANTIC OCEAN

Exuma Sound

Smith Town

Ocean Beach

Fernandez Bay Beach

New Bight
The Bight

Sandy Point

Mt. Alvernia
The Hermitage

Pigeon Bay

Old Bight

Old Bight Beach

Gambier Lake

Greenwood Beach

McQueens

Hawks Nest Point

Baintown

Port Howe

Hawk's Nest Airstrip

Castle Point

Cutlass Bay

The Cave

Vlady's Reef

Columbus Point

Devil's Point

TO TARTAR BANK

Key

Beaches
Dive Sites

Water Depths
-25ft deep
-50ft deep
-100ft deep

0   10 mi

0   10 km

Island's amazing range of dives: from wrecks to walls, and reefs with amazing visibility, all from a 22-foot catamaran. Diving spots can be reached within 5 to 30 minutes. Well-maintained equipment is available for rent. ⊠ *Shannas Cove Resort, North of Orange Creek, Arthur's Town* ☎ *242/354–4249, 242/359–9668 cell* ⊕ *www.shannas-cove.com* ⊙ *Closed Sept.*

Old Bight and New Bight

In this small residential village, just over 8 miles south of New Bight Airport, beaches, historic ruins, and gas stations are what necessitate at least one stop from visitors. Five miles of undisturbed pink-speckled beach can be found on the southwestern coast of Cat Island. Although there is access to basic amenities on **Old Bight Beach** at the boutique **Rollezz Villas Beach Resort,** the light-touch development from the southern end of **Joe Sound Creek** across the crescent-shape beach ensures absolute solitude for most beachgoers. Top up at **Favor's Service Center** (☎ *242/342–4107*), a gas station, car rental, beauty salon, and plant nursery, or at **Pilot Harbour Service Station.**

Yachts anchor off the coast of Regatta Beach, and boaters dingy in to the Custom House amid a cluster of government buildings in this quaint community, the largest town on the island. Houses face the Queen's Highway, which twists through green hills. Yachties and visitors stock up at the small grocery store and the bakery. The island's most well-known sight is **Mt. Alvernia,** which is crowned with a historic little abbey. There's also a colorful **Fish Fry,** a collection of restaurants and take-out places, including **Blue Waters** on Regatta Beach, that are lively hangouts at nights and on weekends, lovely old churches, and eerie abandoned stone cottages, many of which are plantation ruins. Just a minute drive away is

Olive's Bakery, where you can get freshly baked loaves, coconut tarts, pineapple tarts, and Cat Island's well-known flour cakes, as well as jams and preserves made by others on the island. The town sits along a thin, Australian pine–lined white beach on the west coast and has peaceful saltwater estuaries that are nesting areas for great blue herons, egrets, and pelicans. **Hidden Treasures,** on the main road, is also worth a visit, if only for a refreshing daiquiri or smoothie.

Sights

★ The Hermitage
MOUNTAIN | At the top of 206-foot Mt. Alvernia, the highest point in The Bahamas, The Hermitage is the final resting place of Father Jerome, who lived quite an astonishing life. Born John Hawes, he was an architect who traveled the world and eventually settled in The Bahamas. An Anglican who converted to Roman Catholicism, he built many structures, including this hermitage on Mt. Alvernia; St. Peter & St. Paul's Church in Clarence Town, Long Island; and the St. Augustine Monastery in Nassau. He retired to Cat Island to live out his last dozen years as a hermit, and his final, supreme act of religious dedication was to carve the steps up to the top of Mt. Alvernia. Along the way, he also carved the stations of the cross. At the summit, he built an abbey with a small chapel, a conical bell tower, and living quarters comprising three closet-size rooms. He died in 1956 at the age of 80 and was supposedly buried with his arms outstretched, in a pose resembling that of the crucified Christ.

The pilgrimage to The Hermitage begins next to the commissioner's office at New Bight at a dirt path that leads to the foot of Mt. Alvernia. Don't miss the slightly laborious climb to the top. The Hermitage provides a perfect place to pause for quiet contemplation, with glorious views of the ocean on both sides of the island. A caretaker clears the weeds around the

The Hermitage on Mt. Alvernia is Cat Island's most iconic sight.

tomb—islanders regard it as a shrine—and lights a candle in Father Jerome's memory. ⊠ *New Bight*.

Beaches

Ocean Beach
BEACH | On the eastern Atlantic side, 4 miles from Queen's Highway at Smith's Bay is Ocean Beach, 1.8 miles of pink sand and cool breezes. This is a stunning beach that sits below a towering sand dune. There's no shade here, and you should bring whatever water-sports equipment you want. When conditions are right it's good for surfing and, when calm, paddleboarding, kayaking, and snorkeling on the nearby reefs. Bring water and snacks. Only reasonably accessed with a four-wheel-drive vehicle due to the rugged off-road that leads to this beach. **Amenities:** none. **Best for:** snorkeling. ⊠ *4 miles east of Smith's Bay*.

Old Bight Beach
BEACH | Fall asleep on this beach and be completely undisturbed. Walk the five-mile stretch and find only your footprints. The peace and solitude you find at Old Bight Beach is due to the light-touch development along this southwestern part of Cat Island's coast. If you need access to the basic comforts, a small boutique resort is seamlessly blended into the natural surroundings on the southern end of the beach. **Amenities:** food and drink; nonmotorized water sports. **Best for:** solitude; sunset; swimming; walking. ⊠ *Just south of New Bight Airport near Favor's Service Centre, Old Bight Beach* ☎ *242/557–0005*.

Restaurants

Hidden Treasure
$$ | BAHAMIAN | Cat Islanders and visitors alike love this restaurant for its delicious food, refreshing daiquiris and smoothies, and seating on the beach. You will find seafood favorites, including conch,

lobster, grouper, and shrimp, here, as well as jerk pork. **Known for:** chef's suggestions; daiquiris and seafood; family-run. $ *Average main: $25 ⊠ 1 block off Queen's Hwy., look for the sign, New Bight* ☎ *242/424–9237.*

Hotels

★ Fernandez Bay Village

$$ | RESORT | This owner-run resort is one of The Bahamas' most famous and successful—and one of the best kick-back retreats anywhere. **Pros:** private, spacious accommodations; crescent-shape white-sand beach in shade; lots of water sports on-site and activities off-site. **Cons:** no TV; Wi-Fi in the main clubhouse only; insect repellent needed outside in the evening. $ *Rooms from: $283 ⊠ 1 mile north of New Bight Airport, New Bight* ☎ *242/824–3043, 954/302–7422 toll-free* ⊕ *www.fernandezbayvillage.com ⬏ 17 rooms* ❚❂❙ *No Meals.*

★ Rollezz Villas Beach Resort

$$ | HOTEL | FAMILY | This beautiful, family-run boutique hotel has unmatched island charm thanks to the creativity and talent of the Bahamian owners, who handmade the decor and furniture with Bahamian fabrics, native straw plait, and other natural material. **Pros:** secluded beachfront villas; 12-mile stretch of stunning beach; kayaks, paddleboard, pedal boat. **Cons:** insect repellent needed outside in the evening; limited supplies in hotel boutique; limited entertainment. $ *Rooms from: $259 ⊠ Joe Sound Creek* ☎ *242/557–0005, 305/280–5719* ⊕ *rollezz.com ⬏ 8 rooms* ❚❂❙ *No Meals.*

Nightlife

FISH FRY

Regatta Beach Fish Fry

GATHERING PLACES | For an authentic Bahamian experience, don't miss the Regatta Beach Fish Fry on Regatta Beach, just south of the government buildings in the town center. On weekends, at least two fish shacks open late in the afternoon and stay lively into the night. It's a great place for sunset watching and mingling with locals. ⊠ *Regatta Beach, New Bight.*

Shopping

SOUVENIRS

Pam's Boutique

SOUVENIRS | This little shop at Fernandez Bay Village has reasonably priced resort wear, including sarongs, Havaianas flip-flops, logo hats, and T-shirts. They also sell jewelry, bags, coffee mugs, postcards, local art, and books. This is one of your few chances to get a Cat Island T-shirt. ⊠ *Fernandez Bay Village, New Bight* ☎ *242/824–3043, 954/302–7422.*

Activities

FISHING

Cat Island Fishing

FISHING | On Cat Island you have myriad ways to fish: deep-sea, bone-, fly-, and bottom-fishing. Several expert guides can do all, but each has his own specialty. Mark Keasler is great for bonefishing, Nathaniel Top Cat is great for deep-sea trolling, and Carl Pinder is great for reef fishing. Call Rollezz Villas, Fernandez Bay, or the local tourist office to let them find out who is available for which type of fishing. They also do snorkeling tours and beach picnics. ⊠ *New Bight* ☎ *242/338–8668.*

TOURS

Cat Island Experience

GUIDED TOURS | C&O Tours, comprising Pastor Chris, son Danny, and wife Olive King, have eight-seater air-conditioned vans for guided tours of Cat Island. They have customizable tours, both for the north and the south, which include much of the same sites. The tour in the south includes beaches, Mt. Alvernia and its minimonastery, a step-down well, bat caves, cotton plantations and ruins, the old cotton railroad, an old lighthouse, churches, and also the modern structures and utilities. Chris and family can answer your many questions and give good, historical background. It's one of the most rewarding activities, giving you a lasting connection to the island. ✉ *New Bight* ☎ *242/464–6193, 242/474–8462 Danson King, manager* 🌐 *catislandexperience.com/booking-info.html* 🎫 *$200 for half day, $350 for full day.*

Port Howe

At the conch shell–lined traffic roundabout at the southernmost end of Queen's Highway, head east toward Port Howe, believed by many to be Cat Island's oldest settlement. Nearby lie the ruins of the **Deveaux Mansion,** a stark two-story, whitewashed building overrun with vegetation. Once it was a grand house on a cotton plantation, owned by Captain Andrew Deveaux of the British Navy, who was given thousands of acres of Cat Island property as a reward for his daring raid that recaptured Nassau from the Spaniards in 1783. Just beyond the mansion ruin is the entrance road to Greenwood Beach Resort, which sits on an 8-mile stretch of unblemished, velvet pink-sand beach.

Beaches

Greenwood Beach

BEACH | An 8-mile stretch of pink sand on the Atlantic Ocean makes this one of the most spectacular beaches on Cat Island. Hypnotized by the beauty, most visitors walk the entire beach, some going even farther to an adjoining sandy cove accessible only by foot. After such a long walk, a dip in the shallows of the turquoise ocean is pure bliss. The beach is on the remote southeastern end of the island and is home to just one hotel, Greenwood Beach Resort, which is a good place for a bite and a drink. **Amenities:** none. **Best for:** solitude; snorkeling; swimming; walking. ✉ *Greenwood Beach Resort, 3 miles northeast of Port Howe along a bumpy road, Port Howe* 🌐 *www.greenwoodbeachresort.com.*

Hotels

Greenwood Beach Resort

$ | HOTEL | Set on an 8-mile stretch of pink shell-strewn sand, this remote resort is about 35 minutes from the Bight airport, but the peaceful solitude is what brings regulars back. **Pros:** gorgeous, private Atlantic beach location; swimming pool in beautiful setting; lots of ocean breeze. **Cons:** long drive to explore other parts of the island; must reserve air-conditioned rooms in advance; rooms have charm but are dated. [$] *Rooms from: $144* ✉ *Port Howe* ✣ *Go to Port Howe and take the northeast road* ☎ *242/464-6816, 242/808-1846* 🌐 *www.greenwoodbeachresort.biz* 🛏 *16 rooms* 🍴 *No Meals.*

Activities

SAILING

★ Calvert Catamaran Charters

SAILING | Between November and June, you can experience the joy of sailing and exploring Cat Island and the beautiful Bahamian waters with one of the world's great sailors. Captain Dave Calvert and his wife Trish offer half-day or full-day cruises from Port Howe and, even more enjoyable, longer Bahamas-wide cruising and exploring expeditions. Their spacious and well-equipped 46-foot catamaran, the *Destiny III*, is a 2007 Leopard 46, built in South Africa by a leading manufacturer. It sleeps six for overnight charters and up to 12 for day charters, and as few as two guests can book it all to themselves—chef-prepared meals and soft drinks are included. Full-day charters start at $1,200 for the vessel, with an additional $100 per guest, and increase depending on the selected island, Cat Island, Long Island or Exuma. (Consult their website for more rates and timing options.) It's a safe bet that cruising with the Calverts will be your vacation highlight or one of the best

Fernandez Bay Beach is a perfect, calm cove for swimming.

vacations you'll ever enjoy. ✉ *Port Howe Harbour, Port Howe* ☎ *242/342–5155 in Bahamas, 305/664–8056 in U.S.* ⊕ *www. calvertcatamarancharters.com* ✉ *From $1,200 for full-day charters* ☞ *Closed July–Oct.*

SCUBA DIVING
Greenwood Beach Dive Shop
SCUBA DIVING | With this full-service center, divers can take trips to more than 20 dive sites—mainly drop-off and wall diving—on the southern tip of Cat Island or go diving at a coral-reef garden just off the beach. Dive training begins at $100, while daily excursions range from $75 to $600, plus 12% VAT, for up to a standard 10-tank dive trip. You can also take guided snorkeling trips and go kite-boarding on Greenwood Beach. ✉ *Greenwood Beach Resort, Port Howe* ☎ *242/464–6816* ⊕ *www.greenwoodbeachresort.biz.*

Devil's Point

The small village of Devil's Point, with its bright-walled, thatch-roof houses, lies at the southern tip of Queen's Highway, 9 miles southwest of Old Bight. Beachcombers will find great shelling on the pristine beach; keep an eye out for dolphins, which are common in these waters. From Devil's Point, drive north through the arid southwest corner of the island to **McQueens,** then west to the area's biggest resort, Hawk's Nest Resort, which has an airstrip, marina, restaurant, and bar. This resort is well-known to serious anglers and divers, who often fly in to the resort's private airstrip and stay a week to do little else but fish or dive. The southwest end of the island teems with great diving walls, reefs, and wrecks with an abundance of marine life and coral heads.

Restaurants

Hawk's Nest Dining & Clubhouse

$$ | BAHAMIAN | High-beamed ceilings, tiled floors, blue-and-lime-green walls, and blue ceramic-topped tables create a cheerful vibe to go with the Bahamian comfort-food menu. If you have your heart set on a menu item, be sure to call your order in by 3 pm. **Known for:** fresh-squeezed juices; poolside dining; TVs showing sports and news. $ *Average main: $30* ⊠ *Hawk's Nest Resort, Devil's Point* ✛ *7½ miles by road northwest of Devil's Point* ☎ *242/342–7050, 954/376–3865* ⊕ *hawks-nest.com/activities/dining/* ⊘ *Closed mid-Sept.–Oct.*

Hotels

Hawk's Nest Resort & Marina

$ | RESORT | Catering to private pilots, yachties, and serious fishers, this small laid-back resort at Cat Island's southwestern tip has its own 3,100-foot runway and a 28-slip full-service marina with a dive shop for guests. **Pros:** three meals served daily; fully stocked honor bar; great dive spots and shallow walls. **Cons:** long drive from other places on the island; good swimming beach a few yards from main clubhouse; afternoon shark feeding can interrupt swimming at the dock. $ *Rooms from: $175* ⊠ *Devil's Point* ✛ *From Devil's Point village, go 4 miles north and 3½ miles west along white road* ☎ *242/342–7050 resort, 954/376–3865 in U.S. and Canada* ⊕ *hawks-nest. com* ⊘ *Clubhouse and hotel closed Sept. and Oct.* ➳ *10 rooms.*

Spirit House

$$$ | HOUSE | This Bahamian-owned 3,000-square-foot, five-bedroom house is completely off the grid, solar powered with a generator as backup. **Pros:** ecofriendly; beach access; large indoor and outdoor spaces. **Cons:** fairly remote; need a car; can't rent single rooms. $ *Rooms from: $350* ⊠ *Devil's Point*

☎ *242/810–7104* ⊕ *www.facebook.com/ spiritcatisland* ➳ *1 house* ❍ *No Meals.*

Activities

FISHING

Hawk's Nest Marina

FISHING | Blue-water angling boat owners make a point of using Hawk's Nest Marina to access the dynamite offshore fishing. Look for wahoo, yellowfin tuna, dolphin, and white and blue marlin along the Exuma Sound drop-offs, Devil's Point, Tartar Bank, and Columbus Point. March through July is prime-time, with multiple annual fishing tournaments on the books. Winter fishing, from December through February, is also good for wahoo. You can arrange bonefishing with a top guide through the marina. ⊠ *Hawks Nest Resort and Marina, Devil's Point* ☎ *242/342–7050, 954/376–3865* ⊕ *hawks-nest.com/marina/.*

SCUBA DIVING

Cat Island's south coast offers some of the country's best diving. The walls start from very shallow depths, allowing for long dives and great photography. Some of the area's best dive sites are easily reached from Hawk's Nest Marina. **Hole in the Wall** (12 miles, 50–100 feet) features a spectacular break in the wall, an impressive archway and an entrance to a small channel; you might see lobster, spotted drum, black coral, stingrays, sharks, dog snapper, barracuda, and grouper, plus all kinds of soft and hard coral. **The Oz** (7 miles, 55–100 feet) has tunnels and canyons overgrown with soft corals, turtles, reef sharks, reef fish of every color, hogfish, Nassau and other grouper, and oceanic triggerfish and is spectacular when approaching the wall. **Tartar Bank** (6 miles, 40–60 feet) has strong currents and is therefore for pro divers only, with an offshore pinnacle, reef sharks, white-tip sharks, big turtles, and more. **Fish Bowls** (20–30 feet) takes you from micro to macro in a photographer's paradise that includes schools of goat fish, Atlantic spadefish, yellowtail, and mutton snapper. White-spotted eels are numerous, along with nurse sharks and lobster. See a spider crab refuge and cleaning station as you follow the reef's ledge. Dives at Hawk's Nest must be booked a month in advance.

Hawk's Nest Marina Dive Shop

SCUBA DIVING | Hawk's Nest at one time was the only PADI-certified dive operation on Cat Island. The running time to dive sites off the southern tip of the island is 15 to 30 minutes in the shop's 43-foot custom dive boat, outfitted with VHF and GPS. Call ahead for bookings. Dives must be booked one month in advance; it's a $250 minimum to take the dive boat out. Ask for package rates. ⊠ Devil's Point ✛ From Devil's Point, go 4 miles north and 3½ miles along white road ☎ 242/342–7050, 954/376–3865 ⊕ hawks-nest.com.

San Salvador

On October 12, 1492, Christopher Columbus disrupted the lives of the peaceful Lucayan natives when he landed on the island of Guanahaní, which he renamed San Salvador. Apparently he knelt on the beach and claimed the land for Spain. (Skeptics of this story point to a study published in a 1986 National Geographic article in which Samana Cay, 60 miles southeast, is identified as the exact point of the weary explorer's landing.) Three monuments on the island commemorate Columbus's arrival, and the 500th anniversary of the event was officially celebrated here.

The island is 14 miles long—a little longer than Manhattan Island—and about 6 miles wide, with a lake-filled interior. Some of the most dazzling deserted beaches in the country are here. Most visitors come for Club Med's unique blend of fun and activities; others for the peaceful isolation and the diving. There are more than 50 dive sites and world-renowned offshore fishing and good bonefishing. The friendly locals have a lot to be proud of for their special island, and their warmth shows it.

GETTING HERE AND AROUND
AIR

The island has one airport, in Cockburn Town (ZSA), which is modern, comfortable, and has a long runway. A new fuel depot and FBO by Odyssey Aviation means even more long-haul flights will commence and private aircraft can easily refuel here. Air Caraïbes, the French airline, flies from Paris on Thursday, Air Canada from Montreal on Tuesday, and American Eagle or Bahamasair once a week from Miami. From Nassau, Bahamasair has daily flights. A host of charter companies fly in from Florida and Nassau. Club Med's website has packages that include air charters, and Riding Rock Resort & Marina can arrange them as well.

CONTACTS San Salvador Cockburn Town Airport. ☎ 242/331–2131.

BOAT

Mail boats that bring supplies to the island each week make for an adventurous mode of transportation. M/V New G and M/V Lady Francis sail from Nassau on Tuesday at 1 pm and arrive the next morning, with stops in Deadman's Cay, Long Island, and Rum Cay. You'll ride with groceries, large and small appliances, automobiles, and sometimes even livestock. All boats depart from Potter's Cay in Nassau. Schedules change frequently so it's best to call the Dockmaster's Office in Nassau to get the latest information.

CONTACTS Mailboat Port/Dockmaster's Office in Nassau. ⊠ Potter's Cay, Nassau ☎ 242/393–1064 Dockmaster's office, 242/394–1237. M/V Lady Francis Mailboat Contact. ⊠ Potter's Cay, Nassau ☎ 242/467–2156. M/V New G

Mailboat Contact. ✉ *Potter's Cay, Nassau* ☎ *242/341–3466.*

BIKE
For a short visit to Columbus Cross or the lighthouse, a bike is a sufficient mode of transportation. Bike rentals are available at Club Med and Riding Rock Resort.

CAR
If you want to see the entire island, rent a car. Queen's Highway forms an oval that skirts the island's coastline, and road conditions are excellent. Car rentals are about $85 a day.

CONTACTS D&W Car Rental. ☎ *242/331–2484, 242/331–2488, 242/331–2184.*

SCOOTER
Scooters are a fun, breezy, and convenient way to get around the entire island.

CONTACTS K's Scooter Rentals. ✉ *Cockburn Town Airport* ☎ *242/331–2125, 242/331–2651, 242/452–0594.*

TAXI
Club Med meets all guests at the airport. Riding Rock, five minutes away, provides complimentary transportation for guests. If you want to take your own taxi, it's approximately $10 to either resort.

CONTACTS Clifford Snake Eyes Fernander. ☎ *242/331–2676, 242/427–8198 cell.*

Fernandez Bay to Riding Rock Point

In 1492 the inspiring sight that greeted Christopher Columbus by moonlight at 2 am was a terrain of gleaming beaches and far-reaching forest. The peripatetic traveler and his crews steered the *Niña, Pinta,* and *Santa María* warily among the coral reefs and anchored, so it is recorded, in **Fernandez Bay.** A cross erected in 1956 by Columbus scholar Ruth G. Durlacher Wolper Malvin stands at his approximate landing spot. An underwater monument marks the place where the *Santa María* anchored. Nearby, another monument commemorates the Olympic flame's passage on its journey from Greece to Mexico City in 1968.

Fernandez Bay is just south of what is now the main community of **Cockburn Town,** midisland on the western shore. This is where the airport is, and where the weekly mail boat docks. This small village's narrow streets contain two churches, a commissioner's office, a police station, a courthouse, a library, a clinic, a drugstore, and a telephone station.

On the way from Cockburn Town to Club Med, you'll pass **Riding Rock Point.** All fish excursions leave from their marina. Riding Rock Resort makes a good spot to stop for a drink, meet locals and divers, and buy a local T-shirt.

 Beaches

★ **Bonefish Bay Beach**
BEACH | The 3-mile beach in front of Club Med has bright white sand as fine as talcum powder and water that is such a bright neon shade of turquoise, it appears to be glowing. There are activities such as waterskiing, snorkeling, sailing, kayaking, and paddleboarding in front of Club Med, but the beach is long enough that you'll be able to find an isolated spot. To join in all the fun activities and partying, buy a day pass at the front desk. **Amenities:** food and drink; showers; toilets; water sports. **Best for:** partiers; snorkeling; swimming; windsurfing. ✉ *Club Med—Columbus Isle, Cockburn Town.*

 Restaurants

The Christopher's at Club Med
$$$$ | ECLECTIC | The Christopher's open-air restaurant has buffets during breakfast, lunch, and dinner, with the latter changing themes nightly: Caribbean Night has

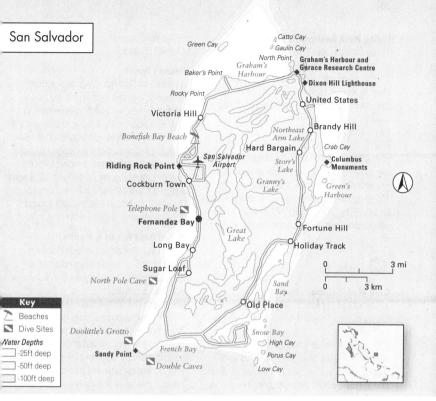

San Salvador

Green Cay
Catto Cay
Gaulin Cay
North Point
Graham's Harbour and
Gerace Research Centre
Baker's Point
Graham's Harbour
Dixon Hill Lighthouse
Rocky Point
United States
Victoria Hill
Brandy Hill
Bonefish Bay Beach
Northeast Arm Lake
Crab Cay
Hard Bargain
Columbus Monuments
San Salvador Airport
Storr's Lake
Riding Rock Point
Green's Harbour
Cockburn Town
Granny's Lake
Telephone Pole
Fernandez Bay
Great Lake
Fortune Hill
Long Bay
Holiday Track
Sugar Loaf
0   3 mi
North Pole Cave
Sand Bay
0   3 km
Old Place
Snow Bay

Key
⤢ Beaches
◩ Dive Sites
Water Depths
-25ft deep
-50ft deep
-100ft deep

Doolittle's Grotto
High Cay
Porus Cay
Sandy Point
French Bay
Double Caves
Low Cay

ocal fare such as conch and fresh fish, nd other themes include French, Mexican, and Mediterranean. Carving stations nd European pastries and breads are mpossible to skip, and simple pastas nd pizzas are mainstays for the finicky ater. **Known for:** themed dinner buffets; inner pass includes open bar; nightly ntertainment. ⓢ *Average main: $64* ⊠ Club Med—Columbus Isle, Cockburn own ⊹ *3 miles north of Riding Rock oint* ☎ 242/331–2000, 855/261–2290 ⊕ *www.clubmed.com.*

⚓ Guanahani Beach Club Restaurant
\$\$\$ | ITALIAN | At this resort restaurant, esh fruit smoothies, panini on crusty rench bread, fresh salads, and various uthentic four-course Italian dinners are l made to order by owner/chef Elena parta. Try the mille-feuille of smoked almon and tomatoes; fettuccine with

crab; shrimp with lime, basil, and herbs; lemon and rosemary risotto; or duck breast in Cointreau and orange sauce. **Known for:** nonguests should call ahead; outdoor patio over Snow Bay; cozy interior lounge. ⓢ *Average main: $70* ⊠ *Snow Bay, Sunrise Rd., Cockburn Town* ☎ 242/452–0438 ⊕ *www.guana-hanibeachclub.com/dining/* ⊟ No credit cards ⊗ *Often closed June–Oct.*

Paradis Restaurant and Bar
\$ | BAHAMIAN | A typical Bahamian enclosed restaurant, Paradis has a daily changing menu written on a chalkboard. Home-cooked Bahamian and American food such as burgers, conch, ribs, and the fresh catch of the day are tastily prepared. **Known for:** popular with locals; free Wi-Fi; fresh seafood. ⓢ *Average main: $15* ⊠ *Cockburn Town* ⊹ *Just north of airport near Club Med* ☎ 242/331–2400.

Riding Rock Seafront Restaurant
$$$$ | **CARIBBEAN** | This 100-seat restaurant offers seating indoors, by the pool, and on the back patio overlooking the ocean. During slower seasons or depending on resort guests, the restaurant is not always open, and each meal is set between certain hours—make sure to call ahead. **Known for:** tasty conch chowder; fresh catches grilled with lemon and butter; fresh-baked bread at breakfast. [$] *Average main: $45* ✉ *Riding Rock Resort and Marina, Cockburn Town* ☎ *242/331–2631, 800/272–1492* 🌐 *www.ridingrock.com* 🕒 *Sometimes closed during slow season.*

Hotels

Club Med–Columbus Isle
$$$$ | **RESORT** | **FAMILY** | After a long closure, this 89-acre oceanfront village reopened in 2022 and remains one of Club Med's most luxurious resorts, with state-of-the-art dive facilities and every water sport and activity imaginable. **Pros:** gorgeous beachfront location; revolving dinner themes; full-service dive shop. **Cons:** no children under age two; long walk to outlying rooms; fee for in-room Wi-Fi. [$] *Rooms from: $1299* ✉ *Cockburn Town* ✥ *½ mile by road from airport terminal* ☎ *888/932–2582, 242/331–2000* 🌐 *https://www.clubmed.co.id/r/columbus-isle/y* 🛏 *256 rooms* 🍴 *All-Inclusive.*

★ **Guanahani Beach Club**
$$$ | **RESORT** | This cozy, small, owner-operated resort is elegant and sophisticated, offering both quiet solitude on a stunning private beach and serious adventure for sports enthusiasts. **Pros:** excellent on-site restaurant; simple and chic villas; private beach adorned with loungers and hammocks. **Cons:** no children under 16; credit cards not accepted; far from other island amenities, so you will probably want a rental car. [$] *Rooms from: $365* ✉ *Snow Bay, Sunrise Rd., Cockburn Town* ☎ *242/452–0438* 🌐 *www.guanahanibeachclub.com* 💳 *No credit cards* 🕒 *Closed mid-June–late Oct.* 🛏 *3 villas.*

Hanna's House
$ | **B&B/INN** | **FAMILY** | This beachfront property, owned and operated by the Hanna family, is an affordable option on San Salvador with simple and comfortable cottages. **Pros:** directly on the beach; spacious rooms with en suite kitchens; free snorkeling. **Cons:** limited entertainment; basic accommodations. [$] *Rooms from: $130* ✉ *Queen's Hwy., Cockburn Town* ☎ *242/452–8365* 🛏 *20 rooms* 🍴 *No Meals.*

Riding Rock Resort & Marina
$ | **HOTEL** | Good for serious divers, this modest motel-style resort is a long-standing property on San Salvador and has a restaurant on-site serving breakfast, lunch, and dinner (included with the all-inclusive dive package). **Pros:** budget-friendly alternative to other resorts; friendly, accommodating staff; rooms are standard but clean. **Cons:** limited entertainment based on occupancy; diving is not daily and dependent on resort guests; rocky beachfront. [$] *Rooms from: $190* ✉ *Cockburn Town* ✥ *½ mi. southwest of airport terminal* ☎ *800/272–1492, 242/331–2631* 🌐 *ridingrock.com* 🛏 *24 rooms* 🍴 *All-Inclusive.*

Nightlife

DANCE CLUBS

Club Med–Columbus Isle
DANCE CLUBS | Evening passes to Club Med cost $90 and include themed dinners, nightly entertainment, and all you can drink from 7 pm to 1 am. The predinner cocktail parties and beachside tiki hut parties are lively affairs with skilled DJs and rapid-fire, charming bartenders. This place is big enough to slink away to a romantic spot on your own. Entertainment gets going after dinner with staff shows in the open-air theater. ✉ *Club Med, Cockburn Town* ☎ *888/932–2582, 242/331–2000.*

Isolated French Bay is on the southern end of San Salvador.

Shopping

SOUVENIRS

Club Med—Columbus Isle

SOUVENIRS | Club Med has a boutique that's clearly the best souvenir, swimsuit, and resort-wear shop on the island. It's an independent French franchise chain that offers excellent shopping. Browse 45 Club (Club Med's logo brand), Hip Way, Fila, Carrera, Le Mar, gorgeous Colombian swimwear, Havaianas flip-flops, sunglasses, hats, and souvenirs. Great gifts to return home with are the Bahamian-made John Waltling's fine rums and Red Turtle vodka. ⊠ *Club Med, Cockburn Town* ☎ *242/331–2000* ⊕ *www.clubmed.us/r/columbus-isle/y.*

Simply Bahamian

SOUVENIRS | A small local crafts and liquor store across the street from the airport sells locally made purses and sarongs featuring Andros batik. ⊠ *Cockburn Town.*

Activities

SCUBA DIVING

San Salvador is famous for its vibrant wall dives and abundant marine life, including hammerhead sharks, sea turtles, eagle rays, and more. **Telephone Pole** is a stimulating wall dive where you can watch stingrays, grouper, snapper, and turtles in action.

Riding Rock Resort & Marina

SCUBA DIVING | The dive operation here (both SSI- and PADI-recognized) uses mostly buoyed sites to avoid damaging the marine environment by dropping anchor. The 42- and 46-foot dive boats are spacious and comfortable. Resort and certification courses are offered, and all-new computerized dive gear is available for rent. Complete dive packages, including meals and accommodations, are available. However, dive trips are not offered daily, so book well in advance. ⊠ *Riding Rock Resort & Marina, Cockburn Town* ☎ *800/272—1492, 242/331—2631* ⊕ *ridingrock.com/bahamas-diving.*

San Salvador has several popular diving sites.

TOURS

Fernander Tours

GUIDED TOURS | In addition to being a taxi driver and island tour guide extraordinaire, Clifford Fernander is friendly and full of information for the inquisitive tourist. He and Bruno Fernander offer tours for Club Med guests. Afterward, you'll feel San Salvador is like a second home. ✉ *Cockburn Town* ☎ *242/331–2676*.

Lagoon Tours

BOAT TOURS | **FAMILY** | Cruise through secluded Pigeon Creek, on the island's beautiful southeast corner, in a flat-bottom boat that maxes at five people to view baby sharks, sea turtles, and starfish, and top off the trip shell hunting on High Cay. Lagoon Tours caters to all interests, from nature walks and historical tours to bird-watching and excursions through the quiet waters of the lagoons. This family-run company is very proud of San Salvador Island and they are happy to show you their favorite off-the-beaten-path spots, with a smile and a cooler full of refreshments. They also conduct kayaking, nature, and bird-watching tours. ✉ *Cockburn Town* ☎ *242/452–0101 cell, 242/331–2459*.

WATER SPORTS

Club Med—Columbus Isle

WATER SPORTS | If you're not a guest at Club Med, you can buy a day pass for $150, which gives you access to water sports (including daily guided snorkeling trips, Hobie Cat sailing, paddleboards, kayaks, and windsurfing) and regular sports activities (including group power walks and jogging, beach volleyball, tennis, various aerobics classes, yoga, and tai chi). The day pass includes lunch, dinner, and all you can drink and is good from 10 am to 1 am. An $80 day pass inclusive of all the above except for dinner gets you access from 10 am to 6 pm. ✉ *Club Med, Cockburn Town* ☎ *242/331–2000* ⊕ *www.clubmed.us/r/columbus-isle/y*.

Guanahani Surf & Sail Center

WINDSURFING | San Salvador is referred to as one of the last "uncrowded kitesurfing paradises," with ideal wind conditions and year-round warm waters. Licensed by IKO (International Kiteboarding Organization), the Guanahani Surf & Sail Center offers in-depth kiteboarding instruction for every level. Led by qualified trainers with Cabrinha kites and boards, courses last anywhere from 3 to 10 hours, and are best done over the course of a few days. The flat, calm, shallow waters in Snow Bay offer the perfect practice and play area. ⊠ *Snow Bay, Sunrise Rd., Cockburn Town* ☎ *242/452–0438* ⊕ *www.guanahanibeachclub.com/activities* ☞ *www.guanahanibeachclub.com.*

Elsewhere on San Salvador

Sometimes you just don't want to stay put at the resort. San Salvador's off-the-beaten-path places require some work to get to, but make for interesting sightseeing. The Gerace Research Centre and the lighthouse are not difficult to reach, but the "other" Columbus monument requires a little more work and an adventurous spirit.

Sights

Columbus Monuments

MONUMENT | Christopher Columbus has more than one monument on San Salvador Island commemorating his first landfall in the New World on October 12, 1492. The simple white cross erected in 1956 at Landfall Park in Long Bay is the easiest to find, on Queen's Highway just outside Cockburn Town. (Also on the site is the Mexican Monument, which housed the Olympic flame in 1968 on its journey from Greece to Mexico City. The flame has not been lit since, but this location is popular for weekend family picnics and local gatherings.) The older and more difficult to find is the Chicago Herald Monument erected in 1891 to celebrate the 400th anniversary of the explorer's landing. No roads lead to this monument—a sphere hewn from limestone—so you'll have to trek through

East Beach on Crab Cay by foot, which is fun for the more adventurous. ⊠ *Queen's Hwy., Cockburn Town* ⊕ *www.bahamas.com/islands/san-salvador.*

Dixon Hill Lighthouse

LIGHTHOUSE | A couple of miles south of Graham's Harbour stands Dixon Hill Lighthouse. Built around 1856, it's the last hand-operated lighthouse in The Bahamas. The lighthouse keeper must wind the apparatus that projects the light, which beams out to sea every 15 seconds to a maximum distance of 19 miles, depending on visibility. A climb to the top of the 160-foot landmark provides a fabulous view of the island, which includes a series of inland lakes. The keeper is present 24 hours a day. Knock on his door and he'll take you up to the top and explain the machinery. Drop a dollar in the box when you sign the guest book on the way out. ⊠ *Cockburn Town* ✣ *Northeast sector of the island.*

Graham's Harbour and Gerace Research Centre

COLLEGE | Columbus describes Graham's Harbour in his diaries as large enough "to hold all the ships of Christendom." A former U.S. Navy base near the harbor houses the Gerace Research Centre, previously known as the Bahamian Field Station. The GRC is a center for academic research in archaeology, biology, geology, and marine sciences, backed by the University of The Bahamas and affiliated with many U.S. universities. It provides accommodations, meals, and air transportation arrangements for students and researchers from all over the world who come to study in this unique environment. Tourists should call ahead to make arrangements to learn about the research taking place. ☎ *242/331–2520* ⊕ *www.geraceresearchcentre.com.*

Sandy Point

RUINS | Sandy Point anchors the island's southwestern end, overlooking French Bay. Here, on a hill, you'll find the ruins of **Watling's Castle,** named after the

17th-century pirate. The ruins are more likely the remains of a Loyalist plantation house than a castle from buccaneering days. A 5- to 10-minute walk from Queen's Highway will take you to see what's left of the ruins, which are now engulfed in vegetation.

☣ Activities

SCUBA DIVING

⇨ *For more information about these and other sites and for dive operators on the island, contact the Riding Rock Resort & Marina or Seafari at Club Med.*

The wall dives in San Salvador are known to be spectacular, with clear underwater visibility at depths of 100 feet and below. **North Pole Cave** has a wall that drops sharply from 40 feet to more than 150 feet; coral growth is extensive, and you might see a hammerhead or two. **Doctor John's** has a steep drop-off starting at about 35 feet with a system of tunnels and crevices that divers can explore. **Runway 10** is a vertical wall with sloping declines and sharp drops in three main sections between 40 and 200 feet. On this dive you will see sponges in abundance, including barrel and elephant ear sponges, plus companion brittle stars.

Long Island

Long Island lives up to its name—80 gorgeous miles are available for you to explore. Queen's Highway traverses its length, through the Tropic of Cancer and many diverse settlements and farming communities. The island is 4 miles at its widest, so at hilly vantage points you can view both the white cliffs and the raging Atlantic on the east side and the gentle surf on the Caribbean side.

Long Island was the third island Christopher Columbus landed on, and a monument to him stands on the north end. Loyalist families came to the island

Historic Lighthouses

Since the 19th century, sailors' lives have depended on the lighthouse beacons that rotate over the Southern Islands and the treacherous reefs that surround them. But for landlubbers, these lighthouses also offer bird's-eye vantage points. Visit the 115-foot Bird Rock Lighthouse on Crooked Island, the Castle Island Lighthouse on Acklins Island, the Great Inagua Lighthouse, and San Salvador's Dixon Hill Lighthouse.

in support of the Crown, and to this day there are Crown properties all over the island, deeded by the king of England. Fleeing the Revolution, their attempt at re-creating their lives as they were in America was short-lived. The soil and lack of rainfall did not support their crops, cotton being their mainstay. Today you can see wild cotton growing in patches up and down the island, along with the ruins of the plantations.

Fishing and tourism support the 3,000 residents of Long Island. Farms growing bananas, mangoes, papaya, and limes also dot the landscape. Boatbuilding is a natural art here, and in the south you can always see a boat in progress as you travel Queen's Highway.

Progress has come to the island slowly. There is now high-speed Internet and cell-phone service, but shops and modern forms of entertainment are still limited. People who come to Long Island don't seem to mind; they're here for the beauty and tranquility and the friendly people. Deep-sea fishing and diving are readily available, and bonefishing flats attract sportfishermen from all over the world. The beaches provide breathtaking views, shelling, exploring, and magnificent pieces of sea glass. The laid-back lifestyle is reminiscent of a slower, gentler time.

GETTING HERE AND AROUND

AIR

Long Island has two airports: Deadman's Cay (LGI) in the middle south and Stella Maris Airport (SML) in the far north. Bahamasair and Southern Air airlines provide daily service from Nassau to Stella Maris and Deadman's Cay airports. Stella Maris Resort has its own excellent air charter service to and from Nassau and between many Southern Islands, including The Exumas. Other charter services are available from Nassau and Fort Lauderdale. Hawkline Aviation is an FBO at Stella Maris, a good fuel stop for private pilots going farther afield.

Guests staying at Cape Santa Maria or Stella Maris Resort should fly into Stella Maris Airport. Chez Pierre Bahamas's guests can fly into either airport, although the Stella Maris Airport is a bit closer. All others should fly into Deadman's Cay Airport midisland. Flying into the wrong airport will cost you not only an hour's drive, but also $100 or more in taxi fares. Listen carefully to the arrival announce-ment when you approach Long Island; most commercial airlines stop at both airports.

CONTACTS Deadman's Cay Airport. ✉ *Deadman's Cay* ☎ *242/337–1777, 242/337–7077 Bahamasair Office.* **Stella Maris Airport.** ✉ *Stella Maris* ☎ *242/338–2006.*

BOAT

Mail boats that bring supplies to the island each week make for an adven-turous mode of transportation. You'll ride with groceries, large and small appliances, automobiles, and some-times even livestock. All boats depart from Potter's Cay in Nassau. Schedules change frequently. M/V *Mia Dean* travels to Clarence Town weekly in south Long Island and returns Thursday (18 hours;

$60 one way). The *Island Link*, a faster RORO boat, stops in Salt Pond and Simms weekly. Bahamas Ferries, also a RORO that takes vehicles, and with its faster, more comfortable passenger lounge, leaves Nassau Monday and gets into Simms, north Long Island, having stopped in George Town, Exumas.

CONTACT Mailboat Port/Dockmaster's Office in Nassau. ✉ *Potter's Cay, Nassau* ☎ *242/393–1064 Dockmaster's office, 242/394–1237.*

CAR

A car is absolutely necessary to explore the island or visit any place outside your resort. Queen's Highway curls like a ribbon from north to south, ending abruptly at the ocean in the north and at a stop sign in the south. It's narrow, with no marked center line, which makes bikes and scooters dangerous modes of transportation. The highway is easily traversed, but some off-roads require four-wheel drive, such as the road to the Columbus Monument, which is rocky and treacherous. The roads to Adderley's Plantation and Chez Pierre's are rough, but a passable adventure.

Most hotels will arrange car rentals and can have your car waiting on-site or at the airport. Rentals range from $60 to $85. Some include gas; all have a limited number of vehicles. It's best to go for an an SUV or compact SUV with all-wheel drive if you have a choice.

Keep your gas tank full; although there are service stations along the highway, hours can be irregular and some take only cash. Some gas stations are closed on Sunday, so if that's your departure day, be sure to fill up the night before so the tank will be full when you return the car. Gas is expensive in the Family Islands.

CONTACTS Mr. T's Car Rental. ✉ *Mid–Long Island, Deadman's Cay* ☎ *242/337–1054, 242/357–1678.* **Omar's Rental Cars.** ✉ *Cape Santa Maria Resort* ☎ *242/357–1043.* **Seaside Car Rentals.**

✉ *Salt Pond, midisland, Deadman's Cay* ☎ *242/338–0140.*

TAXI

Taxis meet incoming flights at both airports. From the Stella Maris Airport, the fare to Stella Maris Resort is $10 per couple; to Cape Santa Maria, the fare is $30 per couple; and it's $150 to Clarence Town. From Deadman's Cay Airport, the fare to Cape Santa Maria is $110 per couple; to Stella Marris, $90; and to Clarence Town, $60. Winter Haven provides free transportation from the Deadman's Cay Airport. A full-day tour of the island by taxi costs about $350, and a half-day tour about $120. However, all taxis are privately owned, so rates can be negotiated. It is generally cheaper to rent a car for the duration of your trip than it is to pay a taxi fare every time you want to go somewhere.

CONTACTS Omar Daley. ✉ *North Long Island, Stella Maris* ☎ *242/357–1043, 242/338–2031.*

TOURS

Bahamas Discovery Quest

SPECIAL-INTEREST TOURS | This company, owned by Charles Knowles, whose love for his island is obvious, offers full- and half-day snorkeling trips, along with many other unique island escapades, including sponging, crabbing, beach-going, and shelling, as well as different types of fishing. He also has two places to stay in Stella Maris and one in Salt Pond. ✉ *Deadman's Cay* ☎ *242/472–2605* ⊕ *bahamasdiscoveryquest.com.*

Omar's Long Island Guided Tours

GUIDED TOURS | Omar shows you around Long Island at a rate of $180 for 4–5 hours for two people. It's $10 per additional person. ✉ *Cape Santa Maria Resort* ☎ *242/357–1043 cell.*

VISITOR INFORMATION

CONTACTS Long Island Ministry of Tourism. ✉ *Salt Pond, mid–Long Island* ☎ *242/338–8668.*

North Long Island: Cape Santa Maria to Gray's

In the far north you will find two large resort communities: **Cape Santa Maria** and **Stella Maris.** Scattered between are the small settlements of **Seymour's, Glinton's,** and **Burnt Ground.** Columbus originally named the island's northern tip Cape Santa Maria after the largest of his three ships. The beach here is gorgeous, full of private homes and resort villas, with a restaurant, bar, and gift shop that are open to the public. North of the Cape Santa Maria Beach Resort are the **Columbus Monument,** commemorating Columbus's landing on Long Island, and **Columbus Cove,** where he made landfall. Twelve miles south of the Cape, Stella Maris, which means Star of the Sea, is home to the so-named resort. Stella Maris Airport sits on the property, along with private homes, restaurants and bars, the magnificent **Love Beaches,** a full-service marina, and a tackle and gift shop—all open to the public. Just north of Stella Maris, off Queen's Highway, are the ruins of the 19th-century **Adderley's Plantation.**

Traveling south about 8 miles, you'll come to **Simms,** one of Long Island's oldest settlements. The Tropic of Cancer cuts through the island close to here, dividing the subtropics from the tropics.

Farther south are the idyllic communities of **Thompson Bay** and **Salt Pond,** both providing safe harbors for those who visit by sailboat. Salt Pond, a hilly bustling settlement so named for its many salt ponds, hosts the annual Long Island Regatta. Continuing south, you will pass the settlements of **The Bight** and **Gray's** before reaching **Deadman's Cay.**

Sights

Adderley's Plantation

RUINS | Just north of Stella Maris Airport, west of the main road, are the ruins of 19th-century Adderley's Plantation, a cotton plantation that once occupied all of Stella Maris. Clearly marked, the road is marginally passable by car. It's about a mile drive and then a fairly long walk. The walking path is marked by conch shells and leads to the plantation ruins. Seven buildings are practically intact up to roof level, but it is overgrown with vegetation. For history buffs, it is well worth the time. ✉ *North of Stella Maris Airport, Stella Maris.*

Columbus Monument

MONUMENT | Two miles north of Cape Santa Maria is the Columbus Monument, commemorating Columbus's landing on Long Island. The road to the monument is off Queen's Highway, and while the sign is often not visible, any Long Islander will gladly give you directions. The 3-mile treacherous road is too rough for vehicles without four-wheel drive, and most rental car companies won't let you drive it without an SUV, yet it is an extremely long hike. At the end of the road is a steep hill, called Columbus Point, and a climb to the summit affords a spectacular vista. This is the highest point on Long Island and the second highest in The Bahamas. Farther north on Queen's Highway is Columbus Harbour, on Newton's Cay. Columbus made landfall in this cove, protected by limestone outcroppings. The more adventurous can follow the beach to the left, where a rough walking path leads to three other coves, each one a delight. Two coves up, you will find sea glass scattered on the beach like sparkling jewels, and by climbing through limestone formations, you will discover another cove perfect for snorkeling. ✉ *North of Cape Santa Maria Resort.*

Beaches

Cape Santa Maria Beach

BEACH | Known as one of The Bahamas' top beaches and located on the leeward side of the island at Cape Santa Maria Beach Resort, the water colors here range from pale blue to aqua to shades of turquoise. The 4-mile stretch of soft white sand beckons you to stroll, build sand castles, sun worship, or wade into the calm shallow waters. In the early morning, you're likely to see a ray swimming along the shore. The resort has a beachside restaurant and lounge chairs for guests, in addition to kayak and paddleboard rentals, but there's also plenty of sand to find a secluded stretch all your own. **Amenities:** food and drink; water sports. **Best for:** solitude; snorkeling; sunset; swimming; walking. ✉ *Cape Santa Maria Resort.*

Restaurants

After a period of rain, the mosquitoes and no-see-ums come out, so bring mosquito repellent with you when dining outdoors.

Beach House Restaurant at Cape Santa Maria

$$ | **SEAFOOD** | **FAMILY** | Upstairs in the Cape Santa Maria Beach House, guests enjoy sweeping vistas of the turquoise bay during the day and bobbing boat lights in the evening, along with the gentle sounds of the sea. Breakfast can be light with yogurt parfait and a seasonal fruit medley, or a splurge with banana bread French toast topped with caramelized plantains or Bahamian-style eggs Benedict. **Known for:** nightly happy hour with free conch fritters; oceanfront bar; banana bread French toast. [$] *Average main: $30* ✉ *Cape Santa Maria Resort* ☎ *800/926–9704* 🌐 *www.capesantamaria.com/beach-house-restaurant-bar/* 🕓 *Closed Sept. and Oct.* ☞ *Meal plans available.*

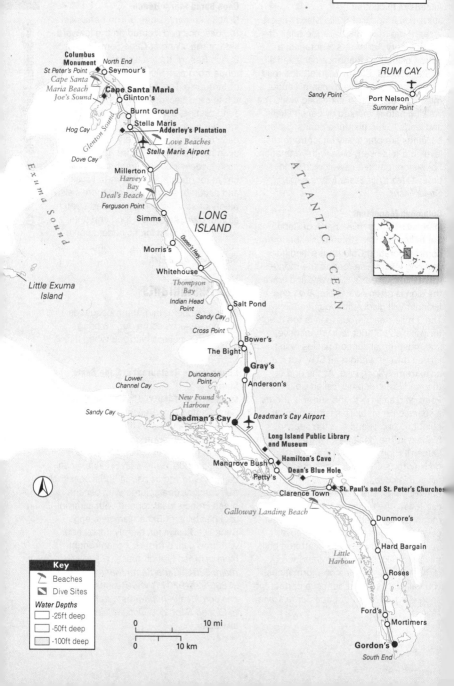

Long Island

Conception
Island
Conception Island
National Park
Wedge Point

RUM CAY

Columbus
Monument
St Peter's Point
Cape Santa
Maria Beach
Joe's Sound
North End
Seymour's
Cape Santa Maria
Clinton's
Burnt Ground
Stella Maris
Adderley's Plantation
Love Beaches
Stella Maris Airport
Hog Cay
Glenton Sound
Dove Cay
Millerton
Harvey's
Bay
Deal's Beach
Ferguson Point
Simms
Morris's
Whitehouse
Thompson
Bay
Indian Head
Point
Sandy Cay
Cross Point
Bower's
The Bight
Gray's
Anderson's
Lower
Channel Cay
Duncanson
Point
New Found
Harbour
Sandy Cay
Deadman's Cay
Deadman's Cay Airport
Long Island Public Library
and Museum
Mangrove Bush
Hamilton's Cave
Petty's
Dean's Blue Hole
Clarence Town
St. Paul's and St. Peter's Churches
Galloway Landing Beach
Dunmore's
Little
Harbour
Hard Bargain
Roses
Ford's
Mortimers
Gordon's
South End

Exuma Sound

ATLANTIC OCEAN

Sandy Point
Port Nelson
Summer Point

Little Exuma
Island

Queen's Hwy.

LONG
ISLAND

Key
Beaches
Dive Sites
Water Depths
-25ft deep
-50ft deep
-100ft deep

0   10 mi
0   10 km

★ Chez Pierre Bahamas
$$ | **ECLECTIC** | At this airy oceanfront restaurant a few steps from the beach, Chef Pierre has been serving sumptuous cuisine since 2002. This curmudgeonly chef serves the best food on the island, hands down. **Known for:** pasta and seafood dishes; delicious pizza; chef expects guests to be punctual. [$] *Average main: $28* ✉ *Miller's Bay* ☎ *242/338–8809, 242/357–1374* 🌐 *chezpierrebahamas.com.*

Moonshine Bar & Grill
$ | **BAHAMIAN** | **FAMILY** | The views surrounding Stella Maris Resort Club's new poolside bar are as beautiful as the frozen fresh-fruit daiquiris they serve. Once a week Rake 'n' Scrape musicians pluck your heartstrings with Bahamian and calypso songs. **Known for:** the Moonshine panini; weekly live music; coastal bluff views. [$] *Average main: $15* ✉ *Stella Maris Resort Club, Stella Maris* ☎ *242/338–2050* 🌐 *www.stellamarisresort.com.*

Stella Maris Resort Club Restaurant & Bar
$$ | **SEAFOOD** | Charming and experienced chef Bruno and his capable team do a superb job pleasing upmarket American and European palates. Dine in the cool inside or on the stone terrace. **Known for:** room-service pizza; delicious liqueur coffees; fresh fish. [$] *Average main: $30* ✉ *Stella Maris Resort Club, Stella Maris* ☎ *242/338–2050* 🕒 *Closed Sept.*

Hotels

C Shells Guest Quarters
$ | **B&B/INN** | **FAMILY** | These quaint, self-catering full-kitchen suites sit just steps away from a quiet private beach on Salt Pond with a large grassy garden space—perfect for family picnics, naps in the hammock, and a vacation without the bustle of a busy resort. **Pros:** friendly, accommodating owners; cable TV, Wi-Fi; affordable. **Cons:** no maid service; no on-site restaurant; rental car is essential to explore the island. [$] *Rooms from: $110* ✉ *Salt Pond* ☎ *242/338–0103, 954/889–5075* 🌐 *www.facebook.com/cshellsguestquarters/* 🛏 *4 suites* 🍴 *No Meals.*

★ Cape Santa Maria Beach Resort and Villas
$$ | **RESORT** | **FAMILY** | This stunning resort consists of spacious beachfront villas that sleep up to eight and beachfront one-bed and two-bed bungalows that each have a screened-in veranda—all overlooking serene turquoise waters on a gorgeous 4-mile-long white-sand beach. **Pros:** only 15 minutes from Stella Maris Airport; friendly staff arranges excursions; great swimming beach. **Cons:** secluded location means you'll need a rental car to explore; no TVs in rooms and no Wi-Fi in bungalows; seven-night stay required during Christmas holiday season. [$] *Rooms from: $239* ✉ *Galliot Cay, off Seymour's* ☎ *242/338–5273, 800/926–9704 toll-free in U.S. and Canada* 🌐 *www.capesantamaria.com* 🕒 *Closed Sept. and Oct.* 🛏 *20 bungalows, 18 villas* ☞ *Kids 12 and under stay free.*

Chez Pierre Bahamas
$ | **B&B/INN** | Lining lovely Millers Bay beach, this rustic, remote resort has six simple cabins on stilts right on the beach, making it a real "get-away-from-it-all" place (guests should be self-sufficient and adventurous). **Pros:** screened-in porches; large private beach; excellent on-site restaurant serves three meals a day. **Cons:** must rent a car to explore the island; no air-conditioning; bathroom water is slightly salty. [$] *Rooms from: $180* ✉ *Miller's Bay* ☎ *242/338–8809, 242/357–1374 cell* 🌐 *www.chezpierrebahamas.com* 🛏 *6 cottages.*

Grotto Bay Bahamas
$ | **B&B/INN** | In the settlement of Salt Pond is this small private hideaway, a labor of love for owners Kris and Jean, who offer two lovely guest rooms with sweeping decks facing the ocean on

Cape Santa Maria Beach Resort is the best on the island.

the lower level of their home, along with a newer beach house that sleeps five guests. **Pros:** centrally located for exploring north and south; personalized service; beautiful lush landscaping. **Cons:** no in-house restaurant, bar, or meals; you need to rent a car to explore the island; owners live right above the guest rooms. $ *Rooms from: $145* ✉ *Salt Pond* ☎ *242/338–0011, 954/840–7724* ⊕ *www.grottobaybahamas.com* ⇨ *2 rooms, 1 beach house.*

★ **Stella Maris Resort Club**

$$ | **RESORT** | **FAMILY** | Stella Maris is more than a resort; it's a long-standing family-fun community that sits atop a hilly ridge offering many accommodations choices (including private homes), complemented by multiple pools, breathtaking views of the Atlantic, fun bars and restaurants, and activities for every interest—it's also within walking distance of Stella Maris Airport. **Pros:** all accommodations have an ocean view or balcony; free activities like island tours and sailing; parties and events hosted by resort for guests. **Cons:** long walks between rooms, clubhouse, and beach bar; rooms somewhat dated but clean and comfortable; not beachfront but free bus to other beaches. $ *Rooms from: $250* ✉ *Stella Maris* ☎ *800/426–0466, 242/338–2050 resort* ⊕ *www.stellamaris-resort.com* ⇨ *26 units.*

 Nightlife

GATHERING PLACES
Stella Maris Resort

GATHERING PLACES | This resort often has live music on the weekends, including Rake 'n' Scrape. Every Thursday night is their Rum Punch Party, which includes rum punch, conch fritters, and dinner ($55 for nonguests). The clubhouse bar has a pool table and foosball, plus a huge rum collection. The restaurant has an excellent selection of wines. Ask about the frequent (in winter) Cave Party, where folks gather round and dine on barbecued treats in a cave. Call ahead to make reservations. ✉ *Stella Maris Resort*

Club, Stella Maris ☎ *242/338–2050* ⊕ *www.stellamarisresort.com.*

 Shopping

MARKETS
Hillside Food Supply
GENERAL STORE | Hillside is probably the largest store on Long Island and the ideal place to stock up if you're self-catering or want snacks in between mealtimes. Here you can find lots of fresh produce and dairy items, dry foods, toiletries, and supplies. In the back of the store you will find just about anything, from snorkeling gear and ice chests to towels and assorted housewares. Hillside can also tell you where and how to get fresh lobster, snapper, grouper, and more. There are seafood vendors living nearby. ⊠ *Salt Pond, mid–Long Island* ☎ *242/338–0022.*

SPORTING GOODS
Bonafide Bonefishing Fly Shop
SPORTING GOODS | This fly-and-tackle shop and souvenir boutique, usually open Monday, Wednesday, Friday, and Saturday, 9 am to 5 pm, is located in Stella Maris on Queen's Highway. In addition to fishing gear, they sell cold drinks and snacks, souvenirs, gifts, apparel, and jewelry. James "Docky" Smith is the fishing guru behind Bonafide Bonefishing. A Long Islander, he is a popular and knowledgeable bonefishing guide who "knows the flats." ⊠ *Queen's Hwy., Stella Maris* ☎ *242/338–2035, 242/357–1417, 242/338–2025* ⊕ *www.bonafidebonefishing.com.*

SOUVENIRS
Cape Santa Maria Beach Resort
SOUVENIRS | There is a small gift shop in the lobby with clothes, swimsuits, island straw works, island books, souvenirs, cold drinks, and sundries. ⊠ *Cape Santa Maria Resort's Beach House lobby* ☎ *242/338–5273, 800/926–9704* ⊕ *www.capesantamaria.com.*

Tingums Boutique
SOUVENIRS | *Tingums* is Bahamian for "I don't know what to call it." This cute gift shop sells clothing, jewelry, gifts, souvenirs, books, and toiletries. ⊠ *Stella Maris Resort Club, Stella Maris* ☎ *242/338–2050.*

 Activities

DIVING AND SNORKELING
Conception Island Wall is an excellent wall dive, with hard and soft coral, plus interesting sponge formations. The M/V *Comberbach,* a 103-foot British freighter built in 1948, sank off Cape Santa Maria in 1984 and was scuttled by the Stella Maris Resort in 1986 to create an artificial reef and excellent dive site. Take a guided diving excursion to **Shark's Reef** and watch a scuba master safely feed dozens of sharks.

Cape Santa Maria Resort
DIVING & SNORKELING | This resort uses expert divers and guides for myriad diving and snorkeling trips to various reefs, walls, and wrecks around Long Island as well as trips to Conception Island; dive and snorkel equipment is available for rent. In addition, visitors can rent stand-up paddleboards and Hobie Cat sailboats to explore the coast of Cape Santa Maria Beach and its surrounding bays. ⊠ *Cape Santa Maria Resort* ☎ *242/338–5273, 800/926–9704* ⊕ *www.capesantamaria.com.*

Stella Maris Resort
SCUBA DIVING | This resort offers diving and snorkeling trips. In addition to daytime dives to some of Long Island's most interesting sites, including Dean's Blue Hole, you can do an overnight dive cruise. They also offer PADI Resort Dive and Open Water Certification courses and Advanced Open Water upon request. Equipment is available for rental. ⊠ *Stella Maris* ☎ *242/338–2050* ⊕ *www.stellamarisresort.com.*

FISHING
Bonafide Bonefishing
FISHING | James "Docky" Smith is highly regarded as one of the best bonefishing guides in The Bahamas. He does full- and half-day bonefishing excursions, as well as reef-fishing trips. He is also an expert fly-casting instructor. Book well in advance. His operation is based out of the Bonafide tackle shop in Stella Maris, open three days a week, which rents conventional and fly-fishing gear, prepares snacks and box lunches, and sells a range of tackle, clothing, and flies. Full days of bonefishing are $550 (maximum two anglers); reef, bottom, or deep-sea fishing are $1,200 (maximum six anglers). Call ahead. ⊠ Queen's Hwy., Stella Maris ✛ Near Stella Maris Resort ☎ 242/338–2025, 242/357–1417 ⊕ www. bonafidebonefishing.com.

Stella Maris Resort
FISHING | Stella Maris Resort arranges deep-sea fishing, bonefishing, and reef-fishing trips with well-trained guides. The small fleet includes a 32-foot single engine inboard that can accommodate up to six fishermen, a 38-foot twin engine that can take up to eight for their deep-sea and reef-fishing trips, and a 16-foot Hells Bay or 17-foot Maverick with poling platforms for a half or full day of bonefishing the flats. Rods and bait are available for rent and purchase. ⊠ Stella Maris ☎ 242/338–2050 ⊕ www. stellamarisresort.com.

South Long Island: Deadman's Cay to Gordon's

The most populated area on the island is **Deadman's Cay.** This umbrella-central settlement covers all the communities stretching to **Gray's** and is the social, economic, and educational center of the island. The Deadman's Cay Airport is in Lower Deadman's Cay and the infamous Max Conch Bar is only a short distance to the south. Shops, restaurants, and bars dot this area, along with amazing views of The Bahama Banks.

Clarence Town is the capital of Long Island and home to the Flying Fish Marina in one of the prettiest and safest harbors in the Family Islands. Situated at the top of the highest hills in town are the twin-towered Moorish style churches of **St. Paul's** and **St. Peter's,** designed by Father Jerome. Clarence Town is the last large settlement on the south end of the island.

To the west of Clarence Town is **Dean's Blue Hole,** the second deepest blue hole in the world. Free-diving contests, without use of any breathing apparatus, are held here each year, and divers come from all over the world to challenge the record. Fantastic snorkeling can be had around the blue hole's edges.

South of Clarence Town you will find **Galloway Landing,** a long stretch of amazing beaches and saltwater canals dug into the limestone hills by the now defunct Diamond Salt Mine. From here to **Gordon's** is the most undeveloped stretch of the island. Plantation ruins are at **Dunmone's,** secluded beaches at **Ford's,** and the incredible pink flamingos at Gordon's along with the largest assortment of sea glass.

◉ Sights

Some of the biggest changes on Long Island have taken place at **Flying Fish Marina** (⊕ www.flyingfishmarina.com) in Clarence Town. The full-service, 20-slip marina offers fuel, a new store, and a new, upscale restaurant.

★ Dean's Blue Hole
BODY OF WATER | Known as the second deepest blue hole in the world, with a depth of 663 feet, Dean's Blue Hole is the most amazing sight on the island and one of the most popular photo sites in the land. "Blue hole" is a term for a

water-filled sinkhole with an entrance below the water level. Free divers from around the world gather here annually to take the plunge. In 2016 William Trubridge broke the world record for free immersion diving: to 407 feet without fins. Dean's Blue Hole is surrounded by a pretty cliff and a superb beach. The shallows at the edge of the hole are perfect for snorkeling and swimming, and the more adventurous visitors can jump into the water from the cliffs above. To find the blue hole, watch for the well-marked sign on your left (going east on Queen's Highway). ⊠ *On east coast, just northwest of Clarence Town, Clarence Town.*

Hamilton's Cave

CAVE | The largest cave system in The Bahamas, Hamilton's Cave features stalactites and stalagmites, with passages over 45 feet wide and 9 feet high. The Lucayans were thought to have lived here about AD 500, and many Lucayan artifacts were discovered in 1936. For added excitement, plan to go closer to dusk when the resident bats are most active! ⊠ *Queen's Hwy., Deadman's Cay* ☎ *242/337–0235, 242/472–1796* ⊠ *$10.*

Long Island Public Library and Museum

HISTORY MUSEUM | The Long Island Public Library and Museum is housed in a beautiful little pink cottage with island trees in front. Learn the history of Long Island and see artifacts collected by local Long Islanders in hopes of preserving their cultural heritage. It's a fascinating collection and exhibit, professionally designed by The Bahamas Antiquities, Monuments & Museums Corporation. Island wares, homemade jellies, and other island goods are for sale, in addition to books on Long Island and a popular Bahamian calendar painted in watercolors by local artist Nick Maillis. ⊠ *Buckley's, near Scotia Bank, Queen's Hwy.* ☎ *242/337–0500* ⊕ *www. nlis.bs/publiclibraries/long-island-public-library-and-museum-buckleys/* ⊠ *$3* ⊗ *Closed Sun.*

St. Paul's & St. Peter's Churches

CHURCH | The twin, towered Moorish churches of St. Paul's (Anglican) and St. Peter's (Catholic) are two of the island's most celebrated landmarks. Father Jerome, often referred to as the hermit of Cat Island, built St. Paul's when he was Anglican; later, after converting to Catholicism, he built St. Peter's. The architecture of the two churches is similar to the Spanish missions in California. The churches are open sporadically, but tours are available through the Ministry of Tourism. ⊠ *Atop Clarence Town Hill, Clarence Town.*

 Beaches

Galloway Landing Beach

BEACH | This remarkable beach on the southeast coast of the island, south of Clarence Town, is relatively unknown and visited mostly by the locals. Swim and sun at the first beach, or walk a short distance south to an even more wonderful and secluded stretch of sand. Here, canals carved into the limestone hills by the now-defunct Diamond Salt Mine are filled with the palest blue ocean water and are home to small marine life. It's a wonderful area to kayak, snorkel and swim, and collect sea glass. A bit farther south, a narrow bridge leads to beyond-stunning lagoons and ocean flats. **Amenities:** none. **Best for:** solitude; snorkeling; swimming; walking. ⊠ *Clarence Town* ✛ *2.4 miles southwest of Clarence Town.*

🍴 **Restaurants**

The Forest TakeAway

$ | BAHAMIAN | This family-owned and -operated takeout restaurant is a favorite with locals for tasty island food and value. It offers barbecued ribs, cracked conch, conch burgers, fish fingers, chicken snacks and dinners, and the ever-popular Forest Burger, a hamburger with boneless ribs and sautéed onions. **Known**

for: cold beer while you wait; shaded picnic-table seating; local favorite. $ *Average main: $12* ✉ *Just off Queen's Hwy., Deadman's Cay* ☎ *242/337–1246* ⊟ *No credit cards* ⊘ *Closed Sun. and Mon.*

Max Conch Bar & Grill

$ | BAHAMIAN | This island treasure—and possibly the area's most-recommended dining spot—is praised up and down by locals and visitors alike. Quintessentially Bahamian, it's where you can sit all day on a stool at the colorful roadside hexagonal gazebo or at a table in the garden patio amid chickens and a goat, enjoying beers and nibbling on excellent conch salad prepared right in front of you. **Known for:** warm hospitality; conch fritters; traditional Bahamian recipes. $ *Average main: $15* ✉ *Deadman's Cay* ☎ *242/337–0056* ⊘ *Closed Sun.*

Seaside Village at Jerry Wells

$ | BAHAMIAN | Located at the end of Jerry Wells Road, this charming, authentic conch shack stuck out on a dock in the water is truly local, offering friendly service, fun music, and good food. Sling back in the hammock, catch some tunes and breeze as you (if you're lucky) watch the almost-tame osprey, "Iron," snack on fish morsels. **Known for:** fresh-caught conch; grouper cooked to order; best conch salad. $ *Average main: $15* ✉ *Jerry Wells Rd., on west coast just south of Deadman's Cay Airport, Deadman's Cay* ☎ *242/337–0119* ⊕ *www.facebook.com/ seasidevillagelongisland/.*

 Hotels

Gems at Paradise

$ | HOTEL | Situated on 16 acres of pink-sand beachfront property, overlooking low-lying Clem Cay and the Atlantic Ocean as far as the eye can see, this resort occupies a rare and superb site. **Pros:** gorgeous location and views; easy access to fishing and water sports; car rentals available on-site. **Cons:** many rooms have stairs; no on-site restaurant;

car rental is essential. $ *Rooms from: $152* ✉ *Clarence Town* ☎ *242/337–3016* ⊕ *gemsatparadise.com* ⤵ *10 units* ⏐⊙⏐ *No Meals.*

Harbor Breeze Villas

$ | HOUSE | Long Island's newest luxury villas are nestled among garden pathways atop a hillside, each with private balconies affording views of Clarence Town Harbour and the Atlantic Ocean. **Pros:** owner rents cars and will stock your villa with groceries ahead of your arrival; complimentary transfers to Arthur's Town Airport; laundry facilities on-site. **Cons:** no on-site restaurant or bar; not on beach; office can be hard to reach by phone. $ *Rooms from: $135* ✉ *Lochabar, just south of Clarence Town, Clarence Town* ☎ *242/337–3088* ⤵ *15 villas* ⏐⊙⏐ *No Meals.*

 Nightlife

BARS AND PUBS

Lloyd's Sporting Lounge & Entertainment Center

BARS | The long name is Lloyd's Sporting Lounge & Entertainment Center, and, for Long Island, it has quite a bit. This comfortable and smartly designed sports bar and lounge has big-screen TVs for sports and five pool tables. In a separate room, they also have a disco, where you can dance to the live tunes of the bands and DJs every Friday and Saturday night. Lloyd's hosts frequent pool tournaments, and people flock to enjoy happy hour from 5 to 7 pm weekdays, when beer buckets are four for $12. Their food is also good and affordable: Long Island mutton, chicken, steaks, seafood, and various fettuccine main courses are available. Lloyd's is well-thought-out and rather luxurious for the Family Islands— very enjoyable especially for big-group entertainment and dining, to catch sports on TV, or to dance to some live music. ✉ *Queen's Hwy., opposite Turtle Cove Rd. that leads to Dean's Blue Hole, Clarence Town* ☎ *242/337–5762.*

🛍 Shopping

GENERAL STORES

It's All Under the Sun

GENERAL STORE | As the name suggests, this "department store" has everything from a café with used books and Wi-Fi to office supplies, toys, baby stuff, souvenirs, beach bags, hats, and snorkeling and fishing gear. Owner Cathy Darville also sells fruit smoothies, deli sandwiches, and homemade ice cream. ⊠ *Off Queen's Hwy. in Mangrove Bush, near Cartwright's settlement* ☎ *242/337–0199* ⊕ *www.facebook.com/ItsAllUnderThe-Sun* ☉ *Closed Sun.*

Activities

DIVING AND SNORKELING

Surrounded by a beautiful powder-beach cove, the area surrounding **Dean's Blue Hole** offers a great place for a beach picnic if it's not too windy. Visitors can jump into the blue hole from various locations on the overhanging cliff above, some at 25 feet above the water. Snorkelers will see a variety of tropical fish and marine life, and Stella Maris Water Sports at Stella Maris Marina offers guided dive trips; flashlights included and necessary. Although Dean's Blue Hole is safe for swimming, it is recommended that all swimmers be competent or wear life jackets.

FISHING

Deadman's Cay Bonefish Adventures

FISHING | Since 2002, Samuel Knowles Bonefish Adventures has drawn a loyal following of saltwater anglers from around the globe, earning a reputation as one of the most popular bonefishing programs in the islands. The main attraction is their expert guides, who are Long Islanders, fourth- and fifth-generation bonefishermen, and champions of four of the five Bahamas bonefishing tournaments. Their location at the center of Long Island's pristine shoreline, with unique landlocked flats, creates an unforgettable fishing adventure for all ages and experience levels. They offer stay/fish/dine packages at their lodge: $2,395 for seven nights/six days fishing. ⊠ *Deadman's Cay* ☎ *242/337–0246, 242/357–1178* ⊕ *http://www.deadmans-bones.com.*

Long Island Bonefishing Lodge

FISHING | This modern lodge offers all-inclusive stay/fish/dine packages for fly-fishers. Packages include three meals and fishing from 8 am to 4 pm. LIBL specializes in and encourages DIY fishing, where, although your guide is present, you're mostly on your own with privacy, and he can boat you to other flats to find success. Most of Long Island's vast flats are wadeable shallows. The main clubhouse has gorgeous flats views. The two duplexes are modern and comfortable and sleep a total of eight. ⊠ *Deadman's Cay* ☎ *242/472–2609* ⊕ *www.longis-landbonefishinglodge.com* 🖃 *$1750 per person double occupancy. All-inclusive stay/fish/dine package Oct.–May. Visit must start or end on Sun.*

Winter Haven

FISHING | The Winter Haven inn organizes fishing and boating adventures through various local guides. ⊠ *Clarence Town* ☎ *242/337–3062* ⊕ *www.winterhavenba-hamas.com.*

Crooked and Acklins Islands

Crooked Island is 30 miles long and surrounded by 45 miles of barrier reefs that are ideal for diving and fishing. They slope from 4 feet to 50 feet, then plunge to 3,600 feet in the **Crooked Island Passage,** once one of the most important sea roads for ships following the southerly route from the West Indies to the Old World. If you drive up to the Cove settlement, you'll get an uninterrupted view of the region all the way to the narrow passage at **Lovely Bay** between Crooked Island and Acklins Island. Two lighthouses alert mariners that they are nearing the islands.

The tepid controversy continues today over whether Columbus actually set foot on Crooked Island and its southern neighbor, Acklins Island. What's known for sure is that Columbus sailed close enough to Crooked Island to get a whiff of its island herbs. Soon after, the two islands became known as the "Fragrant Islands." Today Crooked and Acklins Islands are known as remote and unspoiled destinations for fishers, divers, and sailors who value solitude. Here phone service can be intermittent, Internet access can be hard to find, and some residents depend on generators for electricity. Even credit-card use is a relatively new development. The first known settlers didn't arrive until the late 18th century, when Loyalists brought enslaved people from the United States to work on cotton plantations. About 400 people, mostly fishers and farmers, live on each island today. Two plantation-era sites, preserved by the Bahamas National Trust, are on Crooked Island's northern end, which overlooks the Crooked Island Passage that separates the cay from Long Island. Spanish guns have been discovered at one ruin, **Marine Farm,** which may have been used as a fortification. Another old structure, **Hope Great House,** has orchards and gardens.

GETTING HERE AND AROUND
AIR
Crooked and Acklins have one airport each: Colonel Hill Airport (CRI) on Crooked Island and Spring Point Airport (AXP) on Acklins Island. Neither is open unless there's a flight expected. Bahamasair flies from Nassau to Crooked and Acklins Islands twice a week. The flights are quite early in the morning, making it hard to fly in from overseas without staying one night in Nassau. Many Crooked Island visitors have found a solution to

that: fly in on a private aircraft direct from the United States. The private 3,500-foot airstrip at Crooked Island Lodge is complimentary for hotel guests. Nonguests pay landing and parking fees. This airstrip is most convenient for private and charter flights if you're staying in the area of Pittstown and Landrail Point. Ask your hotel to make arrangements for picking you up at the airport in case there are no taxis.

Hotels will arrange airport transportation. Generally someone from even the smallest hotel will meet you at the airport, despite the fact that taxis are usually waiting on flights.

CONTACTS Acklins Island Spring Point Airport. ⊠ *Midway along Acklins Island* ☎ *242/344–3169.* **Crooked Island Colonel Hill Airport.** ⊠ *On northeast side of Crooked Island* ☎ *242/344–2357.*

BOAT
Mail boats that bring supplies to the islands each week make for an adventurous mode of transportation. You'll ride with groceries, large and small appliances, automobiles, and sometimes even livestock. All boats depart from Potter's Cay in Nassau. Schedules change frequently. Three mail boats travel to Acklins Island, Crooked Island, and Long Cay: M/V *Sea Spirit II*, M/V *New G*, and M/V *Vinase* with Captain Tom Hanna, for a fare of $118 one way.

Ferry service between Cove Landing, Crooked Island, and Lovely Bay, Acklins Island, usually operates twice daily on varying schedules between 9 and 4.

CONTACTS Mailboat Captain Tom Hanna. ☎ *242/341–3468.* **Ferry Service.** ☎ *242/344–2197 ferry, 242/344–2415 Island administrator's office.* **Mailboat Port/Dockmaster's Office in Nassau.** ⊠ *Potter's Cay, Nassau* ☎ *242/393–1064 Dockmaster's office, 242/394–1237.*

Crooked and Acklins islands both have a lighthouse. Bird Rock Lighthouse is the newer of the two, built in 1872.

CAR

There are many car-rental operators. To get a good vehicle, reserve a car through your hotel prior to your arrival; even if you have a reservation you should be prepared for the possibility of the car not being there when you arrive. Gas is also not always available on the islands, as it's delivered by mail boats, which are sometimes delayed. Fortunately, it's easy to get a ride to most places with locals, who are friendly and often willing to help.

Sights

Bird Rock Lighthouse

LIGHTHOUSE | The sparkling white Bird Rock Lighthouse (built in 1872) once guarded the Crooked Island Passage. The rotating flash from its 115-foot tower still welcomes pilots and sailors to the Crooked Island Lodge, currently the islands' best lodging facility. This lighthouse is located 1 mile offshore and can only be reached by boat. ✉ *Bird Rock* ✢ *On separate island off northwest point of Crooked Island.*

Hotels

Casuarina Pines Villas

$ | **HOUSE** | Six modern cottages sit on a half-mile stretch of white-sand beach between Landrail Point and Pittstown Point Landings. **Pros:** beachfront location; spacious economical accommodations; great place to hang out, fish, and relax. **Cons:** you need to arrange transportation to do anything; take plenty of insect repellent. [$] *Rooms from: $165* ✉ *Landrail Point* ☎ *242/457–7005, 242/344–2036* 🌐 *www.cpvillasbahamas.com* 🛏 *7 cottages* 🍴 *All-Inclusive.*

Chester's Bonefish Lodge By the Beach

$ | **B&B/INN** | For bonefishing enthusiasts, opportunity is never far away at Chester's Bonefish Lodge, as each room faces a pristine bonefishing flat that takes no more than 60 seconds to wade into. **Pros:** bonefishing flats directly opposite rooms; easy access to amazing outdoor activities; near Crooked Island ferry. **Cons:** unreliable Wi-Fi; limited dining options; distance from airport. [$] *Rooms from:*

$150 ✉ *Chester's Hwy.* ☎ *242/357–4179, 242/225–1500* 🌐 *chestersbonefish.com* 🛏 *4 rooms* 🍴 *Free Breakfast.*

Crooked Island Lodge & Marina

$$ | **HOTEL** | A true anglers' paradise, this is one of the best fishing destinations in The Bahamas and Caribbean for bone- and deep-sea fishing. **Pros:** mind-bending ocean and beachfront location; bar and restaurant serves three meals a day; private airstrip for easy access. **Cons:** insect repellent necessary in this area; might be too remote for some; not all rooms offer sea views. [$] *Rooms from: $225* ✉ *Pittstown Point Landing* ☎ *242/478–8989, 888/344–2507 toll-free in U.S. and Canada* 🌐 *www.crookedislandlodge.com* 🛏 *8 rooms* ☞ *Meal plans available.*

IVel's Bed & Breakfast

$ | **B&B/INN** | **FAMILY** | When staying at IVel's, you are treated to gourmet meals, both Bahamian and American, and island hospitality that makes you feel like family. **Pros:** car rental available; water sports on-site; tranquil residential community. **Cons:** non-alcoholic facility; far from the best beaches. [$] *Rooms from: $150* ✉ *Mason's Bay* ☎ *242/813–1158* 🌐 *www.ivelsbedandbreakfast.com* 🛏 *10 rooms and a cottage.*

Activities

FISHING

Crooked Island has a number of highly regarded bonefishing guides with quality boats and fly-fishing tackle. Most can be booked through Tranquillity on the Bay or the Crooked Island Lodge, but the guides also take direct bookings. Be aware that telephone service to and from Crooked and Acklins Islands is not always operational.

You can stalk the elusive and swift bonefish in the shallows or go deep-sea fishing for wahoo, sailfish, and amberjack.

Elton "Bonefish Shakey" McKinney (☎ *242/344–2038*), **Randy McKinney** (☎ *242/344–2326*), **Jeff Moss** (☎ *242/344–2029*), and **Clinton** and **Kenneth "The Earlybird" Scavalla** (☎ *242/344–2011* or *242/422–3596*) are all knowledgeable professional guides. **Captain Robbie Gibson** (☎ *242/457–7017*) has a 30-foot Century boat and is the most experienced reef and offshore fishing captain on Crooked Island, where astounding fishing in virgin waters is the rule. Many wahoo weighing more than 100 pounds are landed each season with his assistance. Robbie's personal-best wahoo is a whopping 180 pounds. He's also a skilled guide for anglers pursuing tuna, marlin, sharks, barracuda, jacks, snapper, and grouper.

SCUBA DIVING

Captain Robbie Gibson

DIVING & SNORKELING | In addition to fishing expeditions, Captain Robbie Gibson offers scuba diving of wreck sites and wall dives, plus snorkeling and day tours to see flamingos or explore land caves. You can rent gear from him, and a two-tank dive with equipment runs about $100 per person. ☎ *242/457–7017, 242/422–4737.*

Inagua

Inagua does indeed feel like the southernmost island in The Bahamas' 700-mile-long chain. Just 50 miles from Cuba, it's not easy to get to—there are only three flights a week from Nassau, and you must overnight there to catch the 9 am flight. At night the lonely beacon of the **Great Inagua Lighthouse** sweeps the sky over the southern part of the island and the only community, **Matthew Town,** as it has since 1870. The coastline is rocky and rugged, with little coves of golden sand. The terrain is mostly flat and covered with palmetto palms, wind-stunted buttonwoods, and mangroves ringing ponds and a huge inland saltwater lake. Parts of it look very much like the Florida Everglades, only without the alligators and snakes.

Inagua is obviously not a tourist mecca, but those who do visit witness one of the great spectacles of the Western Hemisphere: the approximately 60,000 West Indian pink-scarlet flamingos that nest here alongside rare Bahama parrots and roseate spoonbills. If you're not a bird lover, there's extraordinary diving and fishing off the virgin reefs. Although there are few tourists, this remote island is prosperous. An unusual climate of little rainfall and continual trade winds creates rich salt ponds. The Morton Salt Company harvests a million tons of salt annually at its Matthew Town factory.

GETTING HERE AND AROUND

AIR

Inagua has one airport: Matthew Town Airport (IGA). Bahamasair has flights on Monday, Wednesday, and Friday from Nassau. Hotels will arrange airport transportation. Generally someone from even the smallest hotel will meet you at the airport, but taxis sometimes meet incoming flights.

CONTACTS Inagua Matthew Town Airport. ☎ 242/339–1680 only answered Mon., Wed., and Fri. when a flight is expected, 242/339–1415 airport ⊕ www.bahamasair.com.

BOAT

The M/V Lady Mathilda sails once a week or three times a month, first to Abraham's Bay, and then to Matthew Town, Inagua. Not only is the boat characteristically cluttered with all sorts of cargo, the service is sporadic—so always call the captain on the scheduled sailing day, Thursday, or the Potter's Cay Dockmaster's Office in Nassau to check sailing times. She departs from Potter's Cay in Nassau, and the journey in good seas takes 36 hours and costs $100 one way. If bad weather is approaching, she may not even leave harbor, skipping a week and leaving you stranded. The whole process is an authentic Bahamian adventure. Take your camera!

CONTACTS Mailboat Port/Dockmaster's Office in Nassau. ✉ Potter's Cay, Nassau ☎ 242/393–1064 Dockmaster's office, 242/394–1237.

CAR

You can rent a car for about $80 a day, but there are few rental cars on the island, so call in advance. If you are driving outside Matthew Town, you will need an SUV or truck to navigate dirt roads. If you plan to stay in Matthew Town, you can easily walk everywhere.

CONTACTS Ingraham Rent-A-Car. ✉ Great Inagua Island ☎ 242/225–3933, 242/339–1515. **Triple R Car Rental.** ✉ Matthew Town, Great Inagua Island ☎ 242/453–8018, 242/443–6671.

 Sights

Erickson Public Library and Museum

HISTORY MUSEUM | The Erickson Public Library and Museum is a welcome part of the community, particularly the surprisingly well-stocked, well-equipped library. The Morton Company built the complex in the former home of the Erickson family, who came to Inagua in 1934 to run the salt giant. The museum displays the island's history, to which the company is inextricably tied. The posted hours are not always that regular. The Bahamas National Trust office and the office of Inagua National Park are also here, but hours are unpredictable. ✉ Gregory St. on northern edge of town across from police station, Matthew Town ☎ 242/339–1863 ⊕ www.nlis.bs/publiclibraries/erickson-public-library-and-museum/ 🎟 Free ☉ Closed Sun.

Great Inagua Lighthouse

VIEWPOINT | From Southwest Point, a mile or so south of Matthew Town, you can see Cuba's coast—slightly more than 50 miles west—on a clear day from atop Great Inagua Lighthouse, built in 1870 in response to the number of shipwrecks on offshore reefs. It's a grueling climb—the last 10 feet are on a ladder—but

Deep-sea fishing in the Southern Family Islands

the view of the rugged coastline and Matthew Town is worth the effort. Look to the west to see the hazy mountains of Cuba. Be sure to sign the guest book just inside the door to the lighthouse. ✉ *Gregory St., 1 mile south of Matthew Town, Great Inagua Island.*

★ Inagua National Park

NATIONAL PARK | Nothing quite prepares you for your first glimpse of the West Indian flamingos that nest in Inagua National Park: brilliant crimson-pink, up to 5 feet tall, with black-tipped wings. A dozen flamingos suddenly fly across a pond, intermixed with fantastic pink roseate spoonbills.

It's a moving sight, and because of the island's remote location, few people get to see it. By 1952, Inagua's flamingos had dwindled to about 5,000. The gorgeous birds were hunted for their meat, especially the tongue, and for their feathers. The government established the 183,740-acre wildlife sanctuary and national park in 1963, and today more than 60,000 flamingos nest on the island,

the world's largest breeding colony of West Indian flamingos. The birds thrive in the many salt ponds (owned by the Morton Salt Company) that supply their favorite meal—brine shrimp. Bird-watchers also flock here to spy gull-billed terns, egrets, herons, burrowing owls, pintail ducks, sandpipers, and snowy plovers—more than 130 species in all. The Inaguan lyretail is one of the world's most recently announced species. Wild boar and feral donkeys left here after a brief French occupation in 1749 are harder to see.

To make reservations, you must contact The Bahamas National Trust's office (☎ *242/393–1317*) or Warden Henry Nixon (☎ *242/395–0856*). All visits to the park are by special arrangement. ✉ *Matthew Town ✢ 10 miles west of Matthew Town ⊕ bnt.bs/explore/inagua/inagua-national-park/ 🎫 From: $25 per person. Rates include: park user fee and BNT warden's time. Not included: vehicle rental and fuel and park warden gratuity (optional).*

9

Morton Salt Company

FACTORY | Marveling at the salt process lures few visitors to Inagua, but the Morton Salt Company is omnipresent on the island: it has more than 47 square miles of crystallizing ponds and reservoirs. More than a million tons of salt are produced every year for such industrial uses as salting icy streets. (More is produced when the northeastern United States has a bad winter.) Even if you decide not to tour the facility, you can see the mountains of salt, locally called the Salt Alps, glistening in the sun from the plane. In an unusual case of industry assisting its environment, the crystallizers provide a feeding ground for the flamingos. As the water evaporates, the concentration of brine shrimp in the ponds increases, and the flamingos feed on these animals. Free tours are available by reservation at the salt plant in Matthew Town. ✉ *Matthew Town* ☎ *242/339–1300, 242/457–6000* 🌐 *www.mortonsalt.com.*

Beaches

Collin's Beach

BEACH | In addition to visiting this remove beach to chill in solitude, Collin's Beach is an ideal location to snorkel Inagua's offshore reefs. Casuarina trees provide shade in some areas, but that is about all you will find on this beach besides the sandy coastline and mesmerizing turquoise waters. It is about ten miles north of Matthew Town, so be sure to bring sunscreen, bug spray, umbrellas or portable shade, lots of fluids in a cooler, and some beach toys and snorkeling gear. Every year, a few luxury cruises make winter stops in Inagua and bring their guests to Collin's Beach. **Amenities:** none. **Best for:** solitude; snorkeling. ✉ *Matthew Town.*

Restaurants

Cepigel

$$ | **BAHAMIAN** | **FAMILY** | Vegan menus are hard to come by in The Bahamas on the whole, so it is a rare treat to find vegetarian options and a focus on fresh ingredients in Inagua, the most southern island in the archipelago. Cepigel has that covered. **Known for:** Bahamian staples; intimate space; homemade desserts. [$] *Average main: $20* ✉ *Astwood St., Matthew Town* ☎ *242/339–1227* 🌐 *cepigel.wixsite.com/cepigel* 🕒 *Closed Sat. and Sun.*

Lighthouse Restaurant Bar & Grill

$ | **BAHAMIAN** | Although Lighthouse Restaurant is casual and intimate like Inagua's overall character, it is considered the best high end restaurant on the island. Known for its stunning sunsets, the octagon-shape restaurant overlooks the ocean and the historic lighthouse. **Known for:** oceanfront location; great sunset views; traditional Bahamian food. [$] *Average main: $18* ✉ *Lighthouse Rd.* ☎ *242/453–2277, 242/453–1200.*

★ **S sinn L Restaurant & Bar Lounge**

$ | **BAHAMIAN** | The best spot to dine and even party is at S sinn L in Matthew Town, which becomes Inagua's dance hot spot on the weekend. In a comfortable, smart, air-conditioned dining room, you can enjoy delicious fresh Bahamian breakfasts, lunches, and dinners with some American fare as well. **Known for:** live calypso and Bahamina Goombay; go-to spot for dancing; Bahama Mama cocktails. [$] *Average main: $15* ✉ *East St., Matthew Town* ☎ *242/339–3923, 242/339–1515* 🌐 *www.facebook.com/SnLBar.*

Hotels

Enrica's Inn & Guesthouse

$ | **B&B/INN** | This affordable inn is a block from the sea and consists of three brightly colored, two-story colonial-style cottages with five guest rooms in each.

Pros: inexpensive meals on request; spacious rooms with many amenities; walking distance to town. **Cons:** no pool; no on-site activities; no views. $ *Rooms from: $85* ✉ *Victoria St., Matthew Town* ☎ *242/339–2127* ⊕ *https://enricasinn.com/* 🛏 *15 rooms.*

Great Inagua Outback Lodge

$$ | **B&B/INN** | Great Inagua Outback Lodge is the dream of Inaguan Henry Hugh, who wanted to relax in his own quiet island paradise. **Pros:** comfortable, with modern amenities; right on the water and close to beach and flats; full meals in stay/fish/dine packages. **Cons:** long and extremely bumpy road; remote; no pool. $ *Rooms from: $284* ✉ *Matthew Town* ✛ *15 miles from Matthew Town, along northern road and the beach road* ☎ *716/479–2327 in U.S. and Canada* ⊕ *www.ccoflyfishing.com/greatinagua.html* 🛏 *2 rooms.*

Sunset Apartments

$ | **APARTMENT** | These two spacious apartments seated on a rocky shoreline on Matthew Town's southern side are your only option for a room with a water view—and a great place to watch sunsets. **Pros:** great place for bonefishing; Ezzard is a wonderful host and a top fly-fishing guide; fully equipped kitchens. **Cons:** no Internet; little to do but fish and bird-watch; you need to pay in cash or wire transfer. $ *Rooms from: $150* ✉ *Great Inagua Island* ☎ *242/339–1362* 🚫 *No credit cards* 🛏 *2 apartments.*

Nightlife

BARS AND PUBS

Da After Work Bar

BARS | This local bar on Gregory Street is the most popular hangout in town. ✉ *Gregory St., Matthew Town* ☉ *Usually closed Sun.*

DANCE CLUBS

S sinn L Restaurant & Bar

DANCE CLUBS | No, that's not a spelling error: S sinn L is Inagua's most popular nightclub, with a restaurant, dance room, VIP lounge, and sky booth with a disco on weekends. On Thursday, karaoke is the vibe, and occasionally (during holidays especially), they import live bands from the Turks and Caicos and Nassau; visiting American and Canadian musicians also turn up. Play pool and dine on tasty Bahamian dishes and fresh seafood. The kitchen and bar are open daily. ✉ *East St., Matthew Town* ☎ *242/339–1515, 242/339–3923* ⊕ *www.facebook.com/SnLBar.*

FISH FRY

The Fish Fry

GATHERING PLACES | A collection of fish shacks next to the water is open on weekends, with DJs occasionally playing music in the covered pavilion next door. ✉ *Matthew Town.*

Activities

BIRD-WATCHING

Great Inagua Tours

FISHING | Colin Ingraham has been a tour guide for more than two decades, and while he specializes in birding and island sightseeing, he can also take you fishing for tuna or wahoo or snorkeling on the reefs. ✉ *Matthew Town* ☎ *242/339–1336, 242/453–0429 cell.*

FISHING

Ezzard Cartwright

FISHING | Inagua's only bonefishing and deep-sea fishing guide, Ezzard Cartwright has been featured on ESPN Outdoors shows. He is the only local with access to Lake Windsor, home to tarpon, snook, and bonefish that can only be reached by boat. Reserve early for bonefishing from January to July. ✉ *Matthew Town* ☎ *242/339–1362, 242/453–1903 cell.*

Index

Photo Credits

Front Cover: Pietro Canali/Sime/eStock Photo [Descr.:Bahamas, New Providence, Paradise island, Nassau, Caribbean sea, Atlantic ocean, Caribbean, French Cloisters]. **Back cover, from left to right:** Maurice Brand /Dreamstime. Bicho_raro/iStockphoto. Henrik Landfors/ iStockphoto. **Spine:** Andrii_K/Shutterstock. **Interior, from left to right:** The Bahamas Ministry of Tourism (1). Ray Wadia/The Bahamas Ministry of Tourism (2-3). Montez Kerr/Shutterstock (5). **Chapter 1: Experience the Bahamas:** Thierrydehove/Dreamstime (6-7). Ray Wadia/The Bahamas Ministry of Tourism (8-9). The Bahamas Ministry of Tourism (9). The Bahamas Ministry of Tourism (9). Daniel Budiman/ Dreamstime (10). Ramunas Bruzas/Shutterstock (10). The Bahamas Ministry of Tourism (10). BlueOrange Studio/Shutterstock (10). The Bahamas Ministry of Tourism (11). Worachat Sodsri /Shutterstock (11). Zweizug/Dreamstime (12). Yoga Ardi Nugroho/Shutterstock (12). The Bahamas Ministry of Tourism (12). The Bahamas Ministry of Tourism (12). Jocrebbin/Dreamstime (13). Danita Delimont/Shutterstock (14). The Bahamas Ministry of Tourism (14). The Bahamas Ministry of Tourism (14). Daniel Botha/Dreamstime (15). BlueOrange Studio/Shutterstock (15). Debbi Smirnoff (18). Dwayne Tucker/Tru Bahamian Food Tours (19). Dan/Sea Photo Art (20). Johnandersonphoto/iStockphoto (20). Jimi world/Wikimedia Commons (20). Nassau Paradise Island Promotion Board (21). Courtesy of The Bahamas Ministry of Tourism and Aviation (21). The Bahamas Ministry of Tourism and Aviation (22). Vitalis Arnoldus/Shutterstock (22). Maria Victoria Herrera/Shutterstock (22). Shane Gross/Shutterstock (22). Nassau Paradise Island Promotion Board (23). Nicolasvoisin44/Shutterstock (25). The Bahamas Ministry of Tourism (26). The Bahamas Ministry of Tourism (27). The Bahamas Ministry of Tourism (10). Frantisekhojdysz/Shutterstock (28). The Bahamas Ministry of Tourism (30). The Bahamas Ministry of Tourism (31). Lars Topelmann/The Bahamas Ministry of Tourism (32). Lars Topelmann/The Bahamas Ministry of Tourism (33). Lars Topelmann/The Bahamas Ministry of Tourism (33). Ray Wadia/The Bahamas Ministry of Tourism (33). **Chapter 3: New Providence and Paradise Islands:** Chenyujie1898/Dreamstime (55). Montez Kerr/Shutterstock (73). Jo Crebbin/Shutterstock (74). Jef Nickerson [CC BY-SA 2.0]/Flickr (74). The Bahamas Ministry of Tourism (75). Jo Crebbin/Shutterstock (75). Jo Crebbin/Shutterstock (76). Erkki & Hanna/Shutterstock (77). Montez Kerr/Shutterstock (77). Graycliff Hotel (80). Nenad Basic/Shutterstock (88-89). Lars Topelmann/ The Bahamas Ministry of Tourism (95). Ramunas Bruzas/Dreamstime (100). **Chapter 4: Grand Bahama Island:** DenisTangneyJr/iStockphoto (107). Albo/Shutterstock (110). Thomas Lorenz/Shutterstock (111). The Bahamas Ministry of Tourism (111). BridgetSpencerPhoto/ Shutterstock (119). The Bahamas Ministry of Tourism (123). Robert Holmes/Alamy Stock Photo (125). Our Lucaya Beach and Golf Resort (129). JonMilnes/Shutterstock (134). The Bahamas Ministry of Tourism (136). **Chapter 5: The Abacos:** The Bahamas Ministry of Tourism, Investments & Aviation (141). Matt A. Claiborne/Shutterstock (144). Flickrized/Flickr (145). KatePhilips/iStockphoto (145). The Bahamas Ministry of Tourism, Investments & Aviation (151). Sinn P. Photography/Shutterstock (155). The Bahamas Ministry of Tourism, Investments & Aviation (158). The Bahamas Ministry of Tourism, Investments & Aviation (165). Sinn P. Photography/Shutterstock (168). Charlie Smith/ EarthBeat (172). **Chapter 6: Andros, Bimini, and the Berry Islands:** Troutnut/Shutterstock (175). Hansche/Dreamstime (188). Tiamo Resort (198). FotoKina/Shutterstock (201). Joost van Uffelen/Shutterstock (205). JMichl (208). Ramunas Bruzas/Shutterstock (215). **Chapter 7: Eleuthera and Harbour Island:** The Bahamas Ministry of Tourism (217). Leonard Zhukovsky/Shutterstock (240). Alisa_Ch/Shutterstock (244). **Chapter 8: The Exumas:** Danita Delimont/Shutterstock (253). The Bahamas Ministry of Tourism (256). Ray Wadia/The Bahamas Ministry of Tourism (257). The Bahamas Ministry of Tourism (257). Ramona Settle (267). Cheryl Blackerby (269). Staniel Cay Yacht Club (270). Cheryl Blackerby (273). The Bahamas Ministry of Tourism (275). Staniel Cay Yacht Club (277). **Chapter 9: The Southern Family Islands:** Lora B/Shutterstock (279). Cheryl Blackerby (282). Alexandr Junek Imaging/Shutterstock (283). Stephan Kerkhofs/Shutterstock (283). Jeff Greenberg/Alamy (284). Cheryl Blackerby (285). Mweichse/Shutterstock (285). W Timothy Schaiff/Shutterstock (296). Sergi Reboredo (299). CanonDLee/Shutterstock (305). The Bahamas Ministry of Tourism (306). Greg Johnston/Cape Santa Maria Beach Resort (314). Bill Schild/The Bahamas Ministry of Tourism (321). Greg Johnston/Cape Santa Maria Beach Resort (324). **About Our Writers:** All photos are courtesy of the writers except for the following: Jessica Robertson, courtesy of Scharad Lightbourne.

Every effort has been made to trace the copyright holders, and we apologize in advance for any accidental errors. We would be happy to apply the corrections in the following edition of this publication.

Notes

Fodor's BAHAMAS

Publisher: Stephen Horowitz, *General Manager*

Editorial: Douglas Stallings, *Editorial Director;* Jill Fergus, Amanda Sadlowski, *Senior Editors;* Brian Eschrich, Alexis Kelly, *Editors;* Angelique Kennedy-Chavannes, *Assistant Editor;* Yoojin Shin, *Associate Editor*

Design: Tina Malaney, *Director of Design and Production;* Jessica Gonzalez, *Senior Designer;* Jaimee Shaye, *Graphic Design Associate*

Production: Jennifer DePrima, *Editorial Production Manager;* Elyse Rozelle, *Senior Production Editor;* Monica White, *Production Editor*

Maps: Rebecca Baer, *Senior Map Editor;* David Lindroth, Mark Stroud (Moon Street Cartography), *Cartographers*

Photography: Viviane Teles, *Director of Photography;* Namrata Aggarwal, Neha Gupta, Payal Gupta, Ashok Kumar, *Photo Editors;* Jade Rodgers, *Photo Production Intern*

Business and Operations: Chuck Hoover, *Chief Marketing Officer;* Robert Ames, *Group General Manager*

Public Relations and Marketing: Joe Ewaskiw, *Senior Director of Communications and Public Relations*

Fodors.com: Jeremy Tarr, *Editorial Director;* Rachael Levitt, *Managing Editor*

Technology: Jon Atkinson, *Executive Director of Technology;* Rudresh Teotia, *Associate Director of Technology;* Alison Lieu, *Project Manager*

Writers: Sheri-kae McLeod, Jessica Robertson, Alicia A. Wallace

Editor: Angelique Kennedy-Chavannes

Production Editor: Elyse Rozelle

34th Edition

ISBN 978-1-64097-681-8

ISSN 1524–7945

All details in this book are based on information supplied to us at press time. Always confirm information when it matters, especially if you're making a detour to visit a specific place. Fodor's expressly disclaims any liability, loss, or risk, personal or otherwise, that is incurred as a consequence of the use of any of the contents of this book.

SPECIAL SALES

This book is available at special discounts for bulk purchases for sales promotions or premiums. For more information, e-mail SpecialMarkets@fodors.com.

PRINTED IN CANADA

10 9 8 7 6 5 4 3 2 1

About Our Writers

 Sheri-kae McLeod is a Caribbean travel writer, journalist, and digital producer who has contributed professionally to various magazines, newspapers, and publishing houses across the region. She has worked as a Senior Journalist for *Caribbean National Weekly* in South Florida and Digital Content Producer for Florida Jerk Festival. She has a bachelor's degree in Communications from the University of the West Indies, Jamaica. Sheri-kae updated the Eleuthera and the Exumas chapters for this edition.

 Born in England and raised in the Bahamas, **Jessica Robertson** has traveled the world for work and play but calls Nassau home. She has visited just about all of the populated islands in the Bahamas, as well as some occupied only by hermit crabs and seagulls, and is happiest when she's paddling on, diving under, or lounging beside the ocean. Jessica updated the New Providence and Paradise Islands, Grand Bahama Island, and Abacos chapters for this edition.

 Alicia A. Wallace is a writer and researcher from The Bahamas covering sociopolitical issues, gender and sexuality, travel, and democracy. She has a weekly column in *The Tribune*, a Bahamian daily newspaper, and writes for a wide range of online publications including *Healthline* and *Business Insider*. She produces a monthly newsletter, The Culture Rush, and has a Patreon (@aliciawallace), both covering feminism, human rights, and social justice in accessible ways. More of her work can be found at ⊕ *aliciaawallace. com*, and she tweets as @_AliciaAudrey. Alicia updated Experience, Travel Smart, the Family Islands, and Andros, Bimini, and the Berry Islands for this edition.